SPIRIT OF ENTERPRISE
THE 1981 ROLEX AWARDS

EDITED BY
GREGORY B. STONE

Foreword by
Lord Hunt
President, The Royal Geographical Society, 1977–1980

Preface by
André J. Heiniger
Managing Director, Montres Rolex S.A.

W. H. Freeman and Company
San Francisco

Photographs and art not credited below were submitted by the entrants.

Pages 20, 52, 60, 124, 132, 164, 196, 228, 276, 292, 332, 388: Dale Johnson. Page 2: Franz Lazi/Photo Researchers, Inc. Page 84, top, and jacket: Philip Jon Bailey/Stock, Boston; page 84, bottom, Frank Siteman/Stock, Boston. Page 90 and jacket: BCL/B & C Calhoun. Page 93: Frederick Ayer III/Photo Researchers, Inc. Page 348: BCL/Norman Tamolin. Page 364: Nicholas Chitty. Page 380: top, W. H. Hodge/Peter Arnold, Inc. bottom, Ken Balcomb, courtesy of the Whale Museum. Page 428: P. Tasker/Alpha Photo Associates, Inc. Page 436 and jacket: Dr. Edward S. Ross.

Project Editor: Patricia Brewer; Designer: Gary A. Head; Production Coordinators: Bruce Muncil and Linda Jupiter; Illustration Coordinator: Nancy Benedict; Compositor: York Graphic Services; Printer and Binder: Arcata Book Group.

Library of Congress Cataloging in Publication Data

Main entry under title:

Spirit of enterprise.

    Includes index.
    1. Inventions—Awards.   2.   Science—Awards.
I.   Stone, Gregory B.
T49.5.S68   608   81-3142
ISBN 0-7167-1317-9   AACR2

Printed in the United States of America

CONTENTS

Rolex Laureates are indicated by a gold crown (♛)
and Honorable Mention winners by a black crown (♛).

iv

EXPLORATION AND DISCOVERY   235

THE ENVIRONMENT   339

FOREWORD

Peter the Hermit once observed of his life and age: "We are living in difficult and dangerous times." If that statement was true of one country in Europe some nine centuries ago, it certainly applies with greater force to the whole world we live in, as the twentieth century draws to its close. So vast and complex are the problems, so fearsome the dangers which beset our world today, that it is fatally easy to doubt human capacity to cope with them: even to despair of human nature itself.

Yet whatever the future may hold, at least one constant factor runs through history and gives grounds for hope: the human capacity for greatness in times of trial and danger. Its importance is greater today because of the wider distribution of education and wealth, and because of improvements in communication between the peoples of the world. To a far greater degree than in Peter the Hermit's time, men and women the world over can, if they will, influence the course of events.

Foremost among the qualities which make for greatness are caring, not only for ourselves but about other people whose needs are greater than ours—caring about our common heritage, the land, the oceans, and the creatures which inhabit them; and courage and enterprise to translate caring into deeds. I am among those who believe that, given the will, if enough people display these qualities of caring, courage, and enterprise, ordinary people can stem the tide of danger and act in unison, across man-made frontiers, to create a better world.

Among the numerous projects submitted by people from many countries for The Rolex Awards for Enterprise, my colleagues and I of The Selection Committee have been impressed by the fact that nearly all of them have revealed some of those very qualities which give hope for the future. They are qualities which are to be found in nearly every human being. The problem, and the need, is to encourage and enable people to develop these qualities and to use them to good effect. The need is urgent.

Industrial companies which, having the means to do so, take the initiative to develop in ordinary people these attributes of greatness in human nature are performing a valuable service for us all.

Aston, Henley-on-Thames
May 1981

Lord Hunt
President, The Royal Geographical Society,
1977–1980

PREFACE

When The Rolex Awards for Enterprise were first presented in 1978, they reflected, for us at Montres Rolex S.A., what had been a massive, remarkably worldwide, and heart-warming response to our notion of how to encourage and support—in a variety of fields—what we have long called the "spirit of enterprise."

Our own reaction to that response was that we, as a company, ought to try to keep such fields of enterprising spirits from lying fallow; the decision was made to offer the Awards again. On May 7, 1981, The Rolex Awards for Enterprise were presented for the second time, again to five Rolex Laureates who were invited to attend the Awards Ceremony in Geneva, where each received a check for Swiss francs 50,000, and a gold Rolex Oyster Day-Date Chronometer.

Once again, we had seen an extraordinarily broad global response from enterprising men and women around the world. It therefore became my pleasure, at the 1981 Awards Ceremony, to announce the third Rolex Awards for Enterprise, which we will present in Geneva in 1984.

This book, like its predecessor about the first Rolex Awards, will provide you with a sense of what it is that we at Rolex find to be representative of that "spirit of enterprise" that we believe to be of vital importance to humanity's continuing search for excellence, in innumerable fields. More importantly, perhaps, we now know that it is also likely that this book will stimulate you to reach out to these unusual and enterprising people, encouraging them with your own support and interest, and quite possibly sharing your own spirit of enterprise with them in mutually beneficial ways.

We have learned that The Rolex Awards for Enterprise have an impact that goes well beyond the grants we have been able to provide to the Rolex Laureates (and to a list of 24 Honorable Mention winners, who received gold-and-steel Rolex Oysters in locally held ceremonies around the world). Letters from non-winning candidates, whose projects appeared in the book on the first Rolex Awards, made it evident that this publication brought them new hope, new sources of assistance and interest, and a renewed commitment to their specialized pursuits. It also has been rewarding to receive, from a wide variety of business, academic, and governmental groups, many favorable comments on the value of publishing a selection of the projects submitted. With such support, it behooved us to include a greater number and wider variety of the projects in this new book on The Rolex Awards for Enterprise 1981.

As before, our intention in presenting these people is to encourage them further by helping their ideas to reach a larger audience than they might achieve on their own. Wishing them all well, we commend them to your attention. I shall hope that their examples will kindle your own sense of caring about the quality of life in our world, and that you will bring your own determination, courage, and spirit of enterprise to the attention of our next Rolex Awards.

Geneva
May 1981

André J. Heiniger
Managing Director, Montres Rolex S.A.

INTRODUCTION

If you could assemble all the people you will meet in this book in a single large room, I submit that no more stimulating and challenging group of individuals would have been gathered together ever before. You would be faced with the opportunity to talk with 171 people, from forty-five different countries around the world, about things and places and subjects and ideas in such abundance that your mind and imagination might easily cry, "Slow down; there is too much here to encompass all at once." You would be right, of course. No physical gathering of people such as those in the pages ahead could ever be frozen in place long enough to delve properly into each and every enterprising soul.

This book attempts to capture some portion of that sensation, in its presentation of some of the myriad wise, wonderful, and warming efforts of individually enterprising people around the world who responded to the generous challenge of The Rolex Awards for Enterprise 1981.

Officially opened in late 1979, via announcements in public media, the 1981 Rolex Awards invited individuals with enterprising projects in three different categories (Applied Sciences and Invention, Exploration and Discovery, and The Environment) to write to Geneva for the detailed, 19-page Official Application Form. Thousands of people did so, and each was mailed one of the forms. At the closing date for applications, the end of April 1980, candidates from 83 countries had submitted applications to the Rolex Awards program.

A distinguished Selection Committee had been assembled to review the projects once the forms had been registered, checked, and assembled by categories by The Secretariat of The Rolex Awards for Enterprise. Meeting later in 1980, The Selection Committee was composed of the following people: Mr. André J. Heiniger, Chairman of The Selection Committee and Managing Director of Montres Rolex S.A. in Geneva; Dr. Sylvia A. Earle, American, Marine Biologist and Aquanaut; Dr. René G. Favoloro, Argentine, Cardiovascular Surgeon; Lord Hunt, British, President of The Royal Geographical Society; Dr. Francisco Kerdel Vegas, Venezuelan, Professor of Dermatology; Mr. John H. Loudon, Dutch, President of the World Wildlife Foundation; Professor (Miss) Chie Nakane, Japan, Vice President of the International Union of Anthropological and Ethnological Sciences; Mr. Gerard Piel, American, President and Publisher of *Scientific American;* and Mr. Haroun Tazieff, French, Volcanologist.

Fulfilling their charter when they convened, The Selection Committee chose the five projects that would be acclaimed as Rolex Laureates for 1981. But such was the range and value of the projects submitted, the Selection Committee proposed a further 24 projects for Honorable Mention notice.

On May 7, 1981, at an Awards Ceremony held in Geneva, the five Rolex Laureates, brought to Geneva as the guests of Montres Rolex S.A., were each presented with checks for Swiss francs 50,000, individually inscribed gold Rolex Oyster Day-Date Chronometers, and scrolls attesting their Awards. In subsequent ceremonies, the Honorable Mention winners were awarded gold-and-steel Rolex Oysters and scrolls in their various locations.

Beyond these officially recognized individuals, Montres Rolex S.A. decided that further support and encouragement could be extended to many of the other enterprising candidates who applied to the Rolex Awards by allowing the publication of projects in this book. The book extends to you a very real invitation to join in the exhilarating and satisfying venture of entering into the "spirit of enterprise" by offering you the information necessary to reach out to these unique individuals on your own. They are people with imagination, drive, dreams, and dedication, and they deserve to be encouraged, helped, and recognized.

Three closing thoughts.

To include as many projects as could be reasonably presented within the desired parameters of this book, I have taken the road of editing often lengthy descriptions of projects down to compact chapter lengths. I ask forgiveness of the authors of the projects for this, and their understanding of the attempt to include as many of their peers as possible. Equally, I would ask you, the reader, to let your imagination range beyond these shortened descriptions. Better still, where your own interest is truly piqued, write to the author concerned and offer your own help in return for further details.

Second, the weighting of the book by project categories reflects the proportions of the applications received, rather than any personal bias or the allocation of prizes.

Lastly, and perhaps most importantly, the Spirit of Enterprise will again be encouraged by Montres Rolex S.A. The Rolex Awards for Enterprise 1984 will be officially launched in the coming year. This book can serve no better purpose than to encourage you to apply for these next Awards with a worthwhile project of your own.

Paris
April 1981

Gregory B. Stone
Editor

APPLIED SCIENCES AND INVENTION

The projects appearing in this section were submitted in competition under the "Applied Sciences and Invention" category, which was defined in the Official Application Form as follows:

Projects in this category will be concerned primarily with science or technology and should seek to achieve innovative steps forward in research, experimentation or application.

An Antarctic iceberg.

A STATE-OF-THE-ART SOLUTION TO THE ENERGY CRISIS

GEORGE L. DRAKE, JR.

636 Bradford Road, El Cajon, California 92021, U.S.A.

American, born January 16, 1927. Engineering specialist, Advanced Space Programs Department, General Dynamics Convair. Engineering education in the United States.

Mother Nature long ago laid the groundwork for solving our current energy problems by providing us a safe, regenerable, and abundant energy source—ice. Using seasonal ice as an energy source could dramatically influence our future. This project is keyed to promoting an awareness and providing the impetus needed to spark a worldwide investigation and acceptance of this fundamental ice energy concept. The specific goal of this project is to provide the nucleus of a credible data base so that all interested governments, industries, businesses, and individual citizens can see its potential and use the ice energy concept to lessen the demands for other energy sources.

Changing the world through a re-discovery and use of a unique energy source is an exciting and worthy challenge. Modern society requires an enormous amount of energy for cooling. The United States alone uses about 1000 million barrels of oil a year for cooling.

The new frontier in energy systems might well be the old way of harvesting, storing, and using seasonal ice, which is nothing more than the natural freezing of lakes and ponds, winter snowfall, the ageless buildup of glaciers, the inevitable calving of icebergs into the oceans, or the deliberate ambient freezing of water during the winter months.

The Great Lakes of the United States could easily provide 5 to 10 million acre-feet of ice every year. This could conserve a significant amount of fossil fuel. About $2\frac{1}{4}$ gallons of fuel oil are required to produce enough electricity to make 1 ton of refrigeration (2000 pounds of ice). One million acre-feet of frozen water can provide 1.36 billion tons of refrigeration or, to say it another way, can make an ice cube 3600 feet on a side. With fuel oil costs at one dollar per gallon, the value of that ice cube is more than $3 billion, and its use as an alternative energy source would release 73 million barrels of fuel oil for other purposes.

Implementing this state-of-the-art alternative energy concept requires an in-depth systems analysis to look at various ice energy scenarios and select those that best serve our varied needs. The systematic worldwide use of seasonal ice for cooling, heat engines, and energy storage can have a far-reaching and long-lasting impact upon our future. Ice is one of the few untapped energy sources with the ideal energy profile: (1) non-exhaustible supply, (2) easily obtainable, (3) naturally regenerated, (4) state-of-the-art technology, (5) non-polluting and safe, and (6) valuable and needed by-products.

Of all the energy demands of our modern society, the one for cooling has expanded most significantly—and potentially most dangerously. Dramatically illustrated by the increasing number of brown-outs, the energy load for cooling is based on a series of efficiencies from the electrical power plant to the final refrigeration units. Overall, starting with the net heat energy of the fuel oil, the net efficiency is about 24 percent. To produce 1 ton of refrigeration (288,000 BTU's/day), taking into account this 24 percent efficiency and the Coefficient of Performance (COP) of the refrigeration unit, requires that 300,000 BTU's of fuel oil energy be consumed at the electrical power plant. A gallon of fuel oil contains about 133,000 BTU's of energy, so $2\frac{1}{4}$ gallons generate the electricity needed to produce the cooling equivalent of 1 ton of refrigeration.

In the search for energy resources, it has become apparent that a new and unique relationship exists between energy and water. In 1973, The Rand Corporation defined the feasibility of transporting icebergs from Antarctica to the California coast for their water value. First findings indicated such an effort was feasible, with acquisition and transport costs estimated at around $10 per acre-foot. Today it would probably cost more like $20–$30 per acre-foot, which still compares favorably with 1980 California household water costs of about $200 per acre-foot.

However, if such an undertaking is viewed in the perspective of both water supply and energy supply, some extremely interesting economics emerge. While the 1360 tons of ice in an acre-foot would be worth $200, the energy value would be worth about $3000. This ratio of ultimate value, about $3200, to acquisition cost of $20–$30, is more than 100, translating into a cost-effective and highly desirable enterprise. For example, the iceberg train envisaged in the Rand studies, 300–600 meters wide and 20 kilometers long, weighing 1.345×10^{10} tons, would be worth over \$32 billion. There is obviously more to an iceberg than the tip that meets the eye!

The most direct use of ice as an alternative energy source is to provide cooling. In addition, ice is also a concentrated low-temperature reservoir—a heat sink. This low-temperature heat sink capability can enhance the performance of heat engines that produce electrical energy from industrial or natural waste heat sources. Today there is no systematic way to use this vast store of seasonal ice energy, but the task of developing and implementing an ice energy concept is not as remote or awesome as it may seem. A comparison might be made with natural gas, considered an oddity in pre-1800 times. It became a hazard with the advent of oil drilling, but today more than one million miles of pipeline costing about \$50 billion provide natural gas to virtually every area of the country.

I wish to begin work on a credible data base to provide a firm foundation for exploring the future of this renewable, non-polluting energy source. The initial step would establish the ice source options to be considered and the potential use of these sources for specific applications. Candidate ice energy applications include scenarios of transportation, storage, processing, operations, energy value, and economic impacts. Using these scenarios, several promising concepts will be selected for demonstration units. A demonstration unit program will be needed to provide operational experience and technical data.

The first phase of this systematic approach will be an information and education phase for potential users. Concept reviews with interested governments, industries, businesses, and the general public will update ideas, establish guidelines, define constraints, and in general promote the value of the seasonal ice energy concept. This visibility and interest should provide the spark needed to obtain the broad-based financial and technical support needed to launch a fully structured systems analysis.

The wings of the collapsible, ultralight aircraft. The D-tube and the ribs can be seen.

A MODULAR, COLLAPSIBLE, ULTRALIGHT AIRCRAFT

FRIEDRICH RENTSCH
Avenue de Belmont #17, CH-1820 Montreux, Switzerland

Swiss, born April 4, 1942. Self-employed in advertising and journalism. Educational background in architecture, philosophy, and photography.

The objective of this project is the exploration of the use of new "folding ribs" in the construction of aircraft wings, with the aim of more fully exploiting the potential flexibility of light-aircraft usage through the elimination of ground-handling problems.

The aircraft, now in prototype form, is being developed along the concept of modular parts. These parts will be light and compact enough for easy car-top transportation to and from appropriate flying sites, and they can be assembled and dismantled quickly, without elaborate equipment.

The key design factor has been the development of two wings that are made to perform all the essential control and stability functions needed for proven flying-wing technology. Added to these wings is a structure accommodating the pilot and the provision for attaching propeller and motor. Each wing consists of a structural D-tube (which provides the spar/leading edge assembly), with a chordwise extension to 27 percent of the full chord length. The wing shape over the remaining 73 percent toward the trailing edge is defined by ribs mounted on the rear end of the D-tube by means of hinges. The hinging of these ribs allows them to be swung sideways, so that they can be folded alongside the D-tube for convenient ground handling and storage.

The wings themselves are covered with accurately tailored envelopes of stabilized Dacron. These coverings are tensioned mechanically and are temporarily fastened to the ribs themselves when the plane is set up for flying.

The cockpit cage, the ailerons, and the tip winglets are all constructed as collapsible tubular frame assemblies. When broken down for storage or transport, the aircraft takes up a volume of about 500 centimeters by 20 centimeters by 100 centimeters. It can be carried on a small passenger car without affecting the car's speed and handling characteristics to any significant extent. If need be, the two wings can be separated so that transportability is further improved by the craft breaking down into several parcels.

Thus a high degree of collapsibility is achieved for an aircraft with a rigid wing's contour and surface quality.

The vehicle is configured as an ultralight aircraft with a wing loading of about 10 kilograms per square meter and a minimum speed of about 40 kilometers per hour. It will be used to determine the utility potential of simple and inexpensive aircraft that can be used independently of normal airport facilities. It will also be used in pursuit of two additional objectives: a fuel economy study in comparison with road vehicles of similar transportation capacity, and testing the folding rib design in view of the feasibility of a self-contained, convertible road/air vehicle.

Experimentation will therefore be with the following successive configurations: (1) a glider, (2) a powered glider, (3) an ultralight aircraft with extended speed range.

The Glider

With the D-tubes themselves spanning 9 meters, the total span in the glider configuration is increased to 12 meters by means of wing-tip panels consisting of a tubular frame and containing the ailerons. These tip panels plug into a sleeve that is laminated into the outboard ending of the D-tubes. Foot-launching of this configuration should be possible, although due to the excessive weight of the prototype the absence of a sufficiently strong headwind might render foot-launching hazardous. Sink rate is expected to be somewhat below 1 meter/second, and the glide ratio to be between 10 and 15 with the pilot in open air. A streamlined pod for the pilot might extend the glide ratio to 20, or perhaps beyond 20.

The Powered Glider

A motor drive is added to the glider configuration. Takeoff would be on wheels from flat ground. A 10-horsepower motor is expected to give a climb rate of about 1.5 meters/second.

The Ultralight Aircraft

The wing-tip panels are replaced by a structure ending the wing at the end of the D-tubes, thus reducing the span to 9 meters, and its surface area from 13.5 square meters to 11.25 square meters. Minimum speed would increase to approximately 45–50 kilometers/hour, and cruising speeds of around 80 kilometers/hour should be feasible. With the elimination of the tip panels, the covering envelope would also have to be replaced, and a different aileron would be required. The cockpit cage might have to be replaced, depending on whether correct trim can be realized with the same cage for both configurations. Resorting to the streamlined pod may cut fuel consumption to that of a small motorcycle.

Work on the above configurations began in 1978 and is expected to be completed in 1980.

Project Aircraft Specifications

	Glider	*Ultralight aircraft*
Span	12 m	9 m
Wing area	13.5 m^2	11.25 m^2
Aspect ratio	10.7	7.2
Net weight	$\approx$ 50 kg	$\approx$ 65 kg (w/o fuel)
Wing loading	9.5 $\pm$ 2 kg/m^2	13 $\pm$ 2 kg/m^2
Minimum speed	$\approx$ 40 km/h	$\approx$ 48 km/h

Common		*Common*	
Root chord	1.5 m	Roll and pitch control	Ailerons
Chord end D-tube	1 m	Yaw control	Aerodynamically self-induced
Leading edge sweep	15 degrees	Spar	U-type, fully cantilevered
Spanwise twist		Construction	
Root to end of D-tube	-3 degrees	D-tube and ribs	Composite (glass)
Glider tip panel	Adjustable	Other elements	Steel and aluminum tubular framework
Airfoil	NACA 23012		

COMPUTERIZED, PERSONALLY ADJUSTING, VISION-COMPENSATING LENSES

JOHN WARREN SENDERS
Keneggy West, Columbia Falls, Maine 04623, U.S.A.

American, born February 26, 1920. Professor of Industrial Engineering at University of Toronto, member of numerous professional scientific societies.

I have invented, and wish to develop to practical application, a device that will compensate both for the progressive loss of accommodative vision ability with increasing age and for its complete loss after cataract removal.

As human beings age, they suffer a progressive decline in the accommodative function of their vision. Thus they become less able to focus on objects over a wide range of distance from the eye. Further, there is an ever-increasing incidence of cataracts, and consequent impairment, associated with increasing age. The remedy for the latter is the removal of the crystalline lens and, usually, the substitution of external supplemental lenses that restore a degree of the lost function. In all of these cases, the accommodative function of the eye is totally lost, leaving the patient in possession of a very narrow depth of field for moderately near vision.

To solve this problem, it is possible to provide a spectacle lens of variable power that can be placed under the control of a system of eye-position sensors in such a way as to provide automatic accommodation to whatever distance the user converges his or her eyes. The lens system is based on a microcomputer with a double function: (1) providing a pattern-recognition capability needed to deal with shifts in the position of the spectacle frame on the head, and (2) providing memory and interpolative ability needed to correct its operation on the basis of relatively few inputs from the user. I intend to bring my patented design for this system to a point where it can be used by patients without difficulty or inconvenience.

Although there is no technical problem with respect to the feasibility of the vision-compensation device, it will be necessary to design and construct developmental models and test their utility and acceptability on people of various ages and with a variety of visual problems.

The patent for this vision-compensation device was granted on January 1, 1980, and the abstract describes it this way: "A vision compensation system includes a lens-receiving frame with a pair of lens members, at least one of which has variable optical compensation capabilities. Carried by the frame are means for producing a signal as a function of the relative angular positions of the eyes of the wearer and means responsive to that signal for changing the optical characteristics of the variable lens to provide compensation for impaired accommodative capacity of the wearer's eye."

I plan to construct prototype devices with a variety of variable parameters built in. These will be adjusted to meet the requirements of users for maximum ease of use and adequacy of function. Measurements of power consumption will be made, and a variety of power sources will be tested and considered. Resistance to vibration and shock will be measured, and the design improved to meet high standards. The goal will be to ensure that a production model will be reliable, not require excessive care, and not require frequent and expensive maintenance. Experiments will also be carried out to determine exactly how many user inputs will be required to ensure correct functioning of the computing and interpolating programs built into the microcomputer control system.

The speed of the system's response mechanism will be varied, and the needs of the users measured and weighed against the power required as a function of response speed, in order to optimize power-source life span.

Tests of the acceptability of the device in a variety of design configurations for the different classes of users must also be made. This is particularly important for elderly persons who find problems in adapting to new technologies.

Finally, the device, if it is to achieve wide acceptability by those who need it, must be aesthetically pleasing and light in weight to the greatest extent possible, so that it will be both physically and psychologically easy to wear and to use.

The total development program outlined above will require approximately one year. I expect to start on the developmental phase in June 1981. Though I anticipate development of a workable prototype within one year, governmental approvals for clinical applications will require more time.

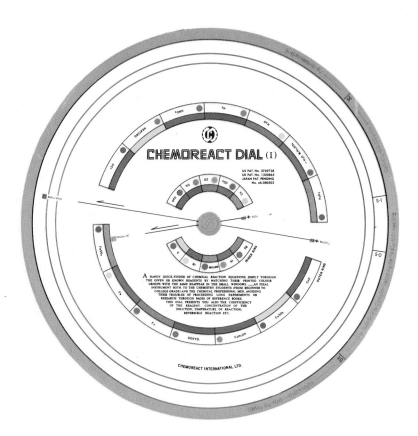

The Chemoreact Dial. The answer to the first example is shown in the right window of the inner ring.

"DIALING" CHEMICAL REACTION EQUATIONS

YUNG-CHEH LU
2460 Southvale Cr. #909, Ottawa, Ontario
K1B 4L8, Canada

Chinese, born June 12, 1919. Chemistry professor, Solar Chemical Company president, and chairman of Institute of Patentees, Inventors & Designers in Hong Kong. Science education background in China, United States, and Japan.

Solving chemical reaction equations without mistakes is an arduous, brain-straining problem for students and professionals in the field of chemistry the world over, no matter what their native language may be. Resorting to reference books and various listings is both time-consuming and tedious.

The search for a better solution to this problem led me to invent my "Chemoreact Dial," which has been patented in the United States and Britain and is pending receipt of its patent in Japan. Using the Chemoreact Dial, solutions to chemical reaction equations can be found in a matter of only a few seconds. The Dial itself will solve over one thousand essential reaction equations and is designed to be learned quickly after a short time of practice.

Its purpose is to give the chemistry student, or the chemistry professional, assistance in rapidly determining the proper chemical products after the reaction of two or more known chemical reactants. Using the Chemoreact Dial, one can derive for each chemical reaction, the following elements of information:

1. Concentration of the solution

2. Reverse reaction

3. Heat required, or heat liberated

4. Number of moles

5. Diffusion or precipitation, if they are produced through the chemical reaction.

   To understand and appreciate the value of the Dial, I will present a few examples.
   Suppose that the chemical problem under consideration involves trying to determine the chemical products produced after aluminum has reacted with carbon dioxide:

$$Al + CO_2 \longrightarrow ? + ?$$

To approach this problem, we go through the following steps:

1. On the Chemoreact Dial, we first locate the reagent "Al" on the *Inner ring,* which has the coloration blue/orange. (The coloration symbols are always read from the inside first.)

2. Turn the Turning plate with your right index finger until you encounter the line marked "S-I." ("S-I" stands for the Setting line of Inner ring chemicals or reagents.)

3. Turn this S-I marking on the Turning plate until it lines up with the other S-I marking found on the outermost part of the Chemoreact Dial.

4. You will then find "Al" on the top section of the S-I on the Turning plate. Follow the direction given by the arrow, and turn the plate slowly counterclockwise.

5. Observe the coloration's change carefully through the smallest window, located near the Inner ring, until the color blue appears.

6. At the same time, observe the coloration through the small window on the left side of the Inner ring, in which orange appears.

7. Turn the Turning plate slowly, observing the names of the chemical reactants in the order of the English alphabet, and you will soon find the reading

$$3CO_2 \qquad (4)$$

and the products appear in the left-hand side window written as

$$2Al_2O_3 + 3C$$

8. The (4) is the coefficient, or the number of moles of the first reactant (i.e., the aluminum). With this information provided by the Chemoreact Dial, the entire and complete chemical reaction equation should be read as

$$4Al + 3CO_2 \longrightarrow 2Al_2O_3 + 3C$$

The same method can be applied to the reactants written in the Outer ring. The only difference in using the Dial for these is that one sets the "S-O" marking in line first, unlike the example given above. (In this case, S-O means the Setting line of the Outer ring.)

With the above method, the user of the Chemoreact Dial can also find out that, in certain conditions, the yield of the products in question will be entirely different. To illustrate this, the Dial is used to give information on what happens with different concentrations of solution:

Concentrated: $\quad Cu + 4HNO_3 \longrightarrow Cu(NO_3)_2 + 2NO_2 + 2H_2O$

Diluted: $\quad\quad\quad 3Cu + 8HNO_3 \longrightarrow 3Cu(NO_3)_2 + 2NO + 4H_2O$

or, similarly, the results of heating the chemicals only:

$$ZnCO_3 \longrightarrow ZnO + CO_2$$
$$2Pb_3O_4 \longrightarrow 6PbO + O_2$$

or, still another example, of water removed at 160°C:

$$C_2H_5OH \xrightarrow{-H_2O} C_2H_4 + H_2O$$

In bringing the Chemoreact Dial to its present state of readiness, I have consulted with many educators, incurred the patent search and registration expenses, and invested in the necessary molds for the device, which has been made in Japan. Concurrently, I have in development what I call the "Organoreact Balancer," which is a similar device that will help to solve over 4000 organic chemical reactions.

I believe these instruments will be of great assistance to chemistry students around the world, as well as to professional users. They will save many hours of time otherwise lost to a laborious process of searching for information in books and tables, and, at the student level, the enjoyment of working with the Dial will contribute to better, easier, and more pleasant learning about chemical reactions.

THE LIQUID
BARRIER FILTER

WOLF D. SEUFERT
Département de biophysique, Faculté de médecine,
Université de Sherbrooke, Sherbrooke, Qué. J1H 5N4, Canada

Canadian, born April 17, 1935. Associate Professor of Biophysics, educated in Germany, the United States, and France. Numerous publications, multiple patents.

A new concept—the liquid barrier filter—is being developed to eliminate highly toxic particulate contaminants from an atmosphere.

Of all liquids, perfluorocarbons can dissolve the greatest quantities of gases. For example, they absorb and pass, by diffusion, sufficient oxygen to keep the blood's hemoglobin oxygenated. Several laboratories are studying aqueous fluorocarbon dispersions in attempts to formulate a preparation which, compatible with whole blood, could be infused into the circulation as a blood substitute. This project explores another application of this same quality of fluorocarbons. As a liquid, a perfluorocarbon phase constitutes a nearly impenetrable barrier to contaminants in a gas that itself can freely pass through it. Thus, a perfluorocarbon liquid could form a "liquid barrier filter" (LBF).

It is already apparent from theoretical considerations confirmed by a few preliminary experiments that an LBF is far superior in performance (particle collection and retention during prolonged charging, etc.) to conventional filters. I propose to perform the experiments necessary for the design of an LBF in the form of a disposable cartridge for a facial mask. Such a filter has important applications: it provides the best available personal protection against the inhalation of highly toxic particulate contaminants.

Particulate material polluting a gas stream is caught with nearly ideal efficiency in a liquid barrier filter. Gas molecules can diffuse freely through these perfluorocarbon liquids, requiring only a minimal pressure gradient, while pollutant particles in the gas stream collide with the molecules of the liquid and lose their momentum in it. Such an LBF will, therefore, collect contaminants from a gas with a very high yield: the filtering liquid as a condensed phase of close molecular packing severs completely the continuity between input and output gas phases that exist in all conventional filters. Thus, the probability of intercepting pollutant particles is vastly increased, giving LBF's the promise of becoming the most efficient filters yet available.

A number of experiments [Ed. note: the experiments are quoted and explained in some detail in the application form.] have established that gas transfer across a perfluorocarbon phase is sufficient for sustained respiration, and that the liquid phase constitutes a barrier for particulate pollutants in a gas stream. There remains the question of possible toxicity of perfluorocarbons to be answered before the actual design of an LBF is discussed.

A liquid film by itself would not be able to support the pressure loads existing in a realistic filtration system, so the LBF will have to contain a carrier matrix to soak up the filtering liquid. This matrix will absorb the fluorocarbon by rotating continuously through a reservoir at low speed. This renews the system, prevents clogging or the increase in flow resistance with charging time through the accumulation of particles on the filter, and always presents a new surface of filtering liquid to the input gas.

A functional LBF is very easily constructed. Strength and porosity of the matrix are matched to the applied pressure, and its thickness determines that of the LBF. Several matrix sheets can be stacked to form a single multi-lamellar barrier filter. The filter matrix rotates slowly through a perfluorocarbon reservoir. Tests demonstrate that 75 percent of the filter area can be exposed to the incoming air; the surface activity of the perfluorocarbons assures that the entire filter area is always wetted, even at very low reservoir levels. The filter can be set into a circular cartridge to be attached to a regular gas mask. A small battery provides enough power to rotate the disc, and a brush attached to the circumference of the rotating disc pulls liquid into a groove in the cartridge housing and seals the inner "clean" compartment from the contaminated outside.

On the basis of results to date, the objective of the project now is to determine with greater accuracy the size of the filter and the thickness of the liquid phase necessary for proper functioning of the envisaged LBF.

The applications of a liquid barrier filter derive from the advantage of a collection yield approaching the ideal. A mask incorporating an LBF will completely protect people who have to work in environments containing highly toxic particulates. Small, light, and inexpensive, it will eventually be accessible to a much greater number of people than could be equipped with the only alternative to guarantee a similar protection, namely, a portable source of compressed air.

FINDING DROUGHT-RESISTANT PLANTS WITH CHEMISTRY

PATRICK MOYNA
Missisipi 1634, Apto. 104, Montevideo, Uruguay

Uruguayan, born Novermber 1, 1938. University Professor of Chemistry at two institutions. Uruguayan, English, Japanese, and Canadian educational background.

C ertain plant species are particularly well adapted to survival in dry climates. Many of the adaptations are chemical mechanisms that enhance a plant's survival possibilities by improving its absorption or retention of water, or by a more efficient metabolism of the water once it has been absorbed.

We propose to complete a project that studies the botanical, biological, and chemical aspects of certain drought-resistant plants native to, or adaptable to, Uruguay. The results should be of value in developing more efficient crops adapted to grow in marginal lands, or crops that can be grown productively with lower water consumption requirements.

As background, we look at the production of foodstuffs as one of the most pressing problems of humanity. Great efforts to obtain better yielding varieties, which grow faster and bear more seeds, have paid off in the so-called Green Revolution. These basic improvements, however, have shed light on related problems. As good planting land has grown scarcer and crop pests have continued to abound, we are being forced to analyze all aspects that might enable us to get better yields by making our crop plants more resistant to pests, less dependent upon fertilizers, and better able to produce in conditions of poor soil and reduced water supplies.

Water is fast becoming one of the major limiting factors in crop production, in both developed and less developed countries. In many areas, poor agricultural practices have led to increasing desertification and the loss of formerly arable lands. For these reasons, it is increasingly important to understand better the process of water economy in plants, because it is a fundamental aspect of their growth and development.

There are several mechanisms—mechanical, physical, and chemical—used naturally by plants adapted to desert and arid environments to ensure their survival. Many involve purely mechanical and physical adaptations (shapes in the plant surface, smaller leaf size, extensive root systems, etc.), but a significant number are related to chemical mechanisms that play their part at molecular levels, or act as foundations for physical adaptations. Under this last type, we can count the internal gums and mucilages present in many arid-climate plants (polysaccharides in cacti, for example), which use their water-retaining properties to make their contributions, and more basic yet, the epicuticular wax layers that cover all green and soft surfaces of plants.

The epicuticular wax layer performs its protective function—avoiding excessive loss of internal moisture—by acting as an impervious layer. It also protects the plant from all kinds of external agression, either mechanical (inorganic agents such as gases) or biological (bacteria or plant pests).

The composition of these protective waxes shows appreciable variation from one species to another. They also show certain variations by season, even within the same plant. The most usual fractions forming these waxes are hydrocarbons (up to 90 percent in certain plants), esters, free fatty acids, alcohols, and a few other components, which have in common their impermeability. We presume a certain adaptation of their composition to the plant's ecological niche, and thus postulate that desert or arid-climate plants will have certain characteristics in common. A better knowledge of these characteristics will enable us to establish goals for current efforts to develop crops better suited to survival in low-water situations.

Work has already started on these studies, with succulent and cacti gums. It includes sample preparation of well-classified plant material, isolation of their waxes (solvent extraction), separation of the different fractions (column and thin-layer chromatography), identification of the different component fractions (analytical thin-layer chromatography, spectrophotometry), identification of the components within each fraction (gas-liquid chromatography), all to form a data base. Once the percentage compositions are established for a series of plants, synthetic simulated waxes will be prepared. These waxes will then be checked to determine their impermeability against water, gases, bacteria, pesticide formulations, as well as their qualities of providing anti-bacterial and insect-repellent characteristics.

If successful, these chemical compounds could be used to greatly increase plants' abilities to maintain good condition in such adverse situations as inadequate water supply, limited fertilizer availability, attack by pests, and poor storage after harvesting.

The collapsible module—collapsed and expanded.

COLLAPSIBLE MODULE FOR USE IN GENERAL ENGINEERING

SUJASH KUMAR BAIN
90B, Shyambazar Street, Calcutta 700 005, India

Indian, born June 1, 1932. Development manager in engineering firm. Engineering education in India, Full Member of Institution of Engineers (India).

The "Module with Collapsible Properties" is an invention using a new principle of collapsibility that possesses unique advantages. The project described here employs this technique of collapsibility in important engineering applications, including such vital fields as energy and air transportation.

As the illustration shows, the invention is conceptually simple (though it carries U.S. Patent Number 4,089,147). Essentially, it is a collapsible module constructed in a new fashion. The tapered side members of the module prevent each others' tendency to collapse in an inward direction, and the module therefore becomes self-locked in a rigid position. Though this may sound simple, its significance is only appreciated when the module is compared with traditional collapsing devices. Of these, there are four main types, each with disadvantages, as follows:

1. *Telescopic Devices.* (A) Require locking at joints. (B) Overlap at joints is required. (C) Must be tapering. (D) Load is limited due to weaknesses. (E) Collapsibility is also limited.

2. *Lazy Tongue Devices.* (A) Hinges float in space. (B) Base and top connections need to be sliding. (C) Need locking. (D) Stability is poor. (E) Load limited due to preceding reasons.

3. *Inflatable Devices.* (A) Inflation is necessary. (B) Resilient material must be used. (C) Chance of leakage persists. (D) Load-carrying capacity is less. (E) Generally costly.

4. *Folding Devices.* (A) Innumerable configurations possible, but these basically are of convenience for quick assembly by locking parts together. (B) Not very stable unless costly design is provided. (C) Each member piece needs separate locking. (D) Generally applicable only to one-tier or one-piece jobs (an example would be a folding table).

As opposed to the above traditional systems, the present invention overcomes the disadvantages of collapsibility with unique features:

1. Self-locking.

2. Auto-stabilizing. A part of the load is transferred inward, providing locking force. Geometric configuration is such that if one frame of a self-locked module is pulled out, the other frames will resist such destabilizing motion.

3. Hinges can be so positioned that loading stress will by-pass them, making it unnecessary for the hinges to be of load-carrying strength.

4. Column or beam configurations can be straight *or* tapering.

5. Once module-by-module erection is completed, the structure becomes an integral structure of the desired configuration.

6. Ratio of full height to collapsed height can be very large.

7. Erection is module by module; operation is at ground level. Unfold one module, nudge the side frames to their self-locking position, and the module is erected. Repeat the operation. The lifting device can be of the limited height required for lifting one module.

8. Height/length can be adjusted by keeping unused modules folded.

9. Heavy load capacity. Because the module gets self-locked, the load is distributed throughout the structure.

10. Respectful of Euler's theorem of the column. A column may be straight, but we have to assume that under load it may bend and thereby set up bending moment. In these modules, a deliberate inward bend is imparted in concentric directions. Thus the bending moment set up is directed toward the axis of the module, with obvious advantages.

The module can be used in three basic modes:

1. *Column.* It can be straight, tapering, or bulging at the middle.

2. *Beam.* Best used as a tied arch, to avoid beam shear forces.

3. *Integral Framework.* Frames of given shapes, such as a hexagonal dome, can be collapsed and erected as a whole.

Some Useful and Specific Applications

Electrical and Electronic Transmission Towers. Conventional towers are made by assembling large numbers of components from ground to higher level, which is time consuming. Collapsible towers can be factory made in several modules or submodules that can be erected at the site very rapidly. Bolted joints are few and all the erection work is done at ground level.

Scaffolding and Shoring Work in the Construction Industry. Heavy load-bearing columns can be made collapsible. Height is adjusted instantly, as required, thus reducing inventory holding. On site assembly work is avoided.

Cheap Hydraulic Jack. By combining an ordinary hydraulic jack with a heavy-duty collapsible column, we get, in effect, a hydraulic jack of larger reach, yet of undiminished strength. Given the great price differentials between a short hydraulic jack of, say, 50-centimeters reach and one of 3-meters reach, both having the same load capacity, using a hybrid jack of 50 centimeters with the performance of 3 meters is very cheap.

Collapsible Poles for Tents, etc. This system enables the making of a folding pole that can be self-locked for use, thus allowing construction of integral tents. Larger tents can be collapsed as one piece, packed, carried, and set up easily.

Perhaps the two most important applications, however, are in the areas of energy and transportation, as follows.

Windmills can be a source of much useful power in many locations, but have not been adequately exploited due to clumsiness, difficulty of erection, and cost. Using this module, with its collapsible and self-locking principle, small, inexpensive, easy-to-construct, pre-packaged windmills can be made for simple do-it-yourself installation, according to our design specifications. Similarly, we have calculated specifications for efficient medium- and large-size windmills, in the latter case using helium-filled modules to form giant wind drums. By inflating the modules on site, and nudging them into position, vast wind drums of little weight can be built, thus requiring towers strong enough to carry only the wind load, not the constructed weight.

Similarly, the use of collapsible modules, helium filled at the site, allows for the simple construction of large, lighter-than-air semi-rigid airships. By using standardized modules, many sizes of airships can be made that can be quickly and easily collapsed by pumping out the helium into storage tanks, thus solving garaging problems. An example from our designs is for a small airship, based on one module running lengthwise. Inflated to 30 meters long and 10 meters across, it collapses to 2.5 meters across and 2 meters thick, but has a net lifting capacity of 1000 kilograms.

RELATING SPACE TO TIME IN TERMS OF ENERGY

CHRISTOPHER B. HEYRING
St. Pierre Golf and Country Club, St. Pierre Park, Chepstow,
Gwent NP6 6YA, U.K.

British, born January 22, 1946. Independent researcher, former lecturer in three-dimensional studies. Architectural education in the United Kingdom.

E leven years ago, I began to investigate symmetry and topology in structures. Five years ago, my personal research program induced me to take a closer look at parity, which strictly speaking is not my field. Parity is a space-reflection mirror symmetry principle that states that no fundamental distinction can be made between a left-hand and a right-hand system of coordinates. Since 1957, however, it has been known that symmetry is violated in nature. A year and a half ago, I found that I was able to establish a model to functionally violate parity.

I now aim to round off my personal research program by constructing two working models of my theoretical model. One model involves making quite simple optical elements from clear acrylic plastic to act as special kinds of prisms in order to demonstrate that the visible part of the electromagnetic spectrum (light) is composed of two independent sets of parity-violating components. The second model involves parity violation in the non-visible part of the electromagnetic spectrum. The evidence (concerning parity in relation to time asymmetry) in these models suggests that there is at the very least a reasonable possibility that (even natural) magnetic sources may be used as efficient but degeneratable energy sources.

The idea that electricity and magnetism are functionally reciprocal was abandoned by Faraday and Henry in 1832, when they independently stumbled on a compromise solution to the generation of electricity involving the relative mechanical motions of copper coil and magnetic field. It is tantamount to an attempt to by-pass the laws of thermodynamics to look for the reciprocal relationship that allows magnetism to induce a current directly into the conductors without relative movements, if the "permanent" magnetic source is *not* expected to be run down correspondingly. No technology has been evolved (since Faraday's findings) that is capable of degenerating a magnetic source, or which transfers magnetic energy directly into an electrical current. Magnets to this day are called *permanent,* but magnetism is still not fully understood. A growing body of evidence suggests that magnetic sources should be regarded as very upgraded voltaic cells, or batteries.

The parity-discriminating characteristics of the electromagnetic device described here [Ed. note: nine pages of illustrations and text accompanied the application.] appear to fit the bill for the hardware needed to prove the reciprocal functions of magnetism and electricity and thus to define space and time.

The working-model concept begins with the established fact that a given current in an electrical conductor has a specific and fixed magnetic field that cannot be reversed without changing the direction of the current. A construction of conductors, involving suitably devious topography and asymmetry, with gaps in between occupied by permeable material, or with the conductors padded out, raises the question whether the interdependence of the electrical and magnetic functions is behaviorally reciprocal, and ultimately enables us to understand, if not use, the fragile conservation properties of parity of electromagnetism.

The approach to the working model begins with the positioning of four electrical conductors, each insulated, which are individually perpendicularly arranged, passing over one and under another in what may be described as a clockwise symmetry. Electricity is limited to flowing along the conductors, while the magnetic flux is free to cross evacuated gaps in order to follow the paths of best permeability. Additional conductors (assumed to be not of copper, but a material with reasonable magnetic permeability as well as electrical conductivity) may be stacked alternately to form a vertical pile, in which the magnetic flux follows a fluent path through the center mesh of wires without ever confronting components that are non-accumulative. Ultimately, by bending the pile into the shape of an annular ring or torus, the two polar faces of the magnetic circuit meet and are connected, and the electrical circuit can be completed also. In practice, it is extremely difficult to fabricate this kind of toroidal wiring system. A more satisfactory approach is to make modular units that have some surfaces treated with insulation material and others that aid electrical conductivity. Stacked in the correct orientation, they can then be fused together. Collectively, the electromagnetic components of force in this arrangement respond to ambient excesses of electromagnetic stresses, and may thus permit magnetism to induce current into idle conductors, even though degenerating the flux.

THE REPOSITORY FOR GERMINAL CHOICE

ROBERT K. GRAHAM
Sycamore Lane, Escondido, California 92025, U.S.A.

American, born June 9, 1906. Lens consultant to Minnesota Mining & Manufacturing Company (3M). Science education in the United States.

The Repository for Germinal Choice is a facility set up to (1) increase the number of offspring of our most creative scientists (Nobelists) and (2) offer to very bright, healthy young women whose husbands are infertile their choice of one of several Nobelists to serve as germinal father of their child or children. The program consists of collecting germinal donations from Nobelists in science who are free of known hereditary defects; preserving the donations under liquid nitrogen; and air-shipping under liquid nitrogen a chosen donation to reach the Recipient or her gynecologist at the appropriate time of the month.

This unique facility, The Repository for Germinal Choice, functions in the same way as Artificial Insemination Donor (A.I.D.), except that, in accordance with the concept of Dr. Hermann J. Muller, the noted geneticist who first proposed this concept:

1. The Donors are unpaid and contribute solely out of willingness to increase the distribution of genes that helped to make them outstanding in their lifetime.

2. The germinal donations (semen) are sealed in ampules and kept under liquid nitrogen ($-192\,°C$) in a cryogenic vessel that is sheathed in lead and kept in a subterranean chamber. Donations to the Repository are thus preserved and protected from mutagenic radiation.

3. The Recipients are genetically selected by a medical panel. They are young women whose husbands are infertile, but who do not wish to be denied motherhood. Recipients may choose from written descriptions of two or more donors the one whose characteristics they would most like to have in the father of their children. Thus, the Repository offers to qualified couples a new resource—the opportunity to choose the father of their child or children from among the most creative scientists of our time.

Semen donations are categorized by every knowable heritable characteristic, but not by name or identity of the donor. Hence, Recipients know the most significant characteristics of the germinal father, but never his identity. Donors never know the identity of the Recipients. Complete anonymity is maintained.

The chosen donations are shipped to Recipients, or to their gynecologists, under liquid nitrogen to arrive at the appropriate time in the Recipient's fertility cycle. The shipping container will hold sperm in viable condition for about 10 days. There is no charge for this service, except for the expenses incidental to the shipping. There is a deposit of $250.00 on the container, which is refunded upon its return.

The first person known to have suggested germinal choice was Dr. Hermann J. Muller, the first American geneticist to win a Nobel Prize. The writer of this application collaborated with Dr. Muller for several years, but at the time of his death, Dr. Muller was still not prepared to proceed with his concept. Neither can the writer claim credit for the technique employed of preserving human semen under liquid nitrogen. This is the contribution of Dr. Jerome K. Sherman, University of Arkansas Medical Center, Little Rock, Arkansas.

The writer's contribution is to have brought the Muller concept to realization. Discussion and planning covered many years, both before and after this writer first proposed the project in his book, *The Future of Man* (1970). It necessitated the setting up of the physical facilities (the Repository), utilizing the Sherman technique for preservation of the donations and shipping them to Recipients, successfully recruiting Nobelists as donors and female Mensans whose husbands are infertile as Recipients. The first collection and preservation of Nobelists' semen was in 1977. The first shipments of semen were made in 1979.

This is an on-going project, intended to be expanded as time and funds permit. I hope that additional Repositories will be established throughout the world and be continued indefinitely. Support for establishing the project has been limited almost entirely to contributions by the writer.

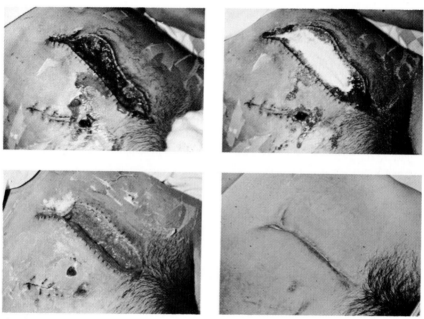

An Argentine woman underwent surgery for acute appendicitis on October 10, 1977. She was reoperated on, because of peritonitis, on October 15. However, the abdominal wall abscessed. On October 21, the incision was reopened (upper left photo); the abscess was drained; use of antibiotics was suspended; and ground sugar treatment (upper right photo) began. After a few days the wound was cleaned and found to be free of infection (lower left photo). Healing was rapid (lower right photo), and the woman was discharged on December 2.

HEALING INFECTED WOUNDS WITH ORDINARY SUGAR

LEON HERSZAGE
Av. Alvear 1864, 3° B, 1129 Buenos Aires, Argentina

Argentine, born December 19, 1931. General and dental surgeon, head of pathology in abdominal walls at Alvear Hospital. Medical education in Buenos Aires.

We are submitting a summary of original research work conducted on the healing of all kinds of infections in wounds, ulcers, and scabs in the field of human medicine through the use of ordinary, commercial-use ground sugar.

Our experience in this area began in January 1976, when the wounds of two young female patients operated on for gynecological problems became infected, destroyed the abdominal walls, and proved impossible to control with the entire therapeutic and laboratory means available to that moment.

We knew of a colleague who had empirically treated some cases of postoperative infection with ordinary sugar, and we decided to attempt his solution. The results were so successful that the young women's wounds healed completely.

In 1977, we began the experience on which this paper is based. We started by analyzing the composition of ordinary sugar, in the belief that some substance or bacteria participated in this apparent bactericidal lysis. We also tried to find literature on the subject, but located only a reference to empirical treatments, and that concerning only ulcers and scabs. We knew that, in earlier times, sugar had been used in a few surgical departments, but never on scientific grounds and that the treatment had been discarded after a short time. On the other hand, folk medicine has made use of sugar as a hemostatic substance for a very long time in the interior of our country. We also found that, in Chile, Bolivia, and Colombia, a powder known as "chanc ca" is used at some centers. This powder is actually the molasses obtained from the first grinding of sugar cane. We tried to find traces of its use in pre-Columbian America and learned that, although it is not documented, a mummy was found in Peru that had apparently been preserved with honey. This led us to study the composition and effects of honey, and this, in turn, to find out why honey is not so effective as sugar.

Finally, in 1977, in view of the limited literature available and subsequent to our own success in utilizing it with a wide variety of patient infections, we decided to undertake the original research needed. We would study the physiopathogenesis of the action of this simple, uncomplicated, and cheap method of healing every kind of infected wound, whatever its etiology.

We began by establishing whether our wounds contained bacteria and then classifying the bacteria. We thus found that all suppurations before the treatment showed a varying polyflora, including mainly *E. coli, Staphylococcus, Streptococcus, Klebsiella, Perfringens, Pseudomonas,* or tuberculosis bacilli, according to the etiology of the wound. Subsequent samples, taken three days after the beginning of the sugar treatment, showed the elimination of all the important bacteria, except *Staphylococcus doradom,* a common skin germ which no longer infected but only contaminated through proximity. The third sample, taken three days later, confirmed the previous findings and additionally showed the absence of inflammation plus signs of clinical evolution toward healing. From the beginning of these treatments, all other therapies were interrupted: general and local antibiotics, antiseptics, washings, etc., and only sugar was used (except where another pathology demanded its own specific treatment). Wound healing was achieved in 100 percent of our cases.

In the bacteriology of food it is well known that any concentration of a sugar in a medium more than 56 percent inhibits the development of germs and forms of resistance; only fungi and yeasts persist. We also found that drugstore syrups are saccharose solutions up to 80 percent and also auto-sterile. A paper by D. J. Kushner shows that bacteria take water from their medium, measured in terms of A/W (Activity/Water), and D. J. Kushner gives a formula with which to measure A/W and the water percentages in which bacteria can survive. Therefore, all bacteria, whatever their type, need water as a vital element. Any solution with a saccharose concentration over 80 percent decreases the A/W to such a low level that the bacteria are completely inhibited.

We also investigated sugar's degree of hygroscopic power. In diabetic patients under hypoglycemic treatment, it struck our attention that their blood sugar level did not vary, even though in the case of one of them, we used 800 grams of sugar due to the size of the wound. This is because sugar cannot be absorbed through the wound: its osmotic action is centrifugal; and even if it got into the bloodstream, it could be metabolized only in the liver.

In general, from seven to ten days after treating the wounds, they were clean and ready for closure. The liquid attracted by the sugar is plasma and lymph, and we started counting the number of macrophages (large cells that remove and consume degenerating tissue and bacteria). In an initial sample prior to treatment, three macrophages were counted per microscopic field; 72 hours after treatment the number had increased three times, and after another 3 days, yet three times again. Therefore, a second characteristic of the effect of the sugar is as a powerful sucker of macrophages, which clean the wound, now no longer infected, and make it ready for healing.

In the case of a new patient, who presented feces on the wound due to the characteristics of his illness, it was enough to remove them with a piece of gauze to see that the open wound was covered with a "glass-like" layer, beneath which the usual healing process continued without overinfection. This led us to initiate a histochemical study that lasted 18 months. We finally came to the conclusion that the layer is made up of 85–90 percent proteic nitrogen. In other words, an organic reaction had taken place in the healing process, with saccharose leading to the formation of a thick collagenous protective layer, which was studied histochemically and with electron microscopy. Thus, a third action of sugar on wounds became established: self-protection against reinfection, with obvious thickening and resistance of the scar thus formed.

Additionally, we have measured the pH in every wound, only to find that it did not vary significantly. We have worked on guinea pigs, rats, rabbits, and mice, with different infection and control procedures, with sterilized sugar, without differences in the results. We have used anhydrous glucose and sodium chloride, with negative results.

We agree with other international authors about the role of macrophages in wound healing, but feel that further studies should be done on the relationship between macrophages and prostaglandins, the collagenous layer and its role in scar resistance, and the theories of membrane phenomena and their relationship with the cell-bacteria process.

The experiments were carried out on 120 patients, though several hundreds have now been treated. In all cases, the wound was only dried with a piece of gauze, and then filled with ordinary sugar. We conclude:

1. Ordinary sugar in high concentrations is lethal to all types of bacteria.

2. The treatment described here has a suction effect on macrophages, and this mechanism eliminates all dead cells.

3. A layer is generated in this treatment that protects the wound, prevents overinfection, and ensures healing.

MEASURING VISION EXACTLY

EASTMAN SMITH
Cranfield Circle, Route 4, Box 460, Mountain Home,
Arkansas 72653, U.S.A.

American, born April 2, 1897. Retired mechanical engineer, presently devoted to subject invention. Mechanical/optical engineering career/education.

For more than a hundred years, the general system of eyesight testing, for eyeglasses, has remained the same. We now have more expensive, automated, and computerized instruments, but the basic system used has remained unchanged—and it is wrong.

It is fatiguing, it is unnatural, and it leads to many poor prescriptions. It is not based on the way in which the eye naturally sees. After thirty years of research, experimentation, and planning for correct instrumentation, I have a totally new and much more accurate method for testing eyes, based on three-dimensional test ranges using pre-focused targets. The instrument which does this is called the Xactometer (U.S. Patent No. 3,825,326).

Present techniques apparently to the contrary, the primary quantities for measurement of the eye's vision are not really independent. They depend upon (1) the shape of the elastic eyeball, (2) the exterior eyeball muscles, (3) the ciliary muscle, (4) the eye lens, (5) the sphericity of the cornea, (6) the warping of the cornea, (7) the angle of this warping, (8) the density or clouding of the lens, and (9) indirectly, but importantly, the ocular nervous system and the physical condition of the patient. An error in one measured quantity may affect the accuracy of the measurement of other measured quantities. This may be due partly to the peculiarities of the light-ray intersections found in astigmatism. None of the quantities can be measured accurately under the conventional systems of testing, until the others are known. This is similar to trying to answer the question, "What three numbers multiplied together give the product 24?" Not one is determined until the other two are known.

The Xactometer is free from these uncertainties, using three-dimensional seeing, with pre-focused targets.

In our invention, a set of targets set at different distances (but proportioned and illuminated to be seen as if all in the same plane) will offer at least one most-distant-target-in-good-focus, when there is no astigmatism. Within the instrument, the power of the test lens required to bring this good image up to a central, standard distance from the eye, is the desired prescription. The standard 6-meter office testing distance is reduced to a few centimeters within the compact instrument.

For astigmatism, there are two foci, or target locations of best focus, each being directional. The directions are mutually at right angles, or approximately so. Each location gives its own "sphere" value. Simply, and uniquely with this invention, the algebraic differences of these two sphere values gives the amount of "cylinder" power to be corrected. Also, their angular directions, shown on the dial, give the "axis" values. This instrument needs no cylindrical lenses for the test lenses, which saves space, expense, and trouble, while providing improved accuracy.

The century-old alphabetic targets are axis-directional, and are therefore inaccurate measuring devices. Only the letter "O" is relatively safe, though incomplete as used in conventional testing systems. One component of the Xactometer has a series of loop-targets, at different distances from the eye (but seen in the same plane). Additionally, an interesting variety of specially designed analytical components can be rotated into testing position as desired. All of them utilize the principles of three-dimensional testing and pre-focused targets. These principles are important because the eye is continually changing (contrary to the artificial situation in which a cycloplegic drug is used to cancel its accommodating power) and must be allowed to roam freely, examining helpfully curious targets, with some part always in focus. Proper use of a "plus lens" overcomes most confusions arising from accommodation, and so far the Xactometer has produced no examples of "instrument myopia," although that could be adjusted for, if ever necessary.

Recent published research on tests of two modern automated instruments and conventional methods of eye testing noted discrepancies of as much as one-half diopter of sphere, and five degrees of axis. With the Xactometer, accuracy is regularly one-eighth diopter (with one-sixteenth possible) for sphere, and one-half degree for axis. Thoughtful analysis and testing should prove that our system affords "true" prescriptions.

Durations of testing with the Xactometer will vary according to the condition of the patient and his special problems. This inventor, with limited time, has made a complete test for his own difficult eyesight within five minutes. The glasses that were made according to this test were perfectly satisfactory.

KIT-FORM AIDS FOR THE DISABLED (K-FADS)

MARLON B. HAYES
20 Fulke House, Brook Road, London E98 AX, England

Barbadian, born March 30, 1956. Special Advisor with London Borough of Redbridge. Educated in furniture design in the United Kingdom and the United States.

Project K-FADS (Kit-Form Aids for the Disabled) is a new pilot project, operating under the purview of the London Borough of Redbridge, that is designed to help improve the quality of life for the disabled by providing physical and psychological comfort through the assembling and utilization of unique self-help equipment and clothing-design kits that will be low in cost and distributed through national and international assistance organizations. The easy assembly of the kits will allow disabled persons, or their friends, relatives, or assistants, to become directly involved in solving the problems of improving quality of life for this disadvantaged section of our population.

We are a three-member team, working together in the K-FAD Project, with our efforts taking place in the environment of the disabled as part of our goal of integrating the disabled in this work. Specifically, we are concentrating on those particular disabilities that have similar characteristics, such as problems of locomotion and general movement, wherein the loss of coordination and mobility may be the first step to a state of mental and physical idleness and withdrawal from society.

The concept of K-FADS is to provide, through appropriate design, the challenge and stimulation that will encourage the disabled person to participate actively in rehabilitation.

My experience in the field of furniture design, assisted by a Travel Grant from the Worshipful Company of Furniture Makers to go to the United States in 1978 to research available examples and trends in furniture for the disabled, has formed the basis of one portion of the effort.

Mrs. Kay L. Wittenborn's experience is first hand: she was incapacitated by polio in childhood, first restricted to an iron lung and later to a body cast, braces, and wheelchair. Now she not only takes care of her school-age children and other home responsibilities without outside help, but she also devotes considerable time and energy to the design and production of clothes that, in easy-to-make or complete form, are specifically attuned to the needs of the physically disabled. Our third member, Mr. Donald P. Romberger, brings to the project much experience with governmental programs that may be able to provide funding and other administrative support for us.

In our designs we have established certain criteria of importance to the disabled: (1) they must be both safe and easy to assemble and use, (2) they much have acceptable aesthetics and comfort, (3) they must be adaptable to multiple environmental and personal requirements, with a minimum of difficulty, and (4) they must be low-cost and easily maintained. Of all these considerations, we believe it is in the area of item (2) that we may make our most effective contributions.

Most hospital and home equipment for the disabled is not attractive and often makes the user feel self-conscious and overly aware of his or her incapacitated state. We believe that our equipment is neither cumbersome nor obtrusive and that, as such, it will better bring the disabled person into the mainstream of life around him or her, and into the community. Clothing made according to our designs is aimed at making irregularities in body shape or movement less noticeable to other people, through the creative, appropriate, and intelligent use of cut, patterns, and color.

Our program involves research and development (assessing and investigating available products, gathering appropriate medical opinions, and most importantly, consulting with disabled persons themselves), production (initially this involves utilization of local resources to make product parts, color-illustrated multilingual directions, etc.), and distribution (given the difficulties of mobility for disabled persons, the K-FADS are being designed for sale on a mail-order basis).

Our purpose in creating and running the K-FAD Project is to bring the disabled person into the mainstream community, by getting them to share with us in the building and designing of equipment and clothing that they themselves wish to have and use. Their insights and wishes should be shared with us, as one means of maintaining human contacts on a two-way basis.

Under the greenhouse, the water wheel powers the fan that draws air from the greenhouse through the concrete-block heat store.

A GREENHOUSE THAT STORES AND RECOVERS ENERGY

ROBERT EDGAR
"Garton," Sundrum, Ayr, Ayrshire, Scotland KA6 6LR, U.K.

British, born June 1, 1930. Professional hydrologist, with engineering education in Scotland.

I n normal or usual greenhouse practice, excess solar energy is not stored for future use within the greenhouse. This project is designed to quantify the equipment and technique necessary to provide storage for excess solar energy with the object of reducing the cost of food production.

The project was originally prompted by the observation that commercial greenhouse practice often had a diurnal heating requirement, which involved energy input from a boiler system during the hours of darkness, followed by the removal of excess solar energy during the periods of bright sunshine. With the cost of the energy necessary to power these activities rising, and now forming a substantial part of the cost of food production, it appeared to be a useful investigation to find out if the energy input could be met, at least in part, by the storage of excess solar energy. Inquiries at the local Agricultural College did not yield any information on this subject; I therefore decided to gain some first-hand knowledge by direct experimentation.

Although the scope of my project was limited by financial considerations, I nevertheless wanted to reduce "scale effects" as far as possible by building a greenhouse of a reasonable size. Accordingly, a greenhouse size of 11 meters by 5 meters was chosen. To expedite and simplify the project, it was further decided that commercially available equipment and materials would be used where possible. From the start of the project, I decided that the logical location for the heat store would be under the greenhouse, although the method of storage was determined by several factors.

Prior to commencement of the project, calculations on the energy requirements anticipated for the greenhouse were made, based on a diurnal cycle, even though I realized that a yearly cycle would be superimposed on these calculations with temperature changes less rapid than that of the diurnal cycle. I also decided that energy taken from the heat store would be used selectively within the greenhouse (i.e., polythene sheeting would be used to create selected enclosures). Since no figures were available on energy requirements, I arbitrarily concluded that the heat store would have to be capable of supplying energy at the rate of 6 kilowatts for a period of 10 hours, with a fall in temperature of the heat store on the order of 10°F.

Initial thoughts on the type of heat store were directed toward the use of water as the storage medium, but further consideration of the hardware for such a system (i.e., heat collectors within the growing zone of the greenhouse, which would reduce the light available for photosynthesis, and the construction of a leakproof tank below the greenhouse floor, which would be expensive) ruled this medium out.

Further thoughts about the whole process of solar energy conversion and collection led to the conclusion that the entire volume contained within the greenhouse structure should be considered as the solar energy conversion zone, and, for the extraction of this energy, the working fluid adopted should be that naturally contained within the zone—the air.

Calculations of air flow for a 6-kilowatt rate of energy transfer based on a temperature difference of 10°F gave flow figures on the order of 56 cubic meters per minute, a flow rate quite capable of being generated by a relatively small fan at low energy expenditure. Accordingly, air was selected as the working fluid.

On the subject of selection of the heat store medium, one of the factors was the energy available from the latent heat of evaporation in the moisture produced by growing plants. To recover this energy in the most efficient manner, I thought that impervious material should be used, so that the latent heat could be recovered by condensation and removal of the precipitated water without subsequent re-evaporation. Availability of suitable material outweighed this factor, and concrete blocks were eventually adopted as the heat store medium.

In preparing the foundation for the greenhouse, hollow concrete blocks were arranged in twelve rows parallel to the long axis of the building, and these formed the support for the concrete slabs which, in addition to providing a floor for the greenhouse, provide the impermeable barrier separating the greenhouse zone from that of the heat store. The air circulation is as follows: air drawn from the general body of the greenhouse by a fan sited at the north end is delivered underground to the heat store, where the flow direction is southward along and among the concrete blocks, where energy transfer takes place dependent upon the relative temperature of the air and the blocks. At the north end of the heat store, a "manifold" type of passage permits selective routing of the air via five holes, each 46 centimeters in diameter, back into the general body of the greenhouse at floor level. Thus, the system works on a closed cycle basis.

The design of the heat store is a compromise between mass and cross-sectional area for air flow. The design adopted gives a total cross-sectional area for air flow on the order of 1.5 square meters, for which a flow rate of 56 cubic meters per minute requires a power input to the fan on the order of 150 watts. The floor of the heat store is sloped so that any water entering the heat store is channeled to a removal point.

A note on the fan may be of interest. The fan is a backward blade radial flow fan from the scrapped aircraft carrier H.M.S. *Eagle.* The power unit itself is a 1.8-meter diameter water wheel.

Results

Work on this project commenced in July 1979, with the system becoming operational in March 1980. Whilst it is early days to assess the system, first results are very promising. At the time of writing this report (April 1980), the weather pattern is such that we are experiencing high daytime temperatures with low nighttime temperatures. This has produced an unexpected result, namely, the cooling effect of the air returning from the heat store. Plants susceptible to high temperatures are being kept cool during the high daytime temperature periods.

Current operation of the system is to direct all the returning air into a polythene enclosed volume on the order of 17 cubic meters, in a method of recovering and storing energy that appears to be practicable for use on a much larger scale.

BANKING THE GENOME
OF ENDANGERED SPECIES

JOSEPH C. DANIEL, JR.
5505 Crestwood Drive, Knoxville, Tennessee 37914, U.S.A.

American, born August 21, 1927. Zoology Professor at University of Tennessee. Educated in the United States, visiting posts in the United Kingdom and Kenya.

T he ultimate goal of this project is to establish a bank of frozen embryos of endangered mammals of the world as a means of preserving the genetic information for the future. I intend to develop reliable procedures for collecting the embryos or gametes of endangered mammals, for storing them by freezing, and for subsequently reproducing the species by supportive embryogenesis in the uterus of a related domestic, or otherwise unthreatened, species.

All the techniques for physiologically manipulating embryos and their mothers that are required for this part of the work are well established. To be able to reinstate these rare animals at some future date, however, will require that their embryos be able to develop in a foster mother of a different species, and the technology for achieving this is not yet available. Thus, the immediate emphasis of this project will be to formulate a reliable procedure for making interspecies embryo transplantation possible. As this will require empirical experimentation, I propose first to use common domestic or laboratory animals, before attempting to use precious and rare endangered species.

My approach to the problem of making interspecies embryo transplants possible emphasizes two areas to maximize the chances of success: first, donor and host will be of closely related species, which share similarities of placentation, length of gestation, breeding behavior, and other significant reproductive phenomena; and second, the host uterus will be made to synthesize proteins common to the uterus of the species donating the embryo. I am an ardent disciple of the hypothesis that these proteins are critical to embryogenesis, and that they must be present at the right time and in the correct concentrations and balance to support particular development stages. Among their many purposes, I am inclined to think that the function of acting as immune response inhibitors may provide essential clues to interspecies embryo transplant failure. If there were a way to make the foster mother's uterus produce the inhibitor characteristic for the embryo donor species, then what may be the essential protection needed could be readily supplied.

The program is designed to progress as follows, using a number of demanding, but currently practiced, techniques to achieve the goal of banking the genomes of endangered animals and recalling them when desired.

First, ova and semen from the respective sexes of a donor species will be collected; the ova will be fertilized *in vitro* and then frozen for storage in liquid nitrogen. At a later date, these zygotes will be thawed, viability tested, and then transferred to the genital tract of a female of a closely related species. Prior to the transfer, the host uterus will be synchronized with the embryos, and induced to produce the specific proteins characteristic of the donor species' uterus during pregnancy, by introducing messenger RNA isolated from the endometrial lining of the donor species' uterus into the host species' lumen. Assurance that a normal donor fetus exists later in the pregnancy will be sought from chromosome analysis of cells obtained through amniocentesis. The major techniques required in this effort are superovulation, ova collection, semen collection, fertilization *in vitro*, culture of cleaving embryos, freeze-preservation, preparation of the host mother, collection of endometrial tissue, and embryo transplantation, all of which I have explained in greater detail in attachments to this application.

One can give many arguments against investing time, money, and effort in trying to bank a gene pool, both scientific and political or social. Perhaps no one can convincingly counter these arguments, but against all of them is the continuing realization that for many animals, there is no longer a natural life in a wild environment. They live only in zoos, or on reservations, where many of the same problems suggested as reasons for not banking genomes are perpetuated by inbreeding, concentration, and the whims of humanity. I applaud and support the establishment of more and larger and more diversified parks and reservations, but other approaches also merit consideration. At this point, we need to draw all our technology into the fight, to try anything that has a chance of working, and do it now; in another decade, we may not even have the opportunity to try.

DEVELOPMENT OF A MICROMINIATURIZED TELEPHONE

ONO HIROSHI
7-10-15, Koyama, Shinagawa-ku, Tokyo (142), Japan

Japanese, born September 5, 1945. Assistant Professor, Department of Otorhinolaryngology, Keio University. Bio-engineering education in Japan.

My project concerns the development of the Micro Telephone, a miniaturized telephone transmitter and receiver that can be inserted into the ear. The Micro Telephone enables an ambulatory individual to communicate with another individual on the opposite side of the globe through the conventional telephone system without holding a receiver by hand. In addition, the Micro Telephone is functional even in extremely noisy environments where the conventional telephone does not function.

The progress of the Micro Telephone has reached the final stages of development where I plan (1) to design and develop the electrical circuits required for the Micro Telephone on a silicon chip in the form of a hybrid integrated circuit, and (2) to develop supplementary product designs that are suited to a variety of applications in the field of communications.

The Micro Telephone has become feasible as a result of my invention of the vibration pick-up type ear microphone. This Ear Microphone is designed to pick up in the external auditory canal of the ear the vibrations of the human voice that are conducted through the bone structure of the face. These vibrations are converted into electric signals through the piezo-electronic element embedded inside the capsule of the Ear Microphone. There are a number of merits to the Ear Microphone itself:

1. *Good Speech Intelligibility.* The patented structure of the Ear Microphone allows good speech intelligibility, similar to that achieved by the conventional telephone.
2. *Easy Attachment.* A small conventional earphone can be attached to the Ear

Microphone, neither interfering with the other's function. This allows the mechanisms for talking and listening to be combined in one device.

3. *No Need to Close External Auditory Canal.* As long as the capsule containing the miniaturized telephone transmitter picks up vibrations from the ear canal wall, there is no need to close the canal. As a result, an individual using the Micro Telephone can still hear ambient sounds and thus feel much more comfortable than he could otherwise.

4. *No Need to Hold the Micro Telephone.* The current state of electronics makes it possible to fit all the required electronic components into a capsule the size of an ear plug, and a small box that can be attached at the back of the ear. As a result, one can effectively "wear" the Micro Telephone in the ear, and need no hand-held receiver.

5. *Immunity to Ambient Noise.* Since the Ear Microphone picks up bone-conducted vibrations directly, the Ear Microphone does not pick up ambient noise, which comes into the external auditory canal by air; this makes it possible for individuals to communicate with others even under conditions of deafening surrounding noise.

The input and output of the Micro Telephone can be connected to a conventional two-way radio system and then to the public telephone system. The dialing function is accomplished through a pocket-sized dialing device. The result is a virtually unlimited communications capability.

Examples of applications include the dramatic improvements possible in the work of firemen, who would be much better able to coordinate their efforts even under chaotic conditions, without any hindrance of activities as both of their hands will be free. Similar applications exist at construction sites, hospitals, and airports. Another application is in making communications from automobiles easier, simpler, and safer; the driver could talk without interference to his steering, have clearer communications in noisy traffic conditions, and even be able to leave the car up to a certain radius and still be able to use this device.

Thus far, I have put together the four circuits needed (Receiver, Transmitter, Voice Control, and Power Generation), combining discrete components for prototypes. To gain design flexibility of the Micro Telephone for various applications, it is now necessary to mount these circuits on a silicon chip in the form of a hybrid integrated circuit. After completing this miniaturization, I plan to design and produce many types of the Micro Telephone—one in a helmet, one in a pocket, and one on an ear tab. I believe that this invention will contribute significantly to the area of communications and that the day will come when people start wearing the Micro Telephone.

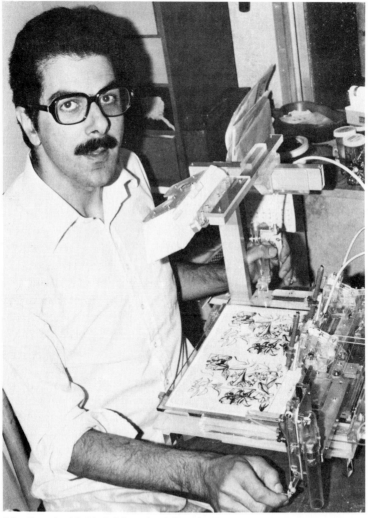

Mr. Tamari with his 3-Dimensional Drawing Instrument.

AN INSTRUMENT FOR DRAWING IN THREE DIMENSIONS

VLADIMIR F. TAMARI
1-36-16 Sakurashimmachi, Setagaya-ku, Tokyo 154, Japan

Palestinian, born July 7, 1942. Painter, inventor, translator. Art education in Lebanon, the United Kingdom, and the United States.

As an artist, I wanted my drawings to "come out" from the paper, in order to better resemble the real world in its solid dimensions. As a result, I invented the 3-Dimensional Drawing Instrument, which is a device that enables anybody to "draw in space." I have worked on this invention continuously for some years, and it has now reached the stage where it can be applied to architecture, education, mathematics, botany, and many other fields. Because it is based on human vision in depth, it is an exciting and useful instrument in any field where drawing is now used, and it might well become the drawing method of the future.

Until now, drawings have been made on flat two-dimensional surfaces: paper, walls, or the sides of caves. The world we live in, however, is solid rather than flat; everything moves and lives and exists in a space that we human beings perceive with two eyes, not one. My 3-D Drawing Instrument is based on human binocular vision (depth perception) and thus enables us to draw our ideas in a realistic relationship to the actual world we see.

The 3-D Drawing Instrument and Its Use

Ordinarily, we use one pen to draw a flat picture on a flat surface. In my invention, however, two pens draw two similar pictures simultaneously, guided by the artist who manipulates a handle suspended in air. According to the depth of the handle or its position at any one time, one of the pens makes a tiny parallax adjustment (which can be as small as 0.01 millimeter) so that the two pictures correspond to the left-eye and right-eye viewpoints of the artist. As the artist draws, he looks in a 2-lens stereoscope, where he sees only one pen drawing only one picture—the two images have become fused into a single, three-dimensional image. The pen itself appears to float *above* the paper and *into* it, creating lines that resemble wire sculptures. By simply moving the drawing handle in any direction in space, a spatial three-dimensional line is created. This simple eyes-hand coordination is one of the basic and unusual features of the invention. It translates ideas instantly and easily into drawings that correspond to the real world in a 1:1 ratio.

Applications of 3-D Drawings and 3-D Drawing Instruments

Until now, a very limited use has been made of 3-D drawings, because the left- and right-hand parallax had to be drawn by hand or by computer, severely limiting the applications and usefulness of this form of artistic presentation. By using my simple instrument, however, drawing in space becomes as simple as XYZ! Even my 4-year-old daughter is able to use the instrument I have built, but, more importantly, the applications abound in many fields. Artists can use it to create a new art form akin to both sculpture and painting. 3-D drawings can clarify the complex and varied shapes encountered in botany, archaeology, mathematics, engineering, architecture, and medicine. Designers and planners can draw their ideas in the actual space they will occupy in real life. I find that this ability to record and communicate with 3-D drawings fills a real need to humanize technology and to add life to works of art. It helps to bridge the gap between the average person and the complex shapes of our modern world.

A Brief History of 3-D Drawing

The importance of this under-utilized area of graphic presentation is illustrated by the following two quotations by two artists of very different epochs:

It is impossible that objects in painting should appear with the same relief as those in a looking glass. (*Leonardo da Vinci, Chapter 24 of* Trattato Della Pittura, 1584)

In our last meeting, we observed to our regret that we have no three-dimensional script. (*Paul Klee, in a lecture given at the Bauhaus, Weimar, 1921, quoted in his book* The Thinking Eye)

The British scientist Sir Charles Wheatstone invented the concept of three-dimensional drawing when he made the first stereoscopic viewers around the year 1838. However, the parallax difference between the two eyes' respective points of view prevented this concept from developing in the field of drawing. Instead, 3-D photography became very popular for a time. Then, in 1939, Professor John T. Rule, of MIT, patented an instrument for drawing in space, but since it was not accurate enough, he abandoned the idea. Professor Richard Gregory has also patented 3-D drawing machines and described them in his book, *The Intelligent Eye,* but these have not gone beyond the prototype stage.

Computers and hand-drawn 3-D drawings have appeared from time to time, but for very limited shapes and uses, and never for the free-hand drawing requirements of artists and illustrators.

My own work in this field was done with no previous knowledge of any of the above developments except Wheatstone's, initially, but this is not surprising due to the basic simplicity of the concept. However, because of my 16 years of effort and dedication to this field, I can say that the instruments I have built are the world's first practical 3-D drawing instruments, thanks to the use of modern plastics and ball bearings that are necessary to obtain the high degree of precision required for satisfactory performance. My work, done with the instrument, has recently toured Japan in an exhibition, but in order that people everywhere can enjoy and benefit from the ability to "draw in space," much cooperative work has yet to be done. This is just the start of what I call the drawing of the future. The reasons are partly historical.

Since the technical advances of the Renaissance, which required the extensive use of drawings, the art of perspective has pervaded much intellectual activity. The drawing, or plan, became a substitute for the mental images held by humanity in earlier, simpler times. The tragedy of this is that we began to refer to these flat images as our reference, *instead* of referring to real life. Of course, it is an exaggeration to blame the world's problems on too much reliance on flat diagrams! But, truly, I feel that this "space blindness" of modern humanity is a serious symptom of the general failure of vision in our global civilization.

My reference to space blindness is not a mere phrase, but something real—a lack in our visual education—resulting from a lifetime of looking at flat pictures and drawing flat drawings. As I began to use the 3-D drawing machines I have developed, I started discovering an exciting awareness of depth, a sense of the solidity of things and of their distribution in visual space. I feel people in every field will benefit from this re-education of the eyes, in order to get some taste of that healthy harmony between idea and actuality, between vision and action, that is so characteristic of simpler societies. I hope that, somehow, my work will be an encouragement for many individuals to open their eyes and rediscover our own environment.

AN ELECTRONIC NOTEBOOK FOR THE SIGHTLESS

WOLFANGO HORN
6, via Pio IX, 40017 S. Giovanni Persiceto, Bologna, Italy

Italian, born August 21, 1956. Student of biological sciences at the Universita degli Studi di Bologna; degree expected in June 1980.

The aim of this project is to provide the blind with a lightweight pocket-size device by means of which they may take notes in Braille during a lesson or a meeting and then re-read them later on at home. At present, in order to take notes, the sightless must carry a bulky Braille slate, punching a card on it with an instrument—a fatiguing and time-consuming task. The Braille notebook of my design will represent a substantial advantage for the blind, allowing them to take notes at considerable speed, without physical fatigue, and without being encumbered by bulky and awkward equipment. A further advantage of the electronic notebook is that the recorded notes, instead of needing to be re-read by the blind person's fingertips, may be transferred automatically to a conventional typewriter or to one encoded with Braille. As an option, a video display may also be used, by means of which a sighted person can assist the blind person's editing. Since the Braille electronic notebook employs MOS (metal on silicon)-semiconductor memories only, its physical dimensions, weight, and power requirements are very small compared with other Braille desk-size writing machines, which memorize the text on magnetic tape.

Basically, the Braille electronic notebook consists of two independent units: the notebook unit and the tactile unit. To take notes, the blind person need only carry the notebook unit, which is about the size of a pocket calculator. It has six small keys, on which the user types the text, arranged according to the conventional 6-dot Braille matrix. Two additional keys are provided, one for "space" (or blank) and a second for "one-step-back" (for erasing), plus two operating switches for "off/on" (which also empties the memory) and "write/read."

The Braille-coded text (binary) becomes memorized into a set of RAM (random access memory) recirculating MOS memories. If 16K × 1 bits wide memories are used, an overall capacity of about 3000 words is achieved, enough for most notetaking tasks. A cheaper, less powerful unit could use a 4K memory.

As mentioned, instead of reading the memorized text on the tactile unit, the user may transfer it to an electric typewriter, for a permanent record, re-charging the nickel-cadmium cells on the notebook simultaneously.

The tactile unit, an electromechanical device, is powered by household current, using electromagnets to activate the small pins that reproduce the Braille code.

Though there are two ways to construct the tactile unit, I believe the better method is that which employs a single 6-dot Braille pin-matrix. The letters, coming in sequence from the notebook's memory, each operate, one after the other, the 6-dot matrix at the speed set into the tactile unit by the user, who may, at will, either stop the sequences, or even back them up for additional review. This solution is the simpler and the cheaper method of design, and psychologically better also. When a blind person reads Braille, letters are recognized by the fingertips, sequentially. It should be the same kind of sensation if, instead of sliding the fingertips along a line, the finger is held steady and the letters flow past under it.

Allowance is also made, with this approach, for the blind person to edit the material, if he or she wishes to record it on paper via the Braille-typing machine, by stopping the machine to change the material if an error occurs.

Besides the pins arrangement, the tactile unit is provided with a reading-speed control unit, a "one-step-back" key, as well as keys that provide fast advance and fast return.

The tactile unit may feed a typewriter or even a video display. This will be accomplished through a code-converter that translates the Braille binary code into the machine's code, for instance, Baudot, ITC, or ASCII. By using the video display, a person with vision, unacquainted with Braille, may read the blind person's editing in Latin characters directly, without transferring the memorized text to the electric typewriter.

Through the design and construction and distribution of this new notebook, we can bring the advantages of the electronic and computer revolution to the sightless members of our society and make their lives easier and more productive.

DETERMINING THE SITE OF RESPIRATORY SOUNDS

STEVE KRAMAN
Veterans Administration Medical Center, CDD, 111-H,
Lexington, Kentucky 40507, U.S.A.

American, born August 30, 1944. Hospital Staff Physician and University Assistant Professor. Medical education in Puerto Rico and the United States.

I wish to substantiate, clarify, and further refine a new technique that is capable of giving information on the site of the origin of lung sounds. This involves the development of an automatic acoustic analyzer, using the principle described below, to aid in lung-sound analysis and, I hope, to perform as a diagnostic tool that is totally non-invasive and that does not expose the patient to ionizing radiation.

The technique of auscultation of the chest and a comprehensive description of the sounds made by breathing was first published by René Laënnec in 1819. Since then, physicians have routinely listened to respiratory noises, and certain correlations have been made between particular sounds and pathological processes.

Initially, these sounds were described in terms of how they were perceived by the ear (amplitude, pitch, etc.). More recently, sound-analyzing equipment has been used to provide a more objective characterization of respiratory sounds. We now know the general timing and frequency characteristics of lung sounds, and this has helped sort them into several categories. Apart from the recognized normal sounds, the abnormal respiratory sounds are further divided into continuous and discontinuous.

Abnormal continuous sounds consist mostly of whistling noises, either high or low pitched, and are referred to as wheezes or ronchi. They are thought to occur due to narrowing of the airways within the lungs or to mucal obstruction of the airflow. Discontinuous sounds are called rales, or crackles, and are quite short. Almost always occurring when the patient is breathing in and not out, they are thought to result from the explosive openings of small airways that may initially have been closed.

Despite our long acquaintance with these noises, and a recent characterization of their frequency and timing, little is known regarding the actual site of the production of these sounds. The subject is not trivial; there are approximately 25 divisions of airways between the trachea and the alveoli, much like a tree, beginning with the trunk and ending with the leaves. The determination of where a particular sound occurs would give information regarding where lung diseases begin or what part of the lung is being affected.

For the past year and a half, I have been using a new technique to study lung sounds, and I have carried out studies on both normal breathing sounds and the abnormal crackles.

The first study, which has been accepted for publication in the *American Review of Respiratory Diseases,* involves the use of a subtraction technique. Normal breath sounds were recorded simultaneously from two sites at varying microphone separations and then played back twice: the first time while mixing the signal from both microphones together in a summing amplifier and displaying the additional signal on an oscilloscope, and again but after inverting the phase of one of them (subtraction signal). The more nearly identical the original signals were in phase and amplitude, the more completely they canceled in the subtraction signal. This process was used to study six normal young people, and the maximum distance between the microphones that would still result in measurable cancellation was determined. Results showed a marked difference between the sounds associated with inspiration and that with expiration, and the distance between the sounds, providing strong evidence that some expiration sounds came from the trachea or larynx.

Present developments suggest that in patients with very early obstruction of the airways (as in early emphysema and chronic bronchitis), the origin of the inspiratory sounds moves farther away from the trachea, and that this movement is measurable. Additional indications of the movement of the origin of crackles derived from the second study.

The significance of this work is two-fold. First, the work done to date has provided information on the site of origin of certain breath sounds and so contributes to our understanding of this aspect of pulmonary physiology. Second, the improved characterization of lung sounds opens the door to correlation with other conventional tests and pathology. These initial studies could form the basis for more sophisticated lung-sound analysis that may aid materially in diagnosis, but not add to the growing number of tests that rely on X rays and radioactive isotopes. The eventual place of this sound analysis in disease diagnosis can only be determined by exploring its limits.

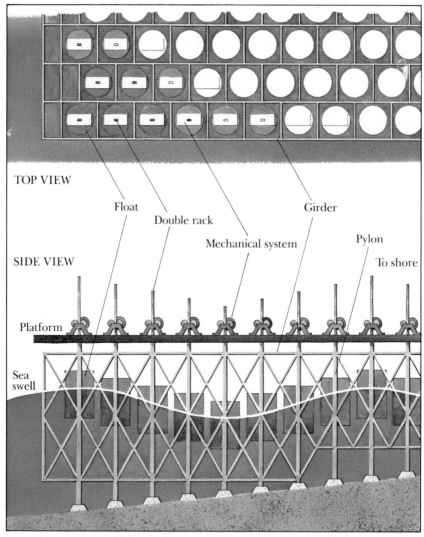

TOP VIEW

Float

Double rack

Girder

Mechanical system

Pylon

SIDE VIEW

To shore

Platform

Sea
swell

Top view and side view of the Energy Conversion Units.

HARNESSING OCEAN WAVES
TO PRODUCE ELECTRIC POWER

GEORGE ANASSONDJIS
Number 139, 3rd September Street, Athens 813, Greece

Greek, born May 28, 1922. Foreign language correspondent in major exporting company. Educational background in five languages.

T he aim of this project is the construction of a special engine whereby the kinetic energy of naturally occurring sea waves is converted into electric power by the action of a particular buoyant structure. Confined in a way that it may only move vertically within a surrounding cluster of upright steel rails, the structure will follow the up-and-down movement of the waves and—through a mechanical device—will activate an electric generator. Several such engines, connected in tandem, will constitute a power plant capable of supplying service to significant urban areas.

The actual installation of such a generating power plant will require only a relatively moderate investment in capital funds, mainly for the purchase of electric generators and other readily available material for the construction of any given number of identical, specially built apparatuses, the Energy Conversion Units (ECU's). Such a power plant, requiring only a very small crew for the maintenance of these ECU's, will run at minimally low costs, once constructed. A further advantage of this system is that it can be built out from virtually any land point, much like a pier, and therefore need not occupy valuable real estate in urban areas.

Each Energy Conversion Unit consists of three main parts: the pylons, the floats, and the mechanical system.

The base part of the ECU is a cluster of three pylons. Each of these simply constructed elements is composed of three straight lengths of railway steel rails. Short lengths of steel piping, placed at regular intervals, are welded to the rails to hold the rails in a rigid vertical position, on top of a concrete base on the sea floor, into which the rails are set. Steel crossbeams and struts join all the pylons together to form a well-balanced girder. Each of these 3-piece pylons enclose one of the floats, with the pylons placed in a clustering pattern that can be extended easily to include additional pylon/float units when desired.

The floats, buoyant and practically unsinkable, are made chiefly of a pre-determined number of ordinary fuel drums, say 21 (in three layers of seven drums each), which are completely filled with polystyrene (in order to be able to disregard watertightness altogether) and are sealed closed. The drums are braced into a sturdily built metal framework, consisting mainly of two circular metal frames that bind the drums inside their thick steel rings. The drums, which are further secured to each other with polypropylene straps, are thus fixed within a steel-ringed "piston," capable of rising and falling within the outer confines of the pylon's steel rails.

The kinetic energy of the floats, acquired as a direct action of the surging seas as they rise and fall within their pylons, is converted into electric power by the mechanical system.

The mechanical system is based on a specially made double-rack device, toothed with cogs of a given gear pitch at two of its opposite sides. It is loosely connected to the center of the top circular frame of the float by means of a freely rotating joint (such as those used on the carriage bumper of a railroad car, around which three fixed but loosely fitting clasps are allowed to move in all directions, though within a limited space).

The double rack is guided to travel in a strictly vertical direction by two pairs of geared wheels to which it is engaged, and which have flanges facing at opposite directions for counteracting any tendency that the rack might have to slip sideways. The lower pair of these geared wheels, of considerably small diameter, serves no other purpose than that of guiding the double-rack device, and it therefore revolves quite freely. The other pair, though also serving the same purpose, has the essential function of conveying the recipro-cating movement of the rack directly to a ratchet wheel.

The two ratchet wheels, however, are adjusted to be acted upon alterna-tively by the movement of the rack; one ratchet responding to the upward strokes only, and the other to the downward strokes only. Nevertheless, both of them will transmit their motion—which will ultimately turn out to be in *one and the same direction*—by means of a chain belt, to a flywheel, which will be coupled to an electric generator.

The axle connecting the flywheel and the generator will be receiving a new surge of motive power with each movement of the rack—whether upward or downward—and with the flywheel maintaining a steady angular velocity, the electric generator will be driven with a satisfactorily constant speed.

The operation of the Energy Conversion Unit is thus based on relatively simple concepts and structures. As a sea wave approaches, the floats are thrust forcibly upward, within the spaces to which they are confined by the surrounding and supporting pylons. Then, as the wave recedes, the floats' own considerable weights will drop them heavily, again within the confining framework of the pylons, until they are once again lifted by an incoming wave. The floats are thus subjected, at regular intervals, to a most powerful reciprocating motion in a vertical direction only, due to the minimization of any sideways deviation by the enclosing pylon frames. Kinetic energy obtained through this action is converted, through the mechanical system, into electric power, with hardly any losses at all, in a process that continues day and night, all the year round.

The concept of floats rising and falling successively within the quasi-cylindrical spaces provided by the pylons could well be compared with that of the steam engine, with the difference that the floats—compared to regular piston engines—will impart motive power with every "stroke" and on *both* directions of their path.

Having in mind the way by which power is obtained from a steam engine as a result of pressure being exerted by steam on the piston, it should be noted that the floats will acquire tremendous impetus with each onrushing wave, due to their important compound mass. This means that they will be heaved powerfully upward and then dropped with equal force downward, at a repeated rate, thus providing the necessary kinetic energy required to drive a relatively large electric generator.

Though the concept of deriving energy from waves is not new, I believe the original mechanical contrivance demonstrated here is, and that Energy Conversion Unit power plants could be made readily available to many coastal locations as cheap, non-polluting sources of much needed power.

"ANTI-BUMPING THERAPY"— A KNUCKLE AGAINST AILMENTS

YUEN-KAY KOON
52-54, Hoi Yuen Road, Kwun Tong, Kowloon, Hong Kong

Chinese, born December 14, 1924. Company Director and Business Manager, founder of Institute of Patentees, Inventors & Designers. Educated in China.

T his project deals with the development and long-term testing of a new therapeutic process that has shown itself to be an effective cure for a number of chronic diseases of humanity, without the application of medicine or injection. More than 2500 patients have received treatment with this method and found relief or cure as its result.

Though not medically trained, I have spent over twenty years perfecting a system of therapy that has proven to be effective in curing or relieving a wide variety of ailments that have resisted other treatments, or which would have required extensive and expensive medical care. The origin of these long-running studies lay in the accidentally twisted leg I suffered some twenty years ago. In nursing the leg, I found that adequate and correctly applied pressure on the leg relieved the pain temporarily. Continuing to apply this pressure a number of times resulted in the total disappearance of the pain, leaving in its wake a great curiosity regarding the means by which it had been eliminated.

In somewhat the same manner as the study of acupuncture's pressure points, a gradual search of the body's key areas of sensitivity was made, resulting in a number of conclusions.

The human body has a variety of mechanisms that are used to fight disease, pain, and other disorders. These mechanisms vary in strength according to state of health, diet, age, stress being endured, and so on. Depending upon the nature of the ailment, certain locations in the body are affected in a way one might consider analogous to a breakdown in the network of an electrical system, with local structures (in the affected area) becoming unable to fully provide the appropriate defense actions. It appears that this local "short-circuit" phenomenon can be repaired, or remedied, through the application of hard, localized pressure in appropriate spots, over varying lengths of time, depending upon the ailment.

Over the years, based on nothing more than word-of-mouth information, numerous patients suffering from a wide variety of ailments have come for the treatment and have been cured. Careful records of these cases have been kept, and among the ailments successfully treated have been chronic headache (179 cases), neurasthenia (111), nasal allergy (159), chronic colds (42), rheumatism (109), strained muscles/ligaments (135), sitting-region neuritis (274), stomach and intestinal indigestion (92), blocking of tear gland (2), high blood pressure (58), insomnia and chronic insomnia (129), nasal sinus inflammation (69), degenerating memory (56), gout (79), strained shoulder and neck nerves (138), trembling hands (30), stomach and duodenum ulcerations (50), and others.

I have kept records on these patients since January 1972, and I am convinced that the treatment is potentially significant for many people around the world. Although I have now studied the principles of acupuncture thoroughly and find certain analogies concerning the pressure points involved, I believe my system may be considered safer, because it does not use needles and because the healing effect derives from the pressure involved. I apply this pressure with my knuckle, forcefully, and it is considerably greater than that which can be achieved safely or comfortably through the use of needles, though the underlying concept of pressure may be similar. Another advantage of this system is that time of treatment is very short, counted in minutes each day, ranging from a few days for a mild case to somewhat longer periods for chronic problems.

Once the "anti-bumping point" is found, the key to the complete cure is in hand. The more frequently the pressure is applied, the more rapidly relief or cure is found. Experience to date has also indicated that there is no relapse into the problem suffered by the patient.

I have given freely of my advice and knowledge of this means of therapy and wish to be able to contribute to spreading its practice as widely as possible. To help in the dissemination of the principles of this "anti-bumping therapy," as I call it, I have printed a small booklet detailing its practice, which is available from the address above, and is entitled "Anti-Bumping Therapy and Health Protection."

TOWARD MORE EFFICIENT HUMAN-POWERED TRANSPORTATION

PETER BOOR

1203 Yale Avenue, Claremont, California 91711, U.S.A.

American, born July 10, 1931. Owner/manager of a bicycle shop. B.Sc. in Physics, educated in the United States.

I wish to encourage the design and development of more efficient human-powered vehicles for transportation on land, water, and in the air. I plan to do this by offering monetary incentives for the accomplishment of certain milestones and by stimulating increased worldwide participation in these efforts. The showcase for demonstrating performances in each of these fields will be the Annual Human-Powered Vehicle Speed Championships presently held in southern California. I am co-President (with Paul Mac-Cready) of the International Human-Powered Vehicles Association.

In 1973, Dr. Chester Kyle, Professor of Mechanical Engineering at California State College, Long Beach, California, was overseeing a student project designed to test the rolling resistance of bicycle tires. The testing was performed in a long hallway, using the coast-down method. In analyzing the data, Dr. Kyle rediscovered that wind resistance was the most important factor in slowing down a bicycle. He began to wonder how fast a human being could go on a bicycle (or on a similar vehicle) if the vehicle were properly streamlined. He built a streamlined fairing, covered a standard bicycle, and with it, Ron Skarin, a United States Olympic Champion, eclipsed all existing records for bicycle speeds over recognized competitive distances.

Others in the United States were thinking along the same lines, among them Dr. Paul MacCready, glider pilot and president of a small aeroscience firm; Jack Lambie, aviation enthusiast; and Dr. Allan Abbott, holder of the world's paced bicycle speed record. With the assistance of others, these men put together the first International Human-Powered Vehicle Speed Championships at Irwindale Raceway in California. This event drew 14 vehicles, which competed through the 200-meter timing traps. The fastest single went 72.08 kilometers/hour, and the fastest multiple went 72.37 kilometers/hour—both speeds faster than any previous 200-meter records.

Since that time, regular yearly events have been held in southern California, with the number of entries now more than 50 annually. In addition to the 200-meter sprints, events now include a Le Mans start road race and hour-distance attempts. Speeds have climbed to 82.00 kilometers/hour for single vehicles and 92.05 kilometers/hour for multiples. These vehicles are now awakening an interest in soft technology, which will ultimately lead to extremely efficient land vehicles.

The International Human-Powered Vehicles Association (IHPVA) was formed in 1976 to encourage open or non-restrictive designs, to hold the annual event where these designs could be tried, and to recognize the records these vehicles were setting. The Board of Directors is a truly international and active one. Wolfgang Gronen should soon hold a European Championship, Frank Whitt will attempt one in England, and Shinichi Toriyama already holds one in Japan. IHPVA's air group boasts our co-President, Dr. Paul MacCready, the Kremer Prize Winner (of the *Gossamer Condor* and *Gossamer Albatross* fame). The IHPVA is the only organized group encouraging competition for human-powered vehicles of unlimited design and is increasingly called upon to promote road races and criteriums on city streets.

I propose a multi-faceted program to encourage human-powered vehicles in all modes, using the yearly Human-Powered Vehicle Championships as the showcase. The Rolex Award would be used to reward or to otherwise assist (1) the first single-rider land vehicle to exceed 55 mph (88.7 km/h) through 200 meters, (2) the first land vehicle to exceed 62 mph (100 km/h) through 200 meters, (3) the first water vehicle to exceed an average of 8.0 meters/second over 2000 meters, standing start, (4) an annual prize for first-year air vehicle competition, possibly over a Kremer type course (1 mile, figure 8), (5) travel expenses for European, Far Eastern, and other competitive vehicles and owners who wish to compete in the annual California championships, and (6) an annual award for road-race winner and hour-distance winner, single and multiple classes.

Monetary incentives have already shown a pronounced effect on the development of more efficient vehicles. The Abbott Prize, offered in 1977 for the first human-powered land vehicle to reach or exceed America's speed limit (55 mph, 88.7 km/h) was captured within two years. The Kremer prizes for human-powered flight stand as beautiful cornerstones upon which have been built the world's most efficient aircraft. I propose to further extend such challenging and beneficial efforts for these fascinating and useful designs.

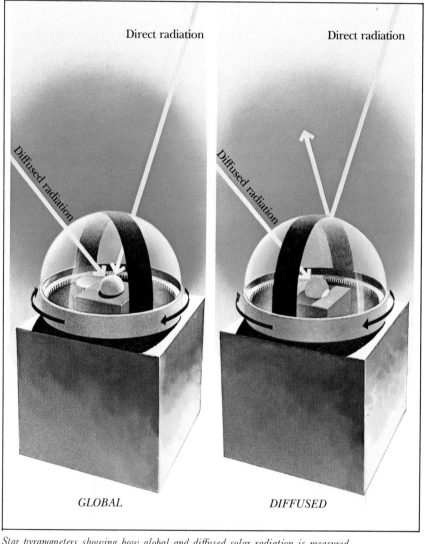

Direct radiation   Direct radiation

Diffused radiation   Diffused radiation

GLOBAL   DIFFUSED

Star pyranometers showing how global and diffused solar radiation is measured.

NOVEL ARRANGEMENTS FOR MEASURING SOLAR RADIATION

VISHNU MAN SHRESTHA
Gopi Newas, Lekh Nath Marg, Kathmandu, Nepal

Nepalese, born December 11, 1936. Teacher in the Physics Department of Tribhuvan University. Received physics education in Russia.

This project is concerned with certain problems in measuring solar radiation through the use of thermocouple-type pyranometers. Solutions to these problems are sought through the help of a clocking-device arrangement and a photoresistor-coupled relay switch.

Before planning for any intensive application of solar energy at any given location, one must know just how much solar energy is consistently available at the location. Solar radiation has two components: direct radiation and diffuse radiation. The usual procedure for determining these parts is to use two star pyranometers to measure separately the global (direct plus diffused) solar radiation and the diffused radiation. Because the star pyranometer is a rather costly apparatus, comparatively few stations can afford to keep two of them.

In the world of solar energy collection, non-concentrating devices, such as the familiar and well-known flat-plate collectors, require of their users only a knowledge of the global radiation available, in order to install them correctly and obtain their efficient application. When the choice is made to use concentrating devices, however, the operator-to-be must possess data on the availability of direct solar radiation if these devices are to be correctly installed and efficiently utilized.

The usual practice for measuring direct solar radiation is to place two similar star pyranometers horizontally and side by side. One of them is positioned at the center of a ring band whose plane extends from east to west, so that the shadow of the ring always falls on the sensitive part of the pyranometer—which is thus activated by the diffused portion of solar radiation only. The other star pyranometer is used in the customary condition for recording global radiation. The difference in the readings between the two devices at any given time will provide the amount of direct solar radiation.

My proposal suggests how to convert a single star pyranometer into a device that will also measure direct radiation, with the help of an attached clock mechanism. As shown in the illustration, a driving clock mechanism runs a toothed wheel, which rotates the outer ring in a clockwise direction, causing the movement of the larger transparent dome of the pyranometer. This larger dome is lined with a black strip equal in width to the diameter of the sensitive elements of the pyranometer, so that its shadow may be cast on the element when it is positioned to block the sun's rays.

With the different speeds available through the driving clock mechanism, the outer ring with the large dome can be made to rotate at different speeds. For example, with the sun advancing 15° every hour, if the outer ring is made to rotate one complete revolution in 57.6 minutes, the diffuse part of the solar radiation will be recorded at every half hour. Thus, a time record will be automatically available in the chart recorder.

According to recent prices quoted by different concerns, the price of the set-up for the recording of diffuse radiation alone is in the neighborhood of about $1200, without the recorder. This project's simple system of coupling the clock mechanism with the star pyranometer certainly costs much less.

Recording the data on the availability of solar radiation is a regular job of continuous monitoring, that goes on day after day, all year through. However, when the sun is below the horizon at night, it is not necessary to have the recorder functioning. Although simply switching the device off for the night is easily done, it is not always practicable to be present to turn the machine on before sunrise in the morning; for this reason, the usual practice is simply to leave the machine running constantly. This process, however, consumes unnecessary amounts of chart paper during the night, when there is nothing to be recorded.

To avoid this waste, a transistor circuit can be used to activate a relay switch, with the help of a photoresistor. When there is no solar radiation, the photoresistor circuit will have almost infinite resistance. Thus, no current will flow through it, meaning no potential drop across it to activate the transistors that operate the relay switch. As the sun rises in the morning, however, the resistance of the photoresistor decreases considerably, which then allows the current to flow through the photoresistor circuit. The resulting potential drop will activate the transistors, which will in turn close the relay switch. This action may be coupled with the recorder, in order to have the desired working of the entire unit.

We have been recording solar radiation here in the Physics Department of Kirtipur Campus of Tribhuvan University both with and without the connection of this device to our single star pyranometer, and we have found it to be an entirely satisfactory solution to a commonly found problem. We hope that other recording stations may be able to benefit from this system.

A GIANT, SELF-PROPELLED POTATO-REAPING MACHINE

JOSE MELA
Acassuso 891, Olivos, Código Postal 1636,
Provincia de Buenos Aires, Argentina

Argentine, born July 21, 1938. Independent worker, trader in land fruits. Self-taught mechanical engineering as hobby, in Argentina.

My project has been the development of a very large, self-propelled and self-contained potato-harvesting machine that allows the automatic reaping of potatoes or other tuber plants. Over a number of years, I have built five prototype machines, each one incorporating certain improvements, resulting in a piece of machinery that is now in operation and that I consider to be unique.

The total machine weighs 4500 kilograms, is 8.5 meters in length, has a maximum width of 2.6 meters, and a height of 2.4 meters. Within the confines of these dimensions, there are what I call removing drums, sifters to separate weeds, and a container for the automatic storing of the product (tubers) until removal at the end of the work cycle.

The machine is operated through electric remote control systems and contains its own engine, which provides the power for propelling all the mechanical actions involved in the harvesting function and the motive power for the entire machine. All of the mechanically moving parts and functions are thoroughly shielded against abrasion, which is a key consideration when working with plants being extracted from the earth. It reaps one ton of potatoes every ten minutes without waste, and performs at good levels even in fields with high levels of moisture and thick underbrush or weeds. Due to the simplicity of all its parts, the machine is operated by only one person.

The machine reaps the entire furrow (potatoes, earth, and weeds, if any) and brings it to a pair of sifters that turn in order to remove earth and weeds from the potatoes. The earth and weeds are removed and expelled into a sieve by a system of hooks, which, by rotation and vibration, return them to the ground. The potatoes are put into boxes and shifted to a carrying system that deposits them, clean and ready to go to market, in a big container, this being the last step before the industrial process.

It is really very simple to understand that this machine is a sum of several elaborations of applied science, and that, though other reaping machines are in use or being tested in different countries, this one is quite new in every way. The most important point I would like to make about it is that no system of complete efficiency is yet known to be in mass production in the world. To my knowledge, no potato-reaping machine can handle the entire serial production of potatoes except this one. I believe that my project should be tested as the basic prototype for agricultural machine "factories" for tubers, equivalent to other reaping machines (for corn, wheat, etc.).

This statement is supported by noting the differences between this machine and other ones now being tested.

Driving. By means of electric control, one man can drive the machine from the tractor cabin.

Efficiency of Tillage. The entire furrow is reaped, and the tubers are held without waste.

Durability or Endurance. This characteristic has been achieved by refining every motion system used in reaping, until these had been reduced to a simplicity that permitted action without any mechanism being worn out easily. All motion commands are performed by means of a system of gear boxes dipped in oil and protected with blindages (Oyster type). It is this characteristic that is the unique advance of this project of mine, without which—after many attempts and reworkings of earlier prototype machines by me—the potato-reaping machine would remain a utopian dream.

The abrasive conditions suffered by mechanisms working in direct earth contact, and under the earth, are the biggest difficulty in such agricultural machines, and have been unsolved in any other prototype up to now.

I consider it important to draw to your attention the fact that I have worked hard for the last 15 years to achieve a high degree of effectiveness and efficiency. Five different models were made and tested by me before I achieved the actual conditions of durability and endurance for 95 percent of the parts in this machine—proven in over 10 years of actual reaping use.

TARGET DROPLET SUFFICIENCY (TDS)— FOR BETTER BUG SPRAYS

MARCO E. C. GIGLIOLI
Mosquito Research and Control Unit, P.O. Box 486,
Grand Cayman, Cayman Islands, West Indies

British, born April 21, 1927. Laboratory Director for governmental research unit. Education in biology in the United Kingdom and Canada.

A ir sprays of insecticide using Ultra Low Volume Concentrates (ULV/C) have been made more effective against adult mosquitoes by using ULV applications of dilute solutions (ULV/S) in oil. Less costly and less polluting, this method increases the number of bioactive droplets available for impact on the flying mosquito.

Research is planned to improve the sufficiency of the target droplets available, in order to make this technique effective against any selected insect. We hope that techniques can be developed to make most of the spray available against the target insect only.

Mosquito-borne disease and epidemics are becoming more frequent in tropical countries, and high-density pest Nematocera often hinder the development of tourism and other economically desirable industries in the Third World. The increasing urbanization of these countries in the last 25 years, and a corollary development of large slums, characterized by poor access and sanitation, have provided mosquito breeding-grounds and led to urban epidemics of dengue, malaria, and eventually yellow fever, in areas where the vector cannot be reached by vehicle-borne insecticidal misters and foggers.

Air sprays to be used against adult mosquitoes are based on the principle of producing parallel, wind-borne mist banks of insecticide droplets which, while drifting downwind, will saturate the air space, penetrate through vegetation, and into buildings. Success depends on producing enough droplets that are too small to be likely to settle and, whilst they remain airborne, are sufficient in number to touch all flying insects in the target zone. This is the concept of Target Droplet Sufficiency (TDS), which is based on the critical relationship between the moving insect and the impact velocity of the droplet—a factor that stresses the need to time the act of spraying to coincide with the times of known maximum activity for the given mosquito species involved. (For urban areas, these times frequently coincide with peak traffic congestion in early morning or late evening, making it difficult for motorized foggers to reach the areas where spraying is most critically needed.)

Previous work had established the need to produce an optimum droplet size related to the target insect, and had defined this as the Biologically Optimum Sized Spray, or what we call the BOSS droplet. Subsequent work on the concept proved that this droplet varies widely in its size depending upon the particular target insect involved. In spite of improvements in centrifugal nozzle sprays, presently available atomizers still cannot produce the smaller droplets required for impact on flying mosquitoes and smaller insects. This renders the ULV/C insecticides very inefficient, even though they have received governmental safety approval for use.

In our experiments in the Grand Caymans, we found that a 36-milliliter Malathion concentrate delivered in a diesel solution of 365 milliliters/hectare gave us excellent results. In light of these observations, it became evident that ULV/C sprays were not as efficient as ULV solutions (ULV/S), provided that the total emitted solution remained a relatively small volume, which we have since standardized at 365 milliliters/hectare. To explain these results, we developed the working hypothesis that as the spectrum being produced by a given atomizer, emitting small volume, was essentially stable, then the BOSS spectrum could be proportionately increased to provide the TDS by: (1) using a stable solution rather than a concentrate, and (2) reducing the viscosity of the emitted formulation.

Repeated tests, even in densely forested mangrove swamps, have demonstrated that satisfactory control requires that at least 96 percent of the target insects be killed. We have found in our work that the TDS system produces kills at the 96+ percent level with much reduced amounts of the active ingredients compared with the recommendations for use given on the EPA-approved labels of the concerned insecticides.

Working with the manufacturers of various insecticides, we have expanded the range of the ULV/S approach to a variety of pest insects and are continuing with this effort.

The ultimate objective is to tailor the spray to a narrow emission spectrum around the BOSS droplet, whilst ensuring a sufficiency of droplets in this part of the spectrum.

68

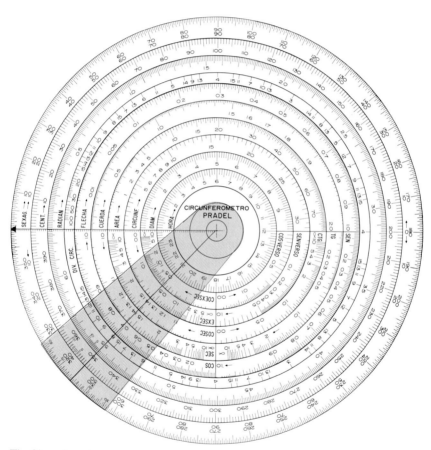

The Circumferometer.

THE CIRCUMFEROMETER

RICHARD PRADEL BULLARD
Calle "P," No. 155, Los Jazmines, Lima 18, Peru

Peruvian, born April 26, 1941. Businessman, engaged in manufacture and sales of auto security devices. Educated in Peru.

I have developed a unique instrument that gives a graphic determination of geometric, trigonometric, and time elements needed to calculate mathematical factors in the outlines of circular curves; conversion of units; measurement of arcs; the division of circles and circumferences into equal parts, arcs, or sectors of circles; and other applications related to circles and circumferences. Moreover, it can resolve triangles and other problems related to the unit measures of circles and circumferences without the need to search through tables.

The Circumferometer consists of a circle divided into concentric circumferences that have geometric, trigonometric, and time scales. It will be made in a transparent material so that we can read and see through it the different functions that can be determined with it. In addition to the circular scales, there is a rotary slider with vernier, also made of a transparent material. Each scale in the Circumferometer is identified with the abbreviation of its respective denomination and has an arrow to indicate the direction in which the scale must be read, according to the respective quadrant or quadrants.

The first circumference for 0 to 360 sexagesimal degrees has been divided into four quadrants; the first from 0° to 90°, the second from 90° to 180°, the third from 180° to 270°, and the fourth from 270° to 360°. Its direct applications are as follows:

To find the center of circles and circumferences to the extent the diameter of the Circumferometer permits.

To convert sexagesimal degrees to centesimal degrees, radians, hours, and vice versa.

To divide circles and circumferences into equal parts.

To find the trigonometric and parameter functions of circular curves.

To find areas, circumferences, and diameters when knowing only one of them.

Description of the Scales

Each of the concentric circumferences is individually graduated with scales, which are described from outside to inside, as follows:

First Circumference, with Two Graduations, one of 360 sexagesimal degrees, the second dividing the first in four quadrants of 90 sexagesimal degrees. The first graduation allows converting sexagesimal degrees to centesimal degrees, plus radian, sagittas, chords, and hours data. The second graduation converts 0–90 sexagesimal degrees, according to quadrant (sine/arc cosine, cosine/arc cosine, etc.).

Second Circumference, of 400 centesimal degrees, for converting from one system to another.

Third Circumference, divided in radians for conversion to degrees, hours, and vice versa, indirectly to trigonometric functions, and to measure lengths of arcs for radius equal to unity.

Fourth Circumference, for direct division of any circumference or circle up to 15 equal parts, indirectly up to 100 equal parts, and conversion of these to either type of degrees, or hours or radians.

Fifth Circumference, of three different sexagesimal degree arcs (one of 180°, two of 90°) for finding values of sagittas or middle ordinates, sines, and cosines.

Sixth Circumference, of three different sexagesimal degree arcs (one of 180°, two of 90°) for finding values of chords, tangents, and secants.

Seventh Circumference, of two arcs (one of 180°, one of 90°) for finding values of the areas of circles and cotangents.

Eighth Circumference, of three arcs (one of 180°, two of 90°) for finding values of circumferences of circles contained between 0 and 10 and vice versa, the values of versed sines and exsecants (externals).

Ninth Circumference, of three arcs (one of 180°, two of 90°) for converting diameters into circumferences, areas of circles and vice versa, and finding values of co-versed sines and co-exsecants.

Tenth Circumference, divided into 24 hours for converting into sexagesimal degrees, centesimal degrees, radians, and vice versa.

Learning to use the Circumferometer takes little time, as the instructions for determining various values are clear and readily understood, once the abbreviations on the scales are grasped.

In general terms, the value of the trigonometric functions and the geometric elements of the circular curves correspond to radius equal to unity (1); for a different radius, multiply the value reading in the Circumferometer by that radius.

The dimensions of the Circumferometer are variable, according to the required level of accuracy and the cost involved in producing different sizes. Obviously, the lengths of the arcs of each one of the scales and the order of same are located within the device, and will vary with the size of the specific model used.

For purposes of reading angles, conversions, trigonometric functions, parameters of circular curves, and the corresponding inverse values, the line of the slider must be used to coincide with numerical value on the slider and on the appropriate circumference. If the angle is already drawn, the instrument is set over the angle, and, reading through the transparent device, the required values are seen.

In order to divide circumferences or circles into equal parts, the center of the Circumferometer must coincide with the center of the circular graph to be divided. The divisions are then marked according to the number required. This operation can be done directly for from 2 to 15 equal parts. For a larger number (up to 100) of divisions, the Circumferometer must be rotated after each mark.

To find the center of a circumference or circle, within the permissible dimensions of the Circumferometer, use the concentric circumferences to obtain equidistant separations in any direction with the aid of the graduated radius.

The illustration of the Circumferometer enclosed is from the original drawing, which has a diameter of 60 centimeters. As noted above, size of the Circumferometer will affect the measuring lengths available, and individual users may wish to have larger or smaller such devices to suit their particular needs.

A SEARCH FOR USABLE MAGNETIC ENERGY

RICHARD J. DESMOND
5435 Dearborn, Mission, Kansas 66202, U.S.A.

American, born May 28, 1923. U.S. Government Quality Analyst in the Social Security Administration. Science education in the United States.

I wish to promote and encourage experimentation in the infant technology of magnetic energy. I am neither mathematician nor physicist and cannot meaningfully and productively experiment in so broad a field as magnetic energy. Surely, however, there are others who *can* do so. My project is to locate these talented and capable persons and encourage them to turn their capabilities to a "new" field of energy that is older than the hills.

The earth is one huge round magnet with energy pouring out from one pole, surrounding the globe, flowing into the other pole and on through the earth. Can this energy be captured and controlled? Can it be intensified? Why is it necessary to use tremendous force to blast a rocket off the surface of the earth when there is an energy source above that might be used to *lift* the rocket?

The key word, perhaps, is *intensification*. For example, the pulling power of a horseshoe magnet on, say, a random collection of paper clips becomes far greater when the magnet is immersed in a container of liquid oxygen. Magnetic energy *can* be intensified. Assuredly, the use of liquid oxygen may be cumbersome, but surely other means can be found for intensifying and controlling this energy source.

For example, can we produce an automobile with magnetized ballbearings in the wheels that we could start, stop, speed up, slow down, or reverse?

How *does* magnetic energy flow through a steel ball, and at what speed? If we were to hollow out the steel ball, would the magnetic energy still flow straight through the center? Would it flow at a slower pace? Or would it follow the metal sides? What happens if we wire the inside of the ball? Can we control the flow of energy? What happens if we nearly flatten the ball? Could we make it move? Revolve? Do we then have the start of a "flying saucer"? There are dozens of such questions regarding this age-old force, and we are not exploring them thoroughly.

We are now entering a new decade, with an energy crisis and many austere predictions for the coming years. Someone has said that the best any government can do is "patch, improvise, make-do, and hold on." We see such alternate energy sources as solar, nuclear, shale oil, and geothermal being pursued. Is there no research being conducted in the field of magnetic energy?

I wrote to Senator Robert Dole to suggest this source of energy, but was advised that no experiments are being conducted through the government sector. He suggested several organizations that I might write to for information. This I did. The Rand Corporation said, "We have done quite a bit of research in the field of energy, but nothing in magnetic energy." The U.S. Chamber of Commerce said that little is known about the possible applications of magnetic energy and suggested that I contact the Physics Department of a good university. The National Academy of Sciences also suggested a local university and mentioned an office elsewhere that would evaluate a well-formulated idea or model, but would not review theories or handle general inquiries on energy matters.

I have also written President Carter but have received no reply. The letter suggested magnetic energy as a possible matter of national defense, with magnetic shields and so on. Perhaps the letter was put aside as the work of a crackpot. This isn't necessarily true. I belong to an organization called Mensa, which is composed of some fairly intelligent people. I intend to call upon them for help in the future and would welcome any interested contributions to the question.

God gave us many natural resources. One of them is not being used.

EARTHQUAKE PREDICTION THROUGH RADIO WAVE ANOMALIES?

LAWRENCE I. COTARIU
8041 N. Hamlin Avenue, Skokie, Illinois 60076, U.S.A.

American, born August 14, 1947. Free-lance writer, licensed Amateur Radio Operator. Self-educated in seismology in the United States.

I am organizing a large group of people, physically located along one of the major geological fault lines of the world, to collect data on any unusual radio frequencies that they may observe in their locations. These data will be made available to the U.S. Geological Survey, or other seismological or earthquake research organizations, for evaluation against known records, in order to determine whether radio waves have the potential of being a viable earthquake prediction source.

This project has come about because of my own experiences as a ham radio operator going back over 10 years and because of reports from other radio operators around the world. These appear to connect variations in radio propagation and "noise" with subsequent occurrences of earthquakes in different parts of the world. Though I had often connected the noise with the thought that an earthquake was due somewhere, the decision to pursue the subject more thoroughly came in August, six years ago, when I picked up persistent loud noise on the 14 MHz frequency. At midnight that night, Chicago had a moderate earthquake, centered on a little known fault line some 30 miles southwest of the city. Blue flashes seen in the direction of the epicenter were subsequently explained as the release of electrical energy during the quake.

Reports from the ham radio world since then have indicated that radio signals go through changes when they pass over major fault lines in the world. In other words, the magnetic field of the planet may change from the fault line up into the atmospheric layers, shortly before the fault jolts.

I have been organizing a large group of people, primarily ham radio operators, within 100 miles of the San Andreas Fault on our West Coast. The objective is to keep records on conditions in various radio frequencies for perusal by appropriate scientific bodies. Evidently this information is of potential interest because I received this response from the U.S. Geological Survey: "I think that your idea to get continuous radio noise records along the San Andreas Fault is a good one. By the way, you would need to look at all the data, not just the month around the earthquake. I would be interested to look at your comparisons of noise and earthquakes as a function of time and position. It would seem that the more information we have, the better our chances of understanding these phenomena. We operate our magnetometers continuously, and thus far, have not seen rapid transient fields just before or following earthquakes."

In another correspondence with the U.S. Geological Survey, a radio operator was quoted as saying, "It appears that the pre-quake phenomenon must be observable at, or near, ground level as well as at ionospheric levels, since the earth's magnetic field consists of flux lines detectable wherever a magnetic compass will function. I believe this convulsion can be large scale, probably global in some instances, since some anomalous propagation conditions observed here in Wyoming were followed by quake reports in Europe."

Over the past several years, I have collected reports from radio operators in Europe and elsewhere that have to do with apparently connected radio noise/earthquake occurrences. To investigate the possible connection further, I have placed a number of announcements in various U.S. ham radio publications and elsewhere, seeking further cooperation from other interested parties. My inquiries to date cover the length of the San Andreas Fault from southern California up to the northwestern portion of the state of Washington. I would like to extend the list of observers to people in Alaska.

In addition to the group of people who are being assembled to monitor and record conditions in various radio frequencies, we hope to have cooperation from the scientists working with the MAGSAT satellite as it orbits the earth for purposes of measuring the magnetic field. We may find connections when MAGSAT flies over faults prior to any given quake, in the possibly detectable change in the magnetic field. Radio signals, of course, are easily passed back and forth between the satellites.

In 1982, the so-called Jupiter Effect will possibly affect the earth, at the moment when the planets and the sun are lined up. Some people theorize that this alignment may cause numerous earthquakes around the globe. I hope to have my group fully organized and collecting data by this time, with the goal of developing our approach into a reliable means of predicting time and location of earthquakes.

The prototype machine with crinkle motor.

THE CRINKLE MOTOR—
A NEW DESIGN CONCEPT

LOUIS STANLEY
22 Ponyara Road, Beverly Hills, N.S.W. 2209, Australia

Australian, born August 26, 1929. Company Managing Director of two development firms. Engineering education in Czechoslovakia.

This project involves the development of a completely new method of manufacturing rotors and stators for electric motors and generators. The method incorporates a unique technique whereby the rotors and stators are produced by a continuous forming of pre-punched metal strips into the finished shape of the desired structure. The required circular shape of the structure is achieved by "crinkling" the pre-punched strip of metal during the forming process and "nesting" these crinkled coils in one another—rather like pieces of corrugated iron placed one on top of the other.

This new method can manufacture the laminated form of structure required to avoid excessive induced eddy currents in electric rotors and stators, while at the same time avoiding the need for *individual stamping* of these laminations, a process that is both expensive and wasteful but nevertheless necessary in today's conventional means of manufacturing rotors and stators.

As background, one needs to understand the conventional manufacturing process in use today for electric motors and generators, particularly for machines above fractional horsepower. In such devices, the machine rotor (for example) is normally formed of many stacked metal disks, or laminations, which are held together by a casting. This method of manufacture contributes considerably to the cost of the completed machine because of the complicated method of assembly employed and, more importantly from the point of view of conservation of natural resources, because of the waste of the metal involved. Conventional stators, although not normally strictly circular in shape, are constructed in similar fashion, which results in a corresponding increase in the cost of the completed motor.

The Crinkle Motor Method of manufacturing for such elements was developed to substantially overcome the disadvantages of increased cost and wastage of material that are associated with the conventional methods of manufacture used today. The Crinkle Motor Method is applicable not only to the manufacturing of rotors and stators, but also to the manufacture of electric transformers.

(I should note that the disadvantages referred to above have already been largely overcome in the case of the Stanley Parallel, or Axial Flux, Motor, which I designed and which is now in development. However, the Parallel Motor is likely to be confined to the fractional horsepower and small horsepower size ranges, whereas I envisage that the Crinkle Motor concept will be applied eventually to the manufacture of motors and generators from the smallest sizes to the largest sizes conceivable.)

The Crinkle Motor concept was conceived by the applicant toward the end of a long period of time spent almost solely in designing and constructing an automatic production machine that would accomplish the production of rotors and stators for the Stanley Parallel Motor. During this time, I experimented with, and tried out, scores of ideas for overcoming the problem of automatically cutting the wiring slots in the disk-type rotors and stators.

Although the designs of the Parallel Motor and the Crinkle Motor concept have nothing in common (beyond both being unique design challenges), the practical experience gained in attempting to overcome the Parallel Motor design problem was of great assistance in overcoming the practical production problems associated with the Crinkle Motor concept. Thus, from the time I first conceived the Crinkle Motor concept, a period of no more than two months elapsed before I had personally designed and constructed a machine capable of producing Crinkle rotors and stators by hand. Once this device for allowing the manual production to be submitted to a method had been perfected, the task of designing an automatic production machine was a simple one.

Enclosed with this application are descriptive materials that better explain the concept of the Crinkle Motor design, for those who would like to have a detailed understanding.

Copies of my notes, "An Introduction to the Crinkle Motor Concept," have been sent to major electrical manufacturers in various overseas countries, and they appear to have created a great deal of interest in these circles. So far, the concept has been inspected in Sydney by, or on behalf of, manufacturers from three different continents. To date, no one I have encountered is aware of the Crinkle concept being used elsewhere in the world.

A copy of the complete patent specification for the invention, "New type electric motors referred to Rotating Machines and Induction Cores," now lodged with the Australian Patents Office, is also included. This specification gives a detailed description of the Crinkle Motor concept.

Also enclosed are photographs showing the prototype machine, in which the rotor and stator coils were pressed out by means of a hand press. We have programmed to produce a sophisticated automatic production machine in the near future. We anticipate no problems in constructing and operating this unique production machine.

No matter where our energy sources may come from for the foreseeable future, the provision of electric power will continue to be an important part of our everyday needs, and electric motors and generators will continue to be needed in increasing quantities. To build these machines today requires unnecessary amounts of precious resources and unduly expensive, wasteful manufacturing methods. In view of the very considerable savings of material achieved by the Crinkle Motor concept, compared with the material required for the construction of conventional type machines, I believe that the development of the Crinkle Motor concept represents a means of resource conservation of worldwide significance.

PRODUCING INEXPENSIVE ANIMAL PROTEIN

PAUL E. CHANLEY
156 Palmetto Avenue, U-21, Indialantic, Florida 32903, U.S.A.

American, born December 3, 1930. Consulting marine biologist, specializing in larval/hatchery operations. Education in the United States.

My interest is in developing methods for producing inexpensive animal protein by farming and harvesting juvenile bivalve mollusks. Bivalve mollusks are widely distributed in both marine and fresh waters and could be produced in many parts of the world. They feed on unicellular algae and efficiently convert solar energy to animal protein. They have many desirable traits for intensive cultivation, and the technology for doing this has developed rapidly in recent years.

Although traditional bivalve mollusk crops are produced in 1–5 years, bivalves grow extremely rapidly as larvae and juveniles. This rapid growth is a key consideration for my project. For instance, oyster larvae increase 125 times in size in only 3 weeks, making juveniles harvestable a short time after birth. This meat could be used in traditional recipes or in new food products, or it could be converted to a protein concentrate for use as a food supplement or as an animal feed.

Specific activities of the project include: (1) determining species and sizes of bivalves that most efficiently produce protein; (2) developing processing techniques for non-traditional products; and (3) improving the technology of hatchery production by developing mass culture systems and standardizing the nutrient value of algal foods.

Apart from the need to expand the world's food supply, a number of considerations speak in favor of developing this particular food source. Bivalve mollusks, low on the food chain, survive easily on readily produced plankton, needing no expenditure of energy to maintain body temperature.

They are relatively immobile, making their cultivation more like that of plants than that of animals. Their enormous reproductive potential (an oyster can produce 100 million eggs annually) and short generation time (bivalve mollusks become sexually mature in a few months) allow for excellent selective breeding activities, and low brood stock requirements. Though some wild species have been farmed for over 2000 years, most shellfish farmers have been able to rely on the abundantly produced wild seed; there are no domesticated species. As harvesting techniques improved and demand rose, wild populations were depleted and bivalve mollusks evolved from a cheap, inexpensive food to a high-priced luxury item—a far cry from 200 years ago in the United States when it was illegal to feed slaves cheap soft clams for more than two meals per day. Today, the still-unfarmed soft clams are a prized delicacy, far more expensive than chicken, which was a delicacy in those colonial times.

Present plans call for research on the oyster, the scallop, and the clam, though non-commercial species will be considered also. Species would be cultivated, and a record of the age and growth rate kept. At a length of 1 millimeter, a sample would be cooked in a known volume of water to separate meat from shell. Average length, drained weight, and dry weight of the meats and juices would be determined, and this sampling repeated at weekly intervals to determine at which size and age each of the species produced the most meat per unit of time.

Processing procedures for juvenile bivalves would be developed: one based on drying and grinding whole juvenile bivalves as a potential livestock feed ingredient, and the second based on separating the shell from the meat—by drying the above powder in an air current that would separate the heavier shell fragments from meat, or by cooking whole animals in a shaker device in which the meat would float and the shells would sink to the bottom.

Hatchery production procedures would be improved to reflect the far greater efficiencies promised in breeding bivalve mollusks only up to the juvenile stage. Much greater volume culture systems (30,000 liters, for example, versus the common 400–1000 liter commercial systems) would significantly increase labor productivity and the profitability of the hatchery.

Further research on algal species would be done to determine the factors affecting their nutritional value for bivalve larvae.

Several scientific papers of pertinent current value for those interested in mariculture could be expected from the project, and experience operating the pilot plant could be transferred easily to larger operations in other parts of the world, where this valuable source of animal protein is vitally needed at an affordable cost.

A NEW APPROACH TO DIAGNOSING AND TREATING UTERINE MALIGNANCIES

RUBEN HERNANDEZ-SANCHEZ
Hospital Central Militar, Ap. Postal #35-548, Mexico D.F., Z.P. 10, Mexico

Mexican, born November 30, 1933. Physician, surgeon, and Professor of Oncology. Scientific and medical education in Mexico.

C arcinoma of the uterine cervix is a significant medical problem in Mexico. A great number of patients are seen in the advanced stages of this dreadful disease. In Mexican women patients, 10 percent show an abnormal cervicovaginal smear, making it imperative that we search for new methods of early tumor detection.

Carcinoma of the uterine cervix can be studied within a continuum of changes: metaplasia (abnormal replacement of cells of one type by cells of another type), dysplasia (abnormal tissue development), intraepithelial carcinoma, and, finally, invasive carcinoma. Until now, the pathologist who diagnosed the degree of dysplasia has determined the treatment; thus, the subjective evaluation of the pathologist who assessed the slides has determined whether the patient will be subjected to a hysterectomy. Practical problems do occur rather frequently with this approach, mainly in borderline cases.

In a study (Hall and Watson) of the evolution of 206 cases of dysplasia (mild, moderate, and severe), only 24 developed into intraepithelial carcinoma. While these observations proved the risk of dysplastic epithelium and intraepithelial carcinoma, they also showed that dysplasia might not be a progressive process toward carcinoma. It follows that a number of women with dysplasia are overtreated with a needless hysterectomy for a lesion that numerically presents a low risk of developing carcinoma and a greater probability of spontaneous involution or stabilization.

We believe it is of great importance to develop new diagnostic procedures leading to the identification of early minimal-risk lesions. Our project seeks to develop a new diagnostic procedure based on the working hypothesis that the malignant potential of abnormal epithelium can be predicted and thus lead to more accurate therapeutic decisions.

We proceed from the following background. Numerous reports describing the growth of solid tumors state that the process is invariably associated with a phenomenon of neovascularization, more vigorous than that observed in tissue reparation and inflammation. Recently, it has been shown that the malignant tumor cells and the endothelial vascular cells form a well-developed ecosystem, in which the mitotic rate of both types of cells depends upon a close intercellular relationship; thus, tumor cells stimulate the proliferation of the endothelial cells, resulting in tumor growth through an indirect effect. Folkman has demonstrated the existence of a diffusible product of tumor cells (known as the Tumor Angiogenic Factor, or TAF) that is capable of stimulating a rapid and vigorous vascular neoformation. Wood has shown that, after 18 hours of injection of a tumor embolus in the auricular chamber of a rabbit, the tumor tissue is invaded by capillaries of new formation.

Other effects associated with the stimulus of TAF are the increase of DNA synthesis and increase of tritiated timidine captation far from the implanted tumoral tissue. This phenomenon of angiogenesis cannot be produced by killed tumor cells, saline, or inflammation. TAF can be obtained from human solid tumors as well as animal solid tumors. It has a molecular weight of 100,000, is degraded by the action of ribonuclease, heating up to 56°C, and it is trypsin resistant. If the lipid component is eliminated, the angiogenic effect increases. TAF contains 25 percent RNA, 10 percent protein, and 50 percent carbohydrates. TAF's effect is species-specific, its action is temporal, and its absence is accompanied by cessation of the angiogenic response.

The study of samples of human breast neoplasms and benign lesions has shown that the angiogenic response is observed only in atypical hyperplastic lesions and malignant neoplasias; thus we see the potential for a new means of diagnosis. By taking tissue samples of the uterine cervix of women with abnormal cytologic findings and implanting them in the iris of rabbits, we will search for angiogenesis. Tissue diagnosis will be correlated with the development of angiogenesis. All cases diagnosed as invasive neoplasia will be eliminated from the study. Cases with positive angiogenesis and cervical intraepithelial neoplasia will be separated at random into two groups. One group will be subjected to definitive treatment, and the other to bimonthly examinations for a minimum of five years. If we are able to evaluate the potential for malignization of hyperplastic tissues through the production and effect of TAF, before structural and morphological changes occur, we will be better able to treat malignant tumors before growth becomes well-established.

Military pilots can learn to fly commercial aircraft.

CONVERTING INDUSTRY FROM MILITARY TO CIVILIAN WORK

 SEYMOUR MELMAN
Rolex Laureate, Rolex Awards for Enterprise
304 Mudd Building, Columbia University,
New York, New York 10027, U.S.A.

American, born December 30, 1917. Professor of Industrial Engineering, Columbia University. Education and Ph.D. in the United States.

T his project involves exploring and defining technical, economic, and organizational methods for the conversion of industrial economy from military to civilian work. It pertains to the actual changeover of industrial equipment and other facilities, as well as the occupational skills of managers, engineers, and production workers from those required for serving the military to the skills and capabilities required for participating in the civilian economy.

Three models are to be formulated for economic conversion: the United States and Western Europe, the Soviet sphere, and less developed countries. These models will include the following major variables: methods for alternative-use planning for military industrial and military base facilities; methods for retraining of strategic military sector occupations; methods for integrating technical and economic conversion planning into the surrounding economy. What is feasible and appropriate for each of these variables is strongly affected by the surrounding industrial-economic environment. Hence the necessity for three different models.

Specifying these methods will required detailed exploration of several technological, managerial, and economic issues. What is the feasibility of converting major machinery in military industry? What methods are applicable to the retraining of military industrial managers and engineers? What economic planning methods are appropriate? Major issues of policy are involved here.

Is centralism in economic control required for economic conversion? Are there limits to efficiency owing to limits on centralism? Under what conditions can local control be more efficient than centralism for economic conversion planning?

Both the design and the feasibility of conversion from military to civilian economy are strongly affected by the particular characteristics of military economy and its relation to the surrounding civilian economy. For example, where the status and pay of military and civilian industry managers are similar (United States model), military managers can be converted by professional retraining. In other economies, where military industry managers may enjoy higher status and pay and have many professional problems eased for them, conversion to civilian work can threaten the professional status of military industrial managers unless the conversion model includes provision for industrial restructuring, changes in priority systems, and so on.

Available data indicate substantial variation in these and allied considerations among major economic systems.

Planning capability at national and local levels for alternative use of industrial and military base facilities varies substantially between the United States/Western Europe, the Soviet sphere, and the less developed countries. *Lead time* is a critical requirement in alternative-use planning and is strongly affected by the availability of trained technicians and of other resources necessary to carrying out the planning function. The diversity and productivity of civilian industry necessarily affect its ability to serve the military sector with new equipment to be used in the conversion process.

The *convertibility of engineering occupations* is strongly affected by the comparability in military and civilian economy of their performance requirements, problems, and rewards. These occupational conditions vary substantially among the three major economic types to be studied. The retraining of technologists is affected by the availability of universities or similar institutions capable of administering appropriate retraining programs.

The possible role of production workers in alternative-use planning varies according to their mode of organization, political and technical sophistication, and tradition of participation in enterprise decision making. Major variation is to be expected among the three types of economies.

Considerable variation may be expected in traditions and capabilities for coping with the retraining of uniformed personnel of the armed forces and for converting military bases and their facilities to civilian work.

The objective of this research, the formulation of three strategic models for economic conversion, will require several classes of data: aggregate (macro) industrial and allied data on the three types of economies; detailed industrial, occupational, and allied data from sampled countries. These should include plant visits (wherever possible at aerospace, electronics and tank/artillery factories); interviews with industrial managers, trade unionists, and government authorities, as well as with technologists with current or prior experience in military economy; and examination of available literature on economic conversion and of related economic performance (comparable to the studies in *Conversion of Industry from a Military to Civilian Economy*, S. Melman, ed., Praeger, 1970).

More data on these matters will be available for the United States than for other areas. There has lately been a surge of activity in Western Europe on these topics that should be helpful to the project. The data for the Soviet sphere will have to be carefully developed. The data base for the less developed countries will require a strategic sampling of countries. The selection of countries may be constrained by problems of access, but this can only be determined empirically.

Building on the analysis of data from diverse economies, I will formulate strategies that can be applied nationally and internationally to facilitate economic conversion planning.

The reason for undertaking such activity is to contribute to the confidence (and therefore the ability) of nation-states to act toward reversal of the arms race. The arms race, conducted in the quest for security, has itself become an ever-greater source of insecurity.

Every political effort to curtail or reverse the arms race requires that the nations concerned have in hand reliable blueprints for industrial-economic conversion from military to civilian economy.

Insofar as ordered inquiry can shed fresh light on ways of solving the intertwined problems of technological, economic, and organizational realities, this work can contribute to greater confidence in the ability of leaders to reverse the arms race by orderly methods that minimize disruption and give promise of net gain to the nations concerned.

HOW DO ANIMALS NAVIGATE?

ANTONIO B. NAFARRATE
1060 Terra Noble Way, San Jose, California 95132, U.S.A.

Argentine, born March 14, 1937. Member of Research Staff, Palo Alto Research Center, Xerox Corporation. Physics education in Argentina and the United States.

The complete project consists of developing, writing, and publishing an inertial theory of animal navigation and biological rhythms, including the search of experimental evidence to support such a theoretical model. The experimental evidence may come from analysis and interpretation of experiments performed by others and reported in scientific literature or from my own experiments specifically designed to test the inertial hypothesis. Presently, the project consists of performing one such experiment by which I will attempt to modify the free-running activity rhythms of cockroaches by manipulation of gravitational cues.

To understand the significance of the proposed experiment, familiarity with the inertial model of navigation and rhythms is necessary; therefore a condensed version of the main ideas in the model follows.

Almost everyone is familiar with the equivalence of geographic longitude and time differences on the globe. Not so familiar or obvious is the mechanical fact that latitude can also be expressed as time differences—if we use an inertial gyroscopic device such as a Foucault pendulum to measure latitude. We can think of the Foucault pendulum as a clock that measures latitude— it is a perfect sidereal clock at either Pole, and it is a very bad clock at the Equator, where it stops completely. A spinning top is the exact complement of the Foucault pendulum; under appropriate conditions, it will generate precessional frequencies related to the latitude. If internal reference oscillators (or biological clocks) are used to compare or monitor the precessional frequencies that correspond to each latitude, it becomes possible to detect changes in longitude, because while motion takes place, there will be Doppler shifts in the precessional frequencies.

An elegant result of this inertial theory lies in the simplicity of description of a migration path on the earth surface: every point has three coordinates given as time differences, not just the migration dates but also the two spatial coordinates are measured in time units. Since experimental evidence indicates that migration routes are genetically encoded, the simplicity of path specification resulting from this inertial model makes it a suitable candidate.

To be useful, and to explain the near incredible accuracy documented in some animal species, notably birds, an inertial navigation system has to detect very small inertial forces. Beause of the nature of inertial and gravitational forces, a demonstration of sensitivity to small gravitational forces should be considered as positive evidence in support of the inertial model.

The actual experiment will be as follows: six to ten adult male cockroaches, half of them experimental and half control, will be individually housed in activity-monitoring cages in continuous total darkness. Each activity cage is pivoted like a seesaw, and the movement of the cockroach from one end to the other actuates an electric switch that produces a signal in an event recorder, a well-known technique.

The experimental animals will be exposed to series of periodic gravitational changes (following different patterns and strategies) produced with lead slabs (up to six slabs of 11 kilograms each). The idea is to observe whether the activity rhythms can be influenced by these small local gravity changes, as new impressed frequencies or activity phase shifts.

A Swiss entomologist, Dr. Fritz Schneider (paper enclosed), using a different technique and insect species, reports sensitivity to such small gravitational cues, and, in fact, all of Dr. Schneider's experimental results can be used to support my inertial model. At the moment, however, Dr. Schneider's interpretation of his results based on what he calls "gravitational waves" is not generally accepted, since physicists have not yet detected such waves. In other words, my inertial model can explain Dr. Schneider's experimental results within the context of accepted physics.

ALCOHOL FOR THE AUTOMOBILE

JOSE M. R. CONCEPCION
30 Melantic, SLV, Makati, Metro Manila, Philippines

Filipino, born December 28, 1931. Businessman, inventor, and consultant in automotive industry. Educated in the Philippines.

My project involves the manufacture and sale of a device that can be attached to an unmodified motor vehicle to enable it to run on denatured 189-proof methyl or ethyl alcohol, or even such alcohol at lower purity levels. It can also run such a motor vehicle in any proportion of alcohol to gasoline in a satisfactory manner.

Alcohol has been used in internal combustion machines in the past, although with difficulty. The main problem has been that alcohol absorbs water from the atmosphere with such voracity that the consequent mixture of alcohol with gasoline caused miscibility problems. Little more than 1 percent water in the mixture would cause the engine to stop. In cold temperatures, starting was difficult, acceleration was poor, and a host of other problems occurred. Suitable ratios of alcohol to gas could not exceed 20 percent alcohol to gas without incurring further deterioration in performance. Additionally, such mixtures required the use of anhydrous alcohol, which is expensive to produce and difficult to store and distribute.

My device solves these and other problems. The system does not use fuel blends, but instead mixes the alcohol and gasoline in vapor form. Any water content is steamed by superheated air from the device and subsequently super-steamed in the combustion chamber and ejected into the atmosphere. The device can utilize low-grade, water-diluted alcohol as low as 160 proof, which can easily be produced by the average distillery anywhere in the world. Key elements in the device include the following:

1. *Alcohol Fuel Tank.* Made of materials impervious to alcohol, and usually placed in the trunk, safety strapped, and vented.

2. *Electric Fuel Pump.* Assures an even flow of alcohol.

3. *Proportionate Valve.* Passes both gasoline and alcohol simultaneously through diagonally opposed identical valves, regulating the fuel flow in desired proportions. When more gasoline flows, less alcohol will flow, and vice versa.

4. *Fuel Filter and Pulse Dampener.* A commercially available filter that contains a pulse dampener emanating from the fuel pump pulsations, thus making the fuel flow more even.

5. *Accelerating Valve.* Directly coupled with the accelerator linkage by a universal type coupling that can be adapted to any motor vehicle, this valve replaces the solenoid valve which stops alcohol flow at idling speeds, and also increases the alcohol supply in metered quantities as speed increases.

6. *Heat Exchanger.* Normally connected in most motor vehicles from the crankcase to the intake manifold and made by manufacturers as part of the system. The device merely superheats the air/oil vapors from the crankcase by coiling these around the exhaust pipe, and bringing them to the vaporizer, where the air and the sprayed alcohol meet.

7. *Vaporizer Assembly.* A Venturi type design, in which the hot air and alcohol (sprayed into a mist by a fine jet) meet immediately prior to the mixture's introduction into the intake manifold.

The device has many favorable attributes. It starts and idles as well as any gasoline engine because it uses only gasoline at these stages. It improves mileage through better vaporization and utilization of the anti-detonating qualities of alcohol, which results in better mileage based on total volume of both fuels. In addition to displacing gasoline, you still save fuel. Power is improved because of alcohol's anti-detonating qualities, which allow production of higher octane, thus permitting engine timing to be advanced. Because alcohol is a supercoolant, the engine runs cooler. The use of non-polluting alcohol lessens emission pollution from the engine.

No adverse effects have been observed in the engine from corrosion or undue wear (the last engine was examined after 30,000 kilometers of use). There is no damage to the existing fuel system, as the device is independent of the stock motor and made of materials impervious to alcohol. Fuel is cheaper. We are using denatured alcohol, which can be produced with only one distillation column and avoids the tax problems present with alcohol used for spirits. Finally, the addition of the alcohol fuel tank, while taking some storage room, allows the vehicle a greater traveling range.

The Yacht Siska.

BUILDING A RADICAL, LIGHT-DISPLACEMENT RACING YACHT

ROLLAND LESLIE TASKER
7 Marlin Court, Dalkeith, Western Australia 6009, Australia

Australian, born March 21, 1926. Yachtsman, educated in Australia.

My project has been the design and construction of a radically new racing yacht that would conform to the maximum International Rating Rule and would be the fastest and safest yacht in the world.

The yacht *Siska*, one of the biggest aluminum sloops in the world, was completed in October 1978 and has achieved outstanding success in 30,600 nautical miles of safe, high-speed record-breaking ocean racing. The yacht embodies unique design features and many new building techniques aimed at providing the lightness, simplicity, and great strength needed to achieve high planing speeds in complete safety under the most testing and severe wind and sea conditions.

In setting out to build the fastest and safest yacht in the world, I decided that I would need to design it totally—the hull, spars, rigging, sails, and fittings—and build it myself in Perth. I also decided that *Siska*, built of aluminum, would displace less than half the normal weight of similar yachts, but be so strongly constructed and so simple in layout that she could be raced in safety across every ocean in the world by a crew of only 12 amateur sailors.

Siska was built in 196 days. She is 23.2 meters long, 5.8 meters wide, draws 3.5 meters, and displaces 18,600 kilograms. Her sail area is 227 square meters.

In one year of ocean racing, *Siska* has sailed through the North and South Atlantic, the Indian Ocean and the Pacific, the Great Southern Ocean and the Tasman Sea, without damage or casualties. She has set a new record for the fastest passage ever made under sail from England to South Africa (37 days), and from South Africa to Australia (19 days). She can cover well over 300 nautical miles in 24 hours, or an average speed of 13 knots. The world press calls her "Supersloop."

To appreciate the challenge of building *Siska,* it's helpful to understand some of the realities of sailing craft design and construction. Yachts (and all other sailing vessels) have, under normal conditions, a maximum speed that is a function of waterline length (about $1.4 \times \sqrt{L}$). At this speed, the addition of more sail (i.e., more driving power) has no effect. The only way to go faster is to design a boat that, in certain wind and sea conditions, will "plane" across the surface of the water. Over the last 30 years, I've built and raced 23 yachts, from dinghies to 19-meter ocean racers, and I have consistently found that the lighter and simpler they've been, the faster I could sail them.

I therefore set out to design a planing hull for the largest yacht I could race under the International Offshore Rules of the International Yacht Racing Union, the governing body of the sport. The calculated and measured rating permitted under the rules is 21.2 meters. Many yachts are racing to this rule limit, with overall lengths of from 21 to 26 meters and displacements between 30,000 and 50,000 kilograms. Though many of them will "surf" down big waves, they will not truly plane. To plane, I calculated I would have to get my total displacement down to no more than 19,000 kilograms, with a very wide, very flat hull shape. No yacht designer had ever attempted to do this with a boat so large, so that I could get no design information or practical assistance. I would have to solve the problem in my own way.

It was the same thing with the mast. Mast failures are so common and yet so disastrous when they occur that one would imagine that designers would by now have found some practical answers. This is not so—the most sophisticated and expensive masts in the world continue to fail, often in quite light winds—so I felt I had no option but to find a way around the mast problem myself. This is really what the story of building *Siska* is all about—finding answers to problems that other designers have failed to solve.

I selected aluminum for the hull and deck. To get form stability with such light displacement, and the planing characteristics needed, I designed a hull with a fine entry, a long straight run aft, and a very shallow, flat underbody having a maximum beam of 5.8 meters. Construction took place around two massive fore and aft main beams 3.5 meters apart, with 43 T-shaped frames welded to them, that required my designing a special hydraulic roller to shape, as each is different. The hull is unique in having no bulkheads to absorb compressive, torsional, and tensile loads, all of which are transmitted by the T-frames to the two main beams and the keelson via the 8–10 millimeter thick hull and deck plating. This plating is pre-formed hydraulically to the compound curvatures required and stress relieved after welding. There have been no problems with it in Force 10 and 11 gales or at temperatures below 0°C at 46° South, where we've encountered sub-arctic gale conditions.

For the mast, I decided on a new type of construction to reduce windage and total mast weight, to lower the center of gravity, and to keep risk of breakage to a minimum. I took a T16 Section (335 mm × 240 mm) for the base portion and progressively tapered this to a point of attachment of the forestay. A T13 Section (250 mm × 174 mm) was then inserted into the top tapered portion, and this in turn tapered to 150 mm × 110 mm at the mast head. The two sections were riveted and welded together. Spreader bases were made in aluminum and then welded to the mast. We have had no mast trouble of any kind, in all of our sailing.

Rigging is of the latest nickel-cobalt rod type, for its excellent physical qualities and high tensile strength of its cross section.

The boom is one of my T13 sections, in two halves, one tapered to fit inside the other. In the boom is a Navtec-type-3 hydraulic system, with 2-way action for controlling the mainsail foot tension. Though the mainsail foot is over 9 meters—normally uncontrollable via purchases and winches—the whole operation is run from one small cockpit lever.

All other controls on *Siska* are non-hydraulic: rope purchases, some assisting deck winches and jammers, and two small "coffee grinder" winches for the headsail and mainsheet.

The sails were all made in my sail loft in Perth. The lightest spinnaker weighs only 11 grams per square meter; the heaviest storm jib is 450 grams per square meter. None has been replaced since launching.

A Perkins 4-cylinder diesel turns a 60-centimeter prop, designed and made in our workshop. Its stainless steel blades are hollow to save weight, and they fold flat when sailing.

Navigation equipment is extensive, as one might guess, for the demands of long-distance racing. It includes a continuous position computer, a satellite weather pattern recorder, powerful radio transmitters and receivers, a VHF telephone, and a comprehensive range of electronic data recorders for boat and wind speeds and headings, and depth and direction finding.

Crew comfort was not limited to save weight. There are 12 saloon berths, in addition to the owner's separate double cabin with its own shower and toilet. The centrally located galley, with gimballed cooker and separate freezer, can provide three cooked meals a day for 16 crew for up to two months at sea.

Most important, however, was my design parameter calling for the yacht to be raced effectively with a crew of 12 amateurs, as opposed to the 20–30 crew members (often professionals) needed on most of today's big yachts. *Siska* can be sailed to any racing venue in the world with only 6 to 8 crew, depending on the length of the voyage, and be raced by amateurs who love sailing. Light and simple design did it.

CLEARING AND FERTILIZING WITH ONE MACHINE

GEORGE A. HENWOOD
Orchard Cottage, The Square, Brightwell, Wallingford,
Oxfordshire OX10 0SB, England

British, born June 20, 1920. Chemical engineering researcher and lecturer.
Mechanical engineering and science education in England.

I have developed a device, now in experimental form, that offers a unique solution to a common agricultural problem, while at the same time holding out the prospect of lessening the farmer's dependence upon imported fuels as a source of power for his agricultural machinery. Specifically, the proposed machine improves the practice of fire clearance on agricultural lands. This includes burning of stubble left after the harvest of cereal crops, destruction of the stems after root crops are lifted, and the top firing of newly cleared or neglected land to reduce weed infestation. Cereal crops are particularly prone to damaging infection from remnants of stubble, which do not readily decay if plowed into the soil.

Though there has been some research into this problem, to the extent of my knowledge, the solution presented here is original. Because of its potential for generating its own power, my device may have application beyond the requirements of technically advanced farming. The device and procedure fit in with the familiar farming routine.

Using a tractor, a broad-swath harrowing operation loosens roots and surface combustible material, which is then collected and conveyed to riddling screens for removal of adherent earth and stone. The remaining material is then fed to a hopper and screw feeder, which gathers and compresses the substance into a tube provided with vents for drainage of free water pressed out during compaction.

The resulting plug of combustible material is pressed along the tube where further drying occurs in a "flame zone." At the nozzle end, the material burns continuously in a forced draft from the air blower. The combustion gases and ash are blown through a shroud tube back past the feed tube. At the exhaust outlet, the sterile, potash-rich ash is blown back over the soil, where it will act as a fertilizing medium.

I am at present working with a small experimental test rig to test the feasibility of the combustion system and to provide thermodynamic data for larger prototypes. The type of material being burned is typical of the remains found in enormous quantities and fired each year in open fields. Apart from the inefficiency of this common firing practice, the environmental damage and pollution caused by the immense volumes of smoke and fumes produced are a perennial cause of complaint. The proposed device could probably provide a complete solution to these problems. Based on the information from the test rig, I envisage a complete attachment rig for a normal tractor. The device will clear and destroy the unwanted roots, stubble, and weeds, and it will return burnt residues to the soil as sterilized, rich ash.

More importantly, if we consider the wider possibilities of using the stubble as fuel, there may be a far greater value in the device.

To date, my investigations have shown that typically there will be about 4.5 kilograms per square meter of wet combustible matter when harrowed to a depth of about 10 centimeters. In turn, this will yield about 1.8 kilograms of dried matter at the device's combustion point. It is difficult to quantify the calorific value of such organic material because of its variability, but a cautious estimate gives a weight-to-weight calorific value of about 25 percent of a typical fuel oil value. Taking the latter to be 43,500 kilojoules per kilogram, then the calorific value of the organic matter will be about 10,875 kilojoules per kilogram. Therefore, the complete combustion of the dried material collected from 1 square meter of a field will generate about 19,575 kilojoules.

To estimate the heat potential in a normal operation, assume a tractor fitted with the proposed device, moving at an average 8 kilometers/hour and collecting stubble over a swath 3 meters wide. In an hour, it will clear about 2.4 hectares. At 1.8 kilograms of dried material per square meter, the heat generated by the combustion will be about 469,000 megajoules per hour.

This energy is far in excess of that required by the tractor and its collecting machinery. Conceivably, a machine could use some of this "free" energy to perform simultaneous clearing, plowing, and cultivating operations, leaving the ground ready for seed drilling. Basic parameters for such a machine suggest a steam-propelled tractor of about 100 brake horsepower (bhp), with a collector/combustion unit, 6-gang plow and cultivator in tow.

Further possibilities can be evolved from the basic concept, but I believe this précis should be sufficient to indicate the immediate practicalities and the reasons for pursuing the project.

TREE RINGS AS
AN ARCHAEOLOGICAL
DATING TOOL

PETER IAN KUNIHOLM
Department of Classics, 128 Goldwin Smith Hall,
Cornell University, Ithaca, New York 14853, U.S.A.

*American, born September 30, 1937. Archaeologist, Assistant Professor, Curator of
Classical Antiquities. Education, Ph.D., in the United States.*

C hronology building in the Aegean and Eastern Mediterranean,
whether by king lists, coinage issues, changing pottery and architectural styles, radio-carbon dates, or any of the various techniques
hitherto employed, is one of the most troublesome and thankless tasks an Old
World archaeologist might undertake. In many cases, the margin for error is
so large that the chronology is virtually unusable: a stratum discovered in the
Taurus Mountains dated *about* the middle of the 2nd millennium B.C., a stratum on the north central Anatolian plateau defined as "somewhere between
Phrygian and Ottoman" (a margin of error of some 2600 years), and so on.
There is no one dating system that, if adhered to consistently, does not cast
doubt on some, or all, of the others.

Ten years ago, the British paleoclimatologist H. H. Lamb, while comment-
ing on the climatic changes that may have put an abrupt end to Bronze Age
civilization in Greece, issued a challenge to researchers in the Mediterranean
and the Near East. He pointed out that there is a body of knowledge on the
three-thousand-year climatic sequence in northern Europe that has been
built up partly from pollen analysis of numerous bogs and lake site deposits,
and partly from analysis of documentary records, especially those that reveal
the incidence of extreme warm or cold, wet or dry seasons. He contended that
a similar record could be pieced together for the classical years of Greek and
Roman times.

Because meteorological records in Greece and Turkey are of fairly recent
vintage, one response to the challenge was to look at such proxy data as

tree-ring chronologies to shed light on the changing climatic conditions in the Mediterranean basin. The relationship between tree growth and climate for each area must be determined as precisely as possible, with the complication of limited meteorological observation in most of the areas.

Since 1973, I have been engaged in developing master dendrochronological scales from climatically sensitive trees in the Aegean area, with the cooperation of the Turkish, Cypriot, and Greek Forest Services. One of the major complications is the absence of trees with the longevity of the 4000-year-old bristlecone pine; any scale assembled must be composed of hundreds of overlapping, shorter-lived specimens, laboriously placed in sequence.

Master chronologies for each microclimatic region and for each species of cross-datable tree within that region must be published, even if in preliminary form, so that researchers can begin to take advantage of the work already done. Our team has cross-dated trees as far as 900 kilometers apart, and we have no idea how much further we will be able to go. Since, under optimum conditions of preservation and collection, it is sometimes possible to determine the *year* in which the wood was cut and since people started living in settled communities (and using large quantities of wood in their architecture) about 7000 B.C. in the Aegean, the promise for establishing long, precise tree-ring sequences is particularly encouraging.

The work is being accomplished via a large network of cooperating institutions and individuals. Foresters, archaeologists, restorers, and many others supply us with the wood itself or the information as to its whereabouts. Each summer, with grant aid, I've been able to take a team of trained students to the Eastern Mediterranean, where we collect and record samples, using photography and drawings when needed. The wood is then brought to our laboratory at Cornell, and more students measure the annual rings and record them in our computer file. In this fashion, hundreds of thousands of pieces of information can be retrieved and analyzed almost instantly.

In the past four years, 670 years of absolute and more than 3000 years of floating tree-ring chronologies have been established for the Anatolian Plateau of Turkey, a 385-year chronology has been established for the Trodos Mountains in Cyprus, and a 311-year chronology for northern Greece.

In effect, we now have a "wood library," which interested researchers can consult for a variety of purposes, including the history of forestation and deforestation, ancient methods of forest management, calibration of radio-carbon time scales, and long-term changes in tree-growth.

The potential exists for a continuous master chronology, extending from the present to ca. 7000 B.C., providing the archaeologist with a dating technique of exceptional accuracy. I am indebted to the Smithsonian Institution for its interest and help in furthering this work.

A small hydroelectric plant newly installed on a South African farm. The outlet pipes show how little water it uses.

SMALL, CHEAP
HYDROELECTRIC PLANTS

MICHAEL C. COTTERRELL
"Ailsa," Thomas River 5311, South Africa

South African, born July 15, 1942. Sheep and cattle rancher, agriculturalist, self-taught engineer. Educated in South Africa.

My project is the designing, manufacturing, marketing, and installing of small, cheap, maintenance-free, efficient, and long-lasting hydro-electric (or hydro-pumping) plants in the more isolated parts of the world where power is unavailable through regular commercial sources and where capital is too limited to enable the building of the usual power plants.

There is nothing new in the concept of building water turbines, which have provided useful energy to humanity for generations. What is unique in my production of turbines, however, can be described in the following way.

I make use of modern materials to build my turbines, which makes them cheaper, longer lasting, more maintenance-free, lighter, and more efficient. I aim at simplicity of design in order to attain my objectives of ease of maintenance (if necessary) by labor that is unskilled. I wish to fill the market for small turbines and Pelton wheels, which does not seem to be catered to by other manufacturers, thus enabling me to deliver plants where transportation problems make the development of hydroelectricity impossible. And I have incorporated certain revolutionary ideas in my turbine designs, which make them highly efficient.

As a physics graduate, I became interested in an old Pelton wheel that had been faithfully serving our farm for some 80 years. It had lasted a long time; but at only 18 percent efficiency, it was taking water I would have preferred to use for gravity irrigation. I designed a new unit and built it myself. Using only 680 liters a minute, with a 49-meter head, it produced 2.2 kilowatts, which was enough to run my farmhouse, workshop, and sheep-shearing-shed lights, with enough to spare for the television, refrigerator, and freezer.

As people began to learn about my machine, orders began to come in from the local area for units adaptable to particular conditions. The first hydroelectric-power unit I built for a neighbor was for a lighting plant; this Pelton wheel runs on 364 liters of water a minute, falling 45.7 meters. Due to friction and the angle of the fall, the effective head (fall of water) is only 41.1 meters, but it drives the wheel at about 500 rpm, and generates 1.3 kilowatts, quite enough to handle the lights, televisions, freezers, and refrigerators of two houses.

With each machine that has been built, I have improved the technology. Virtually all the units I am now building operate at something over 70 percent efficiency, even though each unit generally requires certain particular design alterations to achieve optimum results in converting potential energy to real power. For persons interested in the possibility of this kind of power, I give the following formula:

$$\text{Available kilowatts} = \frac{\text{Water flow (m}^3\text{/hr)} \times \text{Water head (m)}}{360}$$

The best diameter for the wheel depends on the speed at which it is designed to turn. The volume and head of water also affect the shaping, angle, and separation of the wheel's cups, which we now make of fiberglass. I designed a governor to control the units, which takes only three bearings of the five used in the units (the main shaft has two). All these are sealed within the unit, so there is virtually no need for maintenance. With the governor, there is no need to switch the machine off unless there is a need to conserve the water supply or to use it for some other purpose. Stopping the turbine is accomplished simply by turning a stopcock or closing a sluice, to eliminate the water flow.

We are continuing to build Pelton wheels for a variety of needs, mostly for local farm domestic energy supplies, although we have worked on a design for a much larger unit that could provide significant power for a small village. The major limitation to the Pelton wheels is the need for a fall of water (or head) in excess of 25 meters, because efficiencies drop off significantly below that, due to the need for the impulse of the jets (which concentrate and accelerate the water onto the cups) to be strong enough to turn the flywheel.

Having gained experience with these machines, we've begun to develop what are called Francis reaction turbines, which can work on much lower heads, down to 2.44 meters in one of our models. Our second machine of this type generates a steady supply of 2 kilowatts, using a flow of about 7000 liters a minute. These machines, which rotate on a vertical axis as water flows down through their blades, are slightly more expensive to start with (about Rand 6000 for a typical farm installation) than the Pelton wheels (about Rand 3500 to 4000 for the same requirement) though they will, in general, need less piping and other supporting materials. We suggest that users of the systems work on the premise that the cost of water reticulation, necessary piping, transmission lines, and the house for the turbine will cost about the same as the Pelton machine itself. Here in South Africa, a farmer who switches to one of these machines can reasonably expect to save about Rand 1200 per year on his domestic electricity, compared with the cost of equivalent power from diesel fuel and paraffin (for refrigerators), which provides a fairly short-term payout on the investment. The greatest benefit, of course, is that there are no fuel costs at all, once the installation is in, and that little or no maintenance is needed.

I seek to spread the use of these machines to areas where they fit particular needs. As an example of this kind of effort, I've recently returned from a trip to Zambia and Zaire where, through the help of one of the local Rotary Clubs, I have undertaken to install a series of the turbines for the isolated mission stations in these areas. I hope to commission the first of these stations in February 1981. Its purposes will be: (1) to provide power for the local inhabitants to mill their maize, through the mission mill, (2) to provide power for better facilities at the mission hospital, (3) to provide power for the mission houses, student quarters, and the church, and (4) to power a centrifugal pump for irrigation purposes. When the unit is installed, it will mark a significant step forward for the mission, which is now required to transport diesel fuel over 550 kilometers of very poor roads and tracks to power their mill, lighting plant, and pump.

I intend to continue exporting these plants, some of which now work at 90 percent efficiency, largely to the less developed parts of the world, though there are many areas which could use them in addition to locally available power.

TURNING A WEED INTO NUTRITIOUS ANIMAL FEED

NAZARIO J. OMPAD
Even Ventures Company, 10-A Tatlong Bayani Street,
Caniogan, Pasig, Metro Manila, Philippines

Filipino, born July 27, 1935. Mechanical Engineer, Production Manager in grain mill. Engineering/technical education in Philippines and the United Kingdom.

E nsuring an adequate supply of food in the future is a problem that needs to be solved for animals as well as for humans, which has led to a continuing search for new sources of animal feed. In the Philippines, a traditional source of needed protein has been the local ipil-ipil plant, whose leaves, after drying and grinding, could be incorporated in animal feeds. However, this plant is becoming scarcer, which has necessitated the search for acceptable substitutes.

In carrying out research on potential alternatives, we have discovered a common weed, called Alasiman in some regions of the Philippines, that yields good amounts of needed protein when dried and ground. The weed, which belongs to the genus *Lippia* Linnaeus, possesses nutrient protein at levels that make it an attractive feed additive. Using our system of extraction, the Alasiman weed product has been fed to hogs, using a mixture of 70 percent Alasiman product and 30 percent corn bran, and the result is the very satisfactory growth of healthy, meaty animals.

Harvesting of the Alasiman tops is easy and can readily be done even by children. Alasiman is a prostrate creeping vine with roots at the nodes. Branches about 15 to 19 centimeters long can be harvested with productive results. (The plant itself has leaves, almost without stalks, that are larger toward the tip than toward the base, with flowers abounding on every node. This species is found in open and low areas at medium to low altitudes in all Southeast Asian countries, and is especially plentiful in the Philippine lowlands, in coconut or banana plantations. A similar weed is found in the United States.)

To appreciate the potential value of Alasiman, a summary of our analyses of the weed follows, based on standard testing procedures for the various key components. Bear in mind that the plant *is* a weed and that its conversion to a food plant for animals has a doubly attractive result.

The key components of the weed, in a manufacturing/marketing perspective, are:

Protein content	22.7%–24%
Initial moisture content	25%
Final moisture content	12%
Ash	10%–13%

Having previously had experience in the design of machinery (a rice harvester/thresher), I am confident that the designs I have made for the machinery appropriate to the processing of the weed from harvested stage to final bagged product will be feasible.

A SIMPLE, COST-EFFICIENT SOLAR TRACKER

PUSHPENDRA K. JAIN
Physics Department, Birla Institute of Technology & Science,
Pilani 333 031 (Raj.), India

Indian, born September 7, 1946. Teacher and researcher in field of solar energy and physics. Physics education in India and the United States.

T he purpose of this project is to develop and test a solar tracking device that includes the twin requirements of low cost and simplicity of operation. These requirements will allow its use for the generation of solar energy in remote and rural areas, and in agricultural applications in developing countries where resources and skills are limited. The device is based on driving systems that are controlled by a clock mechanism.

Tracking devices that operate with high precision have been developed by various workers and researchers for application to solar energy devices. All such devices, however, in addition to being very expensive, are also highly sophisticated in their technology. This sophistication adds to the cost of their maintenance, thus making these useful devices even further unadaptable for common application at the sometimes primitive levels where they could be of most use in alleviating energy problems.

We believed that a basic solar tracking device could be designed by starting with the simple realization that the motion of the sun is well known and understood. We could thereby avoid the need for introducing solar locating sensors and the associated electronics that add to the cost and the complexity of the system.

We thought that a mechanism that would give solar concentrators a uniform rotation about an axis parallel to the axis of the earth at the rate of one rotation per mean solar day would serve our purpose excellently. A uniform rotation about a fixed axis could be achieved with an accurate clock mechanism, and the motive power would be provided from the gravitational potential energy of falling weights.

This mechanism would, however, require once-a-day manual adjustment to take care of the earth's orbital motion and also for the rewinding of the weights. In view of the simplicity and low cost of the mechanism, this semi-automatic nature of the device cannot be considered a serious disadvantage. It would be particularly suitable for the rural areas of developing nations, like India, where semi-skilled personnel needed to maintain the device in good condition, as well as people required to operate it on a daily basis, will be readily available.

Working on this set of premises, a prototype of this tracking device has been fabricated. The design of this tracking device was presented at the National Solar Energy Conference at I.I.T., Bombay, India, in December 1979. (A reprint of the research paper from the conference proceedings, which gives all the details of the design, is enclosed with this application.)

In the clock mechanism that controls the rate of rotation for the solar tracker, a single lens concentrator is attached for the purpose of rotation. The completed tracking device, including the falling weights used for power, is coupled through a chain drive to a pair of cages meant for mounting solar cells and concentrators. The axis about which these cages rotate has been aligned parallel to the axis of the earth.

Though we have achieved our initial goals with this prototype solar tracking device, we are now proposing to improve this model through the use of better bearings. These will help minimize friction and will also bring improved precision to the functioning of the gears, which will result in close to maximum accuracy in tracking. Further, the system could also be extended to drive larger loads, a highly desirable objective, so that up to 1 kilowatt of power could be produced, using this simple system of concentrators and a single clockwork drive.

With this system, high concentrations of solar radiation can be obtained with minimal need for sophisticated dual tracking (due to the apparent movement of the sun, which derives from the earth's rotation on its own axis once a day, coupled with its orbital motion around the sun each year). Minor daily adjustments of our device can be made in only a few minutes by a layman without any extra equipment and can be viewed simply as part of the general maintenance of the system. Thus, such devices can be used in many locations where cost and complexity of use make ordinary solar trackers impracticable.

The triangulate wooden space frame of Nusatsum House.

NUSATSUM HOUSE: TOWARD A TRIANGULATE ENVIRONMENT

RANDALL G. SATTERWHITE
Box 48, Hagensborg, British Columbia V0T 1H0, Canada

American, born March 18, 1947. Self-employed architect. Civil engineering and architectural education in the United States and the United Kingdom.

N usatsum House is the first in a series of experiments designed to show that a triangulate structure, in this case a space frame, may be inhabited successfully and constructed economically. Further, it is intended to suggest that architects and engineers should exploit the basic stability, beauty, and variety of triangulate housing.

Costs of conventional housing construction are rising much more rapidly than the supply of available capital for building. At the same time, however, housing is in ever shorter supply on a worldwide basis. Though this has led to the manufacture of identical housing units on factory-type production lines, this solution can never hope to respond to the huge variety of site requirements or individual needs and preferences. There is also a widespread reluctance to deviate from expedient and familiar structural forms based on the cube, which may be attributed to an entrenchment of conventional thinking within the building industry.

I propose the exploration of new, triangulate forms as an alternative. They may derive from combinations of the other four platonic solids: tetrahedron, octahedron, icosahedron, and dodecahedron. These forms offer definite structural and aesthetic advantages. On the one hand, they transmit forces through pure tension and compression, so that the structure's mass is not wasted through elements required to resist bending. On the other hand, these structures are beautiful and psychologically stimulating.

It was for these reasons that I chose to build Nusatsum House. I wanted to show that living in a triangulate environment is possible, and I wanted to test a new set of basic structural building components of my own design, which can be mass produced and assembled on site to suit individual needs.

In 1974, a remote building site was chosen, where the experiment could proceed unhampered by restrictive building codes and their concomitant slow approval process. In addition, some important decisions were made at the outset, to ensure maximum likelihood of the experiment succeeding.

First, the entire structure of the house would be a wooden space frame, something which to my knowledge had not been attempted before.

Second, I would design and manufacture a new set of structural components—specifically, a joint and member—since the multitude of space frame systems available commercially were unsuitable for application in Nusatsum House and consisted of components made only of steel. I wanted my system to have as few different parts as possible, and I wished them to be of the utmost simplicity.

Third, I would acquire the skills necessary to fabricate all of the new components myself, using readily available technology. I would then erect the structure myself.

Fourth, and perhaps most challengingly, I accepted the implied designing process problem, that of working with the new language of triangular form, which would mean the abandonment of the conventional drafting board techniques. In its place would be the requirement to make rigorous use of a model, both for visualizing the design and for the construction itself.

Last, it was decided that the space frame would be the offset type, in three dimensions with the geometry of close-packed tetrahedrons and octahedrons, one of the triangulate planes being horizontal. If at all possible, the house should not deviate from this geometry.

Having set out along these lines, there followed a long period of designing, testing, model construction, and finally, the manufacture of the new components to make the house work. Construction began on a part-time basis.

The structural skeleton of Nusatsum House is 12.2 meters in height, and is comprised of nine "layers." Since head height occupies two layers of the space frame, this fixed the member length at 160 millimeters. The new system of construction is composed of only two components: a steel joint and a wooden member. Three steel plates welded together form what I call a trad: eight trads make a joint. The wooden members are hemlock or spruce, with milled ends that are bolted to the joints. The trads act independently, thus squeezing the ends of the members and holding them largely by friction. Where a member is not required to connect at the joint, a plywood spacer is inserted.

Using the model, two men with ordinary mechanic's ratchets and sockets were able to erect the skeleton, with no power tools, in ten days. No drawings were used, as the model was sufficient guideline.

The house is a series of levels spiraling around a central axis, which serves as a focal point in the house and responds to the need for a convection heating system. It has an open plan that allows natural light to reach everywhere. Gentle diagonal stairways connect the different levels.

Nusatsum House shows that a triangulate environment is possible and that it can be more interesting and ambiguous than the rectangular ones to which we have become accustomed. In general, the new joint and member designs have worked, but improvement is necessary. In particular, the nominal dimensions of the joint from inside to outside of the structure should be the same thickness as the member, so that the internal and external membranes may be placed flush with member surfaces. This would eliminate furring on the inside, outside, floors, and ceilings. Existing building components, such as plywood, fiberglass batts, and gypsum board, can cause some difficulty when using the new vocabulary of triangular forms. New components manufactured specifically for these wooden space frames are necessary.

I believe that wooden space frames can become commonplace as the design for connectors improves. The cost of metals and synthetics is increasing faster than the cost of wood since greater amounts of energy are required in their manufacture. As the building industry moves toward the modularization of components, there is no reason why entire kitchen, bathroom, and heating units could not be pre-manufactured and placed inside these structures.

I have progressed as far as I can independently to show that these structures can be beautiful and varied. To continue, I now need financial assistance.

Nusatsum House completed.

A NEW THERMODYNAMIC HYDRAULIC ENGINE

ADOLF P. PINTO
3209 Dalemead Street, Torrance, California 90505, U.S.A.

American, born February 23, 1945. Chemical engineer, working as Project Engineer for industry. Educated in India and the United States.

I plan to build a pilot scale, fractional kilowatt machine that will consist of two Stirling Cycle engines configured to operate on heat from an external combustion process or other heat source. The two engines will be coupled together through a hydraulic pendulum and synchronized with the pendulum's oscillations to impart energy to an oscillating liquid column, sustaining and tending to increase the amplitude of oscillations of the liquid column. Escapement means will transfer this excess energy from the liquid column and stabilize the amplitude of the oscillations within the liquid column.

The Stirling Cycle engine has been studied extensively for use in mobile as well as stationary power production because of its high thermodynamic efficiency for the conversion of heat to work. By using heat regeneration, the efficiency of a Stirling engine can be made to approach the Carnot efficiency, which is the maximum attainable efficiency for the conversion of heat to work. Thus, if a Stirling Cycle engine could be used instead of the steam turbine in a power plant, the thermodynamic efficiency for the conversion of heat to work could be increased from approximately 35 percent to greater than 70 percent. This would open up the possibility of nearly doubling the world's energy reserves.

Efforts at utilizing the Stirling Cycle engine, however, have not as yet met with success. This is because the Stirling Cycle engine results in low compression ratios on the order of 1:3 for the available temperatures of operation. If conventional pistons and cylinders were used, their dimensions would have to be inordinately large to obtain usable power outputs. Any gains resulting from increased thermodynamic efficiency would probably be more than lost in higher friction and other losses due to the large dimensions of the engine components.

In my proposed engine system, I plan to overcome these difficulties through a number of features, briefly noted below.

Rather than basing the system on conventional pistons, I will use a hydraulic piston. Through the proper choice of hydraulic fluid and selection of the hydraulic pendulum U-tube diameter, the frictional losses associated with movement can be minimized.

The entire system I envision can be hermetically sealed, which also means that the system can be pre-pressurized. With pre-pressurization, even though the operating compression ratios will remain on the order of 0.5:3, the net differential pressures, which cause the motion of the power piston (in this case, the liquid column), are appreciable and result in large power output and acceptable power-to-weight ratios.

Because of the inertial nature of the oscillating liquid column, I predict that the engine will operate and produce usable power even when supplied with relatively low temperature heat. Specifically, I have in mind the use of solar heat and other quantities of heat readily available at naturally occurring temperature differences.

The production of electrical energy from solar heat would be accepted more readily if the same piece of machinery could be used to produce electricity from other heat sources, such as fossil fuels or nuclear fuels, when solar energy is not immediately available. This proposed Thermodynamic Hydraulic Engine could be used in this fashion to produce electricity from burning fuels merely by removing the pre-pressurization.

Because of the potential of using low density solar heat for the production of electrical energy and the potential decrease in flue gas pollution and heat pollution that could result from the use of this invention in the generation of power from heat obtained from burning fuels, this project, I believe, is classifiable as a project beneficial to the environment as well as a scientific and technological undertaking.

BUILDING BRIDGES IN RURAL NEPAL

JOHN W. LEEPER

G.P.O. Box 613, Kathmandu, Nepal

American, born November 30, 1956. Civil engineer working on rural construction in Nepal. Engineering education in the United States.

For the last year I have been working on bridge construction in the rural hills of Nepal. I have tried to combine local technologies with engineering judgments. If funds are available, I would like to start work on three local bridges in Lumjung, perhaps employing some new techniques.

As stated by Father Sibaul, S.J., of St. Xavier's School, Kathmandu, in his *Appropriate Technology Handbook*, "In an age when man has flown to the moon, why re-invent the wheelbarrow? Because in most of the world, people need wheelbarrows more than they need rockets."

Nepal is one of those parts of the world. Transportation in Nepal does not mean supersonic transports. It means feet: mule feet, yak feet, and most of all human feet. Reaching one's destinations means walking for days and crossing countless creeks, streams, and rivers. For hundreds of years, Nepalis have used local skills and materials constructing the trail bridges so necessary to aid travelers. For the last year, I have been doing the same thing.

Several features distinguish these construction projects in Nepal.

Foremost, constructing trail bridges requires matching local skills with existing (appropriate) technologies. The strengths of materials and the laws of physics are the same throughout the world. A bridge in Nepal, just like one in New York, will fail if those properties are ignored or those laws are disobeyed. There are no short cuts to building a sound structure. However, construction in Nepal means using the Bronze Age skills of the people in the hills. Often parts are fabricated by the village "Kaami," or blacksmith, who is usually equipped with nothing more than a charcoal fire and a hammer. Stone work and wood work are done by local craftsmen. If blasting is required and dynamite is not available, a local chemist can make gunpowder out of materials from the local bazaar. If rock drilling is required and petrol for the rock drill is not available, that grueling work will be done by hand. The engineer designing these projects must be aware of the applications and limitations of these local technologies if prospects for new construction are to be realistic.

A second factor is sheer remoteness. My first site, for example, was a 90-meter span over the Arun River in eastern Nepal. From that bridge to the closest roadhead was a seven-day walk, fourteen days for a porter. Logistically arranging for every cable, nut, and bolt is a job, but it is nothing compared to the individual porter carrying up to 100 kilograms of steel parts.

An added dimension to this work for a Westerner is the working relationship that develops with the people in the area. When a bridge is finished, the sense of satisfaction shared between us is heartwarming.

Today, however, a number of problems are requiring new approaches to these bridge projects. With inflation, steel parts have risen some 50 percent in cost this year. Steel parts for my current bridge cost 26,000 rupees; today they would cost 40,000. That kind of difference jeopardizes many urgently needed bridges. We are looking for ways to reduce tolerances and safety factors by using more sophisticated designs. A second problem is the general shortage of cement. Strict Indian export quotas and a small domestic supply have combined to force the cancellation of many projects here in Nepal. We are searching to find alternatives—perhaps baked clay, straw, and animal dung will suffice in some applications.

We must also find alternatives to wood planks and beams because this material is most critical, and estimates suggest that 80 percent of Nepal's forest will be cut down in the next 10 years. It would be of enormous assistance if the fabricators of fiberglass, steel grating, or other new building materials would consider the ways their products could be made to fit the needs and realities of these high Nepalese hill communities. One alternative is the use of woven bamboo matting as a possible structural element.

Financing is difficult for these bridges, with many of the smaller ones stalled for want of funds. Cable and volunteer labor are available, but we need funds for other steel parts.

Perhaps such projects sound like re-inventing the wheelbarrow. I know they do not involve high-technology breakthroughs. They involve, instead, the application of older "breakthroughs." These bridges are interesting technical problems, and they are meeting perceived needs. They require technical expertise, a personal commitment of time and labor, and a concern for the well-being of others. In other words, they require enterprise. We have that in abundance at these sites; we need help only to acquire missing materials.

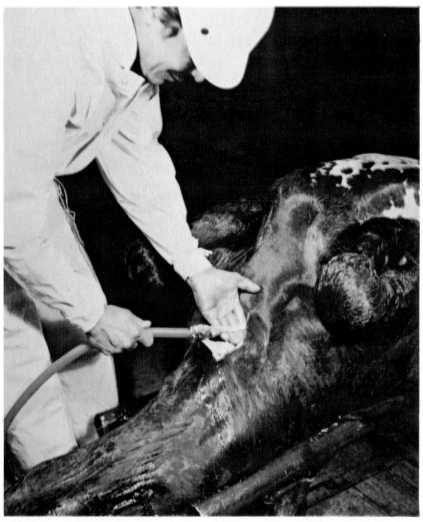

Infusing the solution into the neck of a steer, which lies supine in a metal "cradle."

POST-SLAUGHTER INFUSION FOR TENDERIZING BEEF

GUILLERMO R. MATHEU
8769 Glenwood, Overland Park, Kansas 66212, U.S.A.

Guatemalan, born June 10, 1945. Salesman for livestock supply company. Educated in music (concert pianist) and languages in the United States and Germany.

The present invention (U.S. Patent No. 4,053,963) relates to a post-slaughter infusion for the tenderizing of beef carcasses. It is useful in the treatment of slaughtered animals whether they be beef, including steers, or hogs, chickens, turkeys, deer, or buffalo.

The process, using a solution described below, is as follows. The animal, say a steer, is stunned with a (Koch) knocker and then hung by one or both of its hind legs. The jugular vein is severed on the right side, and the animal is bled. The steer is then laid horizontally on a cradle, with legs pointing upward. Hind legs are then removed at the knee joint. The throat of the animal is opened with a small, six-inch incision, and when the main vein or artery is located, a stainless steel nozzle from the equipment is inserted into the animal. A veterinarian, or the person in charge, controls the quantity of the solution administered in accordance with the live weight of the animal by opening a valve on the solution meter. When a proper amount of solution has been inserted into the animal, the valve is closed and the nozzle removed. While the solution is running through the animal, the remaining and residual blood exits through the severed hind legs and the jugular vein incision. When visual observation indicates the blood has left the animal, followed by the solution, the system is shut down and turned off. Pump pressure behind the solution is approximately the same pressure as that of the heart of the animal to avoid ruptures and high concentrations of the solution. It takes two minutes to process a steer of an average weight of 900 pounds.

Obviously, the solution is important, and I present its ingredients here, which conform with U.S. Government code regulations:

Sodium citrate	37 grams	2.10%
Ascorbic acid	318 grams	18.02%
Milk protein, hydrolyzed	170 grams	9.63%
Maltose or glucose (dextrose)	700 grams	44.76%
Sodium tripolyphosphate	200 grams	11.33%
Sodium tetrapolyphosphate	50 grams	2.83%
Phosphates, hexametaphosphates	125 grams	7.08%
Potassium sorbate	75 grams	4.25%
	1765 grams	100.00%

All these ingredients (1765 grams) are dissolved in 500 liters of sterilized water at a temperature between 27°C and 39°C, and the resulting solution of this temperature is used for the treatment of the animal.

Having processed over 800,000 steers in Latin America, I believe I can state firmly a number of advantages of this system.

First, because most of the blood has been removed, the meat has a much longer durability, as blood is one of the main factors in subsequent contamination. In tests, I have left a full carcass at 32°F for 18 days in a locker, with the disadvantage of other carcasses continuously being brought in and out, creating severe temperature changes. After the eighteenth day, the carcass condition was perfect for human consumption. Because many countries have poor refrigeration facilities, this process will reduce contamination and spoilage for them significantly. And the meat will be tenderized because the application of the process is through the cardiovascular system.

Second, this process increases grading, taking borderline goods and making them choice, up to 4 percent of the herd. Meat takes on a brighter color and is more youthful looking, which is more appealing to the customer, and the process brings out the marbling more rapidly than normally. The user is guaranteed a uniform product, without significant variations in the quality of the meat.

Third, aging time of the meat is considerably reduced because it is already tender and ready to process, which means a savings in refrigeration. The process also saves 5 to 8 pounds of trimmings from the neck of the steer carcass, due to the elimination of blood clots, which also saves time and labor, as one man takes about five minutes to trim a carcass.

One of the greatest advantages of the process, however, is the result of the animal being injected through the cardiovascular system. All of the components in the solution are absorbed by the cellular system, which is why the animal must be processed immediately after de-bleeding, brought down to a cradle and put into a relaxed position. During injection, the animal is rehydrated to its "normal stage" before being killed. It has the same humidity contents as a non-processed animal, but the meat does not shrink during cooking, and the processed animal will render $2\frac{1}{2}$ percent more carcass meat than a non-processed animal.

This process is aimed at the small and middle-sized packer, here in the United States and in other countries where similar operations are already in place. The majority of the smaller and medium-sized packers work with the system called the bed-type operation, and it is therefore not necessary to make any changes in the existing structure of their plants. My units are designed to be either portable or stationary, and they can easily be brought into any plant.

If large packers were to use this process, they would have to make considerable modifications, because they work strictly on rail operations in order to obtain more heads per hour. The only way to process a steer with my method is to lay the animal on the cradle so there will be no stress on any part of the body. To modify a rail operation into a cradle operation can be very expensive. Nevertheless, some large packers may decide to make the necessary change because of the economic advantages it offers.

For example, a Hereford that weighs 900 pounds live will normally render (dress) in full carcass 60 percent of that weight, depending on whether it was feedlot raised or grass fed. An animal from the same herd, put through my processing system, will render out $62\frac{1}{2}$ percent, meaning the production of $22\frac{1}{2}$ pounds more of actual meat. Later, left in the cool room for 24 hours, both animals will have the same shrinkage, normally 1 to $1\frac{1}{2}$ percent. The extra $2\frac{1}{2}$ percent for the processed animal was initially gained when the cellular system of the animal was still alive.

Therefore, any packer using my process obtains an immediate $2\frac{1}{2}$ percent advantage for his business. At current prices, that comes out to about $20.00 per head for cattle in the United States.

With advantages like this, the packer can afford to pay slightly more to acquire better quality cattle, if he wishes, which should encourage cattlemen to raise better quality cattle, and so on. My tests have shown that this system produces better quality meat for human consumption, which is my objective.

ENERGY-EFFICIENT WINDOWS

RONALD P. HOWSON
Department of Physics, Loughborough University of Technology, Loughborough, Leicestershire LE11 3TU, England

British, born September 23, 1935. Senior Lecturer in Physics Department. Physics education and Ph.D. in the United Kingdom.

W e want to take research developed at Loughborough University to the stage where we can demonstrate its practical, energy-saving applications. The research involves a process of coating plastic sheeting at high rates in a vacuum to give a heat-reflecting surface that can be applied to windows to greatly increase their thermal resistance, while still allowing the energy and light from the sun to penetrate into the building.

The most effective use of energy for heating calls for the best possible insulation of the volume of space to be heated. In providing insulation, there are two primary concerns: first, the factor of conduction or convection loss of heat via its transport through an insulating material; and second, the loss of heat through radiation from a hot surface in a cold environment. The ideal system, of course, is the vacuum flask, with conduction loss reduced to the small area of glass that joins the two surfaces; and the emissivity—that ability of a hot or cold surface to emit and receive radiation—is made a very small value by silvering the surfaces.

In buildings, however, insulation needs to be of large area, inexpensive, and durable, and it has generally been reduced to structures that can trap air in small enclosures to provide the insulating medium. Aluminum, vacuum evaporated onto large sheets of polyester in very thin form, has become available for semi-transparent windows, which are widely advertised as a way of reducing solar glare in summer and decreasing thermal loss in winter. This last solution is energy inefficient because, in reducing the thermal loss, the heat input *into* the building, by solar gain through the window, is reduced more, resulting in a net loss.

On the other hand, coating the plastic is very inexpensive when done at high speed, and it gives the surfaces of a very durable and tough sheet plastic the optical properties required, if it is possible to find materials and techniques for these more demanding applications. In our laboratory, we have demonstrated that it is possible to coat polyester with highly conducting oxides that give visible transmitting, heat-reflecting coatings suitable for the radiation insulation of windows.

We estimate that the production cost of such a film could be as low as 32 pence per square meter, which would produce a payback time of only three months, based on our calculations of saved heating costs. Such a film, obviously, has other applications, such as in wallpaper, which can be transparent to allow the pattern to be seen, but heat reflecting to increase the radiant temperature for the individual, allowing the air temperature to be reduced. To date, our experience leads us to believe that it will be possible to produce large-area "heat mirror" samples both of oxides and of thin metals, and that other materials can be developed for insulation and solar utilization.

The technique we have developed uses ion plating, where the plastic substrate is subjected to a radio-frequency bombardment during preparation. This gives us the ability to control the reactivity of the process whereby oxygen is used to react with the metal while depositing. The metal is, in general, vaporized from a planar magnetron sputtering source. The process also adds surface energy to the depositing film that allows structural properties normally associated with high temperature processes to be obtained at the low temperatures necessary with plastic substrates. The unique feature of our roll coater is that it will be operated at radio-frequency potentials. We propose to allow our roll coater to be used to its full potential by having an experienced operator construct large-area samples of materials we have already developed.

We believe that the group at Loughborough is unique in this country in applying sophisticated vacuum-deposition techniques to the rapid coating of plastic film. The vacuum deposition of thin films has been revived with the application of planar magnetron sputtering, the discovery that reactive processes can be easily achieved at high rates, that high adhesion can be achieved with ion-plating techniques, and the use of plasma-deposition techniques. We are applying these techniques to plastic film to reveal a new industry based on the production of large areas of coated plastic, with selected optical properties, at low cost, which are ideally suited to the needs of insulation and solar energy conversion.

AN IMPROVED PROSTHETIC FOOT FOR AMPUTEES

DAVID J. DVORAK
2224 North 26th Street, Terre Haute, Indiana 47804, U.S.A.

American, born January 8, 1962. Mechanical engineering student and an accomplished musician (French horn, harp).

Al present types of artificial feet have toe sections that remain in a fixed, unflexed position in all phases of walking except for "toe off," when the applied forces cause the front section to flex. As soon as the amputee removes his weight from the toe section, it quickly returns to its original position, making the toe section likely to hit the ground as the prosthetic leg is swung forward (swing phase). Amputees compensate for this with gait deviations such as circumduction, excessive opposite-heel rise, or pelvic tilt. This is a serious problem because the limb pulls down in any event as weight is removed from it, and thus, limb fitters may make the limb a bit too short to prevent the toe-stubbing problem.

I have been developing a new type of prosthetic foot, with swing phase dorsiflexion (lifting of the toe), that will help eliminate excessive pelvic tilt, high opposite-heel rise, and vaulting in the gaits of lower-extremity amputees. My design can be used with all levels of amputation, from Syme's (through the ankle) to the highest levels (hip disarticulation, hemipelvectomy), because it requires no connections between the foot's mechanical joints and the knee axis. Standard Syme's, below-knee, and knee-disarticulation sockets could be employed by the limb fitter, greatly simplifying his task, with no new socket-fitting techniques required.

After designing a number of types of prosthetic feet, I came to a design that seemed relatively simple and practical (from a fitting viewpoint) that would meet the objective. This foot consists of articulated toe and heel sections (without an ankle joint), with the heel based on the principle of the SACH

(Solid Ankle Cushion Heel) foot, which is the most widely used and highly regarded foot in America. This particular type of heel cushion simulates the plantar flexion of the ankle at heel strike. My design varies from the SACH foot in that the toe section is not made out of solid rubber. Instead, it has a solid, but articulated, toe section with a constant friction device, which holds the toe (and the shoe) dorsiflexed until the next heel strike, when a connecting rod that is hinged to the top of the heel section would push through a tunnel in the body of the foot, extending the toe section to its original position.

To test this design, I built a prototype, beginning by cutting and shaping a block of basswood to fit the basketball-type shoe (with the high back removed) of a rather active teenage Syme's amputee. After appropriate shaping, trimming, and drilling of the hole for the connecting mechanism, the foot was epoxied and bolted to the amputee's spare Syme's socket, and tested by placing it in the amputee's sock and shoe.

After fifteen minutes of walking, the amputee's comments were that the new foot "allows for excellent flow in walking," "permits smooth swing-through of the leg," and "creates greater ease for walking." Teachers familiar with the amputee's normal gait also noticed the improved smoothness in gait gained from the new foot.

I have been working to develop the design further, in hopes of adding the motions of inversion, eversion, lateral tilt, and so on, in order that the foot will be more comfortable on uneven surfaces. These added motions would also contribute to reducing stress and wear on the biological joints of the prosthesis wearer, such as the knee joint of the below-knee amputee. I am also working on a design with no moving parts in the body of the foot, which relies on fluids moving from one chamber of the foot to another via hydraulic valves.

Beyond this, I anticipate about three workable designs of feet, all having swing phase dorsiflexion, but arriving at this through different systems. For instance, one may have a SACH heel, another an ankle joint, and the third a soft-filled body. This is because of the great variation among amputees' preferences, brought about by different amputation levels, age, activity, sex, or vocation. An athlete or growing child may prefer a simple and sturdy foot, an elderly person may want a foot for slow walking, or a young lady may want a seamless foot that can be hidden under a foam cosmetic cover or that is adjustable for different heel heights of shoes.

I have already won certain honors for the designs of my prosthetic feet, and I would like to be able to develop them further through prototype stages for testing against a broader segment of the amputee population, with a view to determining which ones are the most advantageous to the largest number of amputees, and which ones are most economically feasible.

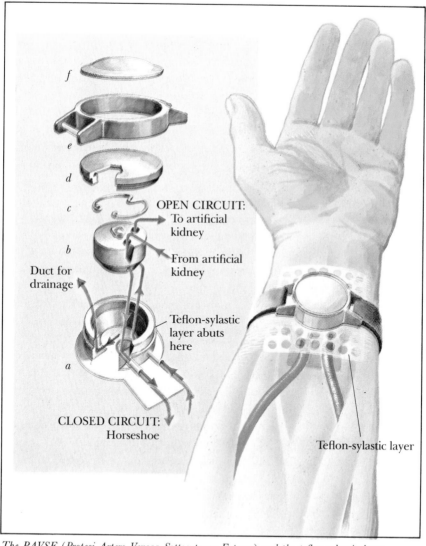

OPEN CIRCUIT:
To artificial
kidney

From artificial
kidney

Duct for
drainage

Teflon-sylastic
layer abuts
here

CLOSED CIRCUIT:
Horseshoe

Teflon-sylastic layer

f

e

d

c

b

a

The PAVSE (Protesi Artero-Venosa Sottocutaneo-Esterna) and the teflon-sylastic layer.

NEW VASCULAR ACCESS FOR DIALYSIS PATIENTS

ROMEO MILANI
Villaggio Piras, La Maddalena, Sassari, Italy

Italian, born March 6, 1935. Head surgeon at La Maddalena (Sassari) General Hospital.

I have been developing a new method of obtaining direct access to vascular interiors through use of a new system that allows externally supplied liquids to be inserted in the bloodstream easily and at will.

The research, conducted to date on dogs, is designed to allow the patient with a chronic hemodialysis requirement to join the artificial kidney to his system simply, surely, and painlessly. This system gives the patient the opportunity to carry out treatment without the need of shunts or via the arterio-venous fistula, which at the present time represent the only vascular accesses for chronic hemodialysis. This instrument also seems to be more durable and to have a lower percentage risk of possible complications. It therefore promises to reduce the need for surgical re-establishment, which is currently required for shunts or an arterio-venous fistula. Successful realization of the project offers undoubted advantages to dialysis patients, especially in the therapeutic phases of self-dialysis at home.

The instrument I have developed has been used successfully several times in experiments with dogs. Based on the results of these experiments, I am continuing to modify the technique, and I am particularly interested in further experimentation with different qualities of implantable material, before choosing a final construction.

The key problem lies in constructing a single physical unit that is separated biologically into an "internal district" (within the organism) and an "external district" (outside the organism). Such anatomical structures as the hair and fingernails are example of this biological separation.

This physical-biological unit, separated into its internal/external districts, is an indispensable part of the system I've been developing, because it allows better support for the two presently available means of providing dialysis. During dialysis, utilizing the instrument as a shunt, we obtain a simple and painless connection between the patient and the artificial kidney. At the same time, between dialysis sessions, the instrument acts as an arterio-venous fistula, giving the patient complete freedom of movement and safety. The simplicity of being able to convert from a shunt to a fistula, and vice versa, allows the patient to control the dialysis personally, without assistance, making it very useful for home therapy.

Because of its functional characteristics and its internal/external nature, I have named the instrument the PAVSE (Protesi Artero-Venosa Sottocutaneo-Esterna). The PAVSE will be constructed of the same kind of implantable materials used in pacemakers, and it is composed of two parts—the upper of which is biologically external to the organism and the lower biologically internal.

I found it possible to do this by dividing the mono-block of the prosthesis with a large stratum of teflon-sylastic, placed transversally and perforated with many holes. The surgeon places the stratum of teflon-sylastic in the subcutaneous tissue in immediate contact with the skin: after healing, thanks to the number of holes in this layer, only one stratum will result, leaving the prosthesis separated into internal and external sections.

As shown in the illustration, the PAVSE itself has six pieces. The base unit (A) has two tubes that connect to the artery and provide for the circulation of blood within the unit. Into the base unit is fitted the solid rotary unit (B), with its small turning key and its internal system of holes that allow for switching the blood flow coming in via the base unit. A fastening spring (C) controls the solid rotary unit, inserted in the base, preventing its random movement. A cover (D) is screwed into place on top of the assembly, and closes against a stopping step on the teflon-sylastic layer. Additionally, a ring with handles (E) is provided, through which a watch strap can be inserted to hold the unit firmly in place. If desired, a cover (F) can be fitted into this ring which could hold a watch, as a means of camouflage for the implaced unit.

The unit functions according to the positioning of the internal rotary cylinder. Moving the handle switches the unit to one of its two positions. In the closed position, the parallel tubes are connected through the horseshoe-shaped circuit. Given that the two small pipes of the cylinder connect respectively with one artery and one vein, this closed position reproduces the function of an aterio-venous fistula. In the open position, the small pipes are connected with the vertical L-shaped tube, and are simultaneously connected, via the first opening of the horseshoe circuit, with the internal opening of the drainage pipe, thus allowing the prosthesis to act as a shunt.

The PAVSE would be in the closed position between dialysis treatments (the interdialytic phase), and it would be in the open position during treatment. The afferent and efferent connections from the artificial kidney insert into the surface openings of the solid rotary unit.

Prototypes of the prosthesis have been used in *in vitro* experiments to demonstrate the perfect hold of the circuits and their easy and fast position changes. We have been able to show that the PAVSE can be inserted into a ring circuit and supports a circulating plasma under the same pump pressure as blood pressure. The *in vivo* experiments with dogs have so far used simulated PAVSE's, in order to study and analyze various types of bio-compatible structures. The teflon-sylastic structures covered the buried layer, which demonstrates the prospect of achieving the physically unified, biologically separated (internal/external) unit I seek. After 6 months of the simulated PAVSE implanted in a dog, we observed on removing the implant that the teflon-sylastic stratum had healed with the skin and formed a biological cover that divided the simulator into internal and external districts.

Having proven this, I believe it is now possible to construct the complete PAVSE, because the unit has shown the capability of carrying the circuits needed to do the work of external shunting or arterio-venous fistula. Such a new method of achieving connection between the artificial kidney and the patient would be a significant advantage to those patients who must take their therapy at home.

CREATING A COMPACT POWER STATION IN SPACE

MILAN POSPISIL
25165 Ondrejov 266, Czechoslovakia

Czech, born April 10, 1936. Researcher in Space Research Department at Czechoslovak Academy of Science. Physics education in Czechoslovakia.

My goal is to persuade the necessary authorities to build an experimental, fully workable compact space power station that can be put into orbit with about thirty flights of the space shuttle during the 1980's.

It has been known for some time that one way to answer the demand for energy on earth would be to build a large structure, placed in a geosynchronous orbit, that would collect solar radiation, convert it to microwave energy, and beam this energy to a receiving station on earth. Until now, the only concept seriously considered has been one based on a planar collecting panel connected with a microwave transmission antenna (the NASA Reference System). Within this system, the collecting panel must rotate in relation to the antenna, two large structures must be built (an area of cells measuring 10 kilometers by 5 kilometers would be needed to provide the targeted 5 gigawatts delivery at the anticipated 7 percent efficiency for the whole space power station's chain of operation), and a lengthy evaluation period will be necessary to launch such power stations beginning in the year 2000. Only this approach (first formulated by P. E. Glaser) is being actively studied and developed. It is clear, however, that many possible Space Power Station (SPS) concepts are available and that we are far from having determined the best model.

I have developed a concept for a compact SPS that, though far from optimal, would make many necessary space experiments possible through use of a fully workable small SPS.

The basic SPS idea is to intercept solar energy in space, convert it, and transmit it to earth. Blankets or bands of photovoltaic cells for receiving and a microwave beam for transmission of energy are currently the preferred means of operation. If we require the optimum exploitation of cells, as in Glaser's concept, the collector must be planar and kept perpendicular to the solar beam. The microwave antenna has to be maintained in the direction of the rectenna on earth. Thus, the collector must rotate synchronously with the earth, and the need for a rotary joint between the collector and antenna is inevitable. The power from all cells is collected, conducted through the interface, and distributed to the converters and microwave sources of the antenna.

In the compact concept, each part of the solar band is rigidly connected to one converter and a source. The solar bands, converters, and microwave sources are fastened to the same structure, immovable with respect to the earth. The shape of its surface can be planar, cylindrical, or other. The power delivery of the compact SPS depends on the shape of the directrix and on the orientation of the SPS surface with respect to the solar beam. An optimal exploitation of cells is not needed with the compact SPS because a fixed cylindrical area would need to be larger than a planar revolving panel to produce the same delivery of energy. Nevertheless, mass/power ratios are not the primary highlight of the compact SPS experiment; we are interested here in the prospect of gaining working knowledge in space during the next 10 years.

The conclusions drawn from the paper I presented on the compact SPS at the 30th IAF Congress (Munich, 1979) included the following key points. Compact SPS is simple, and thus reliable. It is immovable in relationship to earth, its stabilization is therefore easier, and no rotary joint is necessary. Its transmitting antenna is as large as its collector, being on the same supporting structure, and conductors that run between solar elements and microwave converters are very short. To give the compact station the same output as a planar collector kept perpendicular to the solar beam, an area 3.3 times larger would be needed.

Compact SPS can be light, well within the space shuttle capacity, and therefore constructible within the coming decade. As it would be built on a block-by-block basis, the system remains virtually undamaged if one section is hit by a meteorite, and the system can be added to simply by attaching extra blocks. The small power density of the compact SPS makes the operation safer in constructing and handling. When finished, with its diameter of 3.8 kilometers, the critical power density of 230 watts per square meter in the ionosphere will be realized. With this 500 metric ton installation, we could test a wide range of situations to find the one capable of producing usable energy at efficient cost levels.

OBTAINING ENERGY FROM NATURAL RESONANCES

JORGE E. PARDO
20181 Exeter, Detroit, Michigan 48203, U.S.A.

American, born August 13, 1939. Licensed architect, project leader, and consultant. Architecture/science education in Colombia, Sweden, and the United States.

T his project has as its purpose the investigation of natural resonance in different shapes and materials, with the goal of controlling the mechanical vibration of resonators for the production of usable energy. As an architect, my interest in resonance stems from the usually destructive form in which vibration affects man-made structures, particularly suspension structures.

The famous bridge collapse in Tacoma, Washington, has been attributed to Karman vortices (air spirals), some 12 meters long, generated by steady 65 kph winds intersecting the bridge section at right angles to its span. For about two hours the bridge deck oscillated lengthwise at large amplitude, until an increase in wind velocity started it vibrating torsionally. The bridge twisted violently in both directions for nearly an hour until it broke into pieces.

Besides wind, any external pulsating force applied with sufficient force to a mass will set it in motion. If the mode of pulsation corresponds with the natural resonance or fundamental mode of the mass, vibration will follow that, if not controlled, will increase the effect of the pulsating force, augmenting the amplitude of the vibratory waves, and in the case of large structures, possibly causing their eventual collapse and destruction. This is why modern cable structures usually include designing for secondary damping systems, which are "tuned" to a different fundamental mode, thereby canceling any incipient vibration of the primary cable system.

Such powerful effects as these demonstrate the potential of vibratory resonance as a property of matter that could be developed for useful purposes. My research into this area is proceeding in three phases:

1. Development and construction of a natural overtone series resonator array (NOSRA).
2. Resonator design in terms of generating forces.
3. Generation of energy through the use of resonators.

For the NOSRA, two key principles come into play: first, the natural overtone series, which is the sequence of harmonic vibrations that normally ensue from a fundamental frequency; second, the effect known as resonance, which can be defined as the response produced in one body from the vibration in another body (sympathetic vibration). It follows that a device consisting of an array of resonators tuned in sequence to a specific harmonic structure (the overtone series) should maximize the effects of resonance, with each resonator exciting the others through resonance feedback multiplication. I have already constructed a prototype NOSRA, with the aim of optimizing the effects of resonance.

The second phase of the investigation will address itself to the design of specific shapes, suitable for excitation by readily available forces. A classic example of shape affecting the resonating characteristics of a cable is the ice cover on electrical power lines in winter. The asymmetrical ice cover replaces the cylindrical shape of the cable and acts as an airfoil. In this form the wind may cause the cable to vibrate with a wave amplitude in the order of 3.5 percent of its span, at a frequency of around once a minute for a 100-meter long cable, producing the high pitched hum we hear occasionally.

The development of wind-powered resonators in this phase of the work consists of empirical approaches to the design, construction, and testing of shapes and materials that will maximize the effects of Karman vortices.

The ultimate purpose of this line of inquiry is, of course, the application of the data collected in the first two phases to the development of a resonator array that will produce a usable mode of energy.

Mechanical vibration may be transformed into a number of energy forms. Heat itself is vibration at the molecular level. An oscillating conductor moving through a magnetic field may produce the difference potential known as electricity. Another practical application of vibration is in bearing pads, which, acting in lieu of wheels, can be used for the movement of heavy loads.

From all this, it becomes evident that many useful applications could be explored through a better understanding of vibration and resonance. Although the study of vibrating strings goes back at least as far as Pythagoras in the sixth century B.C., most research into resonance has aimed at minimizing its effects, usually considered to be undesirable. Thus, the resonating arrays being developed in this work represent an original approach toward the utilization of untapped properties of matter.

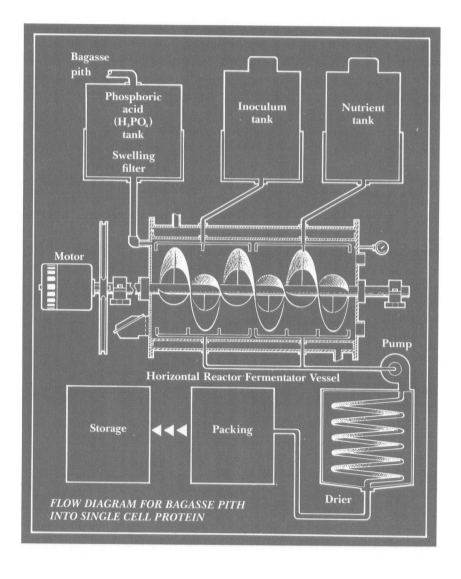

FLOW DIAGRAM FOR BAGASSE PITH INTO SINGLE CELL PROTEIN

TURNING WASTE SUGAR CANE PULP INTO PROTEIN FODDER

NATALINO VITTORI

Av. Las Acacias, Edf. Los Andes, Entrada B, Apt. 901, Sabana Grande, Caracas 1050, Venezuela

Venezuelan, born May 1, 1953. Assistant Professor at two universities, Director in National Scientific/Technological Organization. Educated in biochemistry in the United States and the United Kingdom.

B agasse pith is the fine part of bagasse that is screened and discarded as waste during the preparation of raw material for bagasse (sugar cane) pulping plants. In a modern pulp mill, wet depithing is preferable to produce a better quality product and for better protection of the health of the workers. This process, however, means that the residue is wet and thus not suitable for direct use as a fuel. In Venezuela, over 100,000 metric tons of this wet waste are produced annually and subsequently dumped into the main rivers, creating a serious ecological problem for the country.

I have designed, and experimentally verified on a laboratory scale, a novel process by which a Horizontal Agitated Tubular Bioreactor, acting as a tubular hydrolyzer and fermenter vessel at the same time, will hydrolyze the bagasse pith into its major sugar units, and a recognized fodder yeast will aerobically ferment it in a semi-solid form. The final product is a mixture of highly digestible cellulose and good biological protein. This final paste can be used for animal feeding. Development of this project as an industrial operation will eliminate a serious ecological problem and help alleviate the present food and nutritional crisis.

The proposed investigation offers several important advantages over the conventional processes for the production of microbial protein from animal residues. Among the most important are:

1. The bagasse pith fiber is totally utilized. The process is carried out in a semi-solid form, using all of the hemicellulose and cellulose portions. In addition, no effluent water is produced, thus avoiding the cost of further treatment being required to meet ecological safety requirements.

2. The microorganisms used are yeast species that have been recognized to be safe and have great advantages over the extracellular cellulolitic fungi, which tend to produce aflatoxins during their aerobic growth. The yeast species, *Hansenula anomala* and *Geotrichum candidum,* have been approved for animal feeding for many years by the Food and Drug Administration of the United States.

3. All of the unit operations needed for the process, such as the chemical pre-treatment, the hydrolysis step, the aerobic fermentation, and the final drying operation, can be performed in a single fermentation vessel, as opposed to the present conventional processes in which each step must be performed separately.

The process is described as follows. Bagasse pith is used raw, as it comes from the pulping plants. It does not need to be dried, milled, or screened. The pith is put into the reactor vessel together with a liquid solution of phosphoric acid at 72 percent concentration, in a 1:7 solid/liquid ratio. This semi-solid paste mixture is left at room temperature inside the vessel for 4 hours, a process that induces swelling in the fiber, separating all the hemicellulosic, lignin, and cellulosic chains of the fiber, which will allow the hydrolysis operation to be performed efficiently.

Steam, at 30 psi, is next introduced and circulated rapidly to the external jacket. This heating raises the semi-solid paste's temperature from ambient room level to 170°C, which serves to detach all of the pentosans fraction on the bagasse pith fiber. This contains highly fermentable sugars, such as xilose, arabinose, manose, galactose, and glucose. Next, a 1 percent sulfuric acid solution is introduced into the reactor vessel, while the temperature is held steady at 170°C for 7 minutes. This acid solution breaks the joints of the pentosans and releases all the fermentable sugars in their monomeric forms. The heating period also gives the needed sterile conditions for any aerobic fermentation to be performed without contamination.

After the 7-minute heat period, steam injection is stopped, and normal water starts to circulate in the vessel jacket, bringing the temperature down immediately to 30°C. En route, at 95°C, a calcium hydroxide solution is inserted. This precipitates the decomposed sugars in the forms of furfural and hydroxymethylfurfural, substances known to inhibit the assimilation of the fermentable sugars present in the solution.

In other current processes, the final hydrolyzed solution needs to be cooled, filtered, pumped into other vessels, and heated again, in order to distill the furfural formed. In this process, all these operations are avoided since I have found, experimentally, the optimum temperature and the right hydroxide concentration for the elimination of these undesirable substances, while operating in the same reaction vessel. The use of calcium hydroxide also brings the pH up to the point at which aerobic fermentation can succeed efficiently.

At this stage, the chemical and hydrolysis processes are complete, and aerobic fermentation is ready to start. Once the reactor and its contents are brought to room temperature, an exponential growing solution of *Hansenula anomala* together with a mixture of urea and ammonium sulfate are inserted in the reactor and evenly dispersed over the paste. The specially designed helical ribbon impeller is then switched on, along with the air supply from the manifold gas tube, ensuring an even distribution of fine air bubbles throughout the semi-solid paste.

This mixing provides all the yeast cells with the oxygen needed for the aerobic assimilation of the hydrolyzed sugars. After the sixteenth hour of the fermentation process, all of the single monomeric sugars have been totally consumed by the yeast *Hansenula anomala*. However, some polysaccharides can't be assimilated by the yeast because of the lack of a cellulolitic activity. At this point, an exponentially growing inoculum of *Geotrichum candidum* is added. The lack of single monomeric sugars and the presence of carbon in the form of the polysaccharides induce in the yeast the formation of intracellular cellulolitic enzymes to hydrolyze the remaining sugar chains and thus totally utilize the remaining fiber. At the end of the twenty-sixth hour, the fermentation is completed, and the semi-solid mixture is composed of a biomass rich in biological protein. At this point, the fermentation is ended and the drying operation starts.

Steam is again injected into the external jacket at a low pressure, until the temperature rises to 80°C, sufficient to dry the mixture. The final biomass is then pumped out of the reactor vessel, packed in the form of cubes, and released for animal feeding.

This process can eliminate the serious problem caused by dumping bagasse pith in the nation's rivers. At the same time, this aerobic fermentation can bioconvert this waste pith into usable protein material. The process is simple, economical, and can be established in underdeveloped countries lacking in highly specialized professional human resources. As a low-technology process, it could find appropriate applications on feedlots, where the products could be used to replace the traditional soymeal or fishmeal as animal feed protein supplements, a development that could lead to lower consumer meat prices.

DIRECT CONVERSION OF BIOMASS TO ALCOHOL

STEVEN LEFFLER

435 East 79th Street, New York, New York 10021, U.S.A.

American, born October 17, 1947. Research Assistant Professor, Mount Sinai School of Medicine. Education, Ph.D. (Biochemistry) in the United States.

T his project describes the conversion of biomass into ethanol by genetically re-engineered yeast. This process is designed to be energetically favorable and more economical on a large scale than current fermentation methods. The objective is the construction of two types of yeast: one that converts starch to maltose and the other, cellulose to glucose; and both of which ferment these products to ethanol. The construction of starch-converting yeast begins with restriction enzyme cleavage of DNA from an amylase-producing microorganism, selected for its ability to efficiently digest starch, followed by insertion of the restriction fragments into a yeast-specific plasmid DNA. The latter is subsequently used to transfect (infect with viral nucleic acid) yeast to amylase positive, using DNA from cellulase-producing microorganisms, and is employed for the conversion of cellulosic waste (e.g., corn stalks) to ethanol. Described below is the construction of a yeast that could produce ethanol directly from corn or corn waste.

Starch, consisting of linear amylose and branched amylopectin, is the major carbohydrate component of corn kernels, and is enzymatically digested to maltose and glucose residues by amylases. Corn kernels are ≈ 75 percent starch. Starch consists of glucose residues in α-1,4 and α-1,6 linkage and is digested by amylases, which may number as many as four different enzymes: α-1,4 glucan glucanohydrolase, α-1,4 glucan maltohydrolase, α-1,6 glucan glucanohydrolase (debranching enzyme), and maltase. Using a bacterial source for these enzymes, *Bacillus amyloliquifaciens* (Bam), total DNA is isolated by conventional methods.

The DNA is then subjected to digestion by the restriction endonuclease Eco RI which cleaves the Bam DNA at specific sites, leaving a mixture of "restriction fragments" containing intact amylase activities. The amylase-containing restriction fragments are then ligated to a yeast-transfecting plasmid, which contains a single Eco RI restriction site, leaving a mixture of plasmids containing all or part of the amylase activities.

Following plasmid construction, a receptive host, *Saccharomyces cerevisiae*, is transfected with the plasmid by well-established procedures. Colonies are selected on agar medium containing starch. Only those yeast producing amylases will grow on the selective medium. The selective media used differ in the type of carbon source employed. In type 1, amylopectin (glucose residues in a α-1,4 and a α-1,6 linkage) is used, while type 2 consists of limit dextrins prepared by treatment of starch with α-1,4 glucan maltohydrolase. Type 3 is starch. Using the three selective media, it is possible to determine which of the amylase enzymes is transfected into the *Saccharomyces* host. Maltase activity is not necessary since maltose serves as a substrate for yeast.

Selected colonies are grown in liquid culture and their plasmids purified. A pure plasmid is then inoculated into a fresh host strain, which is then tested for quantity of ethanol production after fermentation. We have experimented with several media, selecting those that have shown the greatest dependence on the added carbon source.

Using the methods described, we have, as a preliminary step, transfected amylase activity from Bam into *Escherichia coli*. The new strain is able to grow on minimal medium supplemented with starch (unpublished studies).

Conversion of corn or corn waste to ethanol by the methods described also yields high-protein feed and carbon dioxide, both very marketable. These by-products also shift the energy balance toward more positive net yield.

Each year, 100 billion tons of cellulose are deposited on the earth, much of it in the form of agricultural waste, such as corn stalks. The conversion of even a small percentage of this material could substantially increase ethanol production. Currently, there are two approaches to the problem of converting cellulosic waste to glucose or cellobiose: first, the hydrolysis of cellulose by acid and base treatment; and second, the development of "super mutants" of cellulase-producing microorganisms, which has yielded some results. However, this second method necessarily dictates a two-step conversion to ethanol (i.e., cellulose to glucose, and glucose to ethanol). It would be more efficient if a single organism could convert cellulose directly to ethanol.

The best method would be a cellulase-producing yeast strain that would allow direct conversion of cellulose to ethanol. We are attempting to do this using methods similar to those discussed for amylase.

LANGUAGE TEXT EDITOR FOR INTERNATIONAL RADIO COMMUNICATIONS

DAVID J. BROWN
Rural Route 5, Box 39, Noblesville, Indiana 46060, U.S.A.

American, born June 27, 1940. Engineering specialist in electronic design. Electrical engineering education in the United States.

C omputers are playing a larger role in communications and now are entering even into amateur radio links. Small hand-held text or language converters (translators) are presently a reality, using integrated technology. I would like to merge the amateur use of these two engineering accomplishments into one piece of electronics, so that the peoples of the world (radio amateurs, to begin with) might freely converse with better understanding.

Initially, these devices could be incorporated at each end of the communications link, but in time there is no reason not to have them become part of communication satellites themselves. Thus, any station could type in a message in its own language, and it could be translated at the receiving station. With a satellite, it would be far more efficient (and less confusing) to use some international machine language, such as ASCII, as the base language for all the others.

The technology currently exists, available to the individual at reasonable rates, to combine the integrated circuitry found in both the digital computer and, more recently, in hand-held language translators. I propose to combine the use of computer-to-computer communications by radio amateurs throughout the world, first through the word-by-word literal translator electronics, and eventually to further extend this network to using some form of phonetic generations system, to produce spoken words in the language of the receiving station. The use of the amateur radio satellites makes the project feasible and attractive to a worldwide group of radio amateurs for whom multi-lingual communication is a normal operating problem.

Our current program is the development of computer-to-computer communication, via amateur radio bands, using the TRS-80, Level II machine, which is broadly available. Because we are familiar with the radio links, hooking in the computers should be no particular problem. The language translator module (we are analyzing several) should require very little work to get it going from the integrated circuit level to a full working module, if the approach (which we have documented for publication in a monthly amateur radio magazine in order to enlist others in the effort) is agreed upon in the beginning. In this fashion, the communications link is always operating in a common machine language (e.g., ASCII), and any given language module need only be able to convert from the common machine language to the language of the user. Anyone could listen to, or join in on, any of the conversations going through the link, because his or her own translator module would convert the machine language to the one of choice, and vice versa. It would be entirely reasonable to have five different individual mother tongue parties conversing through the radio satellite, none having to understand another's language.

The computer can be used for control, and as such, much of what in other circumstances would have to be hard-wired to make the conversion from spoken language to machine language will become "software," or programs, that can be shipped anywhere and fed to an individual's computer to make it interface the keyboard to the transmitter via the translator on transmit, or the reverse on receive. As I said, there are no particularly difficult technical problems involved in bringing the project to fruition.

Keeping the project's initial phases within the realm of the amateur radio operator seems very natural to me. Over the years, with the recent 1979 World Amateur Radio Conference as an example, individuals from around the globe have shown their interest in transcending national borders, language barriers, national politics, and even technological limitations. Perhaps the very nature of trying to reach across sometimes vast distances serves to cement this feeling.

Apart from the technically valuable aspects of this project, there is an underlying belief, held by many radio amateurs, that one of the strongest bulwarks of world peace is better human understanding and that the easiest, openest, freest form of communication is perhaps the best way to achieve that understanding. We see this project as a significant step toward improving that understanding around the world.

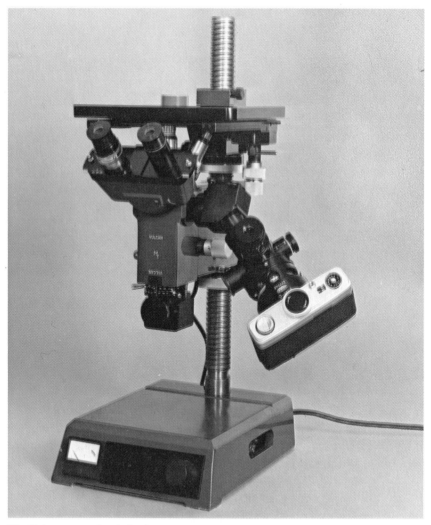

The Vulcan, a metallurgical microscope.

A NEW MICROSCOPE FOR METALLURGY

HAROLD M. MALIES
14, Rye Close, Saltdean, Brighton BN2 8PP, England

British, born October 29, 1920. Managing Director of company, with emphasis on design and technical applications. Science education in the United Kingdom.

T his project involves the further development and commercialization of a new microscope designed exclusively for use in metallurgy and possessing a combination of features particularly useful in the examination of metal structures and metal objects. The microscope, which has been named the Vulcan, was designed, developed to its present state, and made in the workshops of Malies Instruments Ltd.

When most people think of, or refer to, microscopes, they are talking about optical microscopes, which have a long history of service to the world of science. However, optical microscopes were developed principally to meet the needs of the biological sciences, constructed for the examination, by transmitted light, of objects mounted on thin glass slides, of a common, universally accepted size. Because biological microscopes are made in immensely greater numbers than those intended for metallurgy, the instruments intended for use in metallurgy retain certain "biological" features that, from the point of view of the metallurgist, are undesirable.

Specimens for metallurgical examination may vary in size from small resin-embedded samples to large castings or welded components, none of which are suited to examination under the standard microscope. In the Vulcan microscope, the observing and illuminating systems are combined within a unit that is mounted on a very stout pillar, which allows the unit to be raised to accommodate large or awkwardly shaped specimens. Toolmakers' microscopes are mounted in a similar fashion, but unlike them, the Vulcan has a Kohler illuminating system and focusing arrangements that enable it to be used at the highest magnifications available with a light microscope.

The mechanical stage is so designed that its top-plate moves in two directions; this arrangement was adopted out of regard for the varied nature and shape of metallurgical objects. A novel characteristic of our stage is that its mechanical movements can be disengaged by operating only two levers, allowing it then to become a gliding stage, moved directly by the fingers. One or both of the movements can be disengaged this way. The mechanism of the mechanical stage is arranged to permit a specimen to be viewed from either beneath or above, and the stage can be placed above the microscope unit or below it.

Since in metallography there are distinct and separate applications for upright microscopes and for those of the inverted (or Le Chatelier) type, two instruments have been necessary in the past if full advantage were to be taken of the two methods of observation. We have designed Vulcan to allow its assembly in either of these two modes, thus allowing a single instrument to accomplish the tasks previously calling for two separate instruments. The suggestion was made (by Mr. B. C. Cowan of Oxford) that the instrument might be allowed to invert by revolving about an axis; this design feature was incorporated, and the change from one mode to the other is now done in a few seconds, according to the requirements of the work in hand, without tools and without detaching any part of the equipment.

Again, considering the widely varying sizes of the objects one may wish to examine, the conventional "coarse adjustment," which typically ranges between 30 to 40 millimeters of travel, has been omitted in the Vulcan. Instead, the body and stage units can travel the length of the supporting column, and the fine adjustment has an extended movement of 10 millimeters. Operated by a worm and wheel that rotate a scroll, the fine adjustment is linear for the entire length of its travel, and since the whole system must invert, the follower of the scroll is arranged so that the loading on the mechanism remains the same, regardless of the direction in which the force of gravity is acting upon it.

Experience shows that microscopes are often subjected to surprisingly rough use, and the Vulcan is accordingly engineered in a heavier manner than is usual. The focusing motions, for example, take place in relatively massive linear ball bearings. The robust construction adopted has in no way lessened the delicacy of operation under the highest magnifications, and the general rigidity, plus the characteristics of the rolling bearings, enables the instrument to carry easily the side-mounted camera. The focusing motions and the movements of the mechanical stage are protected against damage by being arranged to slip, if accidentally forced against the limits of their travel. Rack and pinion work, which has been used in microscopes since the earliest times, and which is subject to damage and wear, has been eliminated from the Vulcan.

The camera attachment and camera operate in both the upright and inverted modes, and photographs can be taken during actual observation.

If required, the mechanical stage of the Vulcan can have electronic sensing devices added to it, enabling the displacements to be shown in a digital display. A similar device can be added to the focusing motion, thus providing measurement of an object in the $X, Y,$ and Z axes.

In applying for a Rolex Award, our objectives are first, to pursue the further evolution of the instrument, which in the present state of its mechanical development, would be in the field of optics. One avenue we would like to follow is the production of dark ground illumination by utilizing the outer zone of the objective for illumination and the inner zone for observation (or vice versa), effecting this division in the use of zones by means which are external to the objective, so that dark ground observation could be made with any objective. Second, we would anticipate using the Award to help publicize and commercialize the Vulcan, which to date has not been sold to metallurgists.

ANALYZING CHROMOSOMES BY THREE-DIMENSIONAL SCANNING ELECTRON MICROSCOPY

CARL M. M. LAANE
Botanical Laboratory, P.O. Box 1045, University of Oslo, Blindern, Oslo 3, Norway

Norwegian, born July 22, 1940. Assistant Professor of Cytogenetics. Botanical and genetics education in Norway.

W e want to improve the present technique developed by Laane, Wahlstrøm, and Mellem for electron microscopical studies of chromosomes. We aim at a technique for examining the chromosomal fine structure by 3D-high-resolution scanning microscopy that will enable study of the precise arrangement of chromosomal fibers and further analysis of chromosomal arrangement, configurations, chiasma structure, and karyotypes.

We want to improve methods for cleaning chromosomes of adherent cytoplasmic material and stabilize them so that they resist the electron beam during the vacuum in the microscope column and so that they maintain their fine structure. We will further investigate the possibilities for using the methods in analysis of human chromosomes. Today, the *cytogenetic* analysis of chromosome complements is performed almost exclusively by light microscopy. Theoretically, good electron microscopical methods can increase the resolution of the light microscope about 1000 times. This will have immediate effects on cytogenetic studies on disease in humans, cytogenetic studies for agricultural purposes (improvements of strains of plants and animals), and will increase our general knowledge of chromosomes.

Knowledge of the eukaryotic chromosome as the bearer of the heredity factor is fundamental to an understanding of the diverse aspects of biology, and research in this area has been underway for over a century, leading in recent years to the solution of the genetic code. DNA is the major constituent of the chromosomes and contains the genes. A single chromosome in metaphase about 10 micrometers long contains about 10 centimeters of DNA. Somehow, this molecule is packed into the tiny chromosome in a packing ratio of 10,000:1. Under light microscopy, this chromosome can be seen mainly in outline. Due to the optical principles involved, it is impossible to obtain significant enlargements more than 1200 times. Only those structures wider than 0.2 micrometers can be resolved.

The electron microscope, however, has a far better resolution, and current models have a resolution limit of about 2 angstroms. In transmission electron microscopes, chromosomes can be studied whole or in extremely thin sections, and in an essentially two-dimensional manner. Because of difficulties in interpreting two-dimensional sections, or distortion and occasional collapse of biological material, electron microscopy has contributed little to the understanding of chromosomal fine structures, leaving the internal organization of the chromosome as one of the current mysteries in biology.

Some years ago, I discovered a simple chemical treatment that made it possible to obtain pure, clean chromosomes that do not collapse in a vacuum. Since chromosomes usually adhere to each other in most cell stages, it is even possible to obtain electron microphotographs that show their natural arrangement inside the cell in most divisional stages.

In our laboratory to date, we have already shown that a remarkably lifelike chromosome structure is obtainable by the use of a rather crude fixing fluid—acetic acid. The number of plant and animal species we have studied so far has been limited by technical difficulties in removing the cytoplasm in some species. Recently, however, we discovered how, by slight changes in the concentrations of acetic acid, we were able to obtain clean chromosome configurations of *Rhoeo discolor* (complete translocation of the 12 chromosomes) and also of *Drosophila* polytene chromosomes. In any case, the use of the acetic acid as fixing fluid appears acceptable for magnifications up to 10,000 times in the scanning electron microscope, which alone represents a great improvement over light microscopy.

We consider the possibilities for obtaining clean chromosomes and use of better fixatives for preserving chromosomal fine structure as very good. Also, we think that it is well worth while to pay attention primarily to improvements in laboratory techniques in cytogenetics. Once these techniques are available, they can be used by a large community of scientists.

DEVELOPING A
NEW SPANISH STENOGRAPHY

FRANCISCO MEDINA GARCIA
Plaza de Sandoval, num. 5, piso 6°, letra B, Murcia, Spain

Spanish, born November 1, 1936. Teacher and governmental bureau head for national institute. Educated in commercial studies in Spain.

I want to put together a system of rapid typewriting based on the traditional shorthand principles: a phonetic alphabet made up of vowels and consonants, the use of symbols for syllabic groups, the omission of unnecessary sounds, the use of abbreviations, and so on, through the consecutive writing of symbols.

The basis of the project, however, is an initial study of the Spanish language to ascertain the following data: the frequency with which the different vowel and consonant phonemes are used; the breaking down of words into phonemes, letters, and syllables, of syllables into phonemes and letters, and obtaining average frequencies of their occurrence; the classification of sounds according to stenographic criteria and ascertaining the frequency at which each sound occurs; the determination of the words most often used in Spanish; the classification of sounds according to the beginning and end of each word; the reduction of sounds to 90–92 groups; the choice of the symbols that will represent said sounds; the positioning of the symbols, according to their frequency, in the most appropriate parts of the typewriter keyboard; and finally the determination of the saving made on symbols used, provided by the system compared with ordinary typewriting.

The system of shorthand typing would be particularly easy to learn and master, because being a good typist is all that would be required. The benefits could be considerable.

I have reduced a Spanish text, taken at random, 615 words long, with 1198 syllables and 2883 letters, to 1197 strokes, using a version of the system I'm perfecting. This means a typing text of approximately as many strokes as there are syllables, and implies that a typist who only writes at a rate of 400 strokes per minute would produce some 205 words per minute with relative ease. This initial result is encouraging, since shorthand speed is improved and equals the speed of a stenotypist, based on the dexterity of an average typist.

Once the project is completed and the process is systematized, however, with the use of abbreviations, I hope to reduce the ratio (1 word = 1.946 symbols of stenographic typing of the initial text) down to 1.8 or 1.7 symbols per word.

If this result can be achieved, which seems likely, a typing speed of 450 strokes per minute (which is quite normal) would imply a shorthand typing speed of 250 words per minute, which equals 500 syllables—a speed rarely reached by shorthand secretaries, and not very common among stenotypists. Electric typewriters allow the typing of 600 to 700 strokes per minute, and so this new method of shorthand typing, converting a syllable into a stroke, could permit gifted typists to write 600 syllables per minute.

These calculations are based on real facts, witnessed by the author (I served as President of the Spanish Jury at the World Typing Championships in Budapest, in 1975), where entrants averaged speeds over 500 strokes per minute (winners were over 600 and 700 strokes). With the new system, these typists could be shorthand typing more than 250 words per minute, and many average typists could easily be achieving 200 words per minute.

There are four phases to the project. First, a number of Spanish texts, chosen for varied vocabularies, will be culled for a minimum of 60,000 words (more if needed). These will be identified according to their frequency, their syllables, numbers of letters and syllables, and so on. The second phase will research the number of phonemes within the Spanish language that occur in the texts and similarly classify them. Third, the different basic sounds will be studied and symbols chosen for them. Fourth, the number of times a key must be pressed to write the texts initially chosen will be analyzed in terms of the new stenographic symbols, to obtain the best possible placement of the keys on the new keyboard. This will culminate in the comparison of typing speed (wherein a unit equals a stroke) as currently practiced and the anticipated advantages of stenographic typing speed (wherein a unit equals a syllable).

I believe that this process of shorthand typing can be applied to the majority, if not all, of the languages spoken in Europe, and that the advantages it would offer would be undeniable.

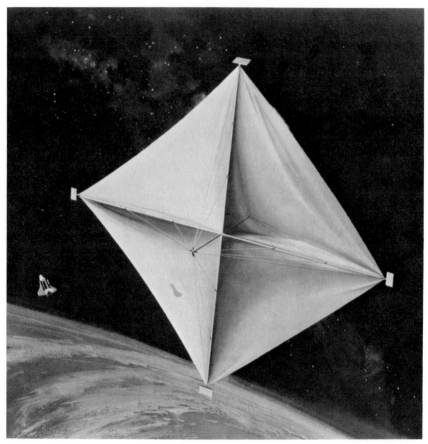

An artist's rendering of the solar sail spacecraft in orbit for a rendezvous with Halley's comet.

SOLAR SAIL DEMONSTRATION PROJECT

JEROME L. WRIGHT
159 South Allen Avenue, Apt. 210, Pasadena, California 91106,
U.S.A.

American, born February 3, 1944. Aerospace engineer and manager. Education and career in aerospace engineering in the United States.

The overall project involves the private development of an experimental solar sail spacecraft. It will use sunlight reflected by a large, light-weight metalized plastic sheet as its only means of propulsion. The project is being developed by aerospace professionals associated with the World Space Foundation. WSF will operate its own private facilities in the Los Angeles area for spacecraft design and fabrication, plus mission opera-tions. Launch is scheduled between 1982 and 1985, followed by a one-year operating test.

The general project objective is to evaluate and gain experience in the design and operation of a solar sail vehicle. Specific mission objectives are to demonstrate deployment of the sail and structure, to verify stability and con-trollability of the vehicle, and to demonstrate orbital energy gain and ma-neuvering capabilities.

The Rolex Award would be used to design, construct, and test the attitude control system and autopilot. This system is crucial to the overall project. It includes the sun sensor (pitch and yaw angles) and a gyroscope plus infrared earth disk detector (roll angle) for determining spacecraft attitude. The on-board computer will implement the autopilot function, which will control spacecraft attitude using solar pressure vanes and a mass displacement arm.

Exploration of the solar system and the rational use of its resources for our expanding civilization require forms of space transportation that are low in cost, high in capability, durable, and modest in the amount of resources consumed by the transportation system itself. The solar sail is a space vehicle outstanding in these areas. It uses sunlight reflected by a large, lightweight metalized plastic sheet as its means of propulsion and uses no expendable propellants. Its only mass is the original structure: sail, miscellaneous control motors, and electronics; it has no engines. This simple design results in low cost relative to other space vehicle concepts; the lack of expendable propellant means high performance capability, long range, and low operating costs. These ships will be useful for the exploration for resources and, much later, in the transportation of mining equipment and the recovered resources.

The solar sail concept has been studied at the Jet Propulsion Laboratory and other institutions, with resulting confirmations of its practicality and capability. Specific designs have been developed through a preliminary design stage. However, there is not now any institutional funding commitment for work on the solar sail, with the exception of the World Space Foundation, for which I am Solar Sail Project Director, with responsibility for managing development and operation of the spacecraft. This organization, a non-profit corporation with the goal of accelerating civilian space activities, has established useful working relationships with the NASA Jet Propulsion Laboratory, the French and European Space Agencies, and several universities and other organizations. Officers of the foundation are experienced aerospace professionals, dedicated to assuring a productive future for space exploration.

The Development Project

The solar sail is now moving to an advanced design and testing phase by people associated with WSF. The intent is to conduct an engineering test in space of a scale prototype solar sail spacecraft, proposed for launch by the European *Ariane* launch vehicle in February 1982, or soon thereafter.

Specific objectives of this test are to obtain data on, and evaluate deployment dynamics of, the sail and vanes; static deflections under solar force, actual vs. predicted force and moments from solar pressure; the dynamic behavior of the structure; electrical charging of the sail; the attitude control system using pressure shift (with vanes) and mass shift; orbit change capabilities and control requirements. The post-mission evaluation is to include a scaling analysis for application to later designs on larger sails.

Our craft, with an area of 1000 to 2000 square meters, will consist of the sail structure itself, a small spacecraft bus containing support subsystems, and an apogee propulsion system. This spacecraft is to be three-axis-stabilized, fully steerable, and capable of autonomous attitude control in a manner desirable for future operational solar sails. Launch mass is approximately 300 kilograms, in an envelope 1 meter long and 2 meters in diameter.

After release from the *Ariane,* in a 200 by 35,800 kilometer transfer orbit, the spacecraft will retain the *Ariane* spin rate and spin axis orientation. At first or second apogee, the apogee propulsion system will be used to raise perigee to about 1500 kilometers to escape the drag effects of the atmosphere. Shortly after burnout, the spacecraft will be despun, oriented toward the sun, and the sail deployed.

As part of the evaluation, the spacecraft will be maneuvered through a spiral trajectory around the earth. The controllability, reliability, and performance of the craft will be evaluated. The autopilot will be evaluated with respect to its ability to steer the vehicle through an optimized attitude profile that will maximize the rate of orbital energy gain. Changing the orbital inclination and raising the perigee altitude are two major engineering objectives of the mission.

The Prospects

If earth-orbit tests of solar sails prove successful, a scaled-up version of the Engineering Development Mission is to be built to carry an unmanned scientific reconnaissance payload on an expedition to one or more of the asteroids that approach or cross the earth's orbit around the sun. These asteroids not only are the subject of considerable scientific interest but also may represent easily accessible sources of raw materials for future space construction and supply. Elements such as iron, nickel, other metals, oxygen, and carbon may be abundant judging from the composition of meteorites found on earth. The solar sail offers a unique capability to mount a multi-asteroid expedition, orbiting several asteroids in succession, without regard to otherwise prohibitive expenditures of propellant, which would be required using other propulsion techniques. The only limitations on mission duration are spacecraft reliability and continued interest on earth.

Further in the future, solar sails are likely to find a place in commerce around the inner solar system, much as maritime sailing vessels supported intercontinental commerce in centuries past. Other privately supported projects of the WSF are likely to form the cornerstones of interplanetary commerce, beginning now with development of transportation techniques, location and study of accessible asteroids, and development of advanced closed-loop life support systems. Freedom from political funding constraints allows the foundation considerable flexibility in choosing projects for their long-term impact on activities in space. With the solar sail, we are in a position to share with private individuals and interested organizations the rising interest in space as a new frontier.

THE INGRID
THOUGHT PROCESSOR

WINSOME R. STRETCH
Global-S.P.S., P.O. Box 2033, Auckland, New Zealand

New Zealander, born September 29, 1950. Computer research and development manager.

We are developing and want to manufacture and market a unique, new decision-making microprocessor—the Ingrid Thought Processor. We coined the term *Thought Processor* to identify and describe the new industry that we believe will inevitably ensue from this project. It involves the logical continuation of data processing and word processing in that the raw material for processing is human thoughts, feelings, or hunches. We see Ingrid as the first stage of a completely new industry of thought processing.

We have developed the Ingrid Thought Processor as a decision-making tool based on psychological theories and analysis procedures derived from the behavioral sciences. It can be used in *any* situation where the decision to be made involves the evaluation of one group of factors or variables in terms of another group of factors or variables. We believe Ingrid will be important enough to effect a widespread and extremely significant change in the whole area of decision making by providing a relatively inexpensive product dedicated to the analysis of the factors in a decision and the presentation of the results in an easily understood form.

The project falls into three major areas: data collection, analysis, and interpretation. Most of our efforts have been concentrated on analysis and interpretation of results. Little effort has been called for in the data collection area since sound, established techniques exist on this in the psychological field.

Our development prototype consists of a keyboard and a screen. The keyboard is detachable and can be positioned at will in relation to a screen. The screen is housed in a small cabinet, which also contains all the circuitry and electronic components. The unit runs on normal household power, and no other equipment is required.

Data collection with Ingrid commences with identification of the variables involved in a decision, which we call the elements. Once these are identified, factors influencing the decision (we call them constructs) are identified. Weighting, or scoring, factors may be applied to each of the elements, in terms of each construct or factor in the decision.

Analysis, once data has been entered in Ingrid, is very rapid. Ingrid produces several displays during the analysis to assist in the final interpretation, such as variations of constructs, variations of elements, relationships between constructs, and relationships between elements. Each display also carries a textual interpretation to elaborate on the actual statistics being displayed.

The most important part of the analysis is the calculation of the underlying components and the location of the elements and constructs within the component space. This section is displayed as a "final picture" of the analysis. It is a pictorial representation of the thought patterns involved in the decision being made. It shows which is the best alternative, provides the underlying reasons for choosing that alternative, and shows the possible results of not following the recommended alternative.

Interpretation is the area into which most of our research and development have been directed. Although there is considerable scope for expertise in the interpretation of the final picture, one of the most attractive features of Ingrid is that with limited interpretative skills a user can arrive at the best possible solution to a problem quickly and simply.

Areas of application for Ingrid range from assessing possible business mergers in terms of potential outcome, evaluating stocks for investment goals, and weighing potential purchasing opportunities, to personal decision making on such questions as what car to buy, where to go on holiday, or which political party to choose.

Benefits accruing from the use of Ingrid Thought Processor include:

(a) Relief of the stress associated with decision making by the provision of objective and rational evidence for a decision.

(b) Enhancement of the decision-making process by providing a level of discipline and structure that ensures that all the important factors are taken into account and that the consideration of these factors is encompassing and substantive.

(c) Reduction of error due to bias or prejudice and the placement of such factors in a perspective where their true importance may be assessed.

(d) Avoidance of costly mistakes by ensuring that the optimum decision is made every time.

NON-INVASIVE EVALUATION OF THE LEFT VENTRICULAR FUNCTION

ANDRÉ E. I. AUBERT
Roelandtsstraat 17, 3200 Kessel-lo, Belgium

Belgian, born April 16, 1943. Lecturer, researcher on Faculty of Medicine, Katholieke Universiteit, Leuven. Physics/science education in Belgium.

A very important aspect of medical investigations, especially in the cardiovascular field, is to develop and improve non-invasive techniques. This means indirect and non-traumatic methods. Such techniques are important for the patient because they do not cause discomfort and can be used as often as necessary, and they are socially valuable because they are not time consuming and costly.

Starting from these principles, our Cardiological Laboratory has started a research project to investigate heart function in a non-invasive way. Major determinants of left ventricular function are pressure, blood flow, and cardiac dimensions. They have to be determined in an invasive way during current techniques of catheterization. Our project will show that these parameters can be replaced by non-invasive ones, namely, pressure by the apexcardiogram, blood flow determined with Doppler techniques, and dimensions measured on echocardiograms.

We should state that overall and local properties of the myocardium are of considerable importance in diagnosing heart disease. This information is mostly obtained from invasive measurements such as catheterization, which introduces a catheter into the heart from a brachial artery. Left ventricular pressure is measured during injection of a radio-opaque contrast medium into the ventricle, and a film is made of the projection of the heart. In this way, dimensions can be measured on the frames of the film, and phase loops of pressure versus dimensions can be made. Our research project will assess cardiac dynamics in a non-invasive way by using dimensions obtained from

M mode echocardiograms and by replacing pressure by the calibrated apex-cardiogram.

In order to evaluate the non-invasive methods for clinical purposes, a series of experiments has been performed on dogs. Left ventricular and aortic pressures are measured with tip-transducer catheters introduced from a femoral artery. The anesthetized dogs are lying on their left side, and the calibrated apexcardiogram (the impulse of the heart that can be felt on the thoracic wall) and the M mode echo are recorded simultaneously, both on opposite sides. The apexcardiogram is recorded with a semi-conductor strain gauge and is calibrated in pressure units. The M mode echo is a technique related to sonar, consisting of a crystal, set on the thoracic wall, that can send and receive ultrasonic impulses. Since distance equals velocity times time, a time measurement gives a dimension. From this work, we reached the following conclusions, which support a reliable means of non-invasive examinations.

A significant correlation exists between pressure and the apexcardiogram, which seems to allow the use of the non-invasive apexcardiogram instead of catheterization as an indicator of overall cardiac behavior.

Dimensions of the heart, needed to investigate its local behavior, can be measured through echo techniques. An ultrasonic impulse (2 to 5 megahertz) reflects from different heart structures and can indicate dimensional changes throughout a cardiac cycle, as the repetition frequency is 1000 hertz.

The efficiency determination of the heart, normally expressed in a pressure volume diagram, can be taken from the calibrated apexcardiogram, on which efficiency is quantified.

To determine blood flow measurements, we are using a transcutaneous pulsed Doppler system, which measures the frequency shift induced by the reflection of an ultrasonic impulse on moving particles or structures.

From these data we can now calculate the wall tension that compensates the pressure in the ventricle. We have shown that the apexcardiogram is also significantly correlated with the wall tension.

We believe that our integrated approach, using dimensions, blood flow, and apexcardiogram data obtained simultaneously and non-invasively, is significant for clinical and fundamental physiological research.

The Teal, *July 30, 1977, forerunner of the* Nene.

THE *NENE*–AN AIRPLANE TO SET WORLD RECORDS

EDGAR J. LESHER
2730 Heatherway, Ann Arbor, Michigan 48104, U.S.A.

American, born July 31, 1914. Aerospace Engineering Professor, holder of four Bleriot Medals for Airplane World Records. Education in the United States.

The Federation Aeronautique International (FAI) is an international aviation organization over 70 years old, with headquarters in Paris. Among its many activities, the FAI sanctions and certifies aircraft world record flights. One of the FAI airplane classes is Class C-1-b, Group I, for airplanes with piston engines, and weighing between 500 and 1000 kilograms.

The *Nene* project consists of the design of an airplane specifically for the purpose of claiming world records in this class, construction of the airplane, the test flying of the airplane, and the claiming of the records. The name of the airplane comes from the nene, the Hawaiian goose.

The airplane design is optimized for claiming the records for (a) distance in a closed course, and (b) distance in a straight line. It appears, however, that the airplane will also be able to claim the records for (c) altitude and (d) speed for 5000 kilometers in a closed course.

The airplane accommodates two pilots, as the proposed flight may take as long as 70 hours. The distance capabilities are somewhat more with only one pilot, due to the additional fuel that could be carried without exceeding the 1000 kilogram weight limit. Nevertheless, the airplane has the capability of claiming the records with two pilots.

The airplane has been designed, and construction of the wing is well under way. The design features a pusher propeller at the rear of the airplane, driven by an extension shaft.

All phases of this project are carried out by the applicant personally. He conceived the project. He made hundreds of pages of design calculations. He is now building the airplane, forming the aluminum sheet, drilling thousands of rivet holes, sealing the wing structure (it will serve as the fuel tank). He will pilot the airplane on its first flight and make the flight tests. He will be the pilot on any solo record flights and the chief pilot on record flights with two pilots. So far, this project has been personally financed by the applicant. Shop facilities are supplied by the Department of Aerospace Engineering, The University of Michigan.

The applicant is well qualified for this project. He has had a consuming interest in airplanes since the age of 7. He has taught aeronautical engineering for 40 years. He has worked in the engineering departments of several aircraft companies. He has been a pilot for 39 years, holds a Commercial Pilot Certificate, and has 3500 hours as pilot in command. He is in excellent physical condition, having jogged for many years. He has always enjoyed working with his hands. He has designed, constructed, and flown two other airplanes, the *Nomad* and the *Teal*.

A high probability of success for the *Nene* is indicated by the success of the *Teal*. This project, conceived in 1961 and still continuing, is similar to the *Nene*, except that the weight class is under 500 kilograms and its object is to claim all nine of the official records for speed, distance, and altitude for its class. This involved a compromised design because an airplane designed for speed is not, due to the laws of aerodynamics, the best for distance. However, the *Teal* aircraft has claimed seven world records, has lost two of them, and still has two to attempt.

The configuration of the *Nene* aircraft follows closely that of the proven *Teal*, but is somewhat larger. The pilots are seated in tandem. The engine is rated at 130 horsepower. The tail pusher configuration has many advantages, such as improved propeller efficiency, reduced fuselage drag, less propeller noise in the cabin, and excellent visibility.

The *Nene* involves many design and construction innovations. For example, the landing gear retraction system requires many hand operations by the pilot. This reduces the weight, and more fuel can be carried. Fuselage skins are developed in the flat, and then rolled up to form the fuselage without the use of jigs. The rivet holes in the main wing skin are punched when the sheet is still flat. Due to special tooling, the holes then match perfectly the holes punched in the ribs in separate operations.

The project involves an extremely wide range of aeronautical activities to be carried out by one person. First, the mental design; then the construction, involving skill with tools and machines. The test flying involves piloting skill and the engineering interpretation of results. Planning and carrying out the record flights involves a knowledge of weather and navigation.

Following are the world records claimed by the *Teal* and certified by the FAI.

1. Distance in a straight line, 2953.89 kilometers, claimed on July 3, 1975. Previous record was 2844 kilometers.

2. Distance in a closed circuit, 2501.4 kilometers, claimed on September 9, 1970. Previous record was 2000 kilometers. This *Teal* record has since been lost.

3. Speed over a 3 kilometer course, 278.579 kilometers per hour, claimed September 29, 1973. Previous record was 219.2 km/h. This *Teal* record has since been lost.

4. Speed over a 15/25 kilometer course, 272.195 kilometers per hour, claimed September 30, 1973. No official record previously set.

5. Speed for 500 kilometers in a closed circuit, 292.17 kilometers/hour, claimed May 22, 1967. Previous record was 271.403 km/h.

6. Speed for 1000 kilometers in a closed circuit, 272.32 kilometers/hour, claimed June 30, 1967. Previous record was 240.519 km/h.

7. Speed for 2000 kilometers in a closed circuit, 228.26 kilometers/hour, claimed October 20, 1967. Previous record was 183.432 km/h.

Following are the record attempts to be made with the *Nene:*

1. For distance in a closed circuit. Present record is 7725.30 kilometers (December 15, 1979). The distance capability of the *Nene* is expected to be 9500 kilometers with two pilots, 12,000 kilometers with one.

2. For distance in a straight line. Present record is 4496.62 kilometers (October 12, 1976). The *Nene* will be able to more than double this record.

3. For altitude. Present record is 9206 meters, claimed January 4, 1951. The *Nene* altitude capability is expected to be over 11,000 meters.

4. For speed for 5000 kilometers in a closed circuit. No official record yet established. The *Nene* would also claim this record on the distance in a closed circuit flight.

The project was started in 1976. Completion is expected by 1983.

THE "ABC" SYSTEM OF PROVIDING MORE FOOD MORE CHEAPLY

VICENTE A. ARANETA
87 Dapitan Street, Quezon City, Metro Manila, Philippines

Filipino, born February 25, 1910. President of two businesses, one in farming, one in development. Agricultural education and Ph.D. in the Philippines.

The ABC triangle of industries (animals, biogas, and crops) when carried out commercially will reduce food prices to unbelievably low levels. I can make this amazing statement because of the Continuous Anaerobic Fermentation Process, which has been granted Philippine Letters Patent No. 11820. This digestion process efficiently produces methane gas, liquid carbon dioxide, and organic fertilizer from animal dung and straw; these presently have little or no value to Filipino farmers. My project is the development of the dairy farming industry in complement with commercial anaerobic digestion of farm wastes, with the objective of producing milk at sharply reduced price levels.

The advanced dairy processing industry in the Philippines imports 99 percent of its milk products, while less than 1 percent is obtained from indigenous production. Subsidies of milk products by foreign governments have prevented the building of a profitable Philippine dairy industry.

This project involves building an integrated dairy farm on a 1144-hectare property in Maapag Plains, Valencia, Bukidnon, located at an elevation of 300 meters above sea level, with a mean temperature of 23°C, considered ideal for the production of milk by the Holstein-Friesian breed of cow. A herd of 1600 cows will be established initially, kept in barns to facilitate easy movement of manure through the installation's integrated energy system.

The digesters around which the system will work require a constant supply of a mixture of 1 pound of manure and 6 pounds of dry straw. The retention period of digestion and stabilization of the sludge is a maximum of ten days, although we anticipate that this can be reduced to about five days with proper control methods. Generated biogas will be at least 7 cubic feet per pound of manure, allowing for a very compact plant.

Biogas is composed of approximately 60 percent methane and 38 percent carbon dioxide; hydrogen sulfide and other unimportant elements make up the remainder. We will scrub the corrosive hydrogen sulfide out in a vessel having ferric oxide in suspension. We will separate methane from the carbon dioxide through pressurization, for purposes of running our 400 kilowatt-hour electric power plant. This plant will run 24 hours a day to serve all the requirements of the integrated farm operations.

Because the total output of the methane will provide fuel for about 3000 kilowatt-hours, we will be able to provide electricity to undeveloped communities in the area to encourage their attempts at local industry. Bottled methane fuel, stored in small oxygen-type containers at 2240 psi, is an excellent substitute for expensive petrol or gasoline. Also, the liquefied carbon dioxide is an excellent refrigerant for the production of dry ice. At its low production cost, a new industry could be developed in the area—the manufacture of small, inexpensive, household dry-ice refrigerator boxes.

Production of perishables, such as fish and meat, will be encouraged through the availability of refrigeration. Crops will benefit from the organic fertilizer discharged from the digester.

Additional benefit to the surrounding community of small farmers lies in the need for an annual 27,800 tons of straw, or the residue from 3475 hectares of ricelands, about 60 percent of the neighboring areas with their two crops annually. The anticipated P 1200 extra income per hectare for the previously wasted straw will be a welcome bonus for the small farmers of the area.

The profitability of the ABC triangle of projects should be of interest to foreign enterprises. In fact, this is the kind of project wherein the more developed countries can provide particularly useful assistance to less developed countries by helping to establish better and more efficient indigenous industries. What is needed, and what we hope to bring to the area with this small industrial/agricultural business, is experienced technology—managerial, supervisory, and communicatory. The objective is to develop among the local staff and program participants the knack for proper handling of milk-producing cows and the ability to make full use of the resources at hand.

We intend to begin in January 1981 with construction of barns and other facilities. Land tillage should start at the same time, to have the grain and forage crops seeded in April. The first of eight monthly arrivals of heifers in-calf, to begin in July 1981, would then be assured of adequate feed. We will welcome any assistance in making this complex model work.

CAN THE COTTON ROOT HERB PROVIDE A SIMPLE NATURAL CONTRACEPTIVE?

PHILIPPUS TEGUHSUSETYA
Widya Mandala Catholic University, 42, Dinoyo Street,
Surabaya, Indonesia

Indonesian, born May 12, 1947. Lecturer, pharmacist, University Assistant in laboratory. Science education in Indonesia and Philippines.

This project involves research into a potential virtue of the root of a cotton plant that has traditionally been used by part of Indonesian society, in the form of a medicinal herb, to induce menstruation when a menstrual period has been missed. I will try to determine whether the medicinal herb from this cotton root could be used as an effective, natural contraceptive. If this turns out to be the case, this product would be of great importance in helping to promote family planning in Indonesia.

As a developing country in Southeast Asia, Indonesia (population 147,000,000 in 1978) faces many problems, such as lack of widespread education, low income levels, and a rapid increase in child birth. Especially in rural areas many families of low income and limited education have many children. The population problem has captured the attention of the Indonesian government, which is implementing a family planning program all over the country, but success has not been easy, partly due to lack of sufficient experts in the field.

As a consequence, there is a lack of information about contraceptives, which are sorely needed in the rural areas. Besides, people do not like to use contraceptive equipment (spirals/IUD's, condoms, caps), because they are not comfortable and easy to use. Women are reluctant to use contraceptive drugs because of fears of side effects. Also, among the uneducated, there is the notion that there is no need to take "the pill" when they are not sick. This may sound amusing, but it is true!

It is the custom in a part of our society that women whose menstruation is delayed for any reason drink a decoction of medicinal herbs—the herbs are boiled or steeped in water—and a few days later they menstruate as usual. One of the herbs in this decoction is cotton root. Based on this custom and a review of existing literature, my theory is that cotton root induces the menstrual flow by contracting the uterus.

The purpose of my research is to find out whether the cotton plants have the potential to be used as a method of birth control. If so, the results of this research could be a great help for the people, since the plant is familiar, cheap, and easy to obtain.

I first plan to complete the identification and selection of the cotton plant that the people use for medicinal herbs, using normal procedures of taxonomy, botanical morphology, and plant anatomy. Next, I will identify the contents of the cotton root, using plant chemistry, chromatography, and spectrophotometry. After these preparatory steps, I will conduct a physiology experiment (to be conducted in the University's physiology lab) along the following lines:

Making a decoction from cotton root similar to that used by the local rural people mentioned above.

Using the intestine of guinea pigs or mice to determine the contraction effect of this decoction in comparison with other known drugs.

Then I will carry out a pharmacology experiment, using fertile female white mice or guinea pigs. After copulation, they will be separated into two groups. One of the groups will be fed the decoction for varying numbers of days following copulation; the other will not be given the decoction at all. The groups will be compared to see relative differences in number of pregnancies and number of offspring delivered. The experiment will be repeated numerous times to provide statistical validity, if initial results seem encouraging.

I am conducting this research on my own, because I believe it may be of importance to my country. If any expert in this field would like to give some suggestions or opinions concerning this research, I would accept them gladly.

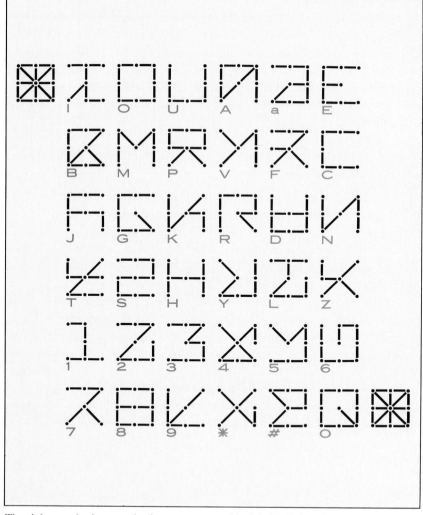

The alphanumeric characters in the new system, with their English equivalents.

MAN AND MACHINE COMPATIBLE COMMUNICATION ELEMENTS

MOHAN KALA
14 Kenilworth Road, Ealing, London W5 3UH, England

British, born November 23, 1940. Technician at Central London Polytechnic. Technical education in South Africa and the United Kingdom.

I t is generally accepted that a single lingua franca will one day eliminate most of the world's communication problems. Numerous attempts have been made to construct a universal second language with a simplified grammar and sound-to-symbol parity acceptable to all inhabitants of the world. All such constructed languages have been derived from one or more existing languages, in an attempt to blend an optimum number of communication vehicles. Of the approximate dozen such constructed languages put forth for international use, Esperanto is by far the most widely known. Constructed by Dr. Ludwik Lazar Zamenhof, a Polish physician, it was first explained in published form in a book that appeared in 1887, under the pseudonym of Doktoro Esperanto. Today around 100,000 people are adherents of Esperanto, but it has no official status.

I believe that Esperanto and other such languages were constructed only with human compatibility problems in mind. In today's technical world, language needs to be made compatible not just with humans, but also with machines (or vice versa!). If the early language inventors had been able to anticipate the importance that machines would take on in our lives, I am sure they would have given consideration to both human and machine compatibilities when they constructed their languages.

My approach to constructing a new language has been quite different from that employed by past inventors. Instead of constructing new words and grammar, I have retained these two components of the most popular language in international use now—English—but have reconstructed the other communication elements from scratch, keeping in mind today's human and machine compatibility requirements.

My first task was to simplify the problem. It seemed that all languages could be subdivided into four major components: (1) alphabet (words), (2) numerals (numbers), (3) basic weights and measures convention, and, (4) basic grammar convention (sentences). Each of these components could be constructed individually, but cohesion between them is extremely important if the total system is to meet the objective of a single unified concept to serve the needs of both humans and machines. Therefore, I have reconstructed the first three components, leaving the fourth in its entirety, with minor changes that can be carried out at a later date. The advantage to such an approach is that, while continuing to speak our own languages, we will have a new form of writing that commences establishment of commonality.

In constructing the alphabet, I had three primary objectives:

1. The alphabetic characters must conform to a singular modular framework to give it preciseness of form and to render it easy to reproduce by humans or by any mechanized or electronic symbol-generating devices.

2. There must be a minimum amount of alphabetic symbols, with sound-to-symbol parity as far as optimal. (It is not possible to construct a perfect phonetic system of writing; too many symbols would be required, and too many would have a very low frequency of use.)

3. The sequence of characters must be logical, vowels first and then the consonants. The sequence should be suited for keyboard devices so that typing skills can be easily acquired in dramatically short time.

In constructing the numeric characters, my four key objectives were:

1. The symbols of the new base must conform to the same modular framework as the alphabetic characters, for the reasons stated above.

2. They should be distinctive in form from the alphabetic characters, with no ambiguity between them.

3. The symbols must be forgery proof, so that they cannot be altered in function once written down.

4. The symbols should indicate their correct functions in one orientation only.

When considering the requirements of a basic weights and measures convention, it became quickly apparent that the counting system we use today, the decimal 10, is a regrettable hangover from our ancestral fixation with our 10 fingers. The efficiency of a counting system depends on the availability of useful factors and the dimension of its base—that is, its numeric value should not be too small or too big. The base 10 in use today has only two factors—2 and 5—and the latter factor is of little use. A base of medial dimension with the best array of useful factors is 12, which has 2, 3, 4, and 6 as its factors. Establishing a duodecimal system involved the creation of two new numeric characters to represent the numbers "ten" and "eleven." Having accomplished this, I then sought a rational basis for weights and measures, which would meet the following provisos:

1. The units of length and time should be derived from the most accurate physical constant available. (Thus the new length unit is 2.0174 centimeters long, correct to four decimal places, derived from the constant expressing the speed of light.)

2. All other units of weights and measures should be extrapolated from the basic time and length units and aligned within the base twelve system of numeration.

3. The size of the units should be human compatible (not too small, not too large). For practical purposes, the centimeter and the gram are far too small for convenient usage.

The last component, that of basic grammar convention, is a task that will take place slowly over the years, with the need to regularize verbs as one of the particularly irksome stumbling blocks to learning the language.

Most important for now, however, is the availability of the new modular system illustrated here. The new set of alphabetic characters, consisting of six vowels [A, E, I, O, U, and a (for a as in arm)] and eighteen consonants is shown in order in the first four lines. Missing from the current Roman alphabet are the characters for Q, W, and X—the lesser used sounds, which can be represented on paper by the use of simple digraphs (i.e., two-letter combinations to represent a single sound value).

The last two lines of the illustration show the numeric characters: eleven numbers and the zero of the duodecimal system. All of these alphanumeric characters can be created with a single module of sixteen bars.

In our increasingly technological world, the need for compatible human-machine communication is becoming a two-way proposition that calls for maximum literacy on both sides. I believe this system proffers an easily learned solution to that problem.

AUTOMOTIVE POWER GRID AND ENERGY STORAGE SILO SYSTEM

JOHN ROSSI
1509 Forest Avenue, River Forest, Illinois 60305, U.S.A.

American, born March 26, 1918. Custom-made automotive vehicles sales engineer. Mechanical engineering education in the United States.

The Automotive Power Grid and Energy Storage Silo System can best be described by its function. I wish to scavenge a tremendous amount of usable energy from some of the passing weight and kinetic energy expended by trucks and automobiles over a given strip of highway, without interfering with the safety, comfort, speed, or purpose of this traffic. Hundreds of geometrically arranged micro-hydraulic pistons, forming a grid, are to be imbedded below the surface of the highway. They protrude about $\frac{1}{2}$ inch above the surface, in the form of round domes about 3 inches in diameter. A grid 200 feet long is envisaged, covering four lanes of traffic. The tires of passing vehicles depress these "pistons," causing oil to be pumped at high pressure into accumulating tanks and then onward to simple turbine electric generators. Surplus energy will be transferred to a unique system of Energy Storage Silos.

The best sources for scavenging this available energy would be on slight downgrades near big cities, where traffic moves at relatively constant speeds. As an example, over a four-lane, slight downgrade site, traffic moving at 40 mph, safely 50 feet apart, would "scavenge" 96 horsepower per second. A conservative estimate gives 22 tons of oil being pumped per minute, at greater than 30 pounds per square inch, or the equivalent of 70,000 watts of electricity.

The heart of the system is a simple 3-inch-diameter piston, with a rounded dome, approximately $4\frac{1}{2}$ inches in length, of which the top, rounded $\frac{1}{2}$ inch protrudes above the road surface. Closed by weather and other sealing rings, the piston is placed in a casing that is embedded in concrete and designed to withstand approximately 150 psi oil pressure plus impact forces when depressed at high speeds by passing tires. At the bottom of each enclosed cylinder is a charging intake ball check fitting and a special discharge pressure fitting. Each piston cylinder is designed to be removable and replaceable by simply turning the entire piston and cylinder 45 degrees. After placing this assembly in the casing and turning it 45 degrees, the discharge and intake outlets couple with the embedded fittings at the bottom of the casing. This connects the piston and cylinder with the piping system located below the pavement surface.

Total displacement of each piston is about 5 cubic inches, or 86 cubic centimeters. The intake charging oil pressure is approximately 2 pounds, to force the piston to rise immediately after being depressed. On depression of each piston, the oil charging the system is forced toward an accumulating tank, through special pressure relief valve fittings set at 25 pounds. Hundreds of these pistons arranged along the traffic lanes form the Power Grid. A 200-foot long grid will have approximately 400 pistons in line, spaced approximately 6 inches apart on center. Using the traffic example given above, some 1000 depressions per second per lane, or 4000/second in four lanes, will occur. This can generate the 70,000 watts—a rather staggering result.

Except for the need to design and produce the piston, all remaining elements (regulators, valves, piping, instruments, and controls) are currently available.

A necessary part of the APG is the Energy Storage Silo System (ESSS), which balances the flow of oil to the electric turbines and stores the surplus energy not directly converted to electricity by the turbines. The ESSS takes the volume of the flow and the pressure from the APG and uses it to raise huge concrete cylinders weighing many tons. These silos, either above or below ground, are constructed by present methods, using current material and equipment. These massive weights, raised via a system of oil-volume-actuated winches connected to pulleys and cables, will be allowed to fall as needed to provide energy to keep the turbines running at constant levels when traffic patterns are diminished.

The APG and ESSS can scavenge an infinitesimal amount of the energy people use to get from one place to another. Drivers should not oppose, but welcome, the grids—they could be met by a sign saying:

> YOU ARE APPROACHING YOUR APG.
> PLEASE HOLD YOUR LANE POSITION
> AND MAINTAIN CONSTANT SPEED.
> THANK YOURSELF

THE ALL-PLASTIC DIKE OF THE FUTURE

CRISOSTOMO G. VILLANUEVA
c/o Mrs. Nenea V. Aniceto, Postal Region VIII, Tacloban City, Philippines

Filipino, born January 27, 1938. Engineer and fabricator of mud digging rig. Business education in Philippines.

The Philippines, like other developing nations, have vigorously faced the challenge of food shortages owing to increasing populations. The nation has been quite successful in developing cereal rice to meet its needs, but we need to do a better job in meeting the demand for protein foods. Fish culture has been one of the more promising opportunities, and the government has encouraged new approaches to fishpond culturing. Large tracts of land in the country remain in a marshland state, and little of this land is developed for what could be a bonanza of fish and shrimp culturing.

The main problem in converting these marshlands to usable ponds is the mixture of salt and fresh water that, in its brackish state, is not fit for proper mariculture. To date, the only means of tackling this challenge has been through the construction of a dike, which has been a manual task for generations, taking a long time and achieving less than perfect results. Manual workers, who cannot afford specially designed machinery to build small fishponds, can only build (using 10 to 20 people working together) about 10 linear meters of dike per week, and the dikes must be added to each six months, because of erosion from below. These problems prompted me to build a dike-building machine and to design a dike-construction method that is promising as a new way of building these structures.

I propose making dikes wholly of hard plastics. Composed of pre-assembled plastic panels of varied sizes, with a specified thickness, length, and width, according to application, these new dike-building units promise significant advantages. When formed, each section in side view looks like the capital letter "A." Averaging in height some 3 meters, the units are designed to conform to the local terrain and mud-base through self-adjusting weight distribution and settling. The sectional plastic forms are pressed into the muddy surface, one after another, connected like a chain, by a specially made assembling machine that I designed for this particular purpose.

The machine cuts into the marshy soil, slicing and paving a base for the A-frame unit, which is then pressed into position at a pre-determined depth. Once the A-frame unit is in place, silt from the surrounding marshy land is pumped through holes in its sides. This river silt is used primarily as dead weight to hold and to stabilize the dike unit against the outside water pressure at high tide, when the pond is dried up, and to contain the desired water level inside the pond at low tide.

By making the elements of the A-frame in various standard configurations and equipping them with pre-determined slots for assembly at the location, the materials for the dike can be transported to sites without great difficulty. Assembly is quick, and work can progress much more rapidly than was the case with manual-effort dikes, made by cutting segments of earth and laboriously moving them into place by hand.

If floodgates are needed, these are also pre-assembled, and resemble the standard wooden or concrete gates used before, except that they are made of plastic and have the same broad A-frame base as the dike walls themselves. A superstructure is placed on the top for controlling the flow of water.

The reason behind the use of the isosceles form for the dike units is akin to the "floating principle" used by the late American architect-builder, Frank Lloyd Wright. The whole dike will float somewhat, along with the movement of the muddy terrain. Here in our locality, a 30 foot long 1-inch pipe will not reach solid ground below, so that any kind of dike structure made of brick, concrete, or steel will eventually sink to the bottom in about three years' time. Earth-filled dikes also sink and erode, so that owners must continually add a meter or so on top each year.

What makes the new A-frame units better is the isosceles principle, where the top of the cone is sealed shut. As the A-frame begins to sink in the mud from its wider-at-the-base starting point, the mud rising in the A-frame gradually compresses the available air until a balance point is reached where the dike unit is stabilized between downward and upward pressures. It will therefore be firm.

The specially designed assembly machine, which will cut sections to a depth of one-third of the height of the dike units, will be a hydraulically operated vehicle, equipped with six balloon-type rubber tires for operating over marshy terrain. I believe this new approach to building mariculture ponds will significantly aid my country.

Before: Lack of cellulose in soil causes erosion.

After: Good pasture results when an eroded soil is treated with cellulose.

"DOMESTICATING" SOIL BACTERIA TO BEAT THE PROBLEM OF SOIL EROSION

 JORGE S. MOLINA BUCK
Honorable Mention, Rolex Awards for Enterprise
Research Center on Microbial Ecology, Obligado 2490,
Buenos Aires (CP 1428), Argentina

Argentine, born June 29, 1919. Full Professor, Chair General Agriculture, Agronomy Faculty, Buenos Aires University. Educated in Argentina.

Our proposition is to domesticate soil microorganisms that can prevent soil erosion at the same time that they fix nitrogen from the air. To realize this big enterprise, knowledge of the ecological conditions needed for the aerobic and the anaerobic bacteria that decompose cellulose and the aerobic and anaerobic bacteria that fix nitrogen from the air is necessary. After more than 30 years of work in laboratory and field practice all over South America, and particularly in the Argentine Republic, Brazil, and the Greater Chaco, this knowledge is nearly complete. The work began in 1946 and has proceeded along two closely aligned areas of inquiry, beginning with the world of cellulose.

Cellulose is the most abundant organic compound in nature. If we could use the enormous amounts of cellulose produced each year by photosynthesis, we could answer some of the most important questions about energy requirements that face agriculture. First, we must find a way to stop soil erosion, and second, we need to find new energy-renewable sources and new (or old) biological processes of nitrogen fixation.

Beginning in 1946, we explored both theoretical and practical aspects of the domestication of aerobic cellulose bacteria, and ways to use them to produce, or "manufacture," large amounts of the polyuronic colloids that are extremely active in developing those properties of soil that help it to resist erosion and exhaustion. In work carried out on more than 2 million hectares, we have obtained very good results in increasing meat production and grain yields through our means of controlling soil erosion. Recently, in a special program on 53,000 hectares of the southern Greater Chaco, we transformed overgrazed and eroded bushland into good pastures—producing large amounts of meat all year round, avoiding soil erosion, and improving soil fertility, without using chemical fertilizers.

We consider this bacterium "domesticated" now, and so since 1973 we have been working on the second aspect of the problem: domestication of nitrogen-fixing soil bacteria to obtain a low-cost biological process that can reap massive amounts of nitrogen from the air.

Nitrogen is vitally important to agriculture, and yet we have not succeeded in taking advantage of our abundant resources of this key element. (Earth was called Planet Nitrogen at the 53rd Congress of the American Society of Agronomy—35,000 tons of nitrogen gas are contained in the air over each acre of earth's soil.) To speak of a nitrogen scarcity seems an absurdity. The air above us is a real mine of nitrogen. But, like all mineral deposits, you must know how to exploit it. Petroleum in the subsoil is of no value until we drill thousands of meters for it, install artificial islands, build pipelines and refineries, and so on.

The same happens with the nitrogen in the air. We have set up costly factories working at hundreds of degrees at very high pressures to capture the nitrogen (N_2) and transform it into products utilizable by plants, animals, and humans.

The present arduous problem is that enormous quantities of energy are required to carry out this task. According to Pimentel (U.S.), the industrial process to obtain usable nitrogen takes 19,200 kilocalories per kilogram of nitrogen fixed from the air. This quantity of energy represents about 2 kilograms of fuel oil, each kilogram having some 10,667 kilocalories. Thus, any increase in the price of petroleum directly translates into an increase in the cost of nitrogen fertilizers.

According to Revelle, the biological processes of nitrogen fixation need a quantity of energy similar to that of the industrial process. Pimentel tells us that in the dry material left over as corn stubble, there are some 4200 kilocalories per kilogram. Larson tells us that there are some 6700 kilograms of stubble per hectare. On a theoretical basis, therefore, we have the possibility of fixing 1465 kilograms of nitrogen per hectare per year. In our investigations, we have proved that aerobic nitrogen-fixing bacteria can use the products of anaerobic decomposition of cellulose to fix large amounts of nitrogen from the air at a very low cost, directly, in conditions very similar to field conditions. The methods used are available to interested parties and promise to be of significance to agriculture in general.

With various processes, including Kjeldahl determinations, gas chromatography, and directly by feeding experimental animals, we have obtained up to 1125 kilos of nitrogen/hectare in only three months using loess subsoil mixed with 22.5 tons of corn stubble per hectare, against only 180 kilos in the control without corn stubble addition (lab experiences). By gas chromatography, Soriano and his co-workers have recorded up to 55.9 kilos of nitrogen per hectare per day.

We have obtained large populations of experimental animals (*Acarus,* a mite) in media totally deprived of nitrogen at the beginning of the experiences.

Just as in the factories that produce industrial nitrogen, the key to the possibility of fixing large amounts of nitrogen through nitrogen-fixing bacteria in our soils lies in the availability and cost of the source of energy. Our agronomic experience has shown that the most abundant and cheap energy source is that contained in the harvest residue.

In the United States, Pimentel (June 1978) demonstrated that from a total of 1403 million tons of dry material hypothetically available in that country for the production of energy, starting with the basic biomass, 430 million tons correspond to farming stubble, surpassing even the remnants of forest exploitation, which reach only 340 million tons. Pimentel at the same time reached the conclusion that *all the farming stubble should be left on the ground because it is essential for the preservation of the soil.* In other words, he does not consider this stubble as a suitable source of energy for industry.

In our studies, we have found that all of the inconveniences of using such stubble for industrial use are, in fact, the major advantages of using stubble as the source of energy for the nitrogen-fixing bacteria in the soil. We have succeeded in domesticating *Azotobacter* and inoculating it with acari, a process that transforms the microbial biomass into an animal biomass which is then used as a source of nitrogen in culture media for anaerobic bacteria of cellulose with excellent results. The same process produces the rapid and abundant formation of polyuronic colloids. This process closes an ecological cycle, reproducing one of nature's most important biological cycles in a petri dish.

We are now at the stage where we can adapt, at least theoretically, these findings to the particular requirements of all types of soil with which we have worked.

CHEMICAL COMMUNICATION IN BOVINE REPRODUCTION

JOHN G. VANDENBERGH
Department of Zoology, North Carolina State University,
Raleigh, North Carolina 27650, U.S.A.

American, born May 4, 1935. Professor and Head of Department of Zoology. Science education in the United States.

T he primary purpose of this project is to extend previous work on the pheromonal control of the ovary in rodents to domestic farm animals. A great deal of basic work in my laboratory and elsewhere has shown that chemical signals (i.e., pheromones) are used by rodents to synchronize ovarian function. I wish to take aspects of this work and apply it to farm animals with the expectation that important advances can be made in the husbandry of cows, pigs, and perhaps sheep. Such advances will improve the efficiency of animal agriculture and contribute to solving the worldwide food shortages we face.

Pheromones are chemical substances that are released by one animal and have a behavioral or physiological effect on another of the same species. We propose to focus on substances that have physiological effects, or what are termed the "priming" pheromones. These are analogous to hormones, except that they act between individuals rather than within an individual.

Previous work on rodents has shown that priming pheromones have strong effects on two reproductive events: puberty and the adult ovulatory cycle. The onset of puberty in the female mouse is hastened by exposing juvenile females to male urine. The active ingredient in male urine is androgen dependent and has been identified as a small peptide or a substance bound to a small peptide. Conversely, puberty in the female mouse can be delayed by exposure to female urine. In adult females, urinary pheromones also influence the timing of the ovulatory cycle. The urine of male mice synchronizes the female's estrous cycle, and the urine of females has an inhibitory effect on the female's cycle. In each of these effects the pheromone is apparently perceived through the olfactory system and acts upon the brain to cause changes in the release of gonadotropin hormones from the pituitary gland. Gonadotropins then act upon the ovary to result in the production of ovarian hormones and ovulation. Though I have here focused on studies using the mouse, similar confirmed or suspected pheromonal effects occur in a variety of other rodents, in pigs, and in sheep.

Stimulated by these findings and by previous work that suggested pheromones might affect the timing of the cow's ovulatory cycle, we initiated a preliminary study to determine if the priming pheromones could be used to synchronize estrous cycles in dairy cows. Using 47 post-pubertal Holstein heifers on two institutional farms of the North Carolina Department of Agriculture, all the animals were injected with 25 milligrams of prostaglandin $F_{2\alpha}$ to bring them all to the follicular phase of the estrous cycle. Then, 25 of them had 1 milliliter of a mixture of urine and cervico-vaginal mucus from estrous cows applied to the nasal and oral cavities at 6, 30, and 54 hours following the $PGF_{2\alpha}$ injection. A similar quantity of water was applied to 22 of the heifers as a control procedure. Estrus was significantly more synchronized and more intense in the treated cows. This study indicated that a priming pheromone could be used to synchronize estrus in a herd, with resulting improvements in conception rates from properly timed artificial insemination following injection of $PGF_{2\alpha}$.

We now wish to extend studies to confirm these initial findings, and to work out the details of pheromone delivery schedules required to induce the greatest response, in order to establish the most appropriate techniques.

Additionally, in separate experiments, we will attempt to isolate the chemical that actually causes the effects on the cow's ovary. In the first stage, we will determine whether urine or cervical mucus contains the pheromone that synchronizes estrus. Identification of the biological fluid containing the pheromone will then permit us to fractionate the substance and test its components. To enter this stage of our research, we will have to develop a sensitive, reliable, and relatively rapid bioassay. This task has proven to be difficult in all work on pheromones but is essential for chemical characterization. We hope that our experiences on the mouse pheromone will enable us to more efficiently separate and identify pheromones in cows.

The potential significance of the work is the contribution to greater productivity in an important part of the agricultural enterprise. If, by a combination of hormonal and pheromonal induction of estrus, more precise control over ovulation could be achieved, artificial insemination could be used in beef cattle, thus helping to meet the challenge of providing more food for the growing human population.

AVIATION DISASTER SALVATION SYSTEM

ANTONIO FRANCO JUNIOR
Rua Vidal Sion No. 214, Apartment No. 11, 11100 Santos, Brazil

Brazilian, born November 6, 1942. Electrician, educated in Brazil.

This project has as its objective the development of a system that would facilitate the location of any plane that crashed in uninhabited areas or at sea. This would accelerate the possibility of prompt rescue of those on board who may have survived the crash.

Following an airplane crash, many survivors of the crash subsequently die because rescue teams have had difficulty locating the exact site of the plane. Perhaps the most dramatic of these occurrences in recent times was the Andes Mountains disaster, a tragic story of the attempt at human survival long after the plane had crashed. The difficulty in locating this plane's wreckage, high in an inaccessible area and virtually impossible to spot visually, produced an agonizing experience of human courage and tragedy that might have been avoided if a fairly simple precaution had been engineered into the body of the plane itself.

To summarize my project, I would like to develop a mechanism that would eject a long, brightly colored plastic band from the tail of an airplane in imminent danger of crashing. The band would be ejected either manually or automatically during a descent, and it would be constructed so that it remains completely extended after the airplane has hit, either over vegetation (land) or on water.

Essentially, the band should be some 300 meters in length, with a width of 50 centimeters and a thickness of 0.1 centimeter. Based on color-recognition experiments and experience, the band should be a combination of fluorescent orange and yellow stripes for maximum visibility. Such a combination of length and colors ought to be visible from considerable altitudes, such as those used by search planes attempting to locate downed aircraft. The band should alternate 1-meter stripes of the orange and yellow colors to provide maximum attention-catching qualities. The material should be a specially chosen plastic, possessing fire resistance, great tensile strength, and a specific weight of less than 1.0 (so that it will float).

To further aid in the identification of the crashed plane, I propose that the plane's identification numbers be printed on the yellow portions of the band; observers who happen to view the signal band can report it to appropriate authorities with proper identification.

Upon selection of the proper fabric for the band, experiments with "parachute-packing" types of folding and compressing will determine the minimum necessary space (a key consideration, especially in the small planes that would be apt to benefit most from this safety feature). The band could be doubled over prior to rolling or folding in order to conserve space and contribute to its optimum pull-away from the aircraft at a given signal. Experiments will be needed to determine whether the band should be rolled or folded for maximum speed of unraveling when the signal is given.

Two systems of ejection would be incorporated into the aircraft, one manual and one electrically operated, depending upon the costs and available space in the aircraft. Obviously, they should be under the control of the crew, for activation when it is apparent that a crash is forthcoming. A simple electromagnetic locking device on an ejection port located at the end of the plane's body could be operated either electrically from the pilot's seat or via manual switching from a close-by location under crew control. It might be feasible to include some kind of firing mechanism that would ensure that the band was properly ejected and extended in only a few seconds, as time would be of critical concern in such a situation.

I believe that such a system could save many lives, at low cost, if it were adopted by aircraft owners.

A diver within the framework of the underwater sculpture submerged near Tague Bay Reef, St. Croix, before accretion began. The central shaft is 21 feet high.

MINERAL ACCRETION FOR UNDERWATER CONSTRUCTION

WOLF H. HILBERTZ
2812 Hemphill Park, Austin, Texas 78705, U.S.A.

West German, born April 16, 1938. Associate Professor of Architecture and company president. Architectural education in West Germany and the United States.

I intend to design, build, and maintain a small underwater research and recreational park in Grand Cayman, British West Indies. A novel technique, mineral accretion, will be employed to provide the greater part of the construction materials needed. This technology employs an electrochemical process that deposits minerals (calcium carbonates and magnesium hydroxides) on negatively charged forms (cathodes) in sea water. Previous work with accreted underwater forms has shown them to serve as excellent habitats for marine fauna and flora, and as unique underwater experiences for humans on recreational, scientific, educational, and aesthetic levels. This underwater facility would be a showplace and test bed for the scientific community, in order to promote the technology of mineral accretion toward a variety of useful applications.

Accretion is an electrochemical process, basically involving the immersion of an electrode pair between which flows a direct electrical current in an electrolyte. The electrolyte in this case is sea water, with its abundance of dissolved minerals. The electrode pair consists of one positively charged anode and one negatively charged cathode. The impressed current, with a varying density of 10–30 milliamperes per square foot produces deposits of calcium carbonates ($CaCO_3$) and magnesium hydroxides ($MgOH_2$) on the cathode. The energy required for the electrodeposition of 1 kilogram of accreted mass averages 1 kilowatt, depending on various parameters (temperature, pressure, etc.). For small-scale accretion tests, we have utilized 12-volt car batteries and battery chargers; for large-scale projects, we installed wind generators (average output 120–360 watts at 12 volts) and solar cell (photovoltaic) banks (peak output 3.8V/2.5A for each 1 foot $\times$ 2 foot unit) as power sources. Solar energy seems especially promising for wide-ranging deployment of the mineral accretion process.

Only recently has thought been given to using this process for artificially stimulated reef components, building components for use on land, beach stabilization, and piling protection. I began experimenting with mineral accretions in sea water some six years ago to explore engineering and architectural potential, and through this work new applications have begun to emerge, including the underwater facility conceived for use in scientific research and as a preliminary means of exploring personal recreational opportunities underwater.

Our research and testing efforts have taken several directions. One major line of study has been the construction of artificially stimulated reef components. In August 1976, we placed several wire mesh reef components in Tague Bay, St. Croix, and in the Gulf of Mexico. Observations indicate the mineral accretion process produces a very suitable substrate for marine growth. With only moderate input of electrical power, a mineral substrate was formed (at times, within one day), which facilitated rapid growth of diatoms and blue-green algae within three days. This, with the availability of shelter in the reef components, attracted various fish populations, indicating that the electrical field has no apparent detrimental effect on marine life.

Another study area has been the production of building components. We have constructed a number of large-scale components ranging from cylinders and columns up to 15 feet tall and 6 feet in diameter, to free-hanging catenary forms. Using double or triple layers of wire mesh, we have been able to accrete components up to an inch or more in thickness, and under low electric field conditions we have produced large architectural or engineering components with a relatively uniform thickness of accreted material. Following standard procedures for concrete testing (compression to the point of breakage) at the University of Texas Structural Testing Lab, samples of electrodeposited minerals on $\frac{1}{2}$ inch galvanized hardware cloth had an average strength of over 4200 psi, which compares with the concrete typically used for stairs and sidewalks at 3500 psi.

Higher strength components are produced using lower current densities and taking more time. Components no longer "under power" and left to cure in sea water after substantial accretion seem to increase in hardness, possibly because of interaction with marine organisms.

Our third major area of experimentation began when we decided to explore the potential for flexibility of form and the creation of unique underwater spaces for recreational and aesthetic purposes. In April 1979, an underwater sculpture, doubling as an artificial reef, was built and submerged outside of Tague Bay Reef, St. Croix, Virgin Islands, at a depth of 35 feet. Consisting of a central shaft 21 feet high and 6 feet in diameter, surrounded by smaller ballast cylinders to produce a base diameter of 18 feet, it allows divers to go into the shaft from above, stand on the floor, and look out of a window cut out above them. Direct current for the sculpture is supplied by photovoltaic solar cells mounted on a metal rack in the vicinity.

Given that the accreted underwater structures attract and shelter marine life, that they can be given a wide variety of shapes and sizes, and that they can be constructed almost anywhere in the ocean, the potential of using such structures for underwater recreational facilities is great.

One possibility for application of the accretion process to underwater recreation is the expansion of existing underwater parks. Within the last year, a municipally operated underwater park in Puget Sound at Edmonds, Washington, was expanded to meet increased use. Even though the local divers expressed the wish for a new reef with some aesthetically appealing form, the traditional method of dumping tires and precast concrete into the water was employed. Not only could the accretion process have allowed for the construction of almost any desired form, it would have precluded the need to transport bulky materials from shore.

Accretion could also enable the creation of interesting new dive sites in areas where large natural underwater reefs do not occur.

Another possibility entails the construction of underwater facilities designed to suit particular instructional needs. Since the mineral accretion process can be employed at any depth within sport diving limits, we can develop facilities for all levels, from beginning to advanced, from cave diving to snorkeling.

The development of underwater zoos also shows promise. With increasing knowledge of marine fauna habitat requirements, it is not unlikely that we can attract specific species through correctly designed structures.

Whether it be for research or for recreation, the provision of an underwater accreted structure park would be a significant first step to a world of almost unlimited opportunities to improve our abilities to live and work underwater, and to enjoy the fascinating world of the sea around us.

THE JOROCTE PLANT:
A POTENTIAL RABIES CURE

PEDRO NORIEGA RUIZ
2a, Calle 50–16 Zona 11, "Molina de la Flores," Guatemala,
Guatemala

Guatemalan, born April 26, 1944. Food, drug, and other products analyst at Unified Laboratory of Central America. Chemistry and pharmacy education in Guatemala.

My project involves a two-year study to discover the active ingredients of a plant called Jorocte by the natives of Coban, one of the northern provinces of Guatemala. Repeated histories from this region indicate that the natives have successfully used this plant to cure rabies, *after* a person has developed the illness. The intention of my research is twofold: first, to scientifically ascertain whether this plant's active ingredients actually do cure this dread disease, and second, through the efforts made in working on this line of research, to encourage and promote both national and international interest in similar research programs for the study of medicinal plants that have been used for many centuries as traditional cures by the natives of our region. Additionally, the research program will contribute to the studies of the overall natural botanical medicine of Guatemala.

I plan to proceed along the following stages in this program. I will summarize each stage in a report.

First, I shall carry out a study of the botanical antecedents of the Jorocte plant. This will include correct botanical classification, and determination of the plant's botanical relations in family, genus, and species.

The second phase will be phytochemical studies. This will involve collection of fresh materials (flowers, fruits, stems, and roots) for subsequent laboratory drying processes. Qualitative analysis of the materials will be made. Then selective studies of the plant extracts will be made by thin layer chromatography, followed by selective comparison of the plant extracts by thin layer chromatography with infusion extracts from the leaves.

Next, initial pharmacological studies will be carried out in two steps. I will determine the oral ingestion effects of selected extracts in rabies-infected laboratory rats first, then in dogs infected with rabies. Following these tests, I will move to the fourth phase.

Taking those selected extracts that indicated pharmacological effects in the previous stage, I will purify them through a number of well-known techniques, including thin layer chromatography and chromatography column purifications. I will then use gas chromatography verifications of the purified extracts. One or more of the compounds will be subjected to infrared and ultraviolet spectral analysis, and to mass and nuclear magnetic resonance spectra. Then I will conduct an analysis of the derivative compounds and determine the chemical and structural identification of the compound(s).

The fifth phase will involve extraction and purification of enough quantities of one or more of the identified compounds with indicated pharmacological effect(s).

The penultimate step in the program will be the continuation of the pharmacological studies. Infected laboratory rats and dogs will be given intravenous or muscular injections of pure compounds in measured dosage at different levels of the compound(s). Similarly, intravenous or muscular inoculations of effective dosage will be given at different infection levels. Metabolic excretion studies will follow.

I will then prepare a written general report based on the partial reports from each stage of the study.

I will work at the Faculty of Chemical Sciences and Pharmacies of San Carlos State University of Guatemala. The public health ministry will provide the biological materials, serums, rabies vaccines, and naturally infected animals. I will obtain laboratory rats from the Nutrition Institute of Central America and Panama, and certain instrumental equipment and information from the Unified Laboratory of Central America and from the Central American Institute for Researching and Industrial Technology.

HIGH-ALTITUDE, PISTON-ENGINE, PROPELLER-DRIVEN PLANE

S. PHILIP CAMMACK
350 E. Rustic Road, Santa Monica, California 90402, U.S.A.

American, born December 27, 1934. Chief of Flight Test Coordination for a helicopter manufacturer. Engineering education in the United States.

The goal of this project is a new world altitude record for piston-engine propeller-driven aircraft. The current record of 56,046 feet was established in a Caproni Biplane on October 22, 1938. This record has not been surpassed, even though, with the application of modern turbocharger technology, altitudes far in excess of it are feasible.

For flight at altitude, the optimum aircraft has minimum weight, a high aspect ratio wing for developing a high lift/drag ratio, and sufficient wing area to permit flight at low speeds. This aircraft is in existence today in the form of sailplanes and powered sailplanes. They are not currently suitable for high-altitude flight because they lack the pressurized cabin, the propeller, and the power plant that would make them high-altitude fliers.

This project will use an existing powered sailplane of front-mounted engine and propeller configuration. Pilot pressurization will be by means of a full pressure suit. The existing propeller will be replaced by a large diameter, slow-turning one required when the tip of the prop turns at low Mach speeds at altitude. The major effort of the project, however, will be development of the engine.

The engine will be liquid cooled by the use of liquid/air heat exchangers. Since heat loss from an engine is approximately 34 percent of the engine shaft power developed, an attempt may be made to recover some of this energy by expanding the cooling air as it leaves the heat exchangers. The total thermal energy in the engine exhaust is about 159 percent of the energy delivered by the engine crankshaft; 47 percent of the fuel energy is exhausted, whereas 29.6 percent of the fuel energy is converted into crankshaft power. Recovery of a substantial portion of the thermal energy in the exhaust by means of turbochargers will be the prime challenge.

Exhaust-driven turbochargers (more efficient than shaft-driven) are widely used on aircraft and cars, with relatively mild compression ratios of $3:1$ (aircraft) and $1.4:1$ (autos). For this project, we seek a compression ratio of $90:1$, which means we will have to get suitable compressors and the power to drive them for supercharging a piston engine.

There will be four stages of supercharging, with intercoolers between the stages. The last three stages will be conventional centrifugal compressors. The first stage may be similar to the last three or may consist of a combination axial and centrifugal compressor, such as that used on small jet engines.

We have determined how large the engine should be on the basis of formulas derived from data about the aircraft. It weighs 1500 pounds and has flown at 53 mph at a lift/drag ratio of 29. At sea level we will fly at an indicated airspeed of 53 mph and maintain this indicated airspeed as we climb, thus maintaining the air pressure felt by the wing, and consequently an unchanged lift and drag. While this would call for 7.33 horsepower in sea level flight, airspeed of 53 mph indicated at 100,000 feet would be a true 449 mph, calling for 62.1 horsepower. As viscosity of air changes drastically at high altitudes, the Reynolds numbers suggest that drag will increase by a factor of 2 to 3. Boosting horsepower by 3 for this, we will require 186.3 horsepower, and since the propeller efficiency may be only 75 percent, the engine power we will need goes up to 248.4 horsepower. We will select the engine so that this power is available at full throttle, unsupercharged, at sea level.

At 100,000 feet, the exhaust gas energy available to the turbine of the supercharger will be about 295 horsepower (at an exhaust temperature of $1500°R$ and an efficiency of .8). The compressors will require about 263 horsepower from the turbines if the efficiency is .8.

If the efficiencies can be kept high, it will be possible to attain altitudes of approximately 100,000 feet. It is interesting that once we are at 100,000 feet, we are traveling at 449 mph, using 248.4 horsepower, while burning 18.6 gallons per hour of fuel. Therefore, we're getting 24.1 miles per gallon. Not bad! And, if we run out of gas, we can glide from 200 to 500 miles.

As the engine, turbocharging, and cooling are critical, we will build, develop, and dynamometer-test the power plant equipment using air tankage equipment to simulate high-altitude conditions. When this work is completed, the engine will be installed in the aircraft for the altitude attempt.

If altitude in excess of 100,000 feet can be attained, many interesting possibilities open up. Speed, distance, climbing records—some 50 to 60 significant ones—could be challenged. My personal ambition is not to claim all these records but to help create the aircraft that would make them possible.

The Evans windmill at the University of St. Andrews, January 1980.

VERTICAL-AXIS WINDMILL WITH HIGH-EFFICIENCY ALTERNATOR

FREDERICK C. EVANS
30, James Street, Pittenweem, Fife, Scotland KY10 2QN, U.K.

British, born April 4, 1929. Senior Lecturer in Electronics, Physics Department, University of St. Andrews. Physics/engineering education in the United Kingdom.

Our group, "Power and Wind," is presently testing a prototype windmill with a novel alternator as load. Our windmill is based on a patented, award-winning vertical-axis windmill of unusual design that has the particular virtues of being self-starting, simply constructed, and possessed of high efficiency. To the windmill, invented by the writer, is being added the alternator, designed by H. Winterbotham, another member of the group. The alternator is designed to run at the same speed as the windmill, so that no gearbox is needed, and to maintain high efficiency over the entire range of working speeds. A third member of the group, P. A. Woolsey, has provided financial assistance and will be organizing the future commercial side of the proposed business.

The present windmill and alternator are the largest that can be made using the personal financial resources of the inventors. Both the windmill and the alternator have been built largely by the inventors themselves.

The prototype structures are of adequate size to prove the principles involved, but the power output is only a few hundred watts. We believe the maximum from this structure will be around 1 kilowatt in a strong wind.

A practicable machine, to be of use in a small holding, or in a remote country house, would have to be rated at a power of about 10 kilowatts. Power output does not increase in direct proportion to the swept area of the windmill, but rather faster than the swept portion, so that this order of power would probably be achieved with a machine about $2\frac{1}{2}$ to 3 times the linear dimensions of the present one.

The reasons for this non-linear scaling are: (1) that we are working in a region in which the aerodynamic properties of the airfoil sections used change rather rapidly with Reynolds number, and (2) that the losses due to friction and drag become proportionately smaller as size increases. The alternator would only have to be made a little larger than at present because it is already capable of converting more power than the windmill currently provides. We therefore wish to build a matched windmill and alternator rated at 10 kilowatts, as a prototype for a production run.

We estimate that production machines will retail for about U.S. $1000 per kilowatt, which is well below the present general level of prices, because of the simplicity of the design. The working prototype, however, will cost considerably more because it will have to be provided with extensive instrumentation and data-logging facilities in order to optimize the design. There will also be some increased cost because we want to locate the next machine in an exposed site to maximize the annual energy conversion, in contrast to the present machine which is located on campus at the University of St. Andrews.

In summary, the project is to build a windmill of similar design to the prototype described below, but with a swept area of about 45 square meters, together with an alternator of about 10-kilowatt capacity.

The St. Andrews windmill design consists of a vertical shaft and 2 or more vertical blades supported by radius arms. Each blade pivots about a vertical axis near its leading edge—the angle through which it turns is controlled by a spring or other controlling force. To minimize pivoting due to centrifugal forces, each blade is balanced, or partly balanced, by a counterweight carried ahead of the blade.

Wind causes the blades to rotate into typical positions, meaning that the aerodynamic force on the two (or more) blades also has a component tending to rotate the windmill in a clockwise direction, except at the two points where the blade is parallel with the wind. When the windmill is rotating at speed, the apparent wind is at a small angle to a given blade, the flow of air over the aerofoil section is non-turbulent, and the blade is working under efficient aerodynamic conditions. This construction also gives an important self-regulating action, which solves the problem of windmills tending to break apart due to centrifugal forces at high speeds unless some kind of braking mechanism is included. With our windmill design, two mechanisms control this problem: (1) As the wind gets stronger, the increasing force on the blades causes them to turn to a smaller angle of attack; and (2) if the blades are only partly balanced, they will tend to swing outward at high rotational speeds and produce their own air-brake effect. This self-regulating action allows the designer to control the maximum power output, which we estimate to be on the order of a few hundred watts per square meter of swept area.

DEVELOPING LOW-COST MEDICAL APPARATUS FOR MONITORING PATIENTS

GÉRARD P. HANUSSE
50, Avenue J. F. Kennedy, 59800 Lille, France

French, born January 1, 1947. General practice physician. Educated in mathematics, electronics, and medicine in France.

This project is concerned with the researching and development of new, low-cost medical apparatus and equipment designed to fill certain needs within the world of medical treatment.

For the proper observation and care of patients, one of two very costly methods is currently necessary: human attendance or costly and sophisticated electronic devices. I propose substitution of lower-cost devices for certain monitoring chores, in an attempt to reduce the costs of medical treatment. Specifically, I have selected four areas for research and development: a heart rate monitor, a standard infusions monitor, an arterial blood pressure monitor, and an artificial kidney monitor. The first two are now developed and ready for production; the artificial kidney monitor is nearly finished with its development phase, and the arterial blood pressure monitor still needs more research.

This work began in July 1973 when I was a medical student, working at night as a nurse. I learned of the numerous difficulties encountered with infusion problems, as much by the patient as by the nurse. I worked for a year to make a prototype of an infusion monitor, but testing showed weaknesses in the system. I returned to my researches and finished my medical studies with a thesis on "Infusion and Its Appliances." Now, six years after the first prototype, I have developed a monitor that is ready for production. In the course of the development work, I began to broaden the concept of making low-cost monitoring apparatuses.

Broadly speaking, when a doctor must watch over and treat a patient, the needs are quite similar whatever the specialty care department may be— monitoring of temperature, heart rate, arterial pressure, the flow of urine, etc., and checking on infusions, injections, oral medicine receipt, etc. To do this monitoring and checking, either human or technological means are employed. The human solution—nurses, for example—has the irreplaceable qualities of human warmth and devotion, yet at the same time unforeseeable mistakes and weariness occur. Shortages in available qualified staff and rising costs of personnel limit nursing care. As a result, technical means are employed as often as possible, and these solutions mean very different things, depending upon the nature of the hospital's departments or mission. What do we propose?

Heart Monitoring

Because of the constant relation between pathology and heart rate, we used to watch over heart rate even in the absence of cardiac injury. More sensible would be to constantly monitor the rate, with an alarm signaling a move away from the basic rhythm. My monitor, about billfold size, without electrode problems, gives an alarm within narrow ranges, chosen in percentages ($\pm 5\%$) or absolute values (± 10 pulse beats). The nurse may place the unit directly under the back of a motionless patient, just to one side of the thorax, or fasten it by means of an adhesive ribbon or elastic belt. There is no switch, no conductive paste, no contact to plug in, no tuning to do. The alarm unit is fixed on the room's wall, and eventually connected to a watching center. The price of the H.R. Monitor could be about $1000 without the alarm unit, which would be common with the other monitors.

Infusion Monitoring

In my thesis, based on 266,231 hospitalization days in 20 Medical and Surgical Services, I showed statistically that one in seven patients is connected to an infusion, receives about 2.1 liters per day, at a cost of FF 19.64 just for the varied tubes. I showed that a good Infusion Monitor could save about FF 4.50 for tubes and an additional FF 8.00 in nursing time. The many systems available for such use (peristaltic pumps, automatic syringes) are applications that are limited to Intensive Care Unit requirements and budgets.

After seven years' work on the subject, I can say that any infusion's apparatus will be unworkable if it doesn't perform simultaneously *two functions:* first, control the infusion pressure between the physiological venous pressures, and second, control the flow rate (not the drops rate, which is too indefinite).

I propose now a lightweight Infusion Monitor that grips directly on any infusion's gallows; the infusion pipe is just introduced on location. Then total volume of the bottle and total duration of the infusion are set on two simple dials. Apart from troubles signaled by the alarm, there is nothing else for the nurse to do. The alarm will call the nurse shortly before the bottle is empty. No contact to plug in, no wire, no switch. No problem with the drops volume, or viscousness of the fluid: the I.M. itself measures the real drops volume, calculates and regulates the ideal drop rate. The infusion pressure is externally controlled, giving an alarm if it increases (choke conditions) or if it lessens (disconnection conditions). I estimate the price for this unit to be approximately $2000.

Arterial Blood Pressure Monitoring

I think it is regrettable that wide awake patients in Middle Care Departments should be forced to support a continuously inflating and deflating armlet as a means of providing a constant watch on this important parameter. I have designed an A.P. monitor whose pick-up would be placed in front of a peripheric and anastomotic artery, and connected to a control unit giving maxima, minima, and middle arterial pressure values, and sending alarms to a common alarm unit. This unit needs more work to increase its artlessness, accuracy, auto-adjust, and stability.

Artificial Kidney Monitoring

Today we can adjust for weight loss in a patient during hemodialysis by acting upon blood flow, blood pressure, concentration or flow of bath, but we can't measure this loss of weight instantaneously. The A.K. monitor I propose is set on the blood circuit and, using an original ultrasonic method, gives and displays weight loss instantly. As with the units above, an alarm sounds if weight loss moves aside from the ordered values.

Conclusion

Born seven years ago in the work on the Infusion Monitor, my project has now become an attempt to bring a wide range of low-cost monitoring appliances into use by Middle Level Medical Departments or hospitals. I believe the project is not simply a number of separate monitor units placed side by side, but that its concept is embedded in the unity of its common alarm and performances. The underlying philosophy is to create useful and low-cost apparatuses for the daily problems encountered in medical treatment and care, wherever such devices could be used to good advantage.

DEVELOPMENT OF AN ULTRALIGHT AIRCRAFT

DONALD R. CRAWFORD

221 Calle de Madrid, Redondo Beach, California 90277, U.S.A.

American, born April 14, 1940. Technical Staff Member, TRW Defense and Space Sciences Group. Aeronautical engineering education (Ph.D.) in the United States.

T he long-range goal of this project is the development of an efficient ultralight personal aircraft. The more immediate goal of this venture is to win the International Birdman Rally at Bognor-Regis, England, in the summer of 1981. The skills and techniques learned in this competitive process should carry over into the design and construction of a practical personal aircraft for the 1980's.

The challenge of the Birdman Rally is to see if it is possible to glide 50 meters from a platform 30 feet high—with the restrictions that the wingspan of the gliding craft can be no larger than 30 feet and that the machine must be launched solely by the pilot. The complicating factor is that there is usually a 10- to 14-knot headwind that must be overcome. I believe this goal can be met if the physics of the problem are understood.

As a theoretical aerodynamicist, I am interested in the mathematical relationships that govern the behavior of a glider in a headwind. As a private pilot, hang glider pilot, and member of the Experimental Aircraft Association, I am curious to know why no one has been able to claim the £1000 prize of the International Birdman Rally—to glide 50 meters from a 30-foot platform in a 10- to 14-knot headwind. This project is designed to do just that, giving me a chance to coordinate theory with the actual design, construction, and test of a glider.

Although this specific contest is a definite goal, I believe that the technology and enthusiasm it generates can be extrapolated to the development of an efficient, practical, personal ultralight aircraft for use in the 1980's. With current trends in the availability of gasoline, the personal airplane as we know it may become obsolete. I propose to continue the development of the ultralight aircraft by first designing a glider to satisfy the requirements of this contest.

A simplified analysis of steady gliding flight in a headwind is described in a paper enclosed with this application. The important parameters are weight, drag area, effective span, and wind speed. The object of the analysis is to optimize the apparent glide angle for the aircraft in the presence of a headwind.

Two concepts must necessarily enter into the problem. The first involves determining the maximum lift-to-drag ratio of the craft in calm air. The second is penetration or, said another way, how well does the aircraft fly compared to the wind speed it is registering. Both of these properties—maximum lift-to-drag ratio in calm air and penetration—are critical if the requirements of the contest are to be met. For example, if the aircraft has a good glide ratio, but the flight speed is too slow, the aircraft may be blown backward, having a terrible glide angle.

To maximize the lift-to-drag ratio, the aircraft must have a large wingspan compared to the square root of the drag area. Obviously, therefore, if the wingspan is to be constrained to 30 feet, the airplane must be suitably streamlined to attain a good glide ratio. The best penetration into a headwind can be attained with the gliding speed large compared to wind speed. For a fixed configuration—one in which drag area and wing area remain constant—a faster gliding speed will be found with a heavier airplane. This is desirable under normal conditions, but not in this particular contest, because the airplane must be self-launched by the pilot. Launching will require a reasonable take-off speed, and this constraint means that the weight of the craft must be reasonably easy to handle by the contestant. In addition, the problems associated with the transition from take-off to the position for achieving the best glide angle must also be carefully analyzed.

With the technical expertise achieved in the pursuit of this well-defined goal, the development of an efficient and practical ultralight aircraft design should proceed quite naturally.

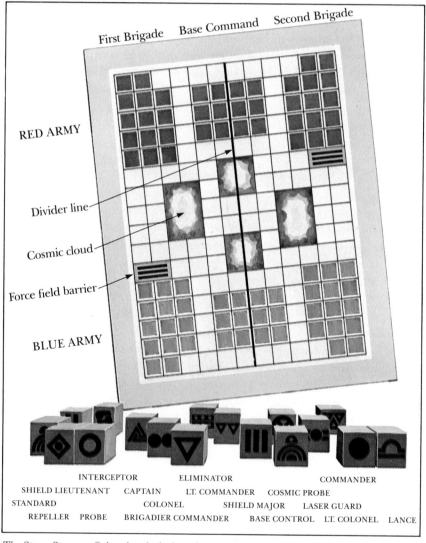

First Brigade   Base Command   Second Brigade

RED ARMY

Divider line

Cosmic cloud

Force field barrier

BLUE ARMY

INTERCEPTOR   ELIMINATOR   COMMANDER
SHIELD LIEUTENANT   CAPTAIN   LT. COMMANDER   COSMIC PROBE
STANDARD   COLONEL   SHIELD MAJOR   LASER GUARD
REPELLER   PROBE   BRIGADIER COMMANDER   BASE CONTROL   LT. COLONEL   LANCE

The Space Stratagem© board and playing pieces.

SPACE STRATAGEM© AND SPASTRACON

ALEX K. DE GUZMAN
7 Evardoni Street, San Francisco del Monte, Quezon City, Metro Manila, Philippines

Filipino, born July 10, 1959. College student (Geology major) at University of the Philippines. Youngest Filipino Inventor in 1974.

With the advent of space exploration, humanity realized the need to extend its frontiers to the limitless reaches of space and to discover new worlds. We will traverse this vastness, facing the unknown with its daunting perils and obstacles. Ultimately, these explorations will necessitate a system of organized space armies to overcome the barriers encountered and to defend against hostile environments.

With these ideas in mind, I first conceived Space Stratagem© as a realistic simulation of space armies battling to gain extraterrestrial colonies. Space Stratagem© is a board game involving effective deployment of space armies to deter opponent aggression and eventually to seize the enemy camp. Strategy is an essential element in winning the game. Surprise and superior mobilization are likewise important components of strategy, which consists of effective planning and organizational coordination among independent forces acting as one space army.

With the invention of Space Stratagem© (Philippine Patent UM 1638), I felt the need to establish an organization that could make the most effective use of its capabilities. This was SPASTRACON (Space Strategists Confederation), which was formally inaugurated in July 1976. Its primary aim was using Space Stratagem© to provide the young people of the world with knowledge of strategy and organization. Furthermore, SPASTRACON aimed to achieve intellectual and creative growth through engaging its members in mental gymnastics and group dynamic techniques within a socially operational atmosphere of intelligence pursued within the ideals of brother-hood and mutual cooperation.

During its first year, SPASTRACON flourished as one of the most success-ful youth organizations. Moves were made to initiate a game production program, with a monthly output of 10 handmade units. Simultaneously, another program on strategic development and self-discovery sessions on cre-ativity were undertaken. With the march of time, we had enough sets among six independent chapters in different prestigious schools to start a tournament in Space Stratagem©. During this period, two "Clash of Minds" tournaments were officiated.

However, during the following year, events proved otherwise. What I had conceived for the organization was becoming more and more difficult to achieve. We were faced with a lack of operating funds to support any massive project within the Confederation. More importantly, we were faced with the physical absence of the games themselves on the Philippine market. In our opinion, the commercial absence of the game is due to its unique complexity, which fails to convince possible investors of its potentially large market. The intellectual significance of the game has not been sufficient to bring it to market, and this has lowered the morale of the members, who have dwindled now to a small group in the University of the Philippines.

I intend to reorganize SPASTRACON with a new perspective and with a new systems design. Space Stratagem© will serve as the basis for various activities in the attainment of the Confederation's objectives. I believe SPASTRACON can be used as the base for relevant, pertinent, and contrib-utory studies and researches in a variety of fields. For instance, as a youth-oriented organization, it can be a laboratory where members would be sub-jected to different testing situations. A psychometric study of reactions to situations can be a foundation for other extensive analysis of correlations between logic, judgment, and skill. Such a study could prove useful in formu-lating new approaches to learning techniques. The principle involved here is the selective monitoring of proper stimuli to elicit *creative reactions*.

Additionally, mathematically quantifying the game is apparently possible, using tools from mathematical game theory. If this is true, then a match of the game can be mathematically mapped out and possibly programmed by computers. This might result in a new branch of game theory, which would find myriad applications in decision making, military strategy, economic forecasts, and so on.

In view of these proposed program studies, the Departments of Mathe-matics and Psychology of the University of the Philippines, working inde-pendently, have committed academic assistance to SPASTRACON. We will, nevertheless, need sufficient funding, perhaps in the form of grants, to carry out these studies.

I also intend to strengthen the organization's capacity to conduct new and effective techniques in group dynamics sessions, to further elicit the creative thinking of the members. In addition, SPASTRACON will again initiate tournaments among Space Stratagem© players, where their skills will be put to demanding tests. Through this, we hope and dream that SPASTRACON will become an international organization of board-game enthusiasts.

All this is but mere speculation at present. None of these goals will be achieved without the game in public circulation. What I need is a chance to prove its worth and value, not as a commercial commodity, but as an intellectually creative device. I need to finance the manufacturing of a few hundred sets to back up the objectives of SPASTRACON.

[Editor's note: The following is a brief, general description of the game of Space Stratagem©, taken from the inventor's rule book.]

The Game Board consists of 192 squares (12 × 16). Four "Cosmic Clouds," two "Force Field Barriers," and a "Divider Line" are already in place on the board.

The Game Pieces comprise two space armies (there are only two players), one red and one blue, each army consisting of 40 pieces. They include a Base Control, Standard, Commander, Lieutenant Commander, Brigadier Commander, Colonel, Lt. Colonel, Shield Major, Captain, and Shield Lieutenant, ranked from highest to lowest. Additional pieces include the Lance, the Cosmic Probe, and the Probe, which are equally ranked. And finally, the pieces identified as Eliminator, Laser Guard, Repeller, and Interceptor are exceptional ranks.

The Objective of the Game is to set up a coordinated strategy of defense and offense to eliminate the opponent's Base Control or both of the opponent's Standards. Occasionally, the objective may be to immobilize the opponent by bringing him or her to the point where only his or her Base Control or Standards can be moved.

Set-up Formation has a Space Army dividing its composition into three commands, known as the 1st and 2nd Brigades and the Base Command. Game pieces of these commands are distinguished by color codes marked within the ranks. At the start of each game, each player positions a Space Army in columns facing each other as shown in the illustration. Ranks of the player's own Space Army face him, and are therefore unidentified to the opponent.

Moves alternate and are described in the author's rule book.

A SIMPLE METHOD FOR FRACTIONATING AMNIOTIC FLUID PHOSPHOLIPIDS

HUGH Y. YEE
Hutzel Hospital, Detroit Medical Center, 4707 St. Antoine, Detroit, Michigan 48201, U.S.A.

American, born September 1, 1931. Clinical chemist, Director of hospital laboratory. Education in the United States.

My project is the development of a relatively simple column chromatographic method for fractionating the amniotic fluid phospholipids. This method will not require any elaborate or expensive instrumentation, so that smaller, lesser equipped laboratories will be able to perform and offer a phospholipid profile. Recent work by Gluck and associates has indicated that the use of a profile has a greater predictive accuracy than the widely used lecithin/sphingomyelin (L/S) ratio test for assessing fetal lung maturity. Knowledge of this test data will enable the physician to manage problem pregnancy patients toward a successful outcome with maximum maternal and fetal well-being. Fractionation and measurement of all of the phospholipids will also help to elucidate how each of these lung surfactants are involved in the development of fetal lung maturity.

The major cause of most lifelong neurological damage, asphyxia, originates during the perinatal period. The incidence of neurological handicaps in children surviving respiratory disease syndrome (RDS) is several times greater than that for the normal population. RDS affects about 10–15 percent of all infants weighing less than 2500 grams ($5\frac{1}{2}$ pounds) at birth. Thus, one of the major factors predisposing to perinatal mortality and morbidity from RDS appears to be prematurity. The majority of the fatal cases of RDS are less than 35 weeks gestation, whereas term infants will only occasionally develop RDS.

The synthesis and release of phospholipids in the lungs is an important factor for fetal lung maturity, contributing to the stability of the peripheral airways by inhibiting the collapse of the alveoli at low lung volume during expiration, and also acting as an anti-edema factor by inhibiting the exudation of liquid from the pulmonary circulation into the airways. Lung surfactant can be recovered either from endobrachial lavage fluid or isolated from lung tissue homogenate. The purified complex contains 85–95 percent lipid and 10–20 percent protein. About 90–95 percent (weight to weight) of the lipids are phospholipids with the remainder being cholesterol. Numerous investigations have proven that measurement of amniotic fluid phospholipids yield a valuable assessment of fetal pulmonary maturity.

At this time, the most widely used assay is the lecithin/sphingomyelin ratio developed by Gluck and co-workers. The L/S ratio can be classified as a measure of the disaturated or acetone-precipitable lecithin. Sphingomyelin is used as an internal marker, because its percentage composition remains relatively constant from a gestational age of 34 weeks until term. Various steps bring the test to measurement of a treated plate by reflectance densitometry. Normally, a value of 2.0 indicates fetal lung maturity. However, with intermediate values of 1.5 to 1.9, approximately 50 percent of the infants will develop RDS, and below 1.5 the risk increases to 73 percent. More recent evidence shows, however, that not just lecithin but several of the other phospholipids are involved in the development of fetal lung maturity, and, as a result, that more accurate testing procedures are needed.

To circumvent many of the problems from analytical variables, I have developed a method for measuring the total phospholipid concentration, expressed as phosphorus (TPP). The current methodology for obtaining an amniotic fluid phospholipid profile involves a two-dimensional thin layer chromatographic technique. Costly, and requiring thin layer plates not commercially available, this process is not readily within the budget or technical expertise of smaller labs, particularly in Third World countries.

My technique is a relatively simple column chromatographic process, and the only instrumentation needed is an inexpensive spectrophotometer. The procedure is basically an extension of my lecithin assay using calcium hydroxyapatite. The additional work required is the separation of lecithin and sphingomyelin, which are now found in the same fraction, and the remaining phospholipids into individual fractions. Quantification would be based upon hot acid digestion to inorganic phosphate and the usual reaction with molybdate followed by reduction to a blue color measured at 660 nanometers. I must investigate to find the appropriate column chromatographic conditions and, in particular, suitable eluting solvent systems, to effect a quantitative separation of all of the phospholipids found in amniotic fluid. Such a system will provide us with significantly enhanced ability to determine the degree to which other factors may affect fetal maturity.

CREATING BETTER CORN VIA A SYSTEMS APPROACH

JON E. HOLTZMAN
4610 Jenewein Road, Suite 6, Madison, Wisconsin 53711, U.S.A.

American, born August 1, 1939. Nutritionist, working on this project. Educated in the United States.

An on-going project began in 1976 when descendants of Reid open-pollinated corn (*Zea mays* L.) produced weight gains in albino rats nearly comparable to that of an opaque-2, floury-2 commercial hybrid corn. The current project seeks to modify the amino acid profile of non-mutant endosperm Reid corn by means of a full sib recurrent breeding program and lab procedures that include ninhydrin dye-binding assays, microbiological assays and rat feeding tests.

I have taken leave, apart from part-time consulting, from a company that produces albino rats in large quantities for scientific purposes. In manufacturing up to 1000 metric tons of a laboratory rat diet for this commercial feeding operation—one million rats per year—least cost formulation techniques showed that cost savings could be achieved by minimizing the amounts of protein supplements purchased from distant suppliers, while maximizing the use of corn that could be grown in nearby fields used for rat manure disposal. However, if corn were to replace some of the supplements, the corn would have to contain higher levels of certain amino acids than present corns can give.

A number of varieties of commercially available corns were tested, and a Reid[2] open-pollinated composite was considered suitable for further breeding and selection techniques.

A program was put into effect, with a complete array of testing procedures to be carried out on various key objectives (level of lysine in seed to be planted and so on). Seed is selected according to a desired amino acid profile. Other factors influencing selection include agronomic fitness, grain drying speed, test weight, fat content, grain yield, and carotene content. Two generations of corn are grown per year; and 2500+ ears of corn are tested per year. No fewer than 100 ears of corn are kept to avoid a rapidly increasing coefficient of inbreeding.

In one selection cycle, up to 30 self-pollinations are made in the progeny of each of about 300 ears selected from up to 15 acres of open-pollinated corn. Next, the best testing 15 ears are intercrossed (intermated) and up to 70 matings are made per cell in the resulting 15×15 matrix grid. Next, the 100 best ears from ninhydrin assays are retested microbiologically for lysine and methionine. Finally, the 30 best ears from the microbiological assays are each grown in isolation, and rat feeding tests are conducted on a portion of the harvest. A fraction of the best feeding corn is inbred or intercrossed further, and the remaining seed is random-pollinated as the start of another improvement cycle.

While the main effort is on developing a corn with an amino acid profile that produces the highest weight gain in rats, three ancillary projects could further explore the diversity of the Reid corn. First, acetylene reduction (an indicator of atmospheric nitrogen fixation). Second, fermentation ethanol yields. Third, evaluation of a quadruple mutant (waxy, opaque-2, floury-2, and sugary-1) in combination with the Reid corn.

I have included a fairly detailed description of the testing procedures, methods used, and results, both of rat feeding and of the agricultural spin-offs of this work.

This project aims at two goals. First, to offer the farmer (including the albino rat producer) an alternative to planting lower commercial hybrids and being obliged to buy extra protein supplements. Second, to maintain as much diversity as possible so that this Reid cultivar may be swiftly adapted to growing conditions around the world. If this project continues beyond 1982, there may be a third desirable result. There are few lines of genetically divergent corn with good general and specific combining ability. In efforts to produce higher yields, agronomists search the world for mutant or isolated species of corn to meet the continuing need for combining ability. For 20 years prior to the inception of my nutrition improvement project, my Reid corn was grown in partial isolation. As a result of my selection, this corn is diverging further from its genetic source. The significance of this project for posterity will be in proportion to the extent that this Reid corn exhibits combining ability.

The preliminary version of the world's fastest sailboat.

THE WORLD'S FASTEST SAILBOAT

PATRICK J. CUDMORE
Box 1243, Duxbury, Massachusetts 02332, U.S.A.

American, born September 12, 1941. Research and development company president. Architectural and design education in the United States.

I intend to build a 1 or 2 man hydrofoil sailboat that will be the fastest sailboat in the world. This sailboat will be manufactured easily and inexpensively, making it the world's first commercially produced hydrofoil sailboat. It will be practical, easy to sail, and will make the experiences of speed and flight in the water accessible to all.

To fly. To go beyond existing limits. To be in harmony with the basic forces of nature. These are desires, perhaps even drives, punctuating again and again the history of human endeavor. My practical hydrofoil sailboat will not only break the existing world speed record for sail but will also partially satisfy these three aspirations.

The dream of flight has been with us from the time of the earliest recorded civilizations. It permeates our myths and fantasies. It could be a recognition of a longing to become again, as we once were, contiguous with nature—with it and of it, not against it.

Our dream, to a large extent, has been realized. We have learned to fly. The evolution of human flight, through air and through water, has followed the same pattern. We mastered aerial flight initially through discovery of buoyant lift, where the pressure of the medium provides the supporting lift. Then dirigibles and hot-air balloons gave way to aircraft whose wings created dynamic lift. The motion through the medium developed the pressure that lifted the craft.

In water, the evolution from buoyant to dynamic lift has been far less successful. The concept of the hydrofoil, which creates dynamic lift, has been around since the late nineteenth century, but so far it has not fulfilled its original promise of faster and more efficient boats. Witness the fact that the current holder of the world's sail speed record is merely a modified conventional hull, employing only buoyant lift. The fastest hydrofoil boats are 30 percent slower.

Hydrofoil boats, in general, have merely added the elements of dynamic lift (hydrofoils) onto the element of buoyant lift (conventional hulls). I have invented the first sailboat that successfully integrates the dynamic and buoyant lift components into a single hull structure.

I have constructed a preliminary version of my design. This boat, in testing, verified my basic design assumptions. It is faster than most conventional sailboats and imparts a unique and exhilarating sensation of true flight. However, this version is not competitive in its low-speed performance. The prototype I wish to build is a modification of the original hull design that will significantly improve both low- and high-speed performance. It is coupled with a breakthrough invention in sail technology, to create not only the world's fastest sailboat, but also a prototype for the world's first commercially feasible hydrofoil sailboat.

This is not an esoteric, experimental design with performance as its only criterion. I have imposed another constraint. I wanted a design that could be mass-produced easily and inexpensively, making the dramatic sensations of flight, speed, and unity with natural forces available to the average person.

Since the sail design is not yet protected, I am withholding it at this time. I can say, however, that it is a sailwing employing the superior lift capabilities of the Liebeck Airfoil. The same principles were used in the airfoils of the *Gossamer Condor* and *Gossamer Albatross,* winners of the Kremer Prizes for human-powered aircraft. If necessary, I will submit my design to the Selection Committee.

Only the final step of this project is incomplete. I have already done a detailed hydrodynamic and aerodynamic analysis of the design. I have shaped the wooden plug from which the mold for the fiberglass modules will be made. Only the actual construction remains to be done—fabricating the hull and making the Liebeck sailwing. My ideas have been proven in prototype and theory; the design is complete. All I need is the money to build it.

The theoretical and mathematical analysis shows that this prototype will be a tremendous advance over current hydrofoil sailboat designs for the following reasons:

1. *Easier Control.* This prototype replaces the classic rudder with a new and simpler control system.

2. *Superior Performance.* In average winds, it can be sailed up to 100 percent faster than current hydrofoils and conventional sailboats.

3. *Wider "Flight" Range.* It will lift out ("fly") at a boat speed of $3\frac{1}{2}$ knots. Current hydrofoil sailboats require speeds three to four times that in order to "fly." Thus, this design will provide far more opportunities to "fly" in light wind conditions.

4. *High-Speed Safety.* The hydrofoils on this prototype cannot ventilate and lose lift at high speed. "Ventilation" (air entrainment) plagues all current hydrofoil sailboats and often precipitates capsizing under high speed.

5. *Simplicity and Unity of Design.* The boat is beautiful as well as being commercially viable.

My hydrofoil's total performance, therefore, will be truly exceptional. It will attain a speed 1.5 to 2.5 times that of true wind speed, while even the fastest conventional sailboats rarely exceed 1.5 times true wind speed. It will surpass the current world speed record for sail of 34 knots, in wind speeds of just 13–21 knots. This is no more than a moderate to fresh breeze.

With this design, the experience of surpassing the existing world speed record will not be limited to a single expert sailor in an intricate and temperamental craft. It can be shared by millions of people. Yet this is not its only benefit. We are in danger of destroying our planet because we do not fully comprehend our relationship to the rest of the natural world. This hydrofoil can teach a vivid lesson: we do not have to subdue and conquer natural forces to use and control them. We *can* have safe access to their awesome energies. A person can cruise with this hydrofoil at power boat speeds, using only wind and water. In fact, this hydrofoil's greatest contribution may be symbolic and intangible—a recognition that we are one with the world we inhabit and that, in harming it, we must thereby harm ourselves.

STEPS TOWARD A FLAT WALL-HUNG TELEVISION

SAKAE TAJIMA
4-2-10, Kyodo, Setagaya-ku, Tokyo 156, Japan

Japanese, born April 13, 1917. Professor in charge of Tokyo University Laboratory of Electrochemistry/Inorganic Chemistry. Science education in Japan.

The two-dimensional electroluminescence (EL), photoluminescence (PL), or electrochromism (EC) of display devices of any size and shape is our goal. We use anodic oxide films on aluminum, and on a laboratory scale we have developed not only liquid state but also solid state illumination in EL and PL, plus an EC color source. We are now attempting to extend these capabilities to large and intricately shaped illumination and display devices of a kind impossible before now. We expect that using any shape or size of aluminum as a substrate material will be possible, thus sharply reducing costs compared with gallium/arsenic (GaAs), zinc/sulfur (ZnS), and activators.

The traditional candle light and Edison's incandescent light are so-called point lights, with very poor heat and energy efficiency. Subsequent developments led to the invention of a linear light source—the mercury fluorescent lamp—which is widely used. The idea of a "flat source" of light, however, is fairly new, although a similar concept exists, for example, in heating and cooling systems, in which two-dimensional flat or wall heaters/coolers have been made.

The concept of a two-dimensional light source has come about only recently with the development of the light-emitting diode (LED) and the numerical liquid crystal display (LCD), using such expensive materials as GaAs, ZnS plus activators or organic materials. These, however, are so small that they can't really be considered illumination or used as flat light sources. Two-dimensional light sources that may be used for illumination as well as for displays of any size and shape are not now available.

This project seeks to achieve such a two-dimensional light source of wet or dry (solid state) type under electric field or ultraviolet (UV) irradiation, with minimal loss of heat energy. The basic material used is aluminum, which can be fabricated as sheet or tubes, in any shape of any size, cast or extruded. I have nearly finished and clarified the basic models of the underlying principles and have published papers in world-recognized scientific journals on the subject; reprint requests have come in from around the globe. (I have about 40 years' experience in scientific research on anodic oxidation of aluminum (anodic alumina films) and was Plenary Lecturer in September 1976 at the Meeting of the International Society of Electrochemistry at Zurich.)

Based on scientific research on liquid state electroluminescence on anodically oxidized aluminum, I have developed a solid state electroluminescence device and a solid state photoluminescence device, in which the light is intensified by suitable heat treatment of alumina film. In an original development, I clarified that the mechanism of luminescence was due to the excited carboxylate radicals under high electric potential during anodic formation and/or to their further excitement by treatment with heat.

Just recently, in my group, we have developed an electrochromic display device (liquid state technology) by immersing the anodized aluminum in a metal-complex solution and then heat-treating it. When this plate is cathodic, it colors blue; when the polarity of the plate is reversed, the color disappears. We are now working to do this with a solid state device for display. Until now, much research in advanced countries has been done on electrochromic devices (ECD's) based on the evaporation of tungsten oxide on silicon or glass. The electric connection is quite difficult to make, and there are other problems preventing success in this particular line of research. Our ECD operates under only 1 DC volt, and energy loss is nil. Weak points still exist with our device, however, such as achieving liquid state ECD and hastening the response time of the color decay.

However, our three devices, taken together, possess unique potential. The earlier-mentioned solid state EL and PL aluminum-based device originally emitted blue light. We have shown that it can emit other colors by putting the element europium in the pores of anodic oxide to achieve reddish light or by alloying manganese with aluminum to achieve an orange color. Based on research to date, therefore, we believe that with further development a flat, wall-hung television is not an impracticable dream.

In short, our final goal, starting from the research described here, using the information on EL, PL, and EC with aluminum as a base metal (by itself an original work), is to put these elements together in a way that provides practical use and a revolutionary new means of illumination.

COULD AN ANTI-GRAVITY SUBSTANCE PROPEL MANNED SPACECRAFT TO THE PLANETS?

DONALD VAN Z. WADSWORTH
1211 Via Granate, Sierra Madre, California 91024, U.S.A.

American, born July 14, 1931. Senior Scientist, Systems Laboratories, Hughes Aircraft Company. Physics education in the United States.

To significantly shorten the timetable for manned exploration of the planets, a radical improvement in spacecraft propulsion is needed. This would be provided if an anti-gravity substance could be found in nature. The proposed project is a methodical search, guided by cosmological and physical theory and sensitive detection equipment, for usable concentrations (one part or more per million) of such an anti-gravity substance in ancient earth rocks, lunar samples, meteorites, chondrules, and so on.

Radical discovery requires boldness to act on the logic of radical ideas and the persistence to leave no corner unturned. Such is the spirit of this proposed research, believed to be the first methodical search for useful quantities of *levitonium,* a conjectured anti-gravity substance that would have all the properties of ordinary matter except for a "negative" gravitational mass. It would be repelled by ordinary matter but is not to be confused with what physicists call anti-matter.

Such a research project might seem to be a long shot indeed, since there is no supporting evidence to date, but neither has there been any thorough search. If both ordinary matter and levitonium originated according to the big bang model of the universe, or even in astronomical black holes, their mutual repulsion would ensure a high degree of separation prior to condensation of the solar nebula. Yet trace amounts of levitonium might be locked into our solar system by molecular or atomic forces. The existence of levitonium is not incompatible with modern physical theories, including Einstein's general theory of relativity (contrary to common opinion).

The hypothesis of levitonium appeals from the standpoint of natural symmetry. Electric charges of opposite sign exist in nature, obeying the law that like charges repel and unlike charges attract. If gravitational forces were to exhibit an analogous symmetry, then gravitational "charges" of opposite type would have to exist, in which like and unlike charges must necessarily complement each other.

To make levitonium compatible with the general theory of relativity, it is necessary to invoke the particle nature of matter, which implies a law of mutual exclusion, and to understand that the principle of equivalence applies to magnitude of the gravitational mass, but not to its sign.

Applicability to spacecraft propulsion can be summarized here as follows. Using a manned mission to Mars for a soft landing and the return of a 5-tonne module would require a chemical propulsion launch vehicle with a mass of over 1000 tonnes. The same mission would require only a 100-tonne launch vehicle using levitonium, and the mission would be much safer.

Detection apparatus for the project is designed to indicate any imbalance in the gravitational-to-inertial mass ratio of a rock sample. It is based on the same principle used by previous investigators: suspend samples with equal gravitational masses from the arms of a torsion balance and observe whether there is a torque due to an imbalance between the centrifugal forces of the orbital motion around the sun and the solar gravitation acting on the samples. Accuracies to one part in 100 million (Eotvos in 1890) to one part in 100 billion (Dicke et al. in the 1960's) have been achieved, so there should be no problem in achieving the one part per million accuracy required for the proposed levitonium prospecting.

With a single detection apparatus, the maximum throughput would be one sample measurement per day, which is governed by the earth's rotation rate and apparatus damping constants. A sketch of the apparatus is available, though the design is straightforward.

The proposed program covers a minimum of three years and would solicit consulting support from local experts in physics, cosmology, and astronomy. The sample testing program would include samples of the most ancient earth rocks, the earth's mantle, meteorites, chondrules, tektites, and lunar rocks.

A search for stars or even galaxies of levitonium would be made by examining the relativistic deflection of electromagnetic energy that passes close to the sun's disk during eclipse. Photons of levitonium would be deflected away from the sun in contrast to ordinary photons. Cosmological and astrophysical models would be developed to estimate the possible retention level of levitonium in a condensing solar nebula. Finally, the implications of levitonium in elementary particle physics and nuclear reactions would be investigated.

VIRBELA FLOWFORMS

ANTHONY J. WILKES
Emerson College, Forest Row, Sussex, England

British, born July 5, 1930. Director of Sculpture Group and Flow Research Group. Educated in flow sciences and art in the United Kingdom and Germany.

Water is the life blood of the earth, with all living things dependent upon it. The life processes themselves involve the rhythmical flow of fluids. We have been engaged in research on the use of structures that generate the rhythmical, lemniscatory movement of streaming water (or any similar fluid), to promote, for instance, the enhanced assimilation of liquid nutrients by organisms.

The method we have developed can be implemented on a small or large scale, with minimum energy requirements, in any situation where life-support systems are involved (oxygenation, irrigation, therapy, etc.). Our proposal is to develop this method further by means of mathematical theory, in parallel with our current practice.

For ten years, we have worked to develop what we call the *Virbela Flowforms,* through which water flows in a characteristic manner because of the mutual relationships of a number of parameters established in a series of such flowforms. In each of the flowforms, a double vortex is formed, resulting in a lemniscatory movement of the water. The parameters consist of (a) the dimension and shape of the outlet and inlet, (b) the distance between these two, (c) the rate of flow, (d) the gradient, and (e) the overall shape of the containing vessel. All of these have to be brought into the "correct" relationship, empirically, which then brings about the oscillating movement. The frequency and character of the movement depend upon the size and shape of the flowform and upon the gradient.

Applications have been developed mainly from the artistic point of view, even though technical and functional problems are involved. For instance, processes of oxygenation and purification of polluted waters from small communities are being investigated. Flowforms were first incorporated in a biological sewage plant on the Baltic Sea at Järna, Sweden, seven years ago. Since then, two more have been built in Norway in similar installations. A large government-sponsored research plant at Warmonderhof in Holland has been running since autumn 1979. At this location, a group of scientists intend to investigate further what effect the rhythmical movements have upon the living organisms that provide the means of purification. For example, if microorganisms, which are "rhythmical" organisms very sensitive to their environment, are embedded in a strongly rhythmical surrounding, this might enhance or speed up their activities.

Even fish have been found to be sensitive to the rhythmical stream ensuing from flowform cascades; perhaps this would be useful in fish culture. Over the last two years, investigations on plant growth using rhythmically treated water have been carried out at a plant research station in Dexbach, Germany, with encouraging results; strong plants and increased harvest have been recorded.

Quite apart from the aesthetic involvements with installations in public areas and school installations, we are interested in raising and transporting liquids, controlling or regulating flows, and studying various mixing processes. This interest is not only directed at large-scale projects, but also is pertinent to the small scale, where sensitive fluids can be easily damaged, such as in therapeutic or pharmaceutical applications or in the treatment of blood.

The motive for this work springs from the conviction that, since life depends upon water, we need to compensate for our increasing industrial use of it by treating it consistent with its own nature. Although water appears to be an amorphous fluid that adapts itself to any container or movement, further examination shows its movement to have inherent laws that are not amorphous. Water naturally forms characteristic vortical movements and eddies, and recent mathematical work has shown that water vortices are a well-defined form that does not immediately arise from conventional fluid dynamics, but from a geometrical and non-differential approach to whole forms.

Water responds rhythmically to external stimuli, such as in wave motion. Conventional theory describes some of these responses, for example, that a natural frequency of oscillation exists in a finite vessel or that a large surface responds to local disturbance. Certain features nevertheless seem to go beyond current theory. Fluid dynamics is not truly founded on a molecular basis but rather on the continuum hypothesis, and our knowledge of the liquid state is still incomplete. There is, thus, adequate room for further development of the scientific theory of fluids, using as a basis the work done by Edwards, in his document, "The Watery Vortex."

The Virbela Flowform work has been largely based on artistic and empirical approaches, which have already borne fruit. Designed surfaces, arranged in the correct relationships within the flowform vessels according to the method described in our group's booklet, can be developed purely empirically from the flow dynamics of any given situation. They can also be derived from forms occurring in nature, such as shell surfaces.

What is needed now is to bring a scientific approach to bear on the problem to see how Virbela Flowforms can be optimized with the aid of exact and calculable theory. We want to be able to determine the correct relationship of the surfaces to each other on other than the purely empirical basis we have been using.

The mathematics envisaged is based on projective geometry, in which phenomena are treated holistically, rather than differentially, following the work of scientists whose methods have already proved fruitful in the study of the forms of plant buds and ovaries. The nature of the forces described by the geometry is unusual, for they are peripheral rather than central—that is, forces acting in a planar fashion of an opposite nature to gravity. George Adams has referred to them as *universal forces*.

The relationship already established between these universal forces and living things reinforces the suggestion of their connection with life. That they are also connected with the way water moves (through the geometry describing them) encourages the view that water is itself directly related to living rhythms. A scientific establishment of this relationship would be of the utmost interest and importance.

IMPROVING ULTRASONIC MEDICAL IMAGING

MARK E. IDSTROM

1440 June Avenue South, Golden Valley, Minnesota 55416, U.S.A.

American, born July 8, 1950. Fellow in Ultrasound Medicine, Coordinator of Cathode Tube Scan. Education in the United States.

U ltrasonic medical imaging is a promising new technique for viewing human tissue without ionizing radiation. However, its use is limited by various "artifacts" of the basic physics involved: gas reflection and non-uniform transducer response are believed to be the primary sources of error in the final image. This project addresses these limitations and will include a pattern characterization of gas reflections, development of methods to remove inaccuracies caused by gas reflection of acoustic energy, and development of methods to remove distortions caused by transducer response. The goal is to correct the data before viewing the display; the approach is divided into three main parts.

One of the significant barriers to the interpretation of ultrasound imagery is the almost complete reflection of a particular acoustic ray by air or gas: no data are obtained at a depth beyond the bubble. (Variations in reflections are discussed by Sample and Erikson in *Basic Principles of Diagnostic Ultrasound.*) The first part of the project will be a pattern characterization study performed by taking frames of gas reflection data from the Sonograf (trademark of the Unirad Corporation) memory, storing them on a secondary storage medium, such as a disk, and reviewing them with a remote computer, which will perform statistical analyses. In addition, the radio frequency data will be recorded to determine if signal amplitude data lost in the original amplitude detector can be used to characterize gas reflections.

Second, the characterization of the gas reflection will be used to identify areas of the image that are unspecified for the particular transmitted ray of energy because of the nearly complete reflection from the bubble. These areas may be filled in by other reflected acoustic rays or not, depending on previous and subsequent angles of transducer placement. The array of picture elements in the Sonograf memory for any given frame will be arranged to contain the best available information and not only the last available data. This is expected to take the form of an external control module performing the image enhancement and sending "corrected" arrays of data back to the Sonograf.

A third part of the project may be accomplished concurrently with the second and employ the same control module. This is an adjustment of the output data for the non-uniform transducer response. Filters will be designed to account for the characteristics. Data may be adjusted before or after the amplitude detector conversion. Both techniques will be examined in order to select the one that gives the more satisfactory results. The geometry correction algorithm developed at NASA's Jet Propulsion Lab for correcting satellite imagery taken at an angle to a spherical surface may very well provide a suitable filter.

We anticipate that each of the three phases will take a year to complete.

We have made plans to meet the project's resource requirements. Professor Samuel B. Feinberg, M.D., the chief of Ultrasound Medicine at the Mayo Hospital and a contributor to this project, has approved the use of a Unirad Sonograf EP (trademark) Medical Ultrasound Imager at the University of Minnesota Mayo Hospital Radiology Department. Ronald West, Chief Engineer of Unirad, has pledged technical support. The University of Minnesota Radiology Department has several minicomputer systems, including DEC PDP-11 and Data General Nova; in addition, the University batch processing system and the computer facilities of Imtech, Inc., will be made available. E. H. Bower, President of Imtech, is a contributing member of the project.

BIOFEEDBACK CONTROL OF FUNCTIONAL MYOPIA

DENNIS M. COLGAN

Psychology Department, University of Auckland, Private Bag, Auckland, New Zealand

British, born May 10, 1942. Lecturer, Psychology Department, University of Auckland. Educated in New Zealand.

The project aims to develop a novel application of biofeedback training for the reduction of functional myopia. Initial experimental demonstrations of such control and new findings in biofeedback conditioning of other autonomic responses suggest that (a) the degree of myopia reduction is clinically significant, (b) myopia reduction can be generalized from the laboratory to the no-feedback condition of everyday life, and (c) the training may be sufficiently rapid and simple for use in the clinic.

While the etiology of simple myopia is unclear, there is evidence that a major factor in the progression of myopia is the accommodative state of the eye. Studies on primates in restricted visual space indicate that, when the eye is accommodated for relatively long periods of time, there is a tendency toward development of this condition.

Studies on humans have attempted to reduce the degree of myopia and its progression by reducing the degree of accommodation. Most work has proceeded along three lines: (a) the use of cycloplegic drugs to paralyze the ciliary muscle, (b) optical correction to influence the accommodative state, and (c) training the visual accommodation system to produce change in the activity of the nerve supply to the ciliary muscle.

Until recently it was accepted that, unlike the skeletal muscle system, the autonomic system could not learn. In the 1960's, N. E. Miller and his colleagues at Rockefeller University used electronic transformations of autonomic responses as response-contingent reinforcing events to produce autonomic conditioning of heart rate, blood pressure, and intestinal response in rats paralyzed by curare to prevent muscular mediations. By 1972, some replication failures raised questions about Miller's work, and many biofeedback researchers began seeking theoretical alternatives. Currently, the two major theoretical camps are the operant conditioners (some of the curarized animal work stands) and the visceral discriminators who draw their models from the motor skills literature.

Which of these models is the better is crucial to the present project. As indicated previously, a major source of myopia is inappropriate activity of the autonomically innervated ciliary muscle. If, as the visceral discrimination model contends, awareness of changes in the muscular response is the criterion for successful conditioning, then biofeedback control of myopia is unlikely. However, if, as the operant model contends, awareness of the response is unnecessary, then biofeedback offers a new and powerful approach to a widespread human problem.

A widening body of research evidence and data, including studies conducted by the author, has provided increasing support for the operant case. For example, with groups matched for acquisition of bi-directional control of heart rate, a group permitted to use their own pulses as feedback rapidly lost control over generalization sessions. Thus, although aware of the response, they lost control. In another case, a group given continued feedback right through acquisition and generalization rapidly lost control during retention sessions when feedback was removed—a process resembling operant extinction, and not what would be predicted by the visceral discrimination model.

These and similar studies indicate that the operant conditioning model better fits the data on biofeedback control of autonomic responses. Further, the data on generalization of the response to a no-feedback condition during retention sessions in the interpolated feedback groups we have studied show the first experimental demonstration of an effect essential for any clinical application of biofeedback. These data suggest not only that functional myopia is an appropriate problem for biofeedback research but also that developing biofeedback training as a treatment is possible.

Following our initial trials, it is necessary to design and build: (1) an accommodometer capable of precise measurement of accommodation changes, (2) extensions to our microprocessor system capable of sensing, analyzing, and feeding back these changes as proportional auditory feedback, and (3) new software to control the equipment and process data.

Studies will then be required to: (1) determine optimum forms of auditory feedback, (2) determine optimum forms for training schedule of trials, duration, intensity, and proportion of feedback trials, secondary reinforcement and bidirectional training, (3) determine optimum form of generalization training, and (4) refine the system for clinical applications.

The Solar Cooker with a reflector (mirror) mounted on one side.

A FLAT-PLATE SOLAR COOKER FOR RURAL AREAS IN THIRD WORLD COUNTRIES

MOHAN PARIKH
Director, Agricultural Tools Research Centre, Suruchi Campus, P.O. Box 4, Bardoli 394 601, India

Indian, born August 24, 1922. Founder/Director of above Centre and Rural Technology Institute. Agricultural studies in India and Japan.

In an agricultural country like India, with 80 percent of its population living in villages, the fuel crisis is a serious problem. In rural areas, up to 98 percent of the fuel for cooking is non-commercial material, such as firewood, dung cake, and agricultural waste. Collecting these non-commercial fuels takes a poor rural family some 200-300 person-days per year. Such collection also leads to serious problems of deforestation, soil erosion, and ecological imbalances. It is said that in the coming 15 years there may be enough food to feed all the mouths that will need it, but that the biggest problem will be finding adequate supplies of fuel to cook this food.

This concern is the reason why the design and development of the Solar Cooker was initiated. The Solar Cooker was not designed to be operated by a technician, but rather by an ordinary housewife. Women in rural areas are potential wage-earners and cannot afford to spend much time cooking. The Solar Cooker is a flat-plate, non-tracking box device that helps solve these problems.

Abundant, inexhaustible, and clean energy from the sun can be the best alternative cooking fuel source for the villages of Third World countries. In thinly populated villages where energy requirements are low, away from industrial centers, markets, and minimum transportation facilities, solar energy can meet local needs in a number of applications. Since domestic fuel is the first and foremost priority in these situations, this Solar Cooker, which presents no problems of overflowing or charring, meets a critical need. Its most important aspect is that it is accessible to the rural poor, whatever its efficiency. *It is the efficiency of utilization that matters most in villages, not absolute efficiency.*

The Solar Cooker is a simple flat-plate collector system. The salient feature of this cooker is that there is no flow phenomenon in the device—it operates under static conditions. Therefore, the governing parameters of this Solar Cooker are different from other solar devices.

The Solar Cooker is made of inner and outer metal boxes, with a top cover of two panes of plain glass. The inner box is painted black with "Boiler Interior Paint" to absorb maximum solar radiation. This paint is dull in finish and can withstand high temperatures as well as moisture. The space between the two boxes is filled with a 75-millimeter-thick layer of rice husk, insulating the inner box from the sides and bottom of the outer box. The top cover contains two plain sheets of glass, each 3 millimeters thick, fixed within a wooden frame that separates the sheets by 25 millimeters. The entire top cover can be opened on its hinges and can be tightly sealed with a padlock hasp. Rubber sealing is provided at the contact surfaces between the top cover and the cooker box. Inner and outer boxes are made of 24-gauge cold rolled sheets.

We selected rice husk as the insulating material for the Solar Cooker because it is almost free of cost, easily available in villages, and insulates the inner box very well. Moreover, due to its high silicon content, it neither attracts insects nor rots easily, and it is not hygroscopic. Partly, the purpose is to make the best use of readily available local materials; alternatives include ground nut shells or coconut shells.

A reflector, equal to the size of the lid, is mounted on one side of the Solar Cooker and positioned facing south. The reflector is a glass mirror fixed in a wooden frame that is hinged to the top cover of the cooker. The mirror's position can be adjusted to any angle to shine directly into the box. A reflector increases the Solar Cooker's collector area, and thus input to the box is boosted by 10–30 percent. This helps raise the temperature inside the cooker box by 15–30° Celsius. The reflector is more useful just when it is needed most, during the winter, when the sun's rays are much inclined to the horizontal surface. If the reflector is hand-maneuvered to track the sun, the Solar Cooker can start cooking earlier and continue until later.

Over the last six months, we have been experimenting with metallized polyester (Mylar) as a reflecting material. Mirror reflectors have been most popular with solar scientists because Mylar does not maintain its reflectivity for long periods. In our discussions with the manufacturers of Mylar, however, we were convinced that this material can give equally good results for long periods if it is properly ventilated from the back side. We fulfilled this condition by mounting it on hard board drilled with many holes for ventilation; for the last six months, this has given us very satisfactory results. The most attractive parameter of the Mylar, of course, is that it is ten times cheaper than the glass mirror, so if it is reliable for at least one year, it is well worth trying. This possibility is under test now, and we are optimistic about it.

Temperature inside the empty cooker is maintained from 80° to 120° Celsius above ambient temperature. This temperature is enough to cook food gradually—steadily but surely, with delicious taste and preservation of nutrients.

All food dishes cooked in pressure cookers or baked in ovens can be prepared in this Solar Cooker. Cereals, pulses, vegetables, roots (like potatoes), meat, eggs, soups, and porridges, as well as the traditional and special Indian dishes, are all deliciously cooked in this Solar Cooker. Bread, cake, and biscuits can also be baked. Potatoes, sweet potatoes, tomatoes, and bringles can be roasted.

Materials to be cooked are mixed with water and the usual spices and placed in cooking utensils with close-fitting lids. These utensils are then placed in the Solar Cooker at a suitable time. We have found that simple aluminum pots with close-fitting lids and painted dull black on the outside are best for cooking. The smaller the depth of the food in the utensil, the faster the cooking. Our experiments show that the maximum thickness of the food layer that can be properly cooked in the Solar Cooker is about 60 millimeters.

In addition to a number of papers prepared and presented at congresses, we have prepared leaflets in three languages—English, Hindi, and Gujarati—for free distribution to visitors to our campus and to others interested in this Solar Cooker. Simple booklets in Hindi (our national language) and Gujarati (local language) explain the basic principles of solar energy, how it can be harnessed for human comfort, and how anyone can design, manufacture, and use the Solar Cooker.

A number of governmental organizations have elected to put this Solar Cooker into various Farmer's Training Centres for popularization and publicity in the villages, to include it in mobile vans that tour the country teaching people how to use this new equipment, and to demonstrate it in solar energy exhibitions.

Though our sales of the Solar Cooker look small (300 at this writing), we are the first agency in our country to market that many. It is only the beginning of something we think can be harnessed for the improvement and benefit of our people's lives.

A PORTABLE
MILKING MACHINE
FOR SMALL SHEEP FLOCKS

WESLEY COMBS
603-225 Lisgar Street, Ottawa, Ontario K2P 0C6, Canada

Canadian, born January 28, 1929. International Consultant in Livestock Development. Animal Husbandry education (Ph.D.) in the United States.

This project proposes to adapt existing milking machine technology to a portable milking machine for sheep that would enable one person to operate two milking units. The objectives are: (1) reduced capital cost to enable economical mechanization of milking in small flocks, (2) reduced physical demands on hand milkers by mechanization, (3) increased number of ewes one milker can milk, and (4) improved sanitation of milk produced in small flocks.

Milk production may well have been the first purpose for which sheep were domesticated, and is today the most important source of income for many sheep producers in those countries bounding the Mediterranean Sea and the next tier of countries beyond. The milking of sheep is described by Homer in some detail in Book IX of the *Odyssey*. The practices used then are essentially the same as those employed today where sheep are milked by hand.

The frequent failure of high-producing dairy cattle introduced from temperate zones into Mediterranean and tropical environments has resulted in renewed emphasis on sheep-milking research and development programs. The availability of sheep breeds and crossbreeds that are adapted to difficult environments makes sheep milking attractive in areas such as the Caribbean, where commercial sheep milking is not now practiced. The high reproductive efficiency of sheep in these environments gives them significant advantages over cattle in the efficient utilization of national feed energy resources. Sheep milk yields twice as much cheese as does Holstein cow milk, and 50 percent more than goat milk. Sheep cheeses, such as Roquefort, feta, and pecorino are widely distributed, and usually at premium prices.

Mechanized milking parlors for sheep are widely used in France, Israel, and Italy. The Système Casse permits one man to milk 100 ewes per hour. Rotary or carousel machines will milk 500 ewes per hour. Single milking units cannot milk more ewes than can a hand milker (about 50 per hour), but the units can milk for more hours, and one man can operate several units.

Unfortunately, the capital cost of these facilities is such that a flock of 200 to 500 ewes, or in some cases 1000 ewes, is needed to justify their purchase. Further, the sophistication of the equipment may often be unsuitable for areas remote from servicing centers or from the usual power sources. A simple milking machine would permit farmers to continue milking their flocks or to enlarge them without increasing the work load.

At the 1979 International Symposium on Sheep Milk Production in Bulgaria, we were shown a relatively simple milking stall. It was viewed with disdain by visiting scientists because it was less labor-efficient (and a technological step backward) when compared with more advanced units designed for large flocks. Yet in international development it is often necessary to move a step down in technology to accommodate local needs and capabilities in economics and management. The Bulgarian milking chute was developed to serve large flocks, but I saw in it the potential for adaptation to serve the needs of small flocks with a portable, low-cost machine, and without disrupting the normal procedure of handling sheep at milking. One man with two of the stalls and a double milking unit could do the milking now being done by two hand milkers. He would sit on a milking stool in his accustomed position as the ewes are crowded to him from behind as with hand milking. He releases each ewe after milking by pulling a cord handle just above his head, which raises the guillotine gate at the front of each stall.

My proposal is to develop this double stall, equip it with existing milking units designed for sheep, and thus enable one milker to milk two ewes simultaneously.

Machine milking improves sanitation levels in milk production by eliminating opportunities for contamination that exist when ewes are hand-milked into open buckets. In many developing countries, families with surplus milk are excluded from marketing channels because they cannot meet minimum sanitation and quality standards. The entry of additional countries into the European Economic Community further increases the necessity of improving milking techniques and milk quality.

Development of appropriate technology for small flocks is essential in this transition. I would like to introduce the techniques in Greece.

POLYMACROMOLECULES— A NEW, LOW-COST ENGINEERING TOOL

ANTONIO B. SIQUEIRA

R. Perdigao Malheiros, 303/302, 30000 Belo Horizonte, M.G., Brazil

Brazilian, born September 19, 1943. Technical Assistant, in company Directory of Development. Engineering education in Brazil and Finland.

T he proposed project is the development of a chemical process to transform unstable and unused macromolecules (by-products of coal and petrochemical processing procedures) into highly stable polymacromolecules that have excellent engineering properties and are low in cost. The polymacromolecules are obtained by reacting the macromolecules with small amounts of special polymers, which yields a compound with a wide range of applications within the engineering field.

One of humanity's oldest searches is that for materials and products that are low in cost and have a wide range of applications and uses. Achieving this goal has always posed technological and economic difficulties because of the need for capital-intensive processing facilities and adequate market demand to support high production levels.

Because of high processing costs, the by-products of the coal and petrochemical industries have generally been used as they are, without further transformations. This is especially true of macromolecular compounds, which retain characteristics of their initial state for only a very short time because of susceptibilities to climatic variations and weathering. The changes in macromolecular characteristics are the result mainly of volatilization, oxidation, and hydration.

The process under development in this project consists basically of a reaction between the macromolecules obtained from coal and oil, and certain special polymers. The result is a reaction product of definite and constant physical, chemical, and mechanical characteristics when conditions such as temperature, pressure, and humidity are constant. The reaction works in a way that blocks groups of macromolecules that could undergo oxidation, hydrolysis, or hydration, and the result is an extremely stable product.

The polymer to be used as a reactant can be of the addition or condensation type, or it is possible that a mixture of polymers could serve the same purpose. As the reaction proceeds, the macromolecules lose their reactive points or groups, form high molecular weight polymacromolecules without reactive groups, and show very little volatilization. The absence of reactive groups or migration possibilities results in constant properties and prevents the reactions that could cause a significant loss of mass. Further, these polymacromolecules show excellent resistance to temperature change.

The process is carried out by reacting the macromolecules with a polymer, or groups of polymers, in a reactor at temperatures of 90°C to 170°C, at pressures ranging from 0.1 kilograms per square centimeter to 12.0 kilograms per square centimeter, with or without agitation and catalysts.

The product thus obtained is a low-cost polymacromolecular substance that possesses constant physical, chemical, and mechanical properties. These properties are such that the product is suitable for a wide variety of engineering applications, including the following:

Rendering organic and inorganic products or materials impermeable.

Preserving wood against decay and insect attack.

Sealing surfaces in canals, pipes, and reservoirs of hydrophilic liquids having acid, basic, or neutral characteristics.

Protecting objects or materials that are subjected to corrosion.

Asphalt coatings where high mechanical strength and resistance to wear are required.

Basic raw materials in processes designed to improve the technical properties of some products and to lower their costs.

Elastomers.

In all the uses proposed here, these polymacromolecules are technically superior to the polymers and macromolecules used today. In addition, they have the advantage of lower cost.

The Indicycle.

THE INDICYCLE—
NEW MOBILITY FOR
HANDICAPPED YOUNGSTERS

ARTHUR W. MITCHELL
"Sandyacre," 18 Ballyardle Road, Kilkeel, County Down,
Northern Ireland, U.K.

British, born May 8, 1938. General Practitioner, one of four senior partners in a Health Center. Medical education in Northern Ireland.

W e were requested to investigate the possibility of evolving an invalid tricycle for spina bifida sufferers, but which could also be used by any invalid suffering from loss of function in the lower limbs. The vehicle should give the invalid independence—it should be a machine capable of operating on all types of indoor and outdoor surfaces. Desirably, the vehicle would possess the speed and maneuverability of a bicycle and the facility for climbing steep inclines. We felt that, in these days of energy conservation, the vehicle should be hand-propelled, a characteristic that could also contribute to the physical fitness and mental outlook of the invalid.

The Indicycle tricycle has been developed to meet the needs of children from 5 years of age who have no use of their lower limbs but who are able to use their arms normally. It is particularly applicable to those youngsters suffering from spina bifida, but it may be used by any youngsters with loss of lower limb control. With only minor alteration, this vehicle would also be suitable for adults with similar handicaps.

The Indicycle is not a toy but a "go anywhere" machine for use indoors or out. It incorporates either a simple forward and reverse transmission for use by younger children or a 2-speed and reverse for older users.

Propulsion is by ratchet levers used in a rowing position as in a boat (but facing forward), and steering is based on the same principle—application of more or less power to either side to correct the castor wheel. Alternatively, partial application of the brakes will achieve the same result. As with oars, the length of stroke is under control of the user.

The machine will traverse soft ground, go up a 75-millimeter curb, and is capable of climbing quite steep gradients in complete safety, without outside assistance or fear of running backward. It will pass through an average size (675 millimeters) door. Forward propulsion on one side and reverse propulsion on the opposite side will turn it in its own length. An added fitting on the Indicycle will carry the user's crutches. The seat is movable for ease in mounting. The vehicle is lightweight at 21 kilograms, which provides a very high power to weight ratio—speeds up to 10 kilometers per hour on level ground. We believe the combination of all these features add up to a vehicle that provides a virtually complete sense of independence for the child and a highly competitive mode of transport.

The geared ratchet principle upon which our patent rests could be adapted to fit many different wheelchairs, but few of these have the mechanical efficiency of a tricycle.

At this writing, we have produced two prototypes of the vehicle and are about to commence work on a third, as soon as a new multi-gear power system is ready. Our first prototype was built from bicycle parts to prove our design principles. It was successful and used constantly for several weeks by youngsters who were not handicapped. The second model was built with new materials and with a single-speed transmission; it has been on evaluation trials in schools for the handicapped.

Complete patent rights on the vehicle have been applied for, and a private company has been formed and registered, Indicycle Ltd. The name Indicycle has been registered as a trademark. To build a further prototype and commence tooling for a pre-production batch of 5 to 6 machines, we urgently need capital to enable us to employ at least one skilled man full time on the project and to clear our existing debt from the development work to date.

We have had some assistance and indications of interest from local governmental bodies, who recognize the urgent need for a vehicle like this. The Indicycle was presented for a Design Council Scrutiny in London, which was extremely enthusiastic about the project and recommended continuing development to production level of the current prototype model, without any radical design changes. We have been further encouraged by gaining access to scientific information comparing ergonomic characteristics of various invalid vehicles. These have confirmed our theories on wheel size, layout, and the desirability of lever operation. This last we have achieved with the Indicycle without the expected unacceptably low road speeds, difficulty of steering, and problems with inclines over 3°. In our design, the vehicle will be able to handle 30° inclines with the 2-speed gear unit and the climbing ratchet device. This ratchet device prevents the Indicycle from running backward down a steep incline between propulsive strokes of the drive levers. The device also can totally lock its wheels for stability in parking.

Perhaps one of our most rewarding experiences has been with our "tester," a 6-year-old girl whose spina bifida makes it impossible for her to "cheat" in her handling of the vehicle. She lives at the top of an unpaved road with a 20° incline, and she has no difficulty traveling up and down it on the Indicycle, whereas this effort would be out of the question with a normal wheelchair.

We wish to begin manufacturing the Indicycle as soon as possible. In the United Kingdom and Ireland, statistics indicate there are 12,000 sufferers of spina bifida. We have prepared the necessary costing figures for the commencement of manufacturing. We would first like to conduct a pre-production run, making 5 or 6 vehicles for testing purposes by various health authorities, which would provide exposure for the vehicle and give us an opportunity to refine the tooling necessary for production. Based on our current plans, we would then go into pilot production of Indicycles, with an output level of approximately 20 vehicles per week.

COBALT CHLOROPHYLL AS A POSSIBLE CURE FOR PERNICIOUS ANEMIA

JOHANNES T. H. ROOS

St. Bede's School, Upper Dicker, Hailsham, E. Sussex, England

South African, born November 11, 1938. Head of School Physics and Chemistry teaching. Physics and chemistry education (Ph.D.) in South Africa.

This project is concerned with the properties of "cobalt chlorophyll"—chlorophyll in which the central magnesium ion has been replaced by an ion of cobalt—both as it resembles vitamin B_{12} in its *in vitro* properties and in the possibility of using cobalt chlorophyll as an inexpensive replacement for vitamin B_{12} in the treatment of pernicious anemia.

The investigations that have been possible to date with the limited equipment available in a school laboratory have shown that, as *in vitro* catalysts, cobalt chlorophyll and vitamin B_{12} catalyze the same reactions. Using elementary colorimetric apparatus, it has further been shown that a given reaction exhibits the same reaction order, and hence probably proceeds via the same mechanism, whether it is vitamin B_{12} or cobalt chlorophyll that is used as catalyst. It now appears to be worthwhile to extend this investigation to include other reactions of biochemical importance and to study both the intestinal absorption of cobalt chlorophyll and the effect of the substance in actual cases of pernicious anemia. If it were shown that cobalt chlorophyll could replace vitamin B_{12} in living systems or even that it provided cobalt in an easily utilizable form, an inexpensive means of treating pernicious anemia would become available.

A method was developed for the preparation of the cobalt chlorophyll from chlorophyll extracted from green leaves. It was found that the cobalt derivative is much more stable than the original material, although it does not possess the latter's ability to fluoresce. Initial investigations involving the aerobic oxidation of thiophenol showed that this reaction was catalyzed by both vitamin B_{12} and cobalt chlorophyll (encouraging an idea originally suggested to the author in the course of adapting certain experiments for his students from articles in the *Journal of Chemical Education*). Further, normal chlorophyll extract and chlorophyll containing copper or iron atoms in the center of the ring system failed to show any catalytic activity. This finding was followed by the investigation of reactions involving the oxidation of different thiol compounds: the anaerobic oxidation of thiols with methylene blue and the anaerobic reduction of riboflavin by thiols, reactions that were previously studied by Schrauzer and Sibert using vitamin B_{12} and several vitamin B_{12} analogues as catalysts. Quantitative measurements with a simple colorimeter have shown that the order of the reaction of the catalyzed reactions is the same using either vitamin B_{12} or cobalt chlorophyll. The results have indicated that the aerobic oxidation of thiols and their anaerobic oxidation with methylene blue are second-order reactions, while the anaerobic reduction of riboflavin is first-order.

The work described above suggests a similarity between vitamin B_{12} and cobalt chlorophyll that invites further investigation. An important biochemical process catalyzed by vitamin B_{12} in living systems is the methylation of homocysteine, which involves the formation of a unique cobalt–carbon bond. With the limited equipment available to the author, it has not been possible to investigate whether or not the cobalt ion in cobalt chlorophyll is able to form such a bond, nor whether cobalt chlorophyll would catalyze the methylation referred to above. It may well be that cobalt chlorophyll would react in the same way as vitamin B_{12} in living systems.

There is, however, another possibility, and that is that cobalt chlorophyll may contain cobalt in a form readily absorbable in the gut and in a form that is non-toxic to humans. Inorganic cobalt is scarcely absorbed during its passage through the intestines, while many simple cobalt complexes, though absorbed, are mildly toxic. If the cobalt in cobalt chlorophyll can be utilized by the body for the synthesis of vitamin B_{12}—even though the cobalt chlorophyll as such is not able to replace vitamin B_{12} in the latter's specific catalytic functions *in vivo*—an inexpensive and readily available method of treating pernicious anemia will have been discovered.

I would like to find myself financially able to investigate further both of the possibilities I have outlined. This would call for equipment and facilities I do not possess nor am I likely to obtain through normal school funds: sensitive analytical equipment for measuring low concentrations of cobalt, a spectrophotometer for more reliable kinetic measurements, and money to cover the cost of cobalt absorption measurements using radioactive cobalt-60.

HONORABLE MENTION WINNERS HAVING NON-RELEASED PROJECTS

The last page of the Official Application Form submitted by candidates for The Rolex Awards for Enterprise 1981 was an "Optional Page—Release Form." With the exception of the five Rolex Laureates, whose projects would be publicly acclaimed, this page afforded all candidates the option of releasing their project details for possible later publication (e.g., in this book), or of maintaining the details of their projects in a confidential status. In choosing the Laureates and the Honorable Mention winners, The Selection Committee had no knowledge of whether a project under review was released or non-released.

Three non-released projects were chosen by The Selection Committee of The Rolex Awards for Enterprise 1981 as Honorable Mention winners:

Clifford M. Anderson, American, born December 15, 1945
1623 6th Street West, Kirkland, Washington 98033, U.S.A.
Patagonian Falcon Expedition

Paul J. Baicich, American, born March 11, 1948
7607 Latham Avenue, Oxon Hill, Maryland 20022, U.S.A.
The 1981 Dotterel Expedition: Search for the Nesting
Grounds of *Eudromias morinellus* in North America

Cesar Vasquez, Argentine, born August 18, 1933
Centro de Virologia Animal, Serrano 661, 1414 Capital Federal, Argentina
An Experimental Vaccine for Foot and Mouth Disease

EXPLORATION AND DISCOVERY

The projects appearing in this section were submitted in competition under the "Exploration and Discovery" category, which was defined in the Official Application Form as follows:

Projects in this category will be concerned primarily with venturesome undertakings or expeditions and should seek to inspire our imagination or expand our knowledge of the world in which we live.

The hot-air balloon on a test flight.

FIVE WEEKS IN A BALLOON
À LA JULES VERNE

 JAUME LLANSANA
Honorable Mention, Rolex Awards for Enterprise
Sant Roc 6, Igualada (Barcelona), Spain

Spanish, born July 12, 1947. Computer science teacher, analyst, and author. Education in engineering and computer systems in Spain.

Our project has been to duplicate Jules Verne's *Five Weeks in a Balloon* in a balloon built by ourselves as closely as possible to the description given by Verne. The novel describes the crossing of Africa in a hot-air balloon that sails with the trade winds from Zanzibar to Dakar.

Jules Verne once said that all that one man is capable of imagining, another man is capable of doing. After having read several of Jules Verne's adventure stories, we decided to realize one of them. After much discussion, we chose *Five Weeks in a Balloon* as the model we wished to follow. In our project, we wanted to do more than simply prove Verne's theories about the technological possibilities of hot-air balloons; we wanted to capture the spirit of the adventure that he described through the characters of his book (written 118 years ago) and live it fully in the present, in the twentieth century.

The total project was subdivided into two parts: (1) the construction of the balloon, and (2) the crossing of Africa.

The project began in 1977 when we commenced designing the balloon we wished to use for the voyage. It had to be a hot-air balloon, because we had to be able to cross Africa in stages, as Verne had described, and it had to be big enough to transport three people and all their equipment.

Based on our calculations, we decided that we would build a balloon with 1300 square meters of nylon fabric, which would give an inflated capacity of 4000 cubic meters (25 meters high, with a diameter of 21 meters). Such a capacity would provide a lifting power of 1400 kilograms, enough to handle our expected load requirements. At this early point in our project, we were fortunate to locate an abandoned warehouse in which we could set up our workshop and carry out the assembly. After the designs were completed, we set about cutting out the panel patterns and then sewed them together with machines that were loaned to us by a factory.

Though we were aware of the lifting capacity we wished to have, a key objective in the design considerations was to make a balloon as efficient as possible in terms of energy consumption in order to maximize the cruising distance available with any given amount of fuel on board. For this reason, we chose a design that incorporated a large quantity of black nylon. This would permit us to anticipate a general savings of 15 percent of our combustibles, and in times of strong sunlight we could anticipate savings of up to almost 100 percent by conserving the hot air in the balloon's interior with the help of solar energy.

The basket was made of wicker, woven in the classical pattern, and of a size very nearly that of the basket in the novel.

With these design configurations decided upon, we turned to our main problem, that of the burner that we would use to heat the air. None of the standard burners used in modern hot-air ballooning would be suitable, since they all used either propane or kerosene as combustibles, and there would be no way for us to be sure of finding such fuels in a flight across Africa. It clearly was going to be necessary to have a burner that could use a substance that we could find fairly easily on our route.

We discarded gasoline for safety reasons, and, after considerable discussion, decided that fuel oil was ideal. The problem with this, however, was that all the fuel oil burners used electricity, which for us was impractical due to the extra weight such an installation would require, and the fact that they do not give the amount of calories we would need. We had, therefore, to invent a fuel oil burner with a capability of 2.5 million calories per hour. Its development cost us a great deal of time and money.

Nevertheless, two years later, in November 1979, the balloon was ready to begin its voyage. We had built it ourselves, from our own designs, including the fuel oil burner, in our own native city of Igualada.

Igualada is an industrial city in Catalonia with a population of 25,000, and it is our home. The whole city had been following our project with interest, and there were many people who gladly collaborated with us along the way. That is why the balloon bears the flag of the city. Its name, *Tramuntana* (meaning North Wind), was chosen by the schoolchildren. On the bottom of the basket, we painted a wind rose and a map of the continent we would cross.

On November 12, 1979, the balloon left Barcelona on a ship heading for Zanzibar, the starting point of our expedition. The three of us making the trip left Barcelona by plane on November 30 to rendezvous with the balloon.

The route of the actual expedition will depend completely on the actual trajectory of the trade winds. We plan to fly only in the mornings, from sunrise until the thermal air currents begin, before midday. Once on the ground, we will set up campsites and live with the natives. We will be carrying very little food in the balloon in order to keep weight down, but we will take all the tools necessary for maintenance and repair during the voyage. We will not take any type of arms.

If we use up all our fuel oil, we will have to search for more. We will not take any land equipment, and no vehicle will follow us. We feel that this is one of the conditions of living out Verne's ideas.

Once the fuel oil is found and transported to the balloon, a process that may well take days, we will begin flight again from the same place in which we landed. The journey will end when we get to the Atlantic Coast.

In his novel, Verne landed in Dakar, but, as for us, only the trade winds can tell.

Sewing the nylon balloon panels.

A SURVEY OF THE LAST HUNTERS AND GATHERERS

JOHAN G. REINHARD
Box 74, New Lenox, Illinois 60451, U.S.A.

American, born December 13, 1943. Research Scientist, Anthropology Department, University of Wisconsin. Anthropological education (Ph.D.) in Austria, England, Germany, and the United States.

For 99 percent of the period that man has been on earth, he has lived as a nomadic hunter-gatherer. Yet this way of life remains one of the least-examined, and, within our lifetimes, will probably cease to exist as an on-going object of study. Not only are the cultures of hunter-gatherers important in themselves as part of humanity's cultural heritage, they also supply information that enables us to think more realistically about past stages of cultural evolution. The aim of this project is to locate as many of the last remaining hunter-gatherers as possible and to conduct an ethnographic survey of the least-known groups. Through publications, the establishment of a comprehensive file, and the archiving of all written, audio, and visual materials in major institutions in the United States and Europe, the data collected will be made available to the international scientific community and serve as a basis for further intensive studies.

It would be tragic if there were any failure on our part to study a way of life that represents so much of our human cultural heritage and that is presently in danger of disappearing forever, because there will be no way to remedy the omission in the future. As S. Washburn and J. Lancaster have noted, "Human hunting is made possible by tools, but it is far more than a technique or even a variety of techniques. It is a way of life, and the success of this adaptation (in its total social, technical, and psychological dimensions) has dominated the cause of human evolution for hundreds of thousands of years."

Given these facts, it would seem that extensive research would now be under way to locate and study the last remaining hunter-gatherers. This is not the case. Despite the boundaries of exploration being constantly expanded in space and under the sea, and despite the massive sums expended for such projects (including archaeology), numerous ethnic groups are allowed to disappear without adequate records of their cultures. I believe that there are two primary reasons. The first is that grants in anthropology are generally directed toward theory testing or to small-scale, intensive projects that help employment in a tight job market. Exploration and discovery are no longer considered important, and the risk factors are often too high, when funds can be spent in more familiar areas. The second reason is that work with the hunter-gatherers is time-consuming, physically and psychologically demanding, and requires a wide range of skills (for example, field linguistics and photography), which means that there are relatively few who are able to conduct such studies. And so the urgency compounds.

What I wish to do is to locate as many of the last remaining hunting and gathering people as possible and to establish the number, distribution, and current situation of the groups surveyed, noting whatever cultural artifacts may exist. Only when such information is available will it be possible to undertake sensibly planned, long-term projects that can then make optimum use of the available resources, in view of the time limitations.

The first step in the project will be to establish a file on hunting and gathering groups. This will be done by making a detailed search through the anthropological literature, contacting individual scholars, publishing a general call for information in the professional journals, and contacting organizations known to be working with these cultures.

Groups will be divided into five categories. The first will be those about which little or virtually nothing is known. The second category will contain those groups for which only outdated or otherwise inaccurate data are available. The third category will be those groups that are little known or are only recently settled. The fourth category will be made up of those who have had some research done among their settled communities, while their nomadic segments remain unstudied. The fifth category will consist of those groups that have been the subject of general study, but whose cultural variation makes research among less-known groups desirable, or those groups in which a particular area of anthropological interest may have been inadequately covered.

The second stage of the project will consist of surveys conducted among the groups that appear to demand the highest priority, and the third stage will be to make the collected material available to the scientific community.

CUMBRIA SCHOOLS EXPLORATION SOCIETY HIMALAYAN EXPEDITION

JOHN R. GRIMSHAW
60 Redoak Avenue, Barrow-in-Furness, Cumbria, LA13 ORN,
England.

*British, born March 9, 1947. School Geography Department Head. Education and
teaching certificate acquired in England.*

T his is a youth expedition sponsored by the Cumbria Schools Exploration Society. The Society's aims are to aid the development of young
people by promoting exploration and adventure in remote areas. This
expedition, a team of ten staff and ten students, with the possible addition of
three Indian colleagues, will visit the Kishtwar Himalaya. While in the area,
we intend to carry out field studies, explore an unvisited valley, and make an
attempt on a number of peaks in the area, notably Arjuna, an unclimbed
peak of about 20,000 feet.

The Cumbria Schools Exploration Society came into existence four years
ago as the result of frustration with regard to the inability of young people to
progress in the field of exploration as easily as they might in many other
fields—for example, in gymnastics, which has a number of sponsors. Certainly there are bodies, for example, the British Schools Exploring Society,
that do sterling work, but in the main they are geared to field study. All too
often, the would-be explorer becomes a caddy for scientific equipment.

Three staff at different schools in the north of England proposed a Society,
and Cumbria County Council agreed to allow us to operate under their
auspices. After staging successful trips to Scotland and Norway, we gained
high degrees of confidence in both the students and ourselves.

We thus conceived an expedition that presented a natural progression for
the Society and its members and that also allowed for the full development
of the capabilities of the youngsters taking part. We chose India to provide

maximum social contrast and because it offers remote, unexplored country that is relatively easy and inexpensive to reach.

We now have a team selected in the main from the schools in Cumbria, which includes two medical doctors, five mountaineers, a biologist, a geographer, and a general assistant, as well as the ten boys and girls, most of whom are experienced on the hill in their own right. We plan to hold a series of meetings in England and a training expedition in the Swiss Alps in the summer of 1980, by way of preparation.

In India, we hope to meet the people—easy enough on the ground as we pass through—but we have also invited the Indian authorities to send two youngsters to join our party. We hope that they will contribute to the social education of our youngsters and, of course, we to theirs.

Once in the area—to the east of Kishtwar, in the Chenab Valley—we will proceed with a variety of projects. This region was chosen for a number of reasons: it allows relatively easy access (the walk in is only some 4 days); we have to use our summer holiday period and the monsoon that lashes the rest of the continent only grazes our area; the mountains are low (by Himalayan standards); and the area is largely unexplored—only a handful of expeditions have been here compared with the numbers that have visited Nepal.

The biologists will record the flora on film and collect specimens and prepare a report on the possibilities for study by similar parties in the area. The geographer has a similar brief. Both parties will stay in the valleys and will be assisted by those youngsters who do not wish to attempt mountaineering.

A trekking group will visit a number of valleys that appear to be unvisited and will produce a report including such map corrections as are necessary. The mountaineering group will attempt one of a series of small peaks that lie on the ridge below Arjuna and then, depending on the level of acclimatization and physical and mental fitness, will attempt Arjuna itself. This group will be monitored at all times by the medical officer and by the staff.

Besides the benefits the youngsters (and adults!) will gain through travel, we hope to provide the foundation for future work. The world grows smaller, and the challenges to youngsters grow greater. We feel that they should be prepared psychologically and physiologically to meet those challenges. The expedition will provide data on physical conditioning and acclimatization and on the effects of training and organization. The project is a difficult one because we do not have the moral right to use youngsters as guinea pigs, but we feel that this expedition, built as it is on work that has gone before, can extend our knowledge without putting at risk the youngsters we seek to encourage. We hope other groups will be encouraged to duplicate these efforts and to spread the challenges of mountaineering to other students.

A female polar pear, Ursus maritimus.

POLAR BEARS—ACTIVE YET HIBERNATING?

RALPH A. NELSON
Clinical Education Center, Carle Foundation Hospital, Urbana, Illinois 61801, U.S.A.

American, born June 19, 1927. Professor of Nutrition and Food Science, and medical consultant. Medical/physiology education in the United States.

I wish to test the hypothesis that the adult polar bear has integrated behavior patterns of physical activity and eating into the state of hibernation, so that in winter it can roam the Arctic wasteland, swim the Arctic Ocean without requiring fresh water, and need no more than dietary fat from seals to support additional energy requirements for physical activity. The hypothesis will be tested in polar bears by observing their winter patterns of intake of food, ice, and snow, and the volume of urine and feces. Their biochemical state will be assessed by comparing collected samples of expired air and blood with established patterns for hibernating and non-hibernating bears. If these animals are in a biochemical state of hibernation (as hypothesized), they should show a decreased urea/creatinine ratio in the blood, from 20:30 (normal) to 4:6; a respiratory quotient below 0.70; hyperlipidemia with a tenfold increase in serum-free fatty acids and no ketosis. Food should be primarily blubber and hide, and the urine/fecal volumes should be low or zero. If the hypothesis is correct, physical activity should not induce ice and snow eating, the consumption of seal carcass meat, an increase in urine/fecal volumes, nor cause any change in the biochemical markers of hibernation listed above.

This project has sparked the imagination of people who have both heard about it and worked on it. It concerns the adaptation of polar bears to the hostile and stressful environment of the Arctic. Their response has the attributes of being the most advanced of any mammal, in an evolutionary sense, as they cope with varying supplies of food, extremes in weather, and lack of fresh water. It appears that the polar bear's adaptation to this changing environment is achieved by combining the biochemical state of hibernation with physical activity and by limiting food intake primarily to fat.

The black and grizzly bears have exhibited the longest documented state of hibernation of any mammal. They hibernate at a near-normal body temperature (30–35 °C), and their dormancy is continuous for three to seven months. Although expending about 4000 kilocalories per day, the bear neither eats, drinks, urinates, nor defecates. Its den has no odor. It is easily aroused into a mobile, reactive state, aware of its surroundings, and able to defend itself. Female bears give birth to cubs and nurse them under these stressful conditions. These characteristics differ sharply from those shown by the mammalian deep hibernators (ground squirrels, woodchucks, etc.) whose body temperatures approach 0 °C. The 13-lined ground squirrel, for example, can hibernate only four to ten days at a time and undergoes periodic arousals, when it then eats, urinates, and defecates. While hibernating, it cannot protect itself from predators.

The polar bear, it is now suspected, differs from black and grizzly bears almost as much as the latter differ from the deep hibernators. For instance, it is now known that polar bears can hibernate in summer, something black bears cannot do. At Churchill Bay, Manitoba, Canada, polar bears have been observed to den when ambient temperatures are elevated. They are also active, although to a much lesser degree than in winter. Food-seeking behavior is at a minimum; some polar bears did not leave their dens at all, in fact, to seek either water or food. In blood samples taken from thirteen of these animals (in dens or active), the biochemical markers of hibernation were found. We have concluded that the biochemical state of hibernation these bears exhibit in summer permits denning, allowing them to keep their body temperatures lowered when ambient air temperatures have risen to levels that impose stress on their thermoregulatory systems.

In winter, however, when the polar bears are extremely active, killing and eating seals, they also hibernate for seven to eight weeks or more. The question arises, "Is the winter state any different from the summer state?" We propose that it most likely is quite similar—a combination of biochemical adaptations of hibernation and physical activity, depending on conditions and the bear's idiosyncrasies.

Arctic activity (swimming, walking) exacts a high price in calories. We now know that adult polar bears meet these needs by restricting food consumption to primarily fat in the form of seal blubber. Fat has no end-products of catabolism that require urinary excretion. It has been estimated that bears kill a seal about once every six days, and that about 50,000 kilocalories are available for energy from the 15 kilograms of blubber eaten. This is about enough to support caloric needs for six days of physical activity. The polar bear's ability to selectively eat only the blubber of seals has been observed, and this specific intake of food would support, rather than disrupt, the biochemical state of hibernation.

If adult polar bears were forced to eat meat, due to limited food supplies, the increased protein intake would necessitate an increased rate of urea excretion, which would in turn mean increased urine volume and the need for water. This circumstance would impose a problem in thermoregulation due to the temperature of the ice and snow that would have to be consumed. If the polar bear consumed enough ice and snow at an ambient air temperature of $-60\,°C$ to excrete 16 liters of urine (a reasonable requirement), about 2000 kilocalories per day would be required merely to warm the ice and snow to the $37\,°C$ body temperature of the bear. Given a 370-kilogram polar bear's metabolic rate of 5905 kilocalories per day, such ice and snow consumption would be a severe drain on the fat stores of its body, thus seriously affecting its ability to survive. Further, excessive meat consumption would disrupt the biochemical state of hibernation.

To test our hypothesis, using the facilities at Point Barrow, Alaska, our experimental plan is as follows. We will identify adult male polar bears, anesthetize them by dart, attach radio collars, and obtain blood samples for urea, creatinine, cholesterol, triglycerides, phospholipids, free fatty acids, ketones, hematocrit, and osmotic pressure. We will catheterize the urinary bladder and obtain urine for ketone concentration. We will also intubate their trachea and collect expired air for the respiratory quotient. We will then allow the bears to recover, follow them on a snowmobile, and observe from a safe distance seal-killing behavior, carcass leavings, ice and snow intake, and urine and fecal losses (from frozen urine patches and scats). After about seven days of such tracking, we will reanesthetize for repeat samples. We have performed these procedures in the past and need no new equipment to test our hypothesis.

Apart from its inherent interest, the study is significant as part of a decade of work aimed at investigating practical applications of hibernating mammals to such problems associated with human beings as long-term flights into space, obesity, and chronic renal disease. Further, oil exploration in the Arctic presents a risk to the seal population, with the commensurate possibility of impact on polar bear survival. The data collected in our study will have direct application to the question of how to support polar bear life if their traditional food supplies are curtailed.

INCREASING THE BIOLOGICAL PRODUCTIVITY OF THE ARABIAN SEA

SANTO H. AJWANI
7-36 C, "DEVRUP" Society, Guru Nanik Road, Bandra,
Bombay 400 050, India

Indian, born November 29, 1927. Science writer. Botany, biology, chemistry, and ecology education in India and the United States.

The Arabian Sea is potentially one of the richest bodies of water in the world in terms of biological productivity. Due to the high intensity of sunlight, the powerful monsoons originating there beat on the agricultural land masses of the Indian subcontinent, picking up nutrients along the way and discharging them into the sea. This unique set of conditions, which should be very favorable for primary production, is, however, underexploited as a result of the strong thermocline separating the upper warm waters of the sea from the lower, nutrient-rich cold depths.

To overcome this barrier, a proposed technique with almost no input of energy could lift the nutrients from the darker depths to the euphotic zone, where they can stimulate production in the form of phytoplankton to the fullest extent possible.

The Arabian Sea possesses a combination of conditions not known anywhere else in the world, all but one of which are favorable for primary production of marine life. With some 4000 hours of annual sunlight, the surface water temperatures fluctuate around 29°C for most of the year, with a range of 26°C to 33°C. The rates of evaporation are high, leading to the strong south-to-west monsoons occurring from June to September. These rains bring soil nutrients into the Bay of Bengal and the Arabian Sea, which stimulate production in the form of phytoplankton. These in turn feed the food chain that results in a thriving commercial fishing business, until the return of the dry season, when the monsoon-generated upwelling currents on the continental shelf decline. The thermocline reasserts itself, leaving the upper layers of the sea warm and light and the lower layers cold and heavy.

The demand of the phytoplankton for nutrients soon leads to depletion of nutrients in the euphotic zone, jeopardizing production at all three trophic levels. Organisms die and sink to the bottom where they decay in the absence of light and oxygen. Anaerobic bacteria break down the complex organic substances into simpler, stable inorganic nutrients such as phosphates and nitrates, which add to the nutrients introduced by river runoff.

A situation now arises in which the light is available where the nutrients are not, and where there are nutrients, there is no light. This is perhaps an oversimplification of a complex phenomenon, but its broad features serve to focus attention on one of the foremost problems in oceanography today.

I propose a virtually energy-free technique for "lifting the water." The job can be done by the gases released in the process of biological degradation of organic matter in much the same manner as sewage sludge gas (methane) pushes its way through a well of water, lifting in the process a heavy steel tank to the desired height.

The requirements for this technique include many polyethylene bags packed in an oceanographic submersible set over an area of active regeneration identified by the International Indian Ocean Expedition on the outer continental shelf, at a depth of about 100 meters. Decomposing matter from the sea floor should then be pumped into the bags, which would then be sealed at their open end and ejected onto the sea floor.

In a matter of days, sufficient gas from the decomposing matter will be generated within the bags to enable them to rise to the surface, where their contents can be released. The nutrients thus discharged will stimulate photosynthesis, and each link in the food chain will come to life.

Initially the proposed experiments will be carried out for a period of three months, during pre- or post-monsoon season, when 20,000 bags of suitable size will be released over an area of 10 square kilometers. Subsequently, the bags will be replaced by polyethylene balloons, similar to the ones used in meteorological research, to lift larger quantities of nutrients.

It is not possible to predict at this stage the magnitude of increase in the biological productivity of the area covered by the proposed project. Nevertheless, the project is technically sound, its validity emanating largely from the foundations laid by the International Indian Ocean Expedition. Consequently, the experiments should succeed in producing evidence of increase in the primary production of the area used in the experiment. This in turn should generate the necessary interest among scientists and financial institutions to participate in the program by expanding the area of operations.

EXPLORING THE LIBYAN SAHARA FOR THE EARLIEST HOMINIDS

 NOEL T. BOAZ
Honorable Mention, Rolex Awards for Enterprise
Department of Anthropology, New York University,
25 Waverly Place, New York, New York 10003, U.S.A.

American, born February 8, 1952. Paleoanthropologist, Assistant Professor of Anthropology and Anatomy. Educated in the United States (Ph.D), field work and exploration experience in Ethiopia, Kenya, and Tanzania.

Since the time of Darwin, there has been a great deal of interest in discovering the earliest creatures to have crossed the threshold of humanity. During the last fifteen years, investigators have documented ever earlier forms of man, but the origin, time, and appearance of the very first members of the hominid family are still unknown. This project is aimed at discovering the "missing links" at a site in the Libyan Sahara Desert estimated to be some 5 to 8 million years old. In 1978, at the invitation of the Libyan authorities, I visited this site and discovered the first primates to be found there. Although the first finds were those of monkeys, a collarbone found in 1979 was that of a hominoid, intermediate in anatomy between apes and humans. If our excavations are successful in recovering hominoids, the discovery will certainly be one of the most important contributions to understanding the beginnings of the human species.

The fossil site of Sahabi (Arabic for "friend of the Prophet") derives its name from a nearby fort, Qasr as-Sahabi, built originally by the Byzantines and later occupied by the Turks and then by the Italians. Italian soldiers began collecting odd fossils at the fort in the 1930's, and the first professional attention was paid to the site in 1934 by Italian geologist Ardito Desio. In that same year, Carlo Petrocchi, an anatomist and paleontologist at the Medical School in Tripoli, led an Italian expedition to the site that lasted several years. This party discovered, among many other fossils, the specimen for which Sahabi was to become famous—a skull of the giant four-tusked elephant Petrocchi named *Stegotetrabelodon lybicus.*

The results obtained from Sahabi thus far have been important and puzzling, partly because of the paleontological vacuum in which the site exists (there are no intensively investigated sites in North Africa from this time range) and partly because of its virtually unique ecology compared to other penecontemporaneous sites—marshes, swamps, and lagoons instead of dry savannas. Sahabi has yielded the earliest known true bear in Africa, *Agriotherium* (bears are no longer present in Africa) and the earliest, or one of the earliest, dogs in Africa. Other animals that are rare elsewhere in this time period are abundant at Sahabi, such as the hippo-like anthracotheres, primitive sea cows, and a number of different species of elephants. The predominance of these species is explained by the proximity of woodlands, marshes, and the sea. Other sites 5 to 8 million years old generally have not preserved denizens of these habitats. The earliest hominids are hypothesized to have inhabited environments similar to those preserved at Sahabi.

The main importance of Sahabi, in my opinion as an anthropologist, is that it documents a virtually unknown time period on hominid evolution—the period when forms evolving from apes in the Miocene Epoch made the transition to hominids in the Pliocene Epoch. Prior to 1978, no primate remains had been recovered from Sahabi, but in that year cranial, dental, and limb bone fossils of two monkey species were found. In March 1979, the first hominoid fossil, a clavicle (collarbone), was unearthed. Now that the presence of hominoids has been documented, it is necessary to investigate intensively to ascertain the nature of the species, which may be new to science. The anatomy of the clavicle is partly chimpanzee-like and partly human-like. Did it belong to a proto-chimpanzee, a proto-hominid, or something different? There will be no answer until further work is done.

Five to eight fossiliferous occurrences at Sahabi will be excavated, depending on results obtained and the number of excavators hired. Each of the major sites has been chosen with a view to providing a cross section of known previous important finds. The research objectives are to discover hominids in this time period, date them, determine their evolutionary affinities, and reconstruct their ecological relations.

If successful, the proposed research will open a new era for paleoanthropology, as the first foray into a heretofore unknown time period. At a minimum, new data will result: on the environmental history of the Sahara Desert, on Upper Miocene vertebrate evolution in North Africa in a number of families, and on primate ecological relations in this period of time. We anticipate that additional hominoids will be recovered by the excavation, which will provide further evolutionary answers for science.

Fijian fire-walkers.

SOLVING THE ENIGMA OF FIRE-WALKING

FRIEDBERT H. KARGER
Walpurgisstrasse 5, 8000 Munchen,
Federal Republic of Germany

German, born May 4, 1940. Scientific Member of Max Planck Institute for Plasmaphysics. Physics, philosophy, and psychology education in Germany.

In an investigation of so-called fire-walking by natives in the Fiji Islands, I filmed and studied a native who stood more than 7 seconds on a stone with a temperature higher than 340°C; the temperature of his soles did not exceed 70°C. Since the conceivable physical explanations of heat insulation and cooling failed, I propose a detailed experiment for scientific investigation of fire-walking, in order to detect the possibly unknown effect involved.

The widespread opinion of natural scientists is that fire-walking can be easily explained by the heat insulation of the ashes, the low heat conductivity and heat capacity of the rocks, the heat transport through increased blood circulation, the cooling effects of evaporation of increased foot transpiration or ointments, the heat insulation of this evaporating fluid (Leydenfrost effect), the short contact time of the feet with the rocks, or, simply, a deceptive trick. At most, the possibility of autosuggestive immunity to pain is admitted. As a result of these many qualitatively plausible explanations, the general feeling has been that there is no need for a detailed investigation of this phenomenon.

The attempt to determine what really happens in fire-walking is, in fact, an enterprise against two fronts: opposition of scientific colleagues and the general secretiveness of the cult groups who practice it. Since I wanted to know the truth, and the phenomenon appeared to me to be of interest both in a medical sense and for physics, in 1974 I went to the Fiji Islands. There I hoped to attend a fire-walking ceremony and possibly to perform initial measurements by using temperature-sensitive paints, which change color irreversibly when a temperature limit is exceeded.

After an intense search I found a fire-walking ceremony open to tourists in the vicinity of Deuba, on the island of Viti Levu. On November 6, shortly before dusk, over twenty natives of the island Bega walked, one after the other, on rocks heated by a charcoal fire. I obtained permission from the priest to film the ceremony and persuaded one of the natives to apply temperature-sensitive paints to his feet in order to determine certain skin-temperature limits. The upper color change points of the two paints used were 70°C and 340°C.

The results of my investigation can be summarized as follows:

1. As measured from the film, the native—in addition to a walk of 4 seconds over hot stones—stood for 7.2 seconds on a rock that 2 minutes later was still over 340°C, the temperature determined by the color change of paint poured over the rock. Since the rocks were glowing faintly red before the 20-minute ceremony, and since the paint gives only a temperature limit, the temperature of the rock was certainly higher during the filming.
2. The soles of the native did not become hotter than 70°C, and there was no perceptible change (burns or wounds) of the skin after the fire-walking.
3. A piece of calloused skin from the native's sole, which I removed and placed on the hot rock, was carbonized within about 2 seconds.
4. As the native stood on the rock, no steam development at the feet could be detected. Steam did appear, however, when another Fijian with a garment of plant leaves lay upon the rock.
5. There were only a few ashes on the rocks, so that direct contact between the soles and the rock was possible.

In subsequent theoretical investigations, I made estimates in which the following parameters were considered: heat capacity and heat conductivity of the rocks and the skin, heat transport of the blood, cooling capacity by evaporation of sweat, sweat production rate, possibility of heat insulation by steam (Leydenfrost effect), and temperature limit for irreversible changes of the skin. Although the exact values of some parameters are still uncertain, the result is well above the measured skin temperature, even if one takes extreme values of the physiological parameters. This means that theoretically the foot skin must show considerable burn damage and carbonization.

One is therefore forced to assume that in this phenomenon an effect still unknown to physics plays a role. This effect produces either heat insulation or a reduction of the person's weight (the natives maintain that they are "lifted" over the rocks). Both possibilities constitute a challenge to physics. I therefore propose the following project.

On one test person among the natives, the foot skin temperature, the foot load, and the electrical conductivity of the skin will be measured by probes attached to both feet during the fire-walking and the results telemetrically recorded. The probe signals will be processed by a multiplexer and an amplitude-frequency converter that modulates a transmitter, all these electronics being carried by the test person. The signals received by a nearby station will be tape-recorded synchronously with the temperature of a certain rock and with the output of a video camera. By this method one can determine how the temperatures of the foot sole and the rock change during fire-walking, whether strong sweat development occurs, and/or whether a reduction of weight in fact does take place. In addition, exact determination of the heat capacity and conductivity of the rocks and the foot skin temperature of the native would be accomplished by conventional methods. Depending on the outcome of the project, further experiments might be necessary to shed more light on the mystery of fire-walking.

The project has interdisciplinary relevance in that not only physics, technology, and physiology but also psychology and ethnology are involved. The trust of the natives must be carefully won, and particular attention must be paid to the statements of the natives about the phenomenon to ensure that they are correctly translated into the semantics of our culture.

The project has certain risks. The electronic equipment must function reliably in a tropical environment. We must obtain the cooperation of the natives, and we must find Fijians willing to perform the ceremony. Based on my experience with experiments in the Philippines and Fijis, the first two risks can be minimized. The third risk, however, dictates that no time be lost, since the fire-walking phenomenon is in the process of disappearing as a result of the influence of Western civilization.

These risks appear worth taking when one considers the possible increase in knowledge in the different disciplines that would result from the successful completion of the experiments. If one does not find an explanation within the realm of known physics—and this seems likely—it is possible that we may discover forces (the natives could help tell us their form) not yet known to physics that might be important for all humanity and that might even make technological and environmental problems appear in another light.

RE-ENACTING THE VOYAGE OF THE FIRST SQUARE RIGGER FLEET TO AUSTRALIA

JONATHAN L. E. KING
Political Science Department, University of Melbourne,
Parkville, Melbourne, Victoria 3052, Australia

Australian, born December 28, 1942. University lecturer, author, and film producer. Educated in England and Australia.

This is an attempt to re-create history for the benefit of the international community and Australia. The plan is to re-create a fleet of eleven square-rigged sailing ships and sail them from the United Kingdom to Australia in 1988, when international attention will be focused on Australia's bicentennial year. As Honorary Director of the First Fleet Re-enactment Committee, I carry a special mission in seeking to achieve this goal. My great-great-great-grandfather, Philip Gidley King, helped organize the First Fleet in 1788 as First Lieutenant on the flagship *Sirius* and Aide-de-Camp to Commander Captain Arthur Phillip. I wish to duplicate that grand and eventful voyage.

As it would not be practical to rebuild the entire fleet, nor necessary, the plan is to create two replicas from the eighteenth-century fleet and charter existing ships to stand in for the remaining nine (next page).

Pre-voyage preparation includes everything from clearances on insurance guarantees to permission from port authorities to allow the ships to enter various harbors. In addition to locating the best shipyard to build our replica ships, there is the task of duplicating as much of the original Fleet's reality as possible, right down to the uniforms, dinner services, and maritime instruments. We will require the help of such British institutions as the Victoria and Albert Museum. With less than seven years to go, we have no time to lose.

The voyage itself is scheduled to run from May 13, 1987, to January 26, 1988. The eleven ships will follow the original route and travel from Portsmouth, England, to Tenerife, Rio de Janeiro, Capetown, and then to Botany

Original Voyage		Re-enactment	
The Two Naval Ships			
1. HMS *Sirius* (540 tons)	Replica built		
2. HMS *Supply* (170 tons)	Chartered	*Royalist*	(United Kingdom)
		or *Beaver II*	(United States)
The Six Transports			
3. *Friendship* (275 tons)	Replica built		
4. *Scarborough* (420 tons)	Chartered	*Bounty*	(New Zealand)
5. *Prince of Wales* (340 tons)	Chartered	*Pamelia II* (*MRFS*)	(United Kingdom)
6. *Charlotte* (340 tons)	Chartered	*Marques* (*Beagle*)	(United Kingdom)
7. *Lady Penrhyn* (335 tons)	Chartered	*Romance*	(Virgin Islands)
8. *Alexander* (270 tons)	Chartered	*Unicorn*	(United States)
		or *New Endeavour*	(United States)
The Three Storeships			
9. *Goldengrove* (350 tons)	Chartered	*Alma Doepel*	(United States)
		or *Pilgrim*	(United States)
10. *Borrowdale* (270 tons)	Chartered	*Regina Maris,*	(United States)
		or *Eolus* (*Black Pearl*)	(United Kingdom)
11. *Fishburn* (270 tons)	Chartered	*Bara Negra*	(United States)
		or *Eye of Wind*	(United Kingdom)

Bay and Port Jackson, Australia, where they will arrive—if modern seamen are as competent as their ancestors—by the appointed date. Permissions have been obtained through the Australian Ambassadors of the countries concerned, and naval escorts are expected to be offered. The ships will travel by wind, and the Commander of the Fleet and each Captain will use the navigational instruments of the day, carrying with them, of course, the modern equipment they would need to save lives in the event of an emergency. The ships will each carry approximately 20 crew members who will perform in the traditional roles of seamen of the day. For the eight-month voyage they will live a modified lifestyle of the period.

After the Australia Day ceremony, the ships will be inspected by the people of Sydney, who will be treated to trips around the harbor. Then the Fleet will sail off, circling the Australian continent and calling on state capitals, returning to Sydney near the end of the bicentennial year. After a final festival the chartered vessels will depart for their homelands.

Once the Fleet has disbanded, the two rebuilt ships will be moored in Sydney and serve as a maritime museum and as a symbol of the great age of the square-rigged sailing ships. They will also be used as sail training vessels and in re-enactments of Australia Day for years to come.

REDISCOVERING AND SIGNPOSTING THE ANCIENT INCA TRAIL

ISMAEL J. ESPINOSA
Castilla 16111 Correo 9, Santiago, Chile

Chilean, born November 27, 1937. Researcher of Latin American iconography; journalist and photographer. Educated in Chile.

I wish to complete the rediscovery and signposting of the ancient Inca Trail. This road, at its peak, led from southern Peru to the Central Valley of Chile, adjacent to the Araucanian territory, in the southern part of the Empire. The Trail, which bordered the Atacama desert or crossed the Andean high plateau, ceased to be used after the first Spanish expeditions during the first half of the sixteenth century. Today, the vestiges of the Trail are almost completely erased, and it is in danger of disappearing. Based on research I have already done, my project consists of exploring the remains of the existing tracks and tracing the erased sections found today in Chile and Argentina. As the segments are located, I plan to signpost them, photograph them, and film them. The final result will be a book with sufficient graphic material to serve as a guide for modern-day visitors to the Trail.

The Inca culture and the Inca Empire have been thoroughly studied by their original countries, notably Peru and Bolivia. Not so much, however, has been done in Chile and Argentina. In Chile, the Empire extended from the Andean valleys to the Atacama desert and through various regions in the Central Valley as far as the border on the Araucanian territory.

At the same time, the Incas spread their influence over the different Indian territories on their borders. For this reason, they built several routes toward the four regions of the Tiahuantinsuyo. The main roads of these routes were partly paved and equipped with stops for food and lodging for messengers who traveled with no provisions. Today, these roads have become known as "El Camino del Inca," or "The Inca Road." It has been calculated that this network extended over some 8000 kilometers in all. Out of this total, the longest and least-known sections are those leading into the Chilean Central Valley; over 3500 kilometers in length, it stretched through immense desert regions on both sides of the Andes.

In Peru and Bolivia, many of these routes survived the end of the Empire, and some of them are still being used. Almost all of their sections have been studied, giving rise to fantastic archaeological discoveries, such as the Machu Picchu citadel (in 1920) and the citadels of the Vilcabamba zone.

The story of the sections leading into Chile has been totally different. The last people to use them were the first Spaniards who arrived in the country. In 1536, Diego de Almagro, who discovered Chile, marched his troops along the route leading through the high Andean plateau. In 1540–1541, Pedro de Valdivia, the first colonizer, used the route through the Atacama desert. The end of the Inca influence in Chile marked the death of the Inca Trail, as the Spaniards coming from Peru preferred to arrive by sea. Subsequent explorations of the route leading into Chile have been fragmented and limited to traditionally known archaeological places. This has led to its virtual disappearance, with only a few sections existing clearly today.

The Inca Trail is significant because it was the most important road network on the American continent. Its ability to tie different communities together, its vastness, and its technology were never exceeded by other Pre-Hispanic cultures. It was the channel through which the Inca culture was transmitted to many hundreds of Indian communities of different origins. In this way, it was possible to obtain peaceful agreements between communities separated by enormous distances, racial differences, and cultural variations. The road expanded agricultural, textile-weaving, and manufacturing technology and gave rise to exchanges of every kind among communities that today occupy the territories of five countries. Numerous paved sections, suspension bridges, roadside "tambos" (inns), and stocking procedures created a relatively safe and wide-ranging means of travel.

Through historical and cartographic research, discussions with archaeologists, interpretation of Andean folklore and legends, and visits to Indian settlements dating back many years, we have approximately established the ancient, primitive route. We propose to follow the anticipated route carefully, seeking to establish its path with assurance.

On confirmed sections of the route, we will signpost it with hard aluminum stakes anchored in rocks or cement. We will prepare a map of the known portions of the route, on a 1:50,000 scale, to provide future travelers and explorers with the information necessary to continue the exploration of this greatest of all ancient American roads.

Descending into one of the potholes in New Britain.

NEW BRITAIN'S GIANT POTHOLES: THE ULTIMATE CAVING CHALLENGE?

 JEAN-FRANÇOIS PERNETTE
Honorable Mention, Rolex Awards for Enterprise
"Pasquet," F-33760 Escoussans, France

French, born September 2, 1954. Student of English and Geography, member and officer of numerous speleological organizations, leader of eight expeditions, discoverer of some dozen caves, and caving writer.

T he aim of my project is to further explore the giant potholes and underground rivers recently discovered in New Britain, Papua New Guinea. These extraordinary hydrogeological systems are so far the largest known in the world. Their exploration is hazardous because of difficulties never before encountered underground, difficulties that call for innovation in techniques and that provide constant challenge.

The study and mapping of the unexplored rivers will help in understanding the hydrogeology of "areas of infinite drainage"—the vague description provided on the currently available maps. The study will contribute to the geographical knowledge of this mostly unknown and remote island north of Australia.

Specifically, my expedition will study the underground network of rivers deep in the Nakanai and Whiteman karsts, by exploring the giant potholes and systems of caves recently discovered in the unexplored areas of New Britain, Papua New Guinea. I shall present the historical and geographical background of the project before describing its objectives and the techniques that will be used.

Papua New Guinea has become, over recent years, the most attractive and appealing place in the world for cave exploration; one could truly call it an "El Dorado" for speleologists. Although the British expedition in 1975 failed to break the world depth record that the 4000-meter-high plateaus seemed to offer, it nevertheless did reveal the incredible speleological possibilities of this vast country, possessed of myriad karst features never visited by speleologists, if indeed ever visited at all. Many expeditions have come—from Australia, Japan, France, Britain, the United States, Switzerland, Spain—each bringing back bits and pieces of results, though often incomplete surveys.

In 1978, a French reconnaissance expedition spent a month in New Britain, where giant systems were discovered. The combination of the speed and the 20-cubic-meter volume of the river flow often precluded further exploration. Two years later, I led a four-month expedition that eventually overcame some of the obstacles. Based on the findings of this expedition, it would appear that the caves of Luse, Kavakuna, Camvuvu may be the largest in the world. Our inability to explore all of them entirely led to the planning of this new expedition, with new objectives of great potential and many further challenges.

There are two main karst areas in New Britain, the Nakanai and the Whiteman Ranges, which together total some 12,000 square kilometers, the largest karst area in all of Papua New Guinea. In height, they rise up to about 2000 meters. They are geologically constituted of carbonated formations (Yalam limestone) that sit directly upon volcanic rocks dating from the Eocene/Oligocene Periods. From the Pliocene Period onward, the island has been gradually rising, leading to a broad anticline oriented southwest to northeast. The overlay of Miocene limestone is 1300 meters thick, but its dip allows a depth potential of over 1600 meters in its extreme points.

To this kind of surface geology have been added the effects of the area's environment. The typical monsoon climate of the region, with its 6000–10,000 millimeters of rain, and the acidity of the tropical rain soil ensure a highly accelerated evolution of the karst landforms—a rate that is certainly one of the most rapid in the world.

Our goal is to erase the "question marks" on the maps of this region. Aerial photos of the Nakanai and Whiteman karsts are lavish in their exposure of the giant potholes, sinkholes, or resurgences, which are easy to locate (if not to reach), but the thick jungle hides many of the surrounding minor dolines. These smaller entrances, still quite impressive by European standards, often lead to major systems that are otherwise unreachable. It will be only through the systematic exploring and documenting of both large and small entrances that we will be able to draw hydrogeological conclusions for the region as a whole.

All these caves have exceptional features in common that imply—indeed, that demand—new techniques of speleological attack and a marvelously new range of challenges. In our desire to be able to explore any cave we may encounter, we will attempt to go beyond the caving techniques of previous expeditions.

These solutions begin long before we actually go underground, as we encounter unique problems well before we get to the caves themselves. First of all, the areas for setting up base camp are hard to reach, due to sporadic and often unsuitable ship services. In Pomio or Kandrian, both of which are District Headquarters, we cannot rely on the availability of goods, food, or the arrival of the next boat. Thus we must organize well ahead of the expedition. Advance camps must be installed, some as far as 50–70 kilometers away (seven or eight days' walk), in order to explore particular areas. The only way to move is through the bush. One usually imagines the jungle as a flat country with a number of well-known discomforts such as inextricable vegetation, suffocating heat, mosquitoes, spiders, and snakes. In New Britain there is all this and more—the rugged karst landforms. Any trek in this area requires a constant pattern of climbing and descending through steep gorges, rough sinkholes, and undulating rocky hills. The paths in the area deserve a description: because of the light thickness of the soil, tree roots most often grow horizontally between projecting rocks with cutting edges. Everything is extremely slippery, particularly when the daily storm turns the track into an unforgettable slough. Orientation in such landforms is almost like blind flying and has to be done with compasses and altimeters.

In addition, due to the lack of manpower and the limited interest in money by the locals, it is difficult to obtain carriers. This problem can be solved only by the reduction of equipment and food or by laborious maneuvering on our own.

Cave exploration in New Britain, then, is very different from standard speleology. The descent into huge potholes 300–400 meters deep is impressive though not technically difficult. Still the danger is always there, due to rock and tree falls, the generally poor quality of the available rigging points, and the impossibility of communicating. More hazardous is the exploration of the underground rivers, with discharges ranging from 5 to 50 cubic meters. To meet these and other challenges, we have designed special equipment to provide us with desired exploring capabilities and safety margins.

New Britain's karsts, its unique rivers and potholes remain one of the last great geographic and hydrogeologic unknowns. Their exploration is the most spectacular and challenging of today's speleological endeavors.

Such an expedition allows no cheating. No helicopter can take you to the cave's entrances; money cannot buy the services of non-existent porters for equipment. You can't afford to forget your shoes or lose a flashlight, or you'll be walking barefoot in the dark. Underground, you don't make mistakes; the water will drown you, or the needed hospital will seem to be in another world. Still, the interest and rewards of such speleology are well worth the difficulties and risks involved.

COLLECTING, GROWING, AND SAVING A TALL CARNIVOROUS PLANT

REINHARD FRENZER

Johann Strausgasse 24, A 2340 Mödling, Austria

Austrian, born September 21, 1953. Medical student at the University of Vienna, following studies in chemistry.

A tropical liane and carnivorous plant, *Triphyophyllum peltatum*, that grows in the hot, seasonally wet forests of Sierra Leone, and possibly in Liberia, is seriously endangered and nearly extinct due to the destruction of forests for wood and agriculture. I wish to go to Sierra Leone to collect specimens of this plant and its seeds, bring them back, and try to cultivate the species. I would attempt the cultivation myself as well as distribute plants among botanic gardens and private collectors who share my interest in trying to prevent the extinction of the species.

First described in 1927 by Hutchison and Dalziel, *T. peltatum* was considered to be a new species of *Dioncophyllum*. In 1951, Airy Shaw did the first modern reworking of this family, which he described as one of the strangest groups of plants to be found in the vegetable kingdom. In 1964, Schmid stated that this family was closely related to Droseraceae, Nepenthaceae, and Sarraceniaceae.

In this family, there are three monotypic genera, all tropical rain forest lianas, growing in Central and Western Africa. *T. peltatum* grows in the hot, seasonally wet forests of Sierra Leone, where only a few inches of mulch and arable soil cover a laterite-pebble hardpan. As the plant's name indicates, it does produce three quite different types of leaves. The juvenile shoot shows quite common oblong-lanceolate leaves. The next stage produces glandular leaves, which resemble the leaves of *Drosera filiformis* or *Drosophyllum* generally. The glands show some resemblance to those of *Drosophyllum*, but there is *no* tentacular movement. All this happens near the ground. Then the plant becomes a climbing liane, producing aglandular, oblong-elliptical leaves, with two hooklets at the tips. Flowers are produced high in the treetops. Little is known about the root system.

From experimentation with plant material from *T. peltatum*, Dr. Y. Heslop-Harrison concludes there is strong support for the idea that the plant is carnivorous, as the glands secrete digestive enzymes, most notably proteases. If this is true, one of the tallest carnivorous plants is in real danger of extinction due to the leveling of its habitat rain forest. At least two previous attempts to cultivate *T. peltatum* have failed (by Kew Gardens and by Marburger). I have therefore decided to try to do something to save this plant. I have cultivated carnivorous plants for more than ten years and now have a collection of 120 species to care for.

I would like to go to Sierra Leone with at least one gardener experienced in growing tropical plants and another expert in growing plants in tissue culture (as there may be no seeds at the time of our visit; there is no information on this factor presently). According to Professor T. L. Green, seedlings appear to transplant well, so we would be attempting to bring back not only live plant material but some seed or seedlings.

With these materials it should be possible to cultivate *T. peltatum* at the *Reservegarten Schonbrunn,* where permission has been given to make the attempt, along with the offer of assistance in the project. I will also attempt to cultivate the plant in my own small greenhouse, and I am sure there will be further interest in the samples from competent private collectors. I would prefer to see the plant in the hands of as many collectors as possible, as quickly as possible, since I do not think it is good to show one's abilities by "cultivating the only plant in the world." Further, I would like to interest botanical gardens in areas of the world with climates similar to that of Sierra Leone in the possibility of cultivating the plant outdoors.

From everything we read about the ongoing destruction of the rain forest habitat of this unusual and rare plant, it seems clear that someone must make the attempt to save it before it disappears, taking with it part of the mystery and fascination about a part of the vegetable kingdom of which we know too little.

AN INSTITUTE TO SAVE
OUR LINGUISTIC HERITAGE

 PIOTR KLAFKOWSKI
Honorable Mention, Rolex Awards for Enterprise
38 Gabels Gate, Box 101, Oslo-2, Norway

Polish, born June 20, 1951. Researcher and adjunct at the Institute of Languages, Adam Mickiewicz University, Poznan. Field work in the Indian Himalayas, editor and translator of Tibetan and Lepcha literary works. Educated in Poland, Ph.D. in Linguistics.

I wish to organize an international institution, or group of scholars, to save the vanishing languages and the "spoken wisdom" of language minorities. The objectives of such a group would be threefold: (1) to make a world register of endangered languages and organize a regular contact with the nationalities in question, (2) to set up a world tape-archive of these languages, and (3) to stimulate and support their maintenance by preparing and implementing language-preservation programs.

If the eighteenth and nineteenth centuries were considered the era of language discoveries, the present century might be called the age of dying languages. Overpowered by the global languages and forced into the game of politics, linguistic minorities are almost totally neglected. While everything else is protected—cultures, monuments, children, endangered animals, and plants—nobody thinks of preserving the human languages. The existence of a "one-world language" is a lovely idea, as long as its use is based on free choice; it is a different situation if it occurs because generations of children may not, or are not allowed to, learn the language of parents.

The three dangers facing linguistic minorities are: (1) total extinction of the language (Cornish, Manx, Manchu, Ainu, those of the American Indians); (2) overpowering by the language of a great population, usually connected with the problem of school instruction (as with Gaelic, Scottish, Tibetan, Hawaiian, Sherpa, Ladakhi, and many others); and (3) neglect of the existing efforts to transmit the language from parents to children (as in the well-documented case of Lepcha).

As the human languages—only a small fraction of which have ever been properly described (if, indeed, at all)—are the storehouses and wealth of unknown literatures (in the broad sense, to include the spoken transmission of literary works) and wisdom (medical lore, field knowledge, historical accounts, etc.), there is the utmost need to preserve as much of it as possible before the generation of the "elders" dies out. Witnesses to most of the major events of this century are still living—and no one is listening to them.

The primary goal of the Human Spoken Heritage project would be to organize a global net of reporters of language-preservation problems and to store in one place all the relevant printed materials available. The field work would be carried out under three headings: (1) Immediate—going wherever the language seems to be on the point of vanishing, to prepare grammars and dictionaries, and to record whatever possible; (2) Language Engineering—assisting, testing, and supervising the implementation of school textbooks in which the target language is the medium of instruction; and (3) Archivistics—setting up an international library of the vanishing languages' books, tapes, and other relevant materials.

In recording the languages, both the spoken and the printed language (where it exists) should be collected. Though the Human Spoken Heritage project should be considered non-religious and non-political, it may well be that recordings of the Bible would serve as a useful common base of comparison in many linguistic cultures.

I would begin my project using sets of Tibetan, Lepcha, and Bhutanese school textbooks; the two editions of the Tibetan Bible; the two manuscripts of the Lepcha tale of Tashe Thing; the Lepcha Gospel according to St. Luke and the Lepcha Story of the Old Testament; the chronological lists of the Bible translations into Tibetan, Mongolian, Manchurian, Lepcha, Hawaiian, Tahitian, Maori, Samoan, and Tongan; and my own personal contacts with experts in the field.

I have already met several qualified men and women who would be willing to join any project along the lines described above. The first step would be the organization of a worldwide mailing program to reach those people who might be interested and to create a group of the first HSH researchers. This program would be addressed to the world's leading universities and linguistic societies, as well as other appropriate organizations.

It is estimated that when the HSH Project is under way, it could support itself, at least partly, through its own publications/journals, reprints of rare or scarce books related to its efforts, and the sale of monographs relating to the field work necessary to fulfill the aims and objectives of the organization.

FIRST NAVIGATION OF THE YANGTZE RIVER, FROM SEA TO SOURCE

MICHAEL E. COLE
High Rising, Linton, Ross-on-Wye, Herefordshire HR9 7RS,
England

*British, born April 10, 1935. Royal Air Force Officer, training officers at RAF
College, Cranwell. Geography/physical education in the United Kingdom.*

I am planning an Anglo-Chinese expedition for 1982 to undertake the first navigation of the Yangtze Kiang River from sea to source, a distance of 3430 miles. A pilot project in 1979 on the Himalayan River Kali Gandaki in West Nepal succeeded for the first time in harnessing the unique potential of lightweight hovercrafts for climbing steep rapids on fast-flowing rivers.

Two new hovercrafts are now being developed and built especially to tackle the previously unnavigable stretches of the Yangtze Kiang. They are specifically intended to overcome the temperamental characteristics of the great rivers of China, which are at present a barrier to their use as a means of communications into the inhospitable areas of the hinterland. In addition, the expedition will be an experiment in Anglo-Chinese cooperation that will break new ground in every direction.

Background to the Expedition

In the developing countries of the world, there are enormous problems of population increase, poor crops, and people permanently living on the brink of ill health and thereby functioning at half pace. Even where aid programs are implemented, lack of communications often ensures that the most needy are never reached.

Over ten years ago, a man walked on the moon. In contrast, many of the inhabited parts of our own planet lack effective communications. The application of appropriate technology in places of need is one solution that could help check world population growth. We have now shown that the lightweight hovercraft is one such application. In our expedition to Nepal in 1979, we proved that these craft are capable of using fast-flowing rivers, previously unnavigable, as highways to areas that were virtually inaccessible prior to the availability of this craft.

The use of the fierce and complex river systems of the Republic of China as a means of regular communication remains one of the most formidable problems of exploration still to be solved.

Outline of the Expedition

Four major rivers and five lesser waterways flow eastward across China from the north. These are the Heilung Kiang, the Hwang Ho, the Yangtze Kiang, and the Si Kiang, plus the Liao, Hai, Hwai, Chientang, and Min. In addition, the southwest of China includes parts of the Brahmaputra, the Salween, the Mekong, and the Red Rivers. On all these rivers, rapids and fast-flowing waters curtail the extent of navigation by boat. A lightweight hovercraft has the potential to penetrate the hinterland deeply (see table). The lightweight hovercraft has the potential to double the navigable length of China's four major rivers. The potential on numerous other rivers is even greater.

River	Length (km)	Navigable by Boat (km)	Exclusive Potential by Hovercraft (km)
Yangtze Kiang	5,500	2,542	2,958
Hwang Ho	4,350	275	4,075
Heilung Kiang	4,700	4,450	250
Si Kiang	3,000	800	2,200
	17,750	8,067	9,483

The Yangtze Kiang is the largest and most challenging Chinese river. Its mood reflects, on its various stretches, all the obstacles to be found on rivers around the world. The planned journey, therefore, will test both men and hovercraft to the limit, over three distinct phases.

The first phase, from the ocean to Ichange, runs over 1000 miles, all fully navigable by boat, and therefore a test of the hovercraft's endurance over long operating conditions.

The second phase, which runs 650 miles upstream from Ichang to the city of Chungking, is normally considered marginally navigable. There are a dozen gorges, one 25 miles long, and a succession of turbulent rapids. Navigation by normal boat is severely hampered by a 13-knot current. Current practice on this stretch is for boats to be pulled through the swifter sections by trackers, a situation that can often prolong the river trip over this section up to two months. A further hazard here is the presence of short-notice floods, during which the river may rise up to 50 feet above normal levels in a day.

The third phase runs from Chungking upriver to the source, a distance of 1848 miles, through great gorges in a wild, sparsely populated area. Round-bottomed skin boats are the only means of crossing the river along this stretch. Two-way navigation possibilities on this last stretch belong exclusively to the hovercraft to the limit, over three distinct phases.

We anticipate a team of fourteen members, consisting of eight British and six Chinese. Our plans call for making the trip during the seven-month period from March to September 1982.

Questions Posed by the Expedition

1. What are the political difficulties of an Anglo-Chinese project? The Chinese authorities have never before been as well disposed toward the introduction of appropriate Western technology. The use of this British innovation has the bold objective of doubling the navigable length of the waterways of this developing country. The joint planning of such a project across cultural, engineering, and political boundaries will be a telling test of character on both sides, as well as a notable adventure of discovery.

2. Are the hovercrafts suitable for the task? The crafts' performance has been successfully validated in the Nepalese expedition, and some improvements are being incorporated into the two craft being built for the operation on the Yangtze.

3. What if there is a major breakdown of the craft on the Yangtze? The two crafts have been specially built in "Meccano" sectional or modular form, to enable repair on long lines of logistics.

4. What rescue plans are envisioned? The upper reaches of the Yangtze are remote and lacking in communications. Radio contact is difficult in the hinterland. A full medical pack set-up will be carried, and it is intended that both British and Chinese medical personnel will be members of the team.

5. What will happen to the craft at the end of the expedition? As an act of international friendship, the two hovercraft will be presented to the Chinese for use on other Chinese rivers.

EARTHPORT: LAUNCHING THE PEACEFUL EXPLORATION OF SPACE

MARK C. FRAZIER
317 "C" Street N.E., Washington, D.C. 20002, U.S.A.

American, born April 17, 1952. Executive Director of Sabre Foundation's International Division. Educated in the United States.

A s humanity reaches into space, a truly international basis for endeavors seems essential. The Earthport Project proposes a unique means to achieve this goal: a launch facility open to peaceful users from all nations. Operating Earthport as a freeport could generate revenues sufficient to strengthen an international presence in space.

Vast new benefits await humanity on the frontier of space. Already, satellites have begun to slash communications costs, survey natural resources and the environment, warn of approaching storms and guide ships to their destinations. The future promises even more. However, significant obstacles stand in the way. The costs of sustained space efforts are extraordinary. The superpowers enjoy an enormous lead over the rest of the world, but more disturbingly, the major powers seem to be increasingly interested in a quest for military advantage. A new approach is needed to promote international, economical, and non-military access to space.

The Sabre Foundation believes it has identified a possible way. It has gathered a team of space scientists and officials from more than two dozen nations, who are preparing a new path for peaceful and productive use of the frontier. The proposal is nothing less than the creation of an international launch site for scientific and commercial users around the world.

Bold as the goal may seem, a number of indicators attest to its practicability. New commercial launch services are being organized to meet demands for orbiting hundreds of satellites in the coming decade. A number of nations have already attained the capability to loft satellites on their own vehicles. Several aerospace corporations are taking similar steps to offer space launch services. In most or all these efforts, there is a common consideration: the cost of launching vehicles into space is directly connected to the location of launch. Many launch organizations are looking to the equatorial belt for optimal sites. At low latitudes, there are the following savings:

1. Greater momentum for boosters. At the equator, the earth's own spin is almost 1600 kilometers per hour to the east. Launches from this region have more inbuilt momentum than from other locations.

2. Simpler orbital paths. Most satellites now launched must make mid-flight corrections to enter an equatorial orbital plane. Launches from equatorial sites avoid this, offer simplified tracking procedures, and can more easily be shifted into other orbital planes.

3. More frequent "windows." Equatorially launched satellites pass overhead on each circuit, allowing easier rendezvous, and simplified landing procedures with a recovery site in the orbital plane.

These and related benefits have prompted some nations to establish equatorial launch zones. The European Arianespace group will use a site in French Guiana, an Italian-American group will use Kenya, and a German enterprise has tested in Zaire.

We believe it makes little sense to duplicate and proliferate these expensive facilities, and we have explored the idea of an international site with numerous expert advisers and interested parties. To respect the idea of Earthport's internationalism, and still be able to provide a neutral international launch site, we have turned to the idea of a freeport and free trade zone, such as those used by many developing countries for economic purposes.

Earthport researchers have moved beyond the conceptual stage. With financial support from Arthur C. Clarke, aerospace firms such as Satellite Systems Engineering, and other advocates of entry to space, over a dozen full and part-time people are developing steps for implementation. We are receiving legal help, university assistance in planning for a training institute, advice from construction and engineering firms, and help in preparing financial proposals.

To date, more than a dozen prospective sponsoring nations have expressed interest in hosting the site for Earthport. Officials and scientists from 26 nations are overseeing preparation of international space efforts that could be funded in the period prior to commencement of launch operations. The Earthport Project has the chance to diminish political confrontations and national rivalries by establishing new and valuable economic and technical relationships between nations in a global effort to use space resources for a more promising future.

EXPEDITION TO STUDY HUMAN PERFORMANCE ON THE SUMMIT OF MT. EVEREST

 JOHN B. WEST
Honorable Mention, Rolex Awards for Enterprise
9626 Blackgold Road, La Jolla, California 92037, U.S.A.

American, born December 27, 1928. Professor of Medicine and Bioengineering. Medical education in Australia and the United Kingdom.

The American Medical Research Expedition to Everest, 1981, of which I am leader, has as its chief objective the obtaining of information on human performance at extreme altitudes including the highest point on earth, Mt. Everest's 8848-meter summit. In autumn 1981, measurements and investigations planned for the climbers on the summit will include barometric pressure, temperature, collection of air from the depths of the lung, continuous electrocardiograms, respiratory rate and volume, and possibly oxygen consumption. A scientific laboratory will be maintained on the South Col (8000 meters), where scientists will measure maximal work capacity and oxygen consumption using a stationary bicycle ergometer. The main physiological camp will be at 6100 meters, where there will be a heated laboratory with electrical power and where measurements will be made of the blood oxygen during maximal exercise and also during sleep.

Though much work has been done on high-altitude physiology, there are only limited data available up to 7440 meters, and almost no information has been obtained at higher altitudes. However, the physiological conditions near the summit of Mt. Everest are of great interest, and it is a remarkable coincidence that this highest point on earth has a partial pressure of oxygen that is precisely sufficient to maintain human life. For many years it was believed the mountain was too high to be climbed without supplementary oxygen. The historic ascent by Reinhold Messner and Peter Habeler in May 1978 demonstrated that humans could indeed perform sufficient physical activity at these extreme altitudes to reach the summit breathing ambient air.

Our expedition, endorsed by the American Alpine Club and having received permission from the Nepalese government, will include approximately nine scientists, many of whom are experienced Himalayan climbers plus an extremely strong climbing team, and about 40 high-altitude Sherpas.

Measurements planned for the 8848-meter summit include barometric pressure, using special digital aneroid barometers. Temperature data will be recorded. Air from the depths of the lungs (alveolar gas) will be collected in pre-evacuated glass ampules. The ampules will be sealed by fusing the flask with an oxybutane flame at the laboratory tent (8000 meters) and analyzed later at sea level. Low-speed portable tape recorders (Medilog) will record electrocardiograms continuously. Ventilation rate and volume will be measured with a turbine flow meter mounted in the inspiratory gas line of the climbing oxygen set. Oxygen consumption will be measured using the Oxylog (Ambulatory Monitoring). This latter is an ambitious measurement, but the instrument is being specially modified for use in these conditions.

Measurements to be made at the 8000-meter South Col will center around a laboratory tent erected at this camp, which will be manned by two scientists each day over a six-day period. The tent will house a stationary bicycle ergometer and associated equipment, for measuring maximal work capacity and oxygen consumption. Venous blood samples will be drawn and taken rapidly down to the 6100-meter camp, where an extensive series of hematological measurements will be made, including PO_2, PCO_2, pH, hemoglobin, hematocrit, P_{50}, oxygen dissociation curve, and the 2,3-diphosphoglycerate concentration.

Measurements at the 6100-meter camp will be made in a scientific lab housed in a pre-fabricated, thermally insulated, rigid hut. Heated to normal lab temperatures by a kerosene heater, with electrical power from solar panels and gasoline generators, this lab will house a Hewlett-Packard ear oxymeter for measuring arterial oxygen saturation during rest, exercise, and sleep, with ambient air and low oxygen mixtures. Respiratory movements will be measured using a variable inductance vest, and one-channel electro-encephalograms and electro-oculograms will also be recorded to determine sleep state. Chest radiographs will also be taken, along with venous blood samples as noted above.

The measurements described here should greatly extend existing knowledge of adaptation to extreme altitudes and the effects of extreme hypoxemia (subnormal oxygen content in arterial blood) on the body. The studies should also improve our understanding of cardiopulmonary function in patients with severe lung and heart diseases.

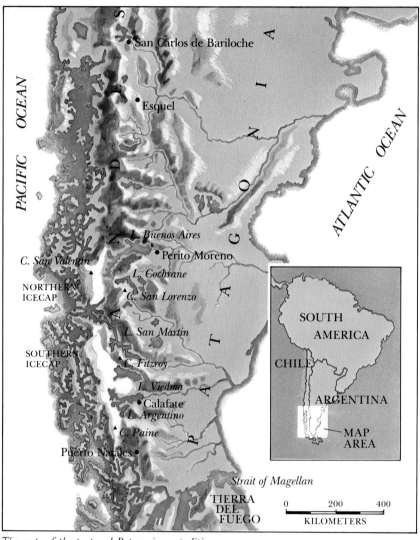

The route of the proposed Patagonian expedition.

PATAGONIAN EXPLORATION EXPEDITION

JANE WILSON
c/o Giobellina, La Citronelle, 1854 Leysin, Switzerland

American, born January 27, 1953. Explorer and mountain climber in North and South America, Europe, and Africa. Art/photography education in the United States.

The Patagonian Exploration Expedition will explore the vast wilderness of Patagonia by two methods. First on horseback, we will explore the eastern slope of the Andes from San Carlos de Bariloche, Argentina, to Puerto Natales, Chile. Second, on skis (a method seldom seen in Patagonia), we will travel from Paine National Park, Chile, to Perito Moreno, Argentina, exploring the full lengths of both North and South Continental Icecaps in the winter season.

Patagonia is a place that, after you have been there, you recall as a place you either love or hate. Its infamous winds, vast deserts, incredible glaciers, and beautiful mountains do not allow impartiality. I love Patagonia. During my two previous trips there, I traveled extensively, studying the wildlife, climbing in the Mount Fitzroy area, speaking with many of the few residents of this isolated world, and looking for Indian artifacts. One expedition took one month to explore the Straits of Magellan and the fjord land on the coast of Chile.

During the Patagonian Exploration Expedition, our aim is to reach and explore the remotest regions of Patagonia, using methods that are particularly suited to both the terrain and the season. We will start on horseback from San Carlos de Bariloche in the early spring. Traveling south in this manner, we will be covering over 1000 kilometers before we reach Puerto Natales. In this stage of the expedition, we will stay primarily on the eastern slopes of the mountains, as glacial travel is obviously not at all practicable with horses. Along this route, we will cross vast, uninhabited areas filled with large lakes, deserts, wildlife (including guanaco, rhea, puma, and condor), and many unclimbed mountains. The latter are one of the main reasons for making this expedition, because there have not even been first attempts on many of these mountains.

The beginning will be the least challenging, since we will find plenty of water and a fair number of towns and villages between Bariloche and Esquel, about 250 kilometers to the south. This will provide us with a margin of safety in the tricky business of buying and selling horses as we move along, before we get into the less inhabited regions.

After Esquel, there are two major stopping points for supplies, one at Perito Moreno, near Lago Buenos Aires, and the other at Calafate, near Lago Argentino. There are also outposts for the *Gendarmerie* at many of the roads near the Argentine-Chilean border, such as the ones at Lago San Martin and Lago Viedma. Finally, isolated estancias provide the opportunity to buy supplies and to get to know some of the interesting characters who carve an existence out of this hostile environment.

Since we all (two women and one man) have a keen interest in climbing, we will spend time exploring in the mountains. Of particular interest will be the regions near Cerro San Valentin, Cerro Fitzroy, and the Paine region. These three areas are well known for their outstanding climbing, but perhaps more exciting will be the possibility of discovering and climbing in new areas.

One of the most important projects during the ride south will be locating good food cache points, and landmarks and escape points for the more difficult second stage of the expedition, that of skiing all along the icecaps in the winter.

We are planning to take at most five months for the ride to Puerto Natales from Bariloche. That will bring us to about mid-February, and we would spend the next month and a half to two months placing food caches and preparing equipment for the skiing.

Toward late April, we plan to leave from Paine National Park, in the vicinity of Puerto Natales, Chile. Soon after Cerro Paine, the immense Continental Icecap starts. We will be basically following this Southern Continental Icecap for 300 kilometers. The icecap itself is a wild place, 300 by 70 kilometers of ice and mountains, bordered on the east by the Patagonian Andes and on the west by rugged, uninhabited fjord lands and the Pacific Ocean.

The icecap is subjected to some of the most ferocious weather in the world, of which the most infamous element is the wind. Local reports indicate that the winter wind is less severe than that of summer, and there is not very much precipitation. In the summer, bad weather can last for more than a month. In general, the few expeditions that have gone to the area in the winter have had better weather than those that have gone in summer. Because of the tempering influence of the nearby Pacific Ocean, we will not expect extreme cold.

Possible exit points from the icecap will include Brazo Rico, a route that leads toward Lago Argentino; Estancia Cristina on Brazo Norte of Lago Argentino; Glaciers Moyano and Viedma, leading to the isolated estancias on Lago Viedma; Pasos del Viente and Marconi, leading into the Cerro Fitzroy area that we know quite well; and Brazo Sur, leading toward the estancias on the south shore of Lago San Martin.

From the Southern Icecap, we will head north across the Northern Icecap for 150 kilometers to the Cerro San Valentin area, from which we will then turn east and head for the north shore of Lago Buenos Aires and our destination of Perito Moreno. Depending on conditions, we might head toward Cerro San Lorenzo from Lago San Martin, travel past Lago Cochrane toward the south shore of Lago Buenos Aires, and into Perito Moreno from that direction.

Our planned schedule for the expedition will have us begin in October 1981 and finish in August 1982.

The three members of the expedition are Jane and Jay Wilson, both American, and Ariane Giobellina, who is Swiss. We are all highly qualified skiers and long-time climbers, and are confident of our ability to survive in this lonely and nearly lost outpost region of the world.

INVESTIGATING THREE ENDANGERED SPECIES IN PERU'S ANDES

V. GRIMALDO MURILLO DUEÑAS
Jr. Alemania 2174, Chacra Rios Norte, Lima, Peru

Peruvian, born April 28, 1935. Operations coordinator/chief guide for Peruvian adventure travel operator. Geology/biology education in Peru.

This project is intended to expand our knowledge of three rare and endangered species of the Peruvian Andes: the Andean condor (*Vulture griphus*), the guanaco (*Lama guanicoe*), and the Andean puma (*Felis concolor*). Little is known about them, since they live far from human civilization, at 4000–5000-meter heights, in extremely remote, inhospitable, and nearly inaccessible places.

The purpose of this project is to observe each of these animals in its native habitat over an extended period of time, in order to add to our very limited knowledge of their behavior, living patterns, and so on.

The information I intend to obtain is basic and unsophisticated compared to most related biologic studies. Nevertheless, these species are so difficult to observe, and live in regions so remote from major academic centers, that the current state of our knowledge of them is sorely lacking. My research has revealed no evidence of extended observations of any of these endangered creatures. As a leader of expeditions to 6000-meter peaks in the Cordilleras for over twenty-four years, I have often seen these species and am concerned about their future.

I intend to hike into three remote regions of the Cordilleras of Peru where I have previously sighted these species, and set up camp. I will maintain my camp for up to a month at a time, while searching for and then observing the animals. I will return to each of the sites at least twice more within the year to observe the animals during different seasons and to observe the development of offspring. Specific plans and aims for observing the species are as follows.

The Andean condor sites are in the Cordillera Vilcanota, Puno department, in southeastern Peru, on the southern exposure of Nevado Kunurana (5700 meters) in the southeastern corner of the range. Base camp will be at 4800 meters at the head of Yuraq Unu Canyon, 25 kilometers from trailhead near the town of Santa Rosa. The search for condors will be at 5300–5500 meters, above a 500-meter-high, 55-degree wall of rock and ice. I plan to spend as many nights as possible above this wall, observing and filming the condor. My first trip will be in June and July, when I hope to find newly laid eggs. I will return in October, then February, then May, to monitor the growth of the young condors, who stay in the nest (or "home"—it is still uncertain whether these condors make nests) for almost a full year before learning to fly.

The guanaco sites are in the Cordillera Vilcanota, 20 kilometers from the 4300-meter La Raya Pass, in an unmapped area of the range. Very few guanacos remain. The young are born between December and February, during the worst of the rainy season in the Peruvian Andes, a key reason why nothing is known about baby guanacos; virtually all sightings are *only* of adults. I plan to set up camp in this area first in August and later in January to observe the newborns. This will require a great deal of patience, for the guanaco is an extremely timid, and also fleet, creature. They run away at the first hint of danger.

The Andean puma, although relatively rare, lives throughout the Peruvian Andes in an altitude zone of 3800–4600 meters. For this reason, I will investigate the puma at the same time as the others. Pumas often live near the herds of alpacas (a prime source of food) that are common in the Cordillera Vilcanota. I will search for their lairs near these herds. I am especially interested in learning about their mating habits, which involve fierce struggles among the males, and how they feed and care for their young.

The only specialized equipment to be used are still and movie cameras, rock-climbing and ice-climbing equipment, and general camping gear. I will use a 35-mm camera with telephoto lenses of up to 300 mm (along with other accessories), and a 16-mm movie camera. The climbing equipment will consist of two 50-meter climbing ropes, crampons, ice axe, ice screws, carabiners, harness, rock-climbing boots, helmet, jumars, pitons, and chocks. The camping gear will include a tent, sleeping bag, stove, and bivouac sack for nights spent above 5000 meters.

The reason I wish to study these animals is my inability to find any reliable information on them, though there have been a number of proposed—but not completed—expeditions by biologists from the United States and Europe. Given my experience in years of learning the mountains that form the habitat of three rare and endangered species, I hope that I will be able to contribute something to the world's knowledge of them.

AFRICAN CRYPTOZOOLOGICAL EXPLORATION

JAMES H. POWELL, JR.

1110 Kokomo Street, Plainview, Texas 79072, U.S.A.

American, born February 2, 1933. Full-time explorer and writer; member of Explorers Club of New York. Educated in the United States.

A s a result of field explorations between 1976 and 1980 in the equatorial African countries of Gabon, Cameroun, and the People's Republic of the Congo, I have become convinced that a large amphibious animal, as yet unknown to science, exists, or did exist until very recently, in certain remote areas of these countries. Specifically, I believe the two most promising areas for exploration are a region in northern Congo, near the headwaters of the Likouala-aux-Herbes River, and the vast region of lakes and swamps bordering and extending south from the lower Ogooué River in Gabon. I wish to return to one or both of these regions to verify the existence or non-existence of this animal, and, if it proves to be a real animal, to establish its identity. In Congo, this creature is known as *mokele-mbembe*, in Gabon as *n'yamala*.

Cryptozoology—the search for animals heretofore unknown to science—is slowly but inexorably evolving from the status of a "monster hunt" into a serious discipline. No doubt the recent discovery of such living fossils as the *Burramys parvus* in Australia and the "extinct" Pleistocene peccary in South America has greatly accelerated this process.

Reports of a large amphibious animal with a long neck and a long tail have emanated from the region of equatorial Africa—roughly the tropical rain forest zones of the above-mentioned countries, plus Equatorial Guinea, the Central African Republic, and adjacent portions of Zaire. Such reports date back at least to accounts by early French Catholic missionaries published in 1776. More recently, German explorers in 1914 and 1938, French explorers in 1934, Scottish explorers in 1932, and my own explorations from

1976 to 1980 have recorded reports of this apparent beast. During 1976, while studying rain forest crocodiles in Gabon and Cameroun, I collected much new information in the form of first-person reports, important local historical tales of encounters with the beast, and vivid descriptions of surprisingly similar consistency from one location to another.

In 1979, I returned to Gabon to follow up the leads obtained during my 1976 expedition, and in the early part of 1980 I made an expedition to the northern part of the People's Republic of the Congo to search for the animal. On the latter expedition, accompanied by Dr. Roy Mackal, a month was spent in the bush in northern Congo, with Impfondo on the Ubangi River as our initial base. Here, at the location of an American Protestant mission, we found the tradition of the mokele-mbembe to be ubiquitous. By questioning numerous informants, we learned that a mokele-mbembe had, about 100 years ago, inhabited a deep pool downstream on the Ubangi, and we were told that, if we really wanted information on the beast, we should go to Epena, a village approximately 50 miles to the west.

We visited the deep pool by day and night without encountering anything unusual, though we did find the alleged favorite food of the mokele-mbembe, the malombo, to be abundant there. Exactly as described by earlier German accounts, it is a liana with a milky-white sap, white blossoms, and nut-like fruits about apple size. Specimens were collected and subsequently identified as belonging to the genus *Landolphia*.

After some effort, we also received permits to visit Epena, which was reachable only by walking overland through 50 miles of swampland. There we spoke with numerous inhabitants who claimed to be eye-witnesses to the beast and who provided us with specific directions to where we might most reasonably expect to find the mokele-mbembe—Lake Tele. This lake, about 4 miles in diameter, is located about 25 miles west of Epena. Unfortunately, with visas due to expire and time too limited, we had to leave the area for the long and uncertain journey back to Impfondo, and thence to Brazzaville, thus turning back only 25 miles from what may have been a remarkable zoological disovery.

I wish to return to Congo, go to Epena with more ample time, and set up a base camp at Lake Tele. From that camp, I wish to explore the lake itself as well as certain adjoining waterways, such as the Bai (or Tebeke) River, which figured in the reports of our Epena informants.

The animal I seek is described in a way that suggests a body similar to a Diplodocus, of massive size, water dwelling, and capable of stopping the flow of a stream when it stands up. Local people are terrified of it, some even to the point of refusing to discuss it. If it is truly there, I wish to find it, and make it known to the world of science.

MEXICO'S FOLKLORIC MUSIC— EXPLORING A CULTURAL TREASURE TROVE

EDUARDO LLERENAS
Rolex Laureate, Rolex Awards for Enterprise
Torresqui 56, Coyoacán, Mexico 21, D.F., Mexico

Mexican, born December 28, 1945. Biochemistry Professor at Department of Biochemistry, Center for Research and Advanced Studies, National Polytechnic Institute. Scientific education and Ph.D. in Mexico, post-doctoral work in the United Kingdom. Conducts basic research, lectures in physical chemistry, tutors graduate students, and publishes professionally.

This project consists of the field collection of Mexican folk music, in the form of magnetophonic recordings. It is an enterprise involving traveling to small, often out-of-the-way villages; the tracing of folk music interpreters; critical listening to both the music and the quality of performance (good and bad musicians are found everywhere); and the actual recording of the music. We have done this collecting in a very systematic way and have thus been able to "sweep out" many ethnomusical zones to what we consider to be completion. A major concern is that we achieve technical standards of recording that are at professional levels, a challenge we believe we have met. We have now completed nearly two-thirds of the project, with some ethnomusical zones still to be fully covered and others yet to be explored for the first time.

It is commonly agreed that Mexican folk music is among the richest in the world. This is partly due to the many native cultures, with very highly developed civilizations, that existed before the arrival of the Spanish conquerors, and to the wide and rich musical heritage that these Europeans brought to the Americas. The mingling of both cultures resulted in a new and vast Mexican folklore. This in turn became more and more individualized in certain regions, given the land's natural configurations—mountain ranges divide the country into well-defined sectors, with resultant heightened variety in musical folklore.

The imprint of modern civilization on Mexican life has been deep and is in many respects irreversible. Musical traditions have not been exempted from this process, and they are disappearing rapidly in nearly all communities. Popular music is taking over the folkloric. The "standardization" imposed by radio, television, and the phonograph, and the recent construction and improvement of country roads, are among the gradual causes of this pending extinction. The pace of standardization is, if anything, accelerating.

In view of this, and the fact that there had been no systematic gathering of folk music in Mexico, we decided to start this enterprise, the primary objective of which is the preservation of our musical heritage in the form of magnetophonic recordings.

We initiated this project ten years ago, making some live recordings in small villages situated in the northeastern part of the country. At that time, we owned only a monophonic cassette recorder. We soon realized that a collection of this caliber and magnitude demanded stringent musical criteria and excellent technical quality in the making of the recordings. Otherwise, we would be bringing back home only nice acoustic souvenirs. The need for recording equipment of the highest standards was evident, and we soon stepped up through better equipment to a point where it became totally professional (Nagra portable stereo recorder, Neumann microphones, mixer, all-monitoring appliances, and so on).

As for musical judgment, the recording team counted on our having a very good knowledge of the music before the start of the first gathering. There are three of us: Enrique, who has an engineering degree and ample experience in electro-acoustics; Beno, who has a long record as a guitar and violin player and also as a musicologist: and Eduardo, who has a deep knowledge of the country terrain and the local people. None of us makes a living from the project, a fact that helped guarantee the endurance, continuity, and high spirit of the enterprise as is reflected in the quality of the results.

To date, we have made about eighty recording trips in Mexico, covering seven ethnomusical areas that include eleven subzones. At least 60 percent of the tours involved long driving over unpaved and dirt roads. Horseback riding and hiking are also part of our explorations. During these trips we taped more than 180 different folk music ensembles, each composed of three to five interpreters. The musicians, as are most of the real folk interpreters, are peasants who play music in their spare time. Nonetheless, they do it in most instances to virtuoso standards. Finding them in their home towns is always an arduous task, since when they are not playing, they are plowing their fields. Normally they play in social celebrations (weddings, birthdays, baptism parties, and so on) and sometimes in the local pubs as well. The music (much of what we have recorded is from the mestizo culture, with its mixture of Spanish and Indian, and strong hints of Andalusian flamenco) is played with stringed instruments such as harps, various guitars, and violins. Percussion instruments are common in some areas. One or two of the players usually sing songs with traditional lyrics.

In addition to our trips in Mexico, we have made eight exploratory recording trips abroad: the Antilles (Dominican Republic) three times, Belize three times, and single trips to Panama and Guatemala. We went to trace their music for comparisons and to start a musical collection from other Central and South American countries. We can proudly say that our Mexican experience worked fine in these other places.

The tape collection includes more than 250 tapes, mostly recorded in half-track stereo at 15 inches per second on low-noise tape. We have also kept a photographic record of the places we visited and the musicians we recorded. On some trips we also taped the musical interpreters talking about the music, the words, and their habitat.

Until now the entire project has been sponsored by ourselves as a private enterprise, carried out in our spare time. Although we have applied for financial help from various state and private organizations, it seems unlikely that we will find assistance in Mexico.

We are convinced that the material we have gathered represents the musical testimony of a considerable part of our country and that it could be utilized in various ways: ethnomusical and historical studies; and wide or narrow scale diffusion of the music as a way of preserving it, both in the places where its tradition is disappearing or already gone and in places where it could be welcomed and learned anew.

Inflation and devaluation have taken their tolls. When we started, a four-day recording trip cost about $100: today it is closer to $800. (A substantial portion pays the musicians for the performances.)

To complete our project, it is imperative that we accelerate the gathering. We envision that it would take us about three more years to tape what is missing, based on making approximately forty more recording trips.

DEVELOPING THE WINGED BEAN IN ASIA

A. N. M. NAZMUL HAQ
Department of Biology, Building 44, The University,
Southampton SO9 5NH, England

Bangladeshi, born January 2, 1942. Leverhulme Research Fellow and Project Coordinator. Educated in Bangladesh and the United Kingdom.

In Asia, particularly in Bangladesh (with 90 million people and a land area of some 133,000 square miles), a chronic food deficit of 20 to 30 percent exists every year. Strenuous efforts have been made to increase production in the agricultural sector, with the emphasis largely concentrated on the cereal crops (rice and wheat). A result of this emphasis is an underdevelopment of plant protein and oil crops. In Bangladesh, the diet is almost devoid of animal protein, and the extent of malnutrition is alarming (about 80 percent of the population suffers from protein calorie malnutrition). Rice alone accounts for all caloric and protein supply for the people. Furthermore, according to a World Bank forecast, $75 million is to be spent to import edible oil in 1980. It is clear that a multiple-purpose crop would be of considerable economic and nutritional benefit to Bangladesh.

One such dual crop is the winged bean (*Psophocarpus tetragonolobus*), which has been grown as a backyard crop in some parts of Bangladesh for the last two centuries. This bean has only recently attracted attention as a potential source of high-quality plant protein for use in the humid tropics, although its cultivation has been known for decades. The plant produces two valuable products—the seed, with 30 to 40 percent protein and 15 to 20 percent oil (70 percent polyunsaturated) and a tuber, with 16 percent protein by dry weight. With an amino acid profile similar to that of the soybean, it has a lower content of antimetabolic products, making it of great value in the prevention of kwashiorkor. Lysine-rich, it naturally complements lysine-deficient, carbohydrate stable foods. Its immature pods and seeds, flowers, and leaves all contain protein and are commonly used as vegetables.

At maturity, the haulm of the winged bean is used as livestock feed, allowing all parts of the plant to be utilized. Additionally, when inoculated with the appropriate strain of *Rhizobium*, it has a great capacity for nitrogen fixation. It is, in all respects, the natural counterpart of the humid tropics to the well-known soybean. In spite of these manifest advantages, however, it is surprising that the winged bean's culture is not more widespread in the humid tropics. Studies of the problem show that its broad cultivation will be neither simple nor straightforward. Yield is low (average 810 kilograms/hectare), and 52 percent of the total input is needed for staking, making the bean of limited appeal to the small farmer. In this project, it is proposed to improve the winged bean to a level that makes it attractive to farmers throughout Asia as a viable and desirable crop.

I propose to hybridize high-yield seed plants and high-yield tuber plants (they are not now similar) and indeterminate dwarf erect-type plants that will minimize the staking cost.

Germplasm evaluation will concentrate on the indeterminate dwarf erect-type plant, already reported to exist within the Indian germplasm, though germplasm collection will continue to be made from different regions of the winged bean's habitat. As the winged bean is closely related to certain other species that grow from 1 to 6 meters tall, certain interspecific crosses will be made with the hope of producing a low-input plant. Once an ideal plant type is achieved, improved yield can be obtained by breeding and selection.

As the winged bean is largely self-pollinating, breeding methods will be similar to those of other autogamous species. These include the collection of germplasm (indigenous and overseas), evaluation and selection (pure line selection), hybridization and selection (using either the pedigree, bulk, or modified bulk-pedigree method), backcrossing, and a modified pedigree method (single seed descent). However, a successful plant breeding program to improve yield will depend on the understanding of the genetics of yield and yield-related characteristics along with other desirable characters.

The actual breeding and selection work will be carried out in the field. During the course of germplasm evaluation, selection will be made for the genotypes with the desired characters. The initial part of the breeding work, hybridization and selection, will be carried out in the greenhouse at Southampton. Once hybrids have been produced possessing desirable characters, these will be put on field trial in Bangladesh. It may be necessary to further adapt plants to specific areas where the winged bean crop will be developed.

The development of low-input, highly productive strains of the winged bean and improvement of its qualities by breeding will be a major step forward in meeting the agricultural and nutritional needs of Asian countries.

AN ICHTHYOLOGICAL EXPLORATION OF BORNEO

 TYSON R. ROBERTS
Honorable Mention, Rolex Awards for Enterprise
Department of Ichthyology, California Academy of Sciences,
Golden Gate Park, San Francisco, California 94920, U.S.A.

American, born June 1, 1940. Research Biologist at California Academy of Sciences. Biology Ph.D. from Stanford University.

I wish to advance the ichthyological exploration of the fresh waters of Borneo and to prepare a definitive account of the rich, extremely diverse, and largely endemic ichthyofauna of this island. Several rivers in southwestern Borneo have never been explored ichthyologically. The important Mahakan and other large rivers in eastern Borneo are poorly known, and the mountainous streams in the complex central highlands, from which arise the headwaters of all the major rivers, are virtually virgin territory. A Rolex Award would permit major ichthyological exploration of one important river, or one important highlands area, and the preparation of a scientific report on the results of this exploration.

In 1976, with support from the Smithsonian Tropical Research Institute and approval of the Indonesian National Research Council, I conducted an ichthyological field survey of the Kapuas River in western Borneo, the largest river and the one possessing the richest ichthyofauna of all the rivers on this island. This effort resulted in an unprecedentedly large collection of specimens representing some 260 species, or nearly two-thirds as many as the total number of freshwater fishes known for the entire island. About 30 of these species were new, that is, not previously described. Several of them represented new genera, and in one instance, even a new family. With sponsorship from the California Academy of Sciences and funding from the U.S. National Science Foundation, I am now preparing a major systematic and biological report, "The Freshwater Fishes of the Kapuas and Sambas Rivers of Indonesian Borneo." This account will include discussion of such ichthyological topics as the zoogeographical relation of the Kapuas ichthyofauna to the rest of Borneo and Southeast Asia, and will be illustrated by 200 high-quality black-and-white photographs.

In the course of collecting material from the Kapuas, I have visited the European museums having important fish collections from Southeast Asia and have examined specimens of almost all fish species ever reported from the fresh waters of Malaya and Sumatra, as well as from Borneo. I have studied entire faunal areas and have consistently worked on all fish groups within them. Consequently, I am now very well prepared to study and report on the rest of the fishes in Borneo.

I propose to use the Rolex Award in order to conduct an ichthyological survey of a significant part of Borneo, possibly of the central highlands area with its extraordinarily specialized torrent-inhabiting fishes, or of the entire Mahakan Basin, in which the level of endemic fish species is very high. A formal institutional sponsorship for the project could be worked out either with the Smithsonian Tropical Research Institute (which sponsored my previous field work in Borneo) or with the American Museum of Natural History in New York (of which I am a Research Associate), and a proposal submitted to the Indonesian National Research Council (which authorized my field work in Borneo in 1976). Field work would be conducted for a period of three months in 1982 (or 1983), after which a twelve-month study period would be spent identifying the material and preparing a comprehensive and extensively illustrated scientific report for publication. This research would be conducted at a laboratory in the San Francisco Bay Area, possibly at the Tiburon Center for Environmental Study of San Francisco State University, where I am now studying the Kapuas material. This would give me access to the research facilities of the California Academy of Sciences, including their important ichthyological research collections where much of the Kapuas material will be permanently deposited. The scientific specimens collected from the field work will be deposited in national museum collections in Indonesia, the United States, and Europe, so that they will be widely available for additional studies by other research workers. Additionally, some of the material will be made available immediately to specialists in particular fish groups, though the responsibility for preparing a comprehensive faunistic and systematic report on the entire material will rest with me.

Land yachts and the proposed route across Australia.

TO "SAIL" BY LAND YACHT ACROSS AUSTRALIA

NICHOLAS E. A. WAINMAN
56 Penn Way, Letchworth, Herts, SG6 2SH, U.K.

British, born May 17, 1948. Chartered mechanical engineer, with own company. Mechanical engineering education in the United Kingdom.

Our project is an expedition for a team of four "land yachts," accompanied by two back-up vehicles, to "sail" across the continent of Australia, from Darwin on the north coast to Adelaide on the south. The six-man team is well qualified for this trip, each individual being a member of the British Land Yacht team for international racing in Europe. It includes three British champions in the sport.

Our main objective, apart from the sheer enterprise and adventure of the trip, is to stimulate public interest in the relatively new sport of land yachting and to show how vast areas of land can be covered using only the motive power of the wind.

The sport of land yachting as we know it today is a relatively recent development, but its antecedents are ancient. The ability to travel over land by sail has been known for centuries, going back to the times of the Chinese war chariots and the ancient Egyptians. Its beginnings as an international sport are associated with the intrepid aviator Louis Blériot, who was involved with its formation as a racing sport on the Belgian coast. Today, a European Championship is held annually, and racing is enjoyed on most continents. As demanding in its sailing and yacht tuning skills as water sailing, land yachting enjoys a basic difference in "downwind" running. Unhampered by the drag effect of water, land yachts will accelerate using the "apparent wind" effect and can thus achieve speeds some two and a half times that of the actual wind speed (recorded speeds of 77 mph have been officially noted).

In our expedition, we intend to use land yachts built by a team member,

John Glen, whose expertise and technical innovation in his designs were demonstrated on BBC's "Tomorrow's World" television program. In addition to having built a European Championship winning yacht, Glen's development of a reversible aerofoil, solid fiberglass sail, puts him in the forefront of land yacht design. Another key team member is Les Damsell, whose own adventures have taken him by land yacht across the Sahara Desert, over all manner of terrain.

The yachts we will be using are three-wheeled craft, with the helmsman, or pilot, seated at the rear and steering by controlling the single front wheel. Unlike normal racing yachts, a main feature of this expedition yacht is its high ground clearance, a proven necessity for traveling over rough, possibly rock-strewn terrain. The pocket-luff sail has an area of 12 square meters, and the body and mast core are of aluminum tubing. Most of the yacht's joints will be clamped instead of welded, as this is easier for running repairs and replacing parts. The tubular body will be covered in canvas for the aerodynamic effect and to incorporate storage pockets. There is a double steering wheel; one is naturally used for steering, the other for controlling the "sheet," or rope, which in turn controls the sail through a series of pulleys to create the purchase required.

The "wing" mast, as used by most land yachts, is an effective and efficient way of creating the aerofoil section required by the sail. The simple construction of this mast, with aluminum sheeting over the aluminum pole core, is designed for the possibility of a yacht's turning over, and its subsequent easy repair.

As with any conventional sailing craft, the land yacht can sail to all points of the compass in any given wind direction, but the time factor is always variable. With this in mind, experience has shown us that, regardless of all the essential pre-planning involved with an expedition of this nature, the day-to-day distance targets depend on the wind conditions and the terrain to be covered. Experience also shows us that, even with the most thorough planning, there can be areas of unnegotiable terrain, not marked on any maps available. To cover this, the expedition will carry winches, floats, and other devices to enable us to carry on regardless of mishap.

Consideration of all these factors helps to formulate the expedition philosophy. It is simply this: to travel from point A to point B, regardless of the time element. With conditions as they are in the Australian outback, safety is of prime importance. To this end, each yacht will carry its own emergency kit, tools, flares, balloons, water, and so on, and will be in constant touch with the back-up vehicles by radio.

As further steps to ensure the safety of the expedition, we intend to arrange with the Australian Flying Doctor Service to keep in regular radio contact. Consultation with this service will also serve to give us advance preparation for various health hazards we might encounter in the outback.

For our route, we plan to follow the path taken by the famed Stuart expedition, only in reverse. There is now a highway that follows this route, although it is only an unsealed track for most of the 3000 kilometers (1800 miles). Our plan calls for one of the back-up vehicles to use this highway, while the land yachts themselves negotiate their own ways through the outback, using the best routes they can find for up to several kilometers on either side of the highway, and followed by the second vehicle.

The vehicle remaining on the highway, with a trailer in tow, will carry the bulk of the expedition's supplies, including a substantial amount of water and fuel. We plan to have this vehicle always within one day's travel to the expedition's moving location.

The whole expedition will leave the highway as a reference point in cases where we need to circle an unnavigable area, such as a mountain range. In any circumstances, a back-up vehicle will be a lifeline in case of emergency or if progress falls so far behind schedule that supplies reach minimum safety levels.

Availability of information from the various Meteorological and Land Survey Departments in the state of South Australia and in the Northern Territory has led to a great deal of interest in the expedition. We have had many offers of assistance, and there appears to be a warm, responsive public interest in the project.

We estimate that the expedition will take up to three months, and we plan to make it during the Australian winter—in June, July, and August.

LOOKING FOR THE MIND

LAZAR STOJANOVIC
Cvijiceva 128, 11000 Beograd, Yugoslavia

Yugoslav, born March 1, 1944. Freelance writer and film director. Philosophy, psychology, and film education in Yugoslavia.

The intention of the author is to spend one year in an environment that provides the maximum possible deprivation of all sorts of perceptual data. The purpose of this project is to obtain a variety of observations of the effects of such deprivation. Outside observers will objectively measure such aspects as the effects of the deprivation on the electrical activity of the brain, the orientation to a sense of time, sleep patterns, and metabolic processes. The effects perceived by the mind will be studied by the author and publicly reported after the end of the exploration. Several experiments concerning concentration, telepathy, and dream control are planned for the deprivation period as well.

The deprivation of perception and communication is likely to isolate and reinforce discrete mental processes and thereby make them more recognizable. Tibetan hermits have used a similar technique for religious purposes, achieving extremely powerful concentration and vivid visualizations.

To provide the maximum possible control of stimuli, a room insulated against light and sound should be used. Equipped with basic facilities, it should be maintained at a constant temperature and be free of as many distinct tactile impressions as possible. Water should be of constant moderate temperature, the lavatory noiseless, and the bedsheets, towels, and clothes should be soft and light. The food should be unchanging, as tasteless as possible, and constantly available, with no "feeding schedule."

Measurements of such things as metabolic functions, electrical activity of the brain, heartbeat, temperature, and blood pressure should be performed by previously planted instruments that do not require any activity by the subject and that cause minimum change in stimulation through their operation. They should not attract the subject's attention in any way. Terms of feeding and sleeping should be recorded, as well as the quantities of food and water taken. The outside staff should be authorized to break the experiment only in the event of a real emergency signaled by the instruments. The subject, on the other hand, should be able to break the experiment at will.

The subjective part of this project will consist mainly of the systematic introspection of the discrete mental processes, observing the movements of the mind and following its spontaneous flow. In addition to this mostly passive examination, some active experimentation will be performed. This activity would cover dream-control attempts, the increasing of single-pointed concentration, sending telepathic messages to different persons (some of them previously notified of the efforts, and some unaware), the visualization of several simple ancient symbols, and other more elaborated exercises in mind control.

A detailed report of the data obtained through the objective measurements and those acquired by introspection would be published in book form after the completion of the project.

Certain previous experience and knowledge that might be needed are already in hand. Through studies in psychology, research into the creative processes, and practical studies of the Tibetan way of meditating, the author believes he has acquired the basic requirements for accomplishing this research project. He has successfully participated in several short-term retreats and different types of sensory and communication deprivations. Though this project might seem simple, easy, and inexpensive, this is not really the case. The stimuli-controlled environment and the objective observations of bodily functions can be achieved only through use of expensive equipment, skillful assistance, and large-scale adaptation of the space to be used. The subject of the experiment should be able to meet certain criteria as well; it requires a calm, well-balanced, and steady individual, without any major attachments that could cause disturbances, someone ready to face unexpected, even strange, mental phenomena. The author believes he meets these criteria.

THE MYSTERIOUS PRE-COLUMBIAN STONE SPHERES OF COSTA RICA

LEO C. SUHOSTAVSKY
Dana Point Marine Research Laboratory. P.O. Box 367,
Dana Point, California 92629, U.S.A.

American, born November 25, 1920. Self-employed physicist and owner of research laboratory. Engineering and physics education in the United States.

This project is concerned with an attempt to solve the riddle of the mysterious giant stone spheres—some weighing up to 16 tons—found, as Pre-Columbian relics, in the southwestern part of Costa Rica. I wish to do a characterization study of these massive and puzzling stone balls, in an attempt to identify the method of their manufacture, the tools used, the procedures for their transport to their current locations, and, if possible, their points of origin, or quarry sites. Further, if time permits, I wish to attempt some conclusions regarding the significance of these giant stone spheres to their original makers and to the traditional local populations in their areas.

The procedures to be followed divide into two phases: the first, desk research at home; the second, field research in Costa Rica.

The first part is currently in process and involves the collection of all available literature on the spheres and the study of these works by other investigators. The information being assembled includes the location of all, or most, known spheres, along with data on their dimensions, composition, weights, and any general characteristics or specific details. Sources of this information include works from the United States, Costa Rica, and other countries in Central America. Apart from this review of the literature, information on petroglyphs occurring in Costa Rica is also being assembled, so that any further references to the stone spheres might be found.

Maps of the area being assembled include terrain maps of the Diquis Delta area, Camaronal Island, the Cordillera Bruquena area, the Pied Blancos area, the Sierpe area, and others all added in the course of locating the spheres. Geological maps of surrounding areas are also being assembled, for purposes of ascertaining geological features that would suggest appropriate quarry sites. Other mapping information, such as aerial photographs of the sphere location points, will also be considered for the clues they may give to potential routes of transportation of the spheres.

With the above information collected, collated, cross-referenced, and analyzed, a correlated location map, or maps, will be prepared of Costa Rica, indicating the location of the spheres and their various composition materials. By matching this with the geological site maps, an attempt will be made to locate the likely quarry areas. As a cross-reference on this search, the likely paths of transportation are expected to be key pieces in the puzzle.

Once this is done, field work in Costa Rica will commence. The surface of existing spheres will be photographed thoroughly and carefully examined for tool marks, fire marks, or other indications of the method of manufacture. Investigation into stone-forming and stone-shaping techniques will be covered, including percussion, pressure flaking, grinding and polishing, fire forming, water pressure, and others.

A specific possibility—the use of metal tools—will be investigated, as the Indians of Columbia used a metal alloy called tumbaga (copper, silver, and gold, with a hardness equal to bronze), and it is possible that bronze tools came to Central America from Bolivia.

While on site in Costa Rica, searches will be conducted in the Sierpe area (and others determined during the course of the study) for additional "undiscovered" spheres, which will be added to the over-all location map to be prepared at the end of the expedition. Using the terrain, geological, and aerial maps, searches will be made for the most likely transportation routes for the giant spheres and for their quarry sites.

A final report on the project will be issued, indicating the most likely method for the manufacturing of the large stone spheres, actual or surmised quarry sites, and the most likely method of transporting the spheres to their present locations. In addition, there will be a narrative describing the possible significance of the spheres to the Pre-Columbian inhabitants of Costa Rica.

Exploring an underwater cave.

EXPLORING THE SUBMARINE RIVER AT CASSIS

 CLAUDE TOULOUMDJIAN
Honorable Mention, Rolex Awards for Enterprise
142, Rue Abbé de l'Epée, 13005 Marseilles, France

French, born March 1, 1942. President of the National Cave Diving Commission of Federation Française d'Etudes et de Sports Sous-Marins, Officer in international caving organizations. Educated in France.

Near Marseilles there is an underground river, yet to be discovered, which flows into the sea through two submarine caves, both of which are completely flooded. The further exploration of these two caves will in the near future lead to the discovery of this fabulous undergound river, whose two arms, the source of Port Miou and the source of Bestouan, form the most important underwater cave network known in the world today. It is the objective of this project to locate this underground river and to explore it as fully as possible.

In southern France, between Marseilles and Cassis, large limestone stretches form the *Massif des Calanques,* from which huge quantities of fresh water drain out through faults and caves. Two of these caves interest us most particularly because of their exceptional size.

The submarine cave of Port Miou, located 2 kilometers from the town of Cassis, opens onto the sea at the extreme point of the creek through two arches. The flow of brackish water at a depth of 12 meters is estimated to be about 2 cubic meters per second in periods of low-water mark. Within the immediate exit of the seaport of Cassis, several breakthroughs yielding a flow estimated at 1 cubic meter per second in periods of low-water mark, at a depth of 1 or 2 meters, compose the spring of Bestouan.

These two cavities were dug in urgonian limestone during the Quaternary Period when sea level fluctuated, varying up to 120 meters. The complete submersion of the galleries occurred on the last transgression of the Flanders.

Because the two caves are completely submerged, their exploration is to be undertaken by means of classic techniques used for subaquatic progression. However, three further factors add to the difficulty of penetration: (1) the complete darkness, which operations must overcome; (2) the presence of a clayey bottom, which inevitably becomes disturbed by the approach of divers, thus creating turbidity that cuts visibility to near-zero levels; and (3) the presence of a ceiling that precludes immediate surfacing, thus obliging a diver to swim back to his entry point in order to find air again.

There are other difficulties, such as the huge dimensions of the caves, strong currents, and very long decompression levels due to lengthy submersion times and depths (the latter extending to –45 meters). In view of these problems, underground diving will be employed, using several waterproof lamps, a guide rope, and two separate air tanks, each equipped with its own regulator. Naturally, such operations require specific training.

Historically, these two springs have been subjected to a number of exploratory expeditions, each seeking to pierce the mystery of the abysses in the *Massif des Calanques,* but none so far has been successful.

Since 1953 explorers at the spring at Port Miou have chosen direct access by means of autonomous diving equipment. Until 1964 the cave had yielded only 280 meters of its distance to divers and had claimed at least one scientist's life. In 1964, in a team of four divers, I reached 320 meters up the main entrance, and in 1966 on a solo dive, I reached a point 350 meters up the main entrance. Subsequent expeditions have now pushed the farthest point back to the cave's actual final point, 1100 meters from its entrance. The cave's dimensions are very important—a diameter running 10–15 meters, and depth increasing from –12 to –30 meters at 950 meters from the entrance, then declining still further from –40 to –45 meters.

At the Bestouan spring, successive groups have similarly pushed the further reaches back. In 1978, as part of one expedition, I solo-dived in a gallery to 855 meters. After its narrow entrance this cave widens at 350 meters, with a depth varying from –15 to –24 meters. The gallery then narrows, goes through a short climb, drops again, though keeping reasonable dimensions of about 2 meters in diameter. Its strong current obliges the diver to crawl on the clayey bottom on the way up and to brake himself on the return trip.

The object of these explorations, with autonomous diving equipment, is to go up the flows through the two entrances as far as possible, with the goal of discovering the main river, which by the look of the flows must be tremendous in size, varying from 5 cubic meters per second on low-water markings to 100 cubic meters per second at full spate. The discovery of this valuable freshwater source, and the ability to divert the flows to avoid the merging that now takes place with salt water, rendering this great potential resource unfit for human or agricultural use, would be of inestimable importance to the surrounding communities.

At present the submerged galleries of Port Miou and Bestouan total more than 2 kilometers. Further underground diving expeditions will allow us to double or treble this network stretch.

Our plan in the first stage is to concentrate on the spring of Bestouan. Though more difficult of access, it is preferred because of its fair depth (–20 meters), its location (which appears to be along the direct axis of the main river), and its salinity, which is half of that at Port Miou. The divers will use a progression method similar to that used by Alpinists—relay camps composed of stocks of air tanks at 400, 700, and 1000 meters from the entrance. For the first relay, two specially adapted submarine "propellers," designed for this expedition, will permit the carriage of air tanks quickly to the relay stations. At the further reaches, each diver will proceed by swimming, carrying his own backpack of 10 cubic meters of air himself.

For the spring of Port Miou, which we anticipate tackling in the autumn of 1982, we plan to have a "wet submarine" built for us, which will be capable of carrying, in addition to two divers and their own equipment, a further load of four to six air tanks fitted onto the body of the submarine. This unique vehicle will be able to travel some 15–20 kilometers at a speed of 4 kilometers per hour, running on batteries, and be perfectly suited to the dimensions of the Port Miou gallery.

There is no doubt that an operation of this type bears some risks in view of the environment in which it will take place. We plan a group of eight highly qualified divers and will have support from a medical team specializing in hyperbarics and diving problems. As we are talking about exceptionally long submersion times (2–3 hours), decompression will be adequately long (2–6 hour levels being envisioned).

In the course of the exploration, we will take color photos, 16-mm films of the expedition itself, and prepare topographic maps of the area covered, all of which will be reported in appropriate forms.

Apart from the pure exploring nature of the expeditions, we will also gain valuable medical data on prolonged submersion and very useful insights into the performance of new underwater equipment, such as the submarine propeller vehicles we plan to use.

Lastly, and perhaps most importantly, we will acquire better knowledge of this important river. Our means of "sourcing" underground supplies of fresh water could have extremely valuable applications in many parts of the Mediterranean coast, as well as elsewhere in the world.

FIRST SUCCESSFUL TRANSATLANTIC CROSSING BY BALLOON

BEN L. ABRUZZO
#10 Tramway Loop N.E., Albuquerque, New Mexico 87122,
U.S.A.

American, born June 30, 1930. Board Chairman and President of several companies; balloonist and pilot. Educated in the United States.

For 105 years, from 1873 until 1978, man has attempted to accomplish the successful crossing of the Atlantic Ocean via balloon. The brave crew of *Double Eagle II,* with the completion of that feat, captured the imagination of the world and provided heroes in a period when heroes were badly needed throughout the planet.

It appears to us that the Rolex Awards are directed to projects in the future; however, in an adventure such as the flight of *Double Eagle II,* the tremendous impact of the enterprise could not have been imagined prior to its successful completion. We were aware that the event would have important historic value; however, the enthusiasm with which the success was met was indeed staggering to us.

The historic flight of *Double Eagle II* has received perhaps more press coverage and has had more journalistic ink devoted to it than almost any other single event since the first man landed safely on the moon. We feel that a detailed description of the project would tend to be laborious to the Committee in that, in all likelihood, the Committee members are familiar with the details at this point. Of the thousands and thousands of words that have been written about the flight, we think that one of the best descriptions appeared in *National Geographic Magazine,* December 1978. A book entitled *Double Eagle* was written by Charles McCarry and published by Little, Brown and Company in 1979, and a 42-minute film entitled "The Spirit of *Double Eagle II*" was made, which provides a great deal of information and visual material concerning the successful crossing.

Should the Committee survey cities and villages throughout the world with populations over 5000, it would be difficult to find many who are not familiar with the flight of *Double Eagle II*, and a tremendous number would be found who followed the flight quite closely. We feel that the manner in which people identified with the crew without regard to nationalities or political interests is the most significant reason for your consideration of our enterprising venture as a potential recipient of one of the Rolex Awards for Enterprise.

At least two of the *Double Eagle II* crew are seriously considering another balloon enterprise, which would also have far-reaching historical ramifications.

Though we believe the broad details of the flight are well known, and thoroughly documented in the attached materials, here are the significant statistics on the flight of *Double Eagle II*:

The Transatlantic Balloon *Double Eagle II* left Presque Isle, Maine, on August 11, 1978 and landed six days later, on August 17, 1978 in Miserey, France.

The length of the flight was 3207.61 miles, or 5001.22 kilometers.

The duration of the flight was 137 hours, 5 minutes, 50 seconds.

Crew members were Ben Abruzzo, Maxie Anderson, and Larry Newman.

This was the first successful transatlantic balloon crossing in history.

TO DISCOVER A LOST ANCIENT CITY IN BRAZIL

GERALDO JORDAO PEREIRA
Rua Cosme Velho, 354 Casa III, 22241 Rio de Janeiro,
RJ, Brazil

Brazilian, born March 11, 1938. Head of Human Resources Department for State of Rio de Janeiro. Educated in Brazil and the United States.

T his project consists of forming an archaeological expedition to locate and discover a lost ancient city in the State of Bahia, which legend suggests was established by Greek travelers around the year 500 B.C. Though many written documents give evidence of its existence, no one has ever undertaken the task of discovering this lost city.

In 1753, a group of "bandeirantes" (adventurers seeking gold and silver mines) ventured into the interior of the State of Bahia. A manuscript, written by their leader, was later found and is now in the National Library in Rio de Janeiro. For several months, I have examined and, to a certain extent, "deciphered" this manuscript, and this is a summary of what it says.

"After following some game animal, we found ourselves in a strange place, with many stones, mostly covered by vegetation. The entry to this place has a great arch, with two small ones on each side. The big arch has inscriptions on it, difficult to read because of their height. Beyond the arches runs a large street, with two-story houses topped by stone slabs, all in a very decayed condition. The street ends in a plaza, in the center of which there is a large black stone column. On top of this column stands a statue of a man, with one hand on hip, and with his right arm extended, pointing to the North Pole. In each corner of the square there is a needle monument [obelisque?], such as the Romans used to have, but in most deplorable states.

"To the right side of this plaza, there is a large building, as if it belonged to the master of these lands, with a great hall and several compartments. On top of the main arch of this street, there is a bas-relief figure, sculptured in the stone, naked from the waist up, crowned with laurels, without a beard, wearing a bandaliere and a shield containing some inscriptions [which are reproduced in the manuscript].

"All around one sees many monuments, one obviously a religious temple for it still bears its magnificent front porch and its large stone halls, with many inscriptions and bas-relief sculptures.

"The nature all around is beautiful and abundant, with many exotic flowers and a very beautiful and large stream, along which we traveled until we reached a falls, where, nearby, we found some stone slabs with the following inscriptions [reproduced in the manuscript]."

The adventurer goes on itemizing his discoveries, inscriptions, and the surroundings, but I feel the most important part has been conveyed.

Almost 100 years later (in 1845), the priest Conego Jose Cunha, who knew of this document, tried to form an expedition to search for the ancient city, but for several reasons did not succeed. Nevertheless, his report, now in the Public Archives of the Museum of Bahia, is very helpful in reaffirming the conviction of the existence of the city, together with a suggestion of its location, that appears to be much more accurate than the one provided by the adventurer.

A later study of this document (1939) was made by the noted Brazilian scholar and archaeologist Bernardo de Azevedo da Silva Ramos. In it, he develops a comparative study of the transcribed inscriptions with ancient Phoenician, Greek, and Coptic writings. The final assumption of this important study is short and definite; he states, "Finally, we believe that these inscriptions reveal that the city is of *Greek origin*, being a valuable archaeological element and testimony thereby."

Therefore, my project is to form an expedition to try to find this lost ancient Greek city. There are several other sites in Brazil with strange inscriptions, but none is so remarkable and none has ever been explored. Nothing, therefore, has ever been proved of the possibility that ancient travelers (Egyptians, Phoenicians, Greeks) have been here, although there is some very eloquent evidence of just that likelihood.

As special techniques, we might need some aerial photogrammetry surveys of the specified area (which is very costly), but otherwise there is just the problem of forming an archaeological expedition, with the appropriate specialists involved. I should like to take about two months to look for this lost city, in the hopes of proving that ancient travelers from across the Atlantic did in fact come to this country and establish themselves in the interior of Brazil.

At the summit of Gasherbrum III (7952 meters) on August 11, 1975. Wanda Rutkiewicz is in the middle, with Alison Chadwick-Onyszkiewicz (standing) and Krysztof Zdzitowiecki. Photograph by Janusz Onyszkiewicz.

THE WOMEN'S EXPEDITION TO K-2: 8611 METERS HIGH

 WANDA RUTKIEWICZ
Honorable Mention, Rolex Awards for Enterprise
ul. Sobieskiego 8/88, 02-957 Warszawa, Poland

Polish, born February 4, 1943. Specialist in automatization of computer equipment designing at the Institute of Mathematical Machines in Warsaw. M.Sc. in electronic engineering from Wroclaw Polytechnic. Eighteen years of major climbing experience, including ascent of Mt. Everest.

Our objective is to climb the 8611-meter mountain K-2, in the Himalayas, the second-highest peak in the world. Our team will consist of women climbers only, who for the first time in history will attempt to climb a very high mountain without any high-altitude porters and without oxygen. It is our intent to break with standard, traditional patterns of alpine sport and to set a new record in women's mountaineering. The success of the venture will considerably expand our knowledge of the capabilities of women climbers, and not just in the area of learning more about female endurance and ability to adapt to extremely rarefied atmosphere. It will also be an inspiring test of self-reliance, daring, drive, and decision making—all areas of great importance in any undertaking requiring exceptional teamwork.

The expedition is being organized under the auspices of the Association of Polish Alpine Clubs and is planned for the summer of 1981 or 1982, depending upon the granting of final permission by the authorities in Pakistan. The team itself will consist of twelve to fourteen women (including a doctor and film crew) and will be led by Wanda Rutkiewicz. Members of the team are experienced Himalayan climbers, with numerous major ascents to their credit. These include mountains such as Gasherbrum II at 8035 meters and Gasherbrum III at Karakorum in Pakistan (the latter having been first ascended in 1975 by the Polish Ladies Expedition, led by Wanda Rutkiewicz), Kanchenjunga at 8595 meters, Rakaposhi at 7788 meters, Makalu at 8481 meters, Lhotse at 8511 meters, and in 1978, Mt. Everest at 8848 meters. Given our objectives for this expedition, it is worth mentioning that the members of the team have excellent records of climbs in all-female parties/ascents without oxygen on both Gasherbrum II and Rakaposhi. Such an outstanding record provides us with invaluable experience for this particularly difficult assault, which has been chosen by us for its specific and demanding challenge.

To put the expedition in perspective, it is generally assumed that the climbing of K-2, the world's second-highest mountain, is a more difficult and perhaps more dangerous assault than climbing Mt. Everest. An indication of this lies in the fact that Mt. Everest has already been climbed by more than a hundred people, while K-2 has been conquered by only fourteen individuals.

We have chosen to take the mountain via the so-called Abruzzi Ridge, named for the Italian team who first ascended the peak. Only two other teams have reached the top of K-2 by this route: the Japanese team that climbed the mountain in 1977, and Reinhold Messner and his partner in 1979.

The mountain itself is not easily accessible. Located at the very end of the Baltoro glacier, one of the biggest in the world outside the polar regions, it requires a lengthy approach. We anticipate some fifteen days of marching to reach its base. The climb itself is technically complex, and we calculate about six to eight weeks to accomplish it. We know that such a venture calls for excellence in preparation, and we are confident that our team brings superb experience to the climb. As a nucleus for the team, we include the following women.

Anna Okopi, nuclear physicist, with fifteen years of experience in expeditions to Pamir (ascents of Peak Korzhenevska, 7105 meters, and Peak Communism, 7483 meters), and Karakorum in the Himalayas (ascents of Gasherbrum II, 8035 meters, Lhotse, 8511 meters, and Makalu, 8481 meters).

Krystyna Palmowska, electronic engineer, twelve years of experience, and Anna Czerwinska, chemist, climbing partner of Krystyna, who have accomplished many hard routes in the Alps (the North Pillar of Les Droites, and a winter ascent of the North Face of the Matterhorn), plus expeditions to Gasherbrum II and III (8035 meters and 7952 meters) and Kanchenjunga, 8595 meters, and the ascent of Rakaposhi, 7788 meters.

Alicja Bednarz, office worker, with twenty years of climbing experience, many expeditions to Hindukush, ascents of three peaks of altitude above 7000 meters, and participation in the expedition to Gasherbrum.

Danuta Wach, shopkeeper, twelve years of experience, with many hard routes in the Alps (North Pillar of the Eiger being one), ascent of Peak Korzhenev-ska and Peak Communism in Pamir, and the expedition to Nanga Parbat, 8125 meters, in the Himalayas.

The total cost of the expedition as planned will be 80,000 Swiss francs, plus 5,000,000 Polish zlotys (equal to about 220,000 Swiss francs). As Polish currency is not convertible outside Poland, the 5,000,000 zlotys will be used internally to cover expenditures that can be made within the country, including such items as purchase of the necessary equipment, food supplies, airplane tickets, and so on. The remaining 80,000 Swiss francs will cover expenditures once we have arrived in Pakistan, including such items as the necessary royalty fees to the government and various authorities, the cost of hiring local porters for the march into the base of the mountain, and necessary local supplies and services.

Up to this point, we have received the 5,000,000 zlotys from local sponsors in Poland—the Sports Councils, Polish Television, Trade Unions, and others. The members of the team will also contribute to the expenses from our own pockets, in our desire to make this expedition. The most pressing problem we face now is to secure the equivalent of 80,000 Swiss francs in some convertible currency, a task that is made more difficult by the present Polish balance-of-trade status.

We very much wish to make this expedition. We believe it will be a major and dramatic accomplishment. There have been no attempts by female parties to climb K-2, and, with the exception of Messner and his partner, none of the male parties has completed the climb without the use of oxygen. Until now, all women's expeditions to high mountains have made extensive use of oxygen and have relied upon the support of male Sherpa high-altitude porters, who have always accompanied the women to the actual summits.

Based on our collective experience and preparation, it is our goal to break with these traditions. Without porters, without oxygen, this female climbing team will try to climb K-2 the hard way.

MASAI LANGUAGE
AND SYMBOLS:
KEYS FOR SURVIVAL

ROBERT E. PEARLMAN
400 East 56th Street, New York, New York 10022, U.S.A.

American, born September 16, 1939. President of advertising agency; member of The Explorers Club. Educated in the United States.

The objective of my project is to write, design, and produce the first communications guide based on the Masai language, utilizing Masai graphics, symbols, and color associations exclusively. The purpose of the project is to develop empathy with the Masai people and to create a lasting understanding of their culture by communicating within a common (Masai) frame of reference.

This has never been done before. As in the past, and until this work is completed, all communication with the 150,000 Masai living in Kenya, Tanzania, and Uganda will continue to be diffused and frequently misinterpreted through third-party perceptions, since the interpreter must translate English and Masai, two languages lacking a common frame of reference, into a third, Swahili. As a result, projects encompassing health, education, and welfare, including United Nations (FAO) programs for legislating land use, increasing crop yields, and improving cattle range land, have failed, thus wasting a great deal of time, energy, and financial resources. With a basic guidebook or Masai primer defining graphics, positive and negative color associations, and a comprehensive understanding of Masai symbols, future projects will stand a far greater chance of success.

In addition, as a secondary objective, I would like this work to establish guidelines or a framework for communicating with other tribes that do not feel compelled to assimilate or absorb external cultures.

Dr. Sixten Haraldson, adviser to the World Health Organization, recently stated that about 2 percent of the world's population are nomads, the most neglected group where international assistance and health services are concerned. A partial explanation of this lies in the extremely low density of their numbers in vast areas through which they roam. Often their cultures and values are little or not at all known to us, necessitating new approaches to communication. Nomadism is the consequence of long historical adaptation by groups to particular climatic and ecological circumstances. Forcing nomads to leave their tribal and migratory lifestyle to settle into community life results in inevitable deculturation, establishment of slum existence, and severe psychosocial disturbance. Such people will tend to rely to some extent on their traditional principles, so that intercultural projects must win local cooperation of the tribe if they are to succeed.

What I mentioned above concerning misinterpretation through third-party perceptions is understated. Unless one is fortunate enough to find an English-speaking Masai (extremely rare, but possible), one must use an interpreter, who will speak Swahili and several other languages, including English. However, a Masai must converse only in Swahili, since the interpreter will not be able to speak Masai. Only a handful of missionaries and other dedicated individuals have ever learned the Masai language. Masai is primitive by definition (the numerical system lacks a zero), and there seems to be a unique word for every object; furthermore, many meanings of objects and symbols have dropped from memory. I have developed a basic working vocabulary of the Masai language, which allows me the rare opportunity to communicate directly with these people. Thus the first phase of my project is completed.

The second phase of my project (First Field Expedition for Orientation) has also been completed. This involved four weeks of traveling alone from Nairobi in Kenya south to Arusha in Tanzania, visiting with individuals and isolated villages. Knowledge of the language was a major asset as the Masai made me feel welcome and allowed me to photograph their jewelry and cattle without making the traditional and obligatory payments.

The third phase of the project (Second Field Expedition) is due in September 1980, encompassing four weeks traveling from Nairobi west to Nakuru with an organized research team. Our objectives are (1) to photograph and/or illustrate graphics and symbols, (2) to document color associations and relationships to the environment, (3) to determine negative/positive associations attached to colors and symbols, and (4) to collect a photographic record of the crude branding of cattle via the Masai system of scarring ears and necks.

Phase four of the project will be the preparation of a text and illustrations during 1982, and phase five of the project will be publishing the results in the spring of 1983.

CANOEING THE
TAMUR RIVER IN NEPAL

BENI MULLER
im Mettel, P.O. Box, CH 8811, Hirzel ZH, Switzerland

Swiss, born July 25, 1950. Freelance filmmaker and producer. Educated in Switzerland, France, and Yugoslavia.

A group of Swiss canoeists, led by Ueli Marty and containing the Swiss champion canoeist Martin Baerlocher, will undertake an expedition to Nepal in September 1980 with the goal of being the first to navigate the Tamur River. I plan to make a 45-minute documentary film of this expedition with the assistance of Ruedi Homberger, who is a Swiss mountain guide and an expert in climbing films, as well as cameraman Willi Notzli and sound engineer Ruedi Muller, both from Swiss television.

The film will stress the following three subject areas: (1) the actual daring feats of the canoe team; (2) the life of the Tamur Valley people, virtually unknown to anthropologists and never before filmed; and (3) the contrast between traditional bamboo bridges and new suspension bridges designed by highly skilled Swiss engineers.

This project was conceived when we first heard, from several Swiss suspension bridge engineers in Nepal, of the wild and untamed Tamur River and of the people living by its upper course at altitudes of 4000–5000 meters. Although very little is known of these people, they are interesting because of their mercantile connection with Tibet.

In August 1980 I will fly to Kathmandu (with one other canoeist) to arrange the final details of the expedition and to survey the Tamur Valley by chartered airplane. In September we will be joined by three more canoeists, an anthropologist, a photographer, three other filmmakers, and a physician specializing in the effect of high altitude on well-trained athletes. The group will reach Taplejung by plane and climb with twelve porters to Walungchung Gola, where we will contact the Tamur Valley people. The descent on the river to Taplejung will be a real white-water adventure. The expedition should be back in Switzerland in October 1980.

The film will be based on a synopsis of the following segments, each of which is designed to provide its own dimension for the viewer:

A. The canoeists forge their way through little-known territory up to an elevation of 4500 meters. What are their motivations? The chance to paddle on a virgin river, for those who come from a country in which all the rivers have been canalized or tamed by dams; the desire to test one's capabilities in extreme and unknown situations; the search for adventure; or just plain curiosity? The ascent will be made on trails that have for centuries connected the Ganges plain with the Himalayan mountain passes. In the descent, emphasis will be given to the special care taken when navigating a river for the first time. The canoeists must acquaint themselves with each section of the river. Difficult and dangerous areas must be reconnoitered. A "guinea pig" navigates the river in advance, then discusses his experiences with his team. A clear picture of the risks and rewards of such an enterprise will be made quite evident.

B. The climax of the ascent will be the arrival in Walungchung Gola, the main village of the Tamur Valley people. Little information is available about these people. I could not find out what they are called even in their own language. We know today that some one hundred years ago they must have emigrated from Tibet. They are presumably related to the famous Sherpas in many ways. The Tamur Valley people trade salt with Tibet and rice with India; therefore an important trade route passes through Walung-chung Gola. Other villages we will visit are Ghunsa, Yangma, and Lungtun. I will show the behavior of the native people and their reaction to the intruding canoeists. The collision between the two cultures will be of great interest. Another white space on the anthropologists' world map will be colored in.

C. Throughout the film, we will see that the Tamur Valley is a real suspension bridge paradise; native bamboo bridges alternate with modern Swiss steel constructions. The traditional bridges are washed out each year by the river, when it is swollen with the monsoon rains, and the bridges must be rebuilt annually. We will be able to film the building of such a bridge. The new bridges will be shown in contrast to the traditional ones, and the engineers will describe their experiences in cooperating with Nepalese technicians. Standardized plans have improved their constructions, and through planning and warehousing the annual output of bridges has risen from two to twenty. Such cooperation is an excellent example of the use of efficient technical assistance with modest means.

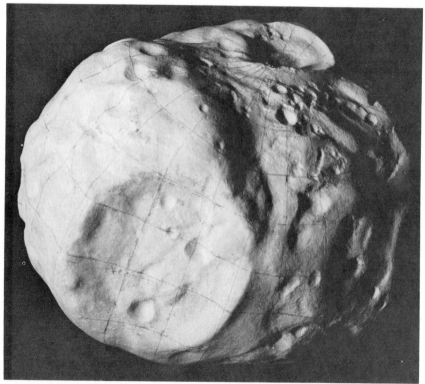

The first Phobos model, sculpted from information in the Mariner IX photographs. The large crater Stickney, left of center, is $6\frac{1}{2}$ to $7\frac{1}{2}$ miles across. The shadow extending from the center to the upper left is cast by Kepler's Ridge. The crater at the top is Hall; the south pole of Phobos is on its near rim. The light area to the left in this view always faces the planet Mars at a distance of 5841 miles, because the satellite orbits every 7 hours 39 minutes.

THE EXPLORATION OF PHOBOS

RALPH J. TURNER
Route 2, Box 167, Sheridan, Oregon 97378, U.S.A.

American, born October 24, 1935. Sculptor/planetologist, with commission work for NASA and business. Art and science education in the United States.

A detailed, three-dimensional model of Phobos, the largest Martian moon, should answer two scientific questions that have some bearing on the genesis and nature of the solar system: (1) What is the density of Phobos? (2) What are the striations on Phobos' surface? Density (and probably composition) results from mass and volume determinations. Tracking by Viking spacecraft has yielded a mass for Phobos. The volume of an irregular body can be found by measuring a three-dimensional model. A method of controlled illumination is available, and a special stage for orientation of the model can be constructed to create an analog with the solar-Phobos-spacecraft orientation. I propose that all of the Viking pictures of Phobos be integrated into a sculpted model—an ideal projection correction, already tested. The generally accepted interpretations that the genesis of the striations is associated with a Stickney event (impact-explosion) can be tested. It may not be the only or the best interpretation. Mapping, crater measurement, and feature exploration would complete a comprehensive study and lead to a publication of the results.

Exploration in our solar system will eventually extend beyond the Apollo missions to most of the planetary bodies. For the near future, however, exploration will continue to be limited to analysis of remote-sensing techniques. These techniques are nevertheless exciting, in their sophisticated ability to carry out mapping, geologic analysis, determination of molecular, atomic, and subatomic knowledge without the actual presence of humans.

Funding for scientific analysis in this area is remarkably limited considering the amount of data accumulated. When artists are invited occasionally to participate in the space program, it is usually within a framework structured to encourage their response to the processes of technology, to the personalities involved, or to obtain an overall philosophical response. My involvement with the actual data, especially the visual information resulting from the remote-sensing technology, has enabled me to respond as an artist as well as an investigator member of a scientific team.

In the last quarter of the twentieth century, the apparent trend in the fine arts has been toward conceptual projects. I am convinced that my work is in a position between the conceptual trend of art and a synthetic trend in science. Scientific disciplines, though apparently more and more specialized, often encompass more than one basic field, for example, biochemistry, astrogeology, and medical sociology. Planetology, for instance, rather than being a specialization of geology or geophysics, has become a field in which geology is a subfield.

The specific conception of this project is a combination of planetology and sculpture in a simultaneous effort and product. Although the project is presented from the standpoint of its scientific *raison d'être,* behind that lies a vision of an exploring artist. A tangible object is sought. A product is being created and sensitivity to the material is maintained. The result could have artistic value even if it does not fulfill all of the requirements of an efficient scientific inquiry. As a result, the artifact communicates with contemporary society (across barriers of language, both verbal and mathematic) and makes a clear record for history of where we are in a particular realm.

As background, one should appreciate that the pictures of Phobos were not made on a systematic basis, as coverage of Phobos had a lower priority than coverage of Mars. Nevertheless, some remarkable views of Phobos have been gathered, even though the stereo coverage is uncontrolled in terms of mapping needs. This is because determination of relief, or elevation, depends on stereo control or shadow measurements from an assumed surface. Phobos' irregularity disallows determination of a reference surface. One *can,* however, be assigned. An accurate, three-dimensional model can be constructed from pictorial data in its present form, with the use of a lighting system and model orientation that matches the conditions existing at the time the pictures were taken. The redundancy, overlapping, and complete coverage required to do this are available from the Viking views.

In the first Phobos model, made from Mariner IX pictures, I had included striations barely visible but occurring in more than one picture. When the Viking views came in, these striations were clearly in evidence—an example of how close analysis and careful model building can provide accurate data useful in subsequent exploration. For purposes of estimating mass of Phobos, I found a volume of 5620 cubic kilometers from two separate measurements of the first Phobos model, one of which was determined by averaging 156 radii taken from the model. A check was made by immersing the model and measuring liquid displacement. A more accurate determination of volume is imperative if the density of Phobos is to be settled. The construction of a new model of Phobos from all of the data now available would achieve this.

The significance of a valid and accurate volume is greater than might be initially imagined. The mass has been determined from Viking orbiter perturbations at close encounters with Phobos. Thus the average density of Phobos can be found. Since the mass is small, very little compression or change of state is likely, and average density would correlate positively with the density of the compounds making up the body. It is already evident that Phobos is not dense enough to be the remnant of a dense planetary interior, so the question of its genesis remains. Was it formed in place from debris such as that revolving around Jupiter, Saturn, and Uranus in rings? Or is it a captured asteroid? The volume of Phobos is a key indicator of its genesis, and to finding any pattern to such formation.

The number of craters, their condition, and distribution of sizes are an indication of age that can be keyed to the earth's moon. Many more than the 260 craters shown on the first model could be placed on the new model and tied in with density measurements. The new model would improve the accuracy of most of the known striations' orientations by a factor of 10, from the first model's "to the nearest 20°." This would provide further clues to density. There appears to be a tendency for the apparent volume of a cratered body to decrease as the measurements of its radius increase. Even though earlier estimates of volume came from the same data and assumed the same triaxial-ellipsoid dimensions, the concave inward surface of Phobos displays less volume as the measurements increase. The theoretical curve, based on silhouettes, yields too much volume. (A silhouette looks like a section, but isn't.) A model automatically accounts for the real shape.

In my modeling procedure, each picture (from at least 139 Viking pictures available) must fit the results of all the others. The model surface is pushed in, or pulled out, to accommodate any seeming inconsistencies, until the true orientation and extent of the linear features match exactly. I use a solar-analog illumination system at my Station, equipped with two small light sources and Fresnel lenses, to duplicate lighting conditions in the photos. The objective is to create a model with 5-millimeter resolution (equal to 300 meters on Phobos) that will be of scientific value for present analyses of Phobos, for future exploration of Phobos, and as a valuable piece of educational art for the public.

CREATING AN ILLUSTRATED MOBILE "ZOO"

REBECCA A. COVALT
3740 25th Street, Apt. 206, San Francisco, California 94110,
U.S.A.

American, born December 19, 1951. Self-employed illustrator and graphic artist. Educated in the United States.

I will design and construct *life-size* original drawings of African animals to be assembled and presented as a traveling zoo. This mobile presentation is designed for the underprivileged children of Appalachia, in the eastern United States. It is my intention to draw a life-size zoo for children who may never have seen an original piece of art or any of the wild animals of Africa.

The first phase of this project will take me to live in Kenya to study the animals prior to the actual design and physical construction of the zoo. I will observe the movement, living patterns, and habitats of each animal selected for the zoo in order to achieve realistic representations of the animals as they might be seen in nature. During this research phase, I will be photographing, sketching, and, when possible, recording the sounds of each animal. Also at this time, I will be able to gather data on each animal from naturalists and zoologists in Kenya.

Underwater life will also be portrayed in my mobile zoo, which will have two life-size aquariums depicting underwater life. While in Kenya, I will study marine life by means of scuba diving and underwater photography.

Following the research phase, I will begin design and preparation work, prior to construction of the zoo, in San Francisco. Each of the images and accompanying habitats for some 40 animals will be drawn to scale. This will be done on Arches watercolor paper, measuring 20 inches by 30 inches, using a Kohinoor rapidograph pen. Each drawing will then be blown up to life size by the process of photomechanical transfer. Also at this time, I will be editing the information gathered in Kenya for incorporation into a book depicting each illustration with accompanying data.

When this is done, I will interview artists and designers to collect a crew to work at the Appalachian construction site. Contacts will also be made at this time with the Appalachian community prior to arrival of the construction team.

The actual construction of the zoo will be accomplished in a warehouse. I will work with 100-foot rolls of watercolor paper and India ink. The particular paper is resilient and textured, and absorbs the ink readily without buckling. The inks retain their brilliance and are permanent. I have worked with these products for ten years and have repeatedly been satisfied with the results.

Images will be transferred from the photomechanical transfer to the paper by a tracing. The result of this procedure will be a true-to-scale life size image on the paper, ready for outlining and then color inking.

Each image will be on panels 6 feet by 4 feet, the number of panels per image depending on the actual size of the animal. Freestanding drawings, independent of the animal illustration, will represent the habitat and vegetation to create a three-dimensional effect. The aquariums and insect/reptile presentations will be done similarly.

After the illustrations are completed, with color, they will be sprayed with an acrylic fixative spray to protect each drawing. Then the drawings will be fixed to 10-ply pressboard with rubber cement. Freestanding plywood frames will support each illustration.

On completion of the zoo, contact with the communities prior to the zoo's visit is essential to ensure receptive audiences. Per capita income in the area is low, making it difficult for people to travel long distances, even to view a new zoo.

The zoo will be presented to as many communities as are physically and financially feasible within the general area. It will be displayed in a circus tent, and there will be no admission fee. The book comprising the illustrations of the Mobile Zoo will be sold at cost, and children will be given coloring books free of charge, containing designs of the animals that are the same as the original drawings.

After the tour, the zoo will be donated to the children of Appalachia, under the auspices of a non-profit organization, "Mobile," which will house the zoo. This will also provide an art and social services center for the community, to encourage creativity and learning.

CROSSING THE SAHARA WITH HOVERCRAFTS

BERNARD R. L. DEVAUX
1 Place Cathédrale, 4000 Liège, Belgium

French, born October 3, 1939. Cineaste and designer of furnishing elements in various materials. Self-educated in the design field.

My project is to demonstrate, with working models operating under severe conditions, that light hovercraft vehicles can be of significant value for transportation and communication in Third World countries.

These machines are simply constructed, easy to drive, and are repaired almost as simply as motorbikes. They can traverse areas unfit for motor traffic (marshes, sands, rivers, rapids) and do so quickly and safely. They can be invaluable in medical efforts for the rapid transport of doctors, medical assistants, and other personnel in times of emergency; and in social areas, such as for agronomists and others working in remote regions in roles of developmental assistance.

The project has developed in steps. To gain familiarity with the terrain, I went to the Sahara in 1976 to make two crossings by car—the first by way of Tamanrasset and Agades, the second from Niamey by way of Gao and Tanezrouft. The purpose of the trip was to allow me to seriously study the ground, in order to set up a precise plan for the future expedition.

Next, it was necessary to learn the hovercraft technology. From studying the existing hovercrafts around the world, I learned that all of them were essentially conceived as pneumatic boats, particularly suited to travel over water or marshy areas. After much research, I decided to design and build my own machine. This one is actually in the final stage of construction. In order to build it according to the objectives of my planned expedition, I had to devise a light engine that is easily dismantled and reassembled, simple to repair and carry. It will be suitable for demonstration purposes, for use as a sport hovercraft, and most importantly as an economical hovercraft for transportation in Third World countries.

Christened the DVX-1, my hovercraft has a light aluminum tubular structure, totally dismountable, connected with cast aluminum joints. The bottom is polyester, and the skirt and cowling are made of tight linen cloth. The machine is capable of moving on terrestrial areas; by joining inflatable bags in the base of the linen cloth, it can be made non-submersible and aquatic.

This hovercraft is very light at 80 kilograms and runs 50–80 kilometers per hour. It can carry either one or two persons without modification and should cost, in production, about the same as an average motorbike. For the expedition we would like to have two of the vehicles ready, depending upon available finances.

The expedition itself is planned to take place in the October–November or February–March periods, to avoid problems with the rising of the River Niger and of the temperature in the Tanezrouft.

The specific objectives of the expedition will be: (1) to cross the River Niger from Mopti, in Mali, to Gao, through Tombouctou, covering a distance of 800 kilometers; (2) to cross the sandy areas, by going through the Tanezrouft from Bordj-Moktar (Algerian border) at Reggane, by Bidon 5, covering a distance of 823 kilometers; and (3) realizing a full-length 100-minute film in 16 mm color on the attempt, in order to document the effectiveness of these vehicles in central African countries.

The hovercrafts will be accompanied by two motor vehicles, which will provide mechanical repair facilities, gasoline, water, food, radio equipment, cinematographic equipment, and so on. The support vehicles will also be available if the hovercrafts encounter impassable terrain (overly steep ground, large rock barriers, overly thick vegetation, etc.).

The light hovercraft is, however, very effective on any liquid surface, any sandy or fine gravels, and any unstable or bumpy surfaces such as corrugated iron or the Sahelian steppes. This was a main reason for my first expedition—to check on the most feasible of the various routes available.

I know the hovercrafts can travel in this part of the world. The filming of the expedition will be a great challenge, and will be made even more interesting by our planned use of a scale-model, radio-controlled airplane for purposes of taking overhead footage. I believe that we will return from the expedition with convincing proof that this kind of small, light hovercraft can open new sporting and economic vistas in many parts of the world.

Sextant sighting aboard the Solo *off Cape Adare, Antarctica, in the 1977–1978 expedition.*

MARITIME RESEARCH EXPEDITION TO ANTARCTICA

DAVID H. LEWIS
Dangar Island, N.S.W. 2253, Australia

Australian, born September 16, 1917. Explorer, sailor, President of Oceanic Research Foundation. Medical education in New Zealand and England.

T he Oceanic Research Foundation, of which I am President, is a nonprofit, tax deductible (in Australia) organization of volunteers dedicated to researching human impact on vulnerable undeveloped areas in general and Antarctica in particular. Our research is expedition oriented and stresses low-cost, energy-saving technology. In 1977–1978 we carried out an Antarctic expedition in our yacht *Solo,* in which a wide range of scientific measurements and observations were made. We are now constructing a unique, 75-foot, ice-strengthened topsail schooner to further these Antarctic research expeditions, commencing with Commonwealth Bay, King George Land, and Macquarie Island in 1981–1982, and continuing with a twelve-month wintering expedition at Commonwealth Bay, Antarctica, in 1982–1984.

Rising populations and depleting world resources will inevitably bring new and increased human activity to the less accessible and sparsely inhabited places near Australia, especially Oceania and the Antarctic. In response to this challenge, the Oceanic Research Foundation was proposed in 1975 by the author and a group of fellow scientists and explorers to undertake independent marine-based research in areas of special concern to Australia. It is a small, independent, adventurous group, determined to use its flexibility and the special experience and resourcefulness of its members to define and solve the problems arising from exploitation of the great remaining undeveloped areas.

Research efforts concentrate on the investigation of certain aspects of natural resources and ecological systems in remote areas and waters in the general region of Australia. Certain critical environmental studies are undertaken. Damage that has already occurred from human settlement and the exploitation of marine and mineral resources is assessed to assist in the development of guidelines for future development in these areas.

Our research is oriented toward learning through adventure and experience. We are able to solve some of the problems we encounter through our own efforts. Areas outside the scope of the Foundation's capabilities that present clear problems are referred to appropriate organizations. We therefore believe that we are taking full advantage of the opportunity that still exists in undeveloped places to foresee and forestall thoughtless and unnecessary damage to the environment.

Our main aim is to determine how man can best adapt to the Antarctic environment. To this end, we will concentrate on: (1) investigating energy-saving, low-cost technologies, including the use of wind power (sail and generating electricity); (2) testing simple prototype sea-ice and land vehicles; (3) beginning to train a nucleus of small ship ice navigators; (4) investigating the logistics and economics of making the long Southern Ocean passages under sail, thus conserving diminishing reserves of fuel oil; (5) undertaking iceberg studies in connection with their possible value as sources of fresh water, collecting ecological data, especially on krill and fish resources, to help ensure that sensibly controlled fishing programs only are allowed; and (6) collecting geological and botanical specimens, together with data on wildlife and weather.

Our underlying satisfaction is in doing all this with a high level of cost effectiveness that is only possible in a flexible organization of active enthusiasts. (As an example of this latter concern, our 1977–1978 Expedition in the yacht *Solo* was able to cover 6266 nautical miles in 79 days of scientific exploration, using only 350 gallons of diesel fuel, sail being the main motive power. The overall cost of the expedition was under $22,000.)

Our present expedition is by far our most ambitious and will be carried out from a base station, the 75-foot auxiliary sailing vessel *Douglas Mawson*. This ship, built of $\frac{1}{2}$-inch steel, is being designed along the lines of Nansen's *Fram;* that is, shaped in such a way that it can and will be squeezed upward by surrounding ice and not crushed by this ever-present danger in the waters of Antarctica. This ship will be unique as an expedition ship today and will have the freedom to survive the polar pack that is shared only by major icebreakers. She will carry twenty people with stores, equipment, laboratories, and more than adequate supplies of food and fuel for eighteen months of summer expeditions. She will be able to feed and provide fuel for a team of ten people for twelve months in wintering-over projects.

Construction commenced in June 1980, and the first voyage to the ice is planned for the southern summer of 1981–1982. This voyage will be to Commonwealth Bay in King Georges Land, where base lines were drawn fifty years ago by Mawson. We will be comparing the ice sheet's limits (retreat or advance), penguin and seal populations, and weather with the observations made and recorded by Mawson, which may well turn out to be of significant interest. We will also be testing simple over-ice and over-snow vehicles, like the sledge-kayak, and investigating wind-power generation units and other living and traveling technology. An important part of the project is being arranged by Dr. George Simeon, who is at present researching Eskimo orientation at Goja Haven in the Canadian Arctic. He is arranging for two Eskimos to accompany our expedition, to advise on traveling and living techniques, should Antarctic conditions parallel their own.

We will spend a month measuring and studying a large iceberg in conjunction with Flinders University. Starting from Macquarie Island in March 1982, we will be following elephant seals tagged by the South Australian Museum.

The wintering-over program of 1982–1983 will be a more ambitious extension of the foregoing. The location will be a sheltered cove off Commonwealth Bay, where the vessel can safely freeze-in for the winter. This technique, much favored by the early explorers, was last used for a large vessel by the schooner *Penola* off the Antarctic Peninsula in 1936–1938, and more recently by the French yacht *Damien II* at Marguerite Bay in 1978. The advantage in this approach, of course, is in being able to position a mobile base for a year's study, and then to be able to depart without having done any harm to the environment.

To sum up our Antarctic past activities and aims, we hope to form a bridge between the present era of high-cost governmental research and more modest and flexible research and adventure expeditions. We believe that this effort can update many of the techniques of the heroic age of exploration and add new conservation-oriented techniques of traveling and living.

FINDING THE PYRAMIDS OF THE AMAZON

CAMERINO O. ANDRADE
Rua Negreiros Lobato 23, Apt. 802, 22471 Lagoa, Rio de Janeiro, Brazil

Brazilian, born February 23, 1938. Brazilian Naval Officer, Bureau of Naval Personnel. Military education in Brazil.

This project involves forming an expedition to conduct archaeological research at the site of three mysterious elevations, long held to be the pyramids of an ancient civilization, that have only recently been photographed from the air.

Approximately 360 miles northwest from Manaus City, capital of Amazon State, in Brazil, there is a valley between the slopes of Gurupi Mountain and the Araca River, a small branch of the Domini River, which empties into the Rio Negro, a main tributary of the Amazon River. In this valley exist three elevations that bear great similarity to the pyramids of Egypt. Based on Indian legends, over the centuries explorers have searched for these elevations, but their location had never been documented until just recently. By chance, they were seen from the air and photographed by the airplane's pilot. Sighting of these elevations, which are approximately 50 feet high, gives rise to new interest in the old Indian legends that tell of a people known as the Mongulala civilization, who supposedly lived in the area more than 2000 years ago, and who were the forebears of the Incas. The photographs show that the elevations have well-formed edges, presenting four converging and smooth faces, now thickly covered with tropical vegetation, which could easily have spread over the surfaces through centuries of the humid climate in the region.

The Indian legends tell that such pyramids harbor the treasures of the old Mongulala civilization; if this is true, finding and excavating the pyramids would be of major scientific interest. As an indication of the possible accuracy of this theory, ceramic pots found in the area by explorers are believed to be some 2000 years old.

Although the exploration to locate the pyramids has been an enticing challenge, and expeditions have been mounted to make the attempt, all have failed in the face of great difficulty in getting to the locale, lack of support resources, and little knowledge of the region. Added to these quite real problems has been the very hostile reaction of the Yanomanis Indian tribe who inhabit the area and strongly resist the approach of any white people.

It may well have been the ancestors of these Indians who created the more than 500 objects of gold exhibited in the Manhattan American Museum of Natural History in late 1979. Most of these treasures were created by Indian goldworkers who lived in the region of the pyramids well before the time of Christ. There may be connections between this work and the association of the Amazon pyramids with the well-known legend of the lost city of Eldorado, with its temples, treasures, and supposed "mountains of gold."

In spite of the quasi-mythical and extraordinary nature of these stories about treasures and ancient civilizations, the photographs of the elevations now afford clear reason to undertake more accurate investigation of the region near Gurupi Mountain. Confirmation of even a portion of the old legends would spread new light on the history of humanity.

In these modern times, there is no longer the need to undertake an expedition to a specific objective through the traditional arduous battle against the obstacles of terrain. Whereas previous expeditions into the region were defeated by the need to struggle up unnavigable rivers, through dense and wild forest, and against unfriendly local Indian tribes, there is no reason today not to make the expedition by helicopter.

By helicopter, a team can easily leave from Manaus and land in Barcelos, a city some 80 miles to the south of the region of the pyramids. With refueling there, the expedition of eight members, equipped with radio, armament, provisions, and equipment for archaeological research could be transported in the same day to the location of the pyramids. After ten days of research, the expedition could be picked up and returned just as easily. Through radio communication, in the event of emergency, the helicopter would be able to perform evacuation rescue nearly immediately.

The expected duration of the project is thirty days, taking the month of November 1981.

THE TRADITIONAL MUSIC OF PAPUA NEW GUINEA

JOHN R. KELSEY
University of Papua New Guinea, Goroka Teachers' College,
P.O. Box 1078, Goroka, Eastern Highlands Province,
Papua New Guinea

American, born June 1, 1932. Lecturer in Music, University of Papua New Guinea. Educated in the United States.

As the only Music Lecturer at the University of Papua New Guinea, my responsibilities include helping in the development of a syllabus for the high schools of Papua New Guinea. In the course of this work, I carry out research and make field trips in order to make the curriculum as varied, interesting, and enlightening as I can. It is this research that provides the genesis of my project.

I propose to gather information on the enormously varied traditional music of Papua New Guinea. I will collect the music using field recording equipment, possibly including videotape machines, taking notes, using accepted recording techniques, and taking photographs when applicable and when allowable. Field trips will be taken in my 4-wheel-drive vehicle. A light aircraft is also available to me, a Cessna 182, ideal for use in such rugged countryside. As I have the required license, I would pilot the plane myself.

Though the variety of music here in Papua New Guinea is immense, I find of particular interest the "Singsing," which can go on unceasingly for days, and the musical instruments, some considered sacred and virtually all most intriguing. The rituals and dress accompanying the Singsing can be truly unique.

Since there are over 700 languages and dialects in this country, communication will be accomplished most often in what is known as Neo-Melanesian (Pidgin), a relatively simple language that I am able to speak. When possible, students from Goroka Teachers' College will accompany me to help with translation from the local vernacular. When the occasion arises, the students will most likely help with arranging surface transportation, as they have done for my research work in the past, using dugout canoes and other forms of local transportation. As part of their course work with me, students frequently bring information and instruments into the College, making possible a larger source of data than would be normally found in any such research project. Furthermore, there is in my office a sizable collection of old tape recordings, some with attending notes, that, to the best of my knowledge, have never been published. I would hope to include some of them with the results of my own research in the overall collection.

Some of the areas to be documented include such things as the Garamut signals. This signal, briefly, is a very old one and has been used for ages to call everyone to the dance-ground for a Singsing, involving both dancing and singing. One such piece, "Paitum garamut," derives its first word (*Paitum*) from the English "Fight him" and indicates the striking of a log drum, a frequently utilized musical instrument here. Yet another of the Garamut signals is "Trabul i kamap," meaning "Trouble has come (up)," and other examples of cross-cultural influences abound.

I have included for your listening a cassette of the music I have already recorded, with appropriate notes. One of the songs is rendered to the accompaniment of the nearly ubiquitous kundu drum. In this particular case, this traditionally hour-glass-shaped drum was made of a lizard skin head, and if you listen carefully, you will hear the musician rubbing the drumhead in order to heat it up slightly to produce the correct pitch.

I must say that I am incredibly fortunate in that the position I hold is very likely to be the perfect situation for pursuing my work. Not only is the immediate work, lecturing and preparing materials for my proposed Papua New Guinean replacement, just what I do best, but the environment is perfect for my own studies. My office is nearly filled with fascinating things: sacred flutes, conch-shell trumpets, sea-shell decorated water drums, etc.

There has not been a book published on the traditional music of Papua New Guinea since the monumental work of Jaap Kunst, whose work took place in the late 1920's and early 1930's. There are other ethnomusicologists working here presently, and perhaps one of them will publish a work soon. Of course, many shorter works are in print, and I am sure, at the very least, I could present several of these. I am intrigued by the possibility of using videotape equipment, as it would serve to provide a stunning archival record, if it were available. The work has begun, and I look forward to completion of the actual research in mid-1983.

The extent of the Wari Empire and current excavation sites.

THE CHICHA ARCHAEOLOGICAL PROJECT IN PERU

FRANK M. MEDDENS
12 Tavistock Place, Flat 8, London WC1, England

Dutch, born October 3, 1956. Director/Trustee of Chicha Archaeological Project. Post-graduate student, Institute of Archaeology, University of London. Educated in The Netherlands, Spain, and the United Kingdom.

The central aspect of the Chicha Project is the study of the Wari Empire (A.D. 500–A.D. 800). This empire was probably the first state to obtain control of the Peruvian culture area through military means. Wari was a hierarchical urban polity that in many ways anticipated the achievements of the Incas. The project began with a field survey in 1978, concentrating on a small part of this empire. In 1980, this survey will continue. Excavations will begin. Environmental archaeology is an integral part of the studies. In addition, a medical and educational program will be carried out.

I resolved to do research on the Wari Empire while working at the site of Huari, Peru, in 1977 as an archaeological supervisor for Dr. W. H. Isbell, from the State University of New York in Binghamton. My undergraduate dissertation was a study of an early phase of urban development at Huari. Returning to Peru in 1978, I was able to obtain a permit to carry out archaeological investigations in the Rio Chicha Valley, an area virtually untouched by archaeologists, containing Huari, the suggested capital of the Wari Empire and what appeared to be the center of the Empire's greatest activity.

The remains of the Wari Empire were first described at the turn of this century by the German archaeologist Max Uhle, who had recognized the existence of two distinct styles of archaeological remains in Peru, belonging to two different ages, now known as the Wari and Inca periods.

The impetus for the Wari Empire came from several areas. Cultural and religious aspects were developed in the Nazca area on the southern coast of

Peru and in the Tiahuanaco culture originating around Lake Titicaca. These came together in the Ayacucho Valley in the central highlands of Peru. Here, combined with local cultural influences, the basis for the Wari Empire emerged.

The site of Huari, near the modern town of Ayacucho, was first occupied around A.D. 350. It probably became the capital of the empire in the seventh century. Areas for special activities, such as the production of turquoise artifacts or religious functions, are recognizable today in the ruins of the site. It is likely that religion formed the moral basis for the period of conquest following the emergence of Huari as a city. During the first period of expansion (circa A.D. 650), Nazca remained in a special—but poorly understood until now—relationship to Huari. At its peak, the Wari Empire reached from just north of the Supe Valley on the northern coast, through the northern highlands, past Cajamarca, and on to the present border with Bolivia in the south.

A sophisticated infrastructure was developed, with a vast road network, way stations, and urban control centers built on typical rectangular grid plans. A state hierarchy and a class system formed the social background to these developments.

Sometime around A.D. 700, the site of Pachacamac, near Lima, gained disproportionately in influence. Certain iconographic themes manifested in high quality crafts, such as pottery and textiles, are associated with the growing importance of this site. The most characteristic motif is the Griffin, perhaps a representation of the site's principal diety. It may be that Pachacamac came to rival the site of Huari.

Around A.D. 800, the Wari Empire collapsed. Huari itself was abandoned, as were many other Wari sites. The reasons for this decline and collapse are unknown. As yet, archaeological evidence does not lend any support to the various theories for this decline, such as foreign invasions, failure of the socio-political structure, epidemic disease, or environmental changes. From A.D. 800 to A.D. 1000, Wari iconographic features continued to linger in the area but clearly not as a reflection of any centralized authority. After about A.D. 1000, independent regional cultures were firmly established with their own characteristic styles in what is now called the Late Intermediate Period.

For my first field work in 1978, I assembled a team of eleven volunteers who were already in Peru, including Monica Barnes, an archaeobotanist who was of great help in organizing the project and who has continued in the position of co-director.

The village of Pampachiri was selected for base camp. The community was willing to provide my team with accommodation and work space for processing finds. In exchange, I raised money in Europe to bring electricity to the town high school. Relationships have become increasingly good, Monica Barnes and myself having been invited to sit on the town council and my becoming godfather to one of the sons of the governor of Pampachiri.

The area of the excavations lies at an elevation of 3200–3800 meters. The river cuts through a series of older natural terraces, and the terrain is geologically very interesting, with mines and obsidian sources, clear signs of volcanic activity in the form of thermal springs, and the presence of glacial deposits.

In 1978, five sites were mapped and surface sherds and lithics systematically collected. Four additional sites were studied in less detail, but diagnostic material was recovered from these also.

Chicha Qasa is a multiperiod site, with approximately sixty house structures, some extremely well preserved, and no buildings with any right angles, a curious builder preference. From this site we have recovered numerous burned, deformed, and vitrified pottery fragments. As ceramics with a true glaze were not thought to be known in Peru before the colonial period, further excavation of the site might provide unique evidence of pre-Hispanic ceramic technology.

The three burial caves of Charrangochayoc are among the most spectacular remains in the Chicha Valley. Due to the extremely dry conditions in these caves, preservation of organic remains has been very good. We have discovered large quantities of artificially deformed and trepanned skulls. The ancient Peruvians distorted the skulls of their infants for cosmetic or status reasons, while trepanation was probably done on medical or ritual grounds.

During the Empire's ascendancy, one or two larger Wari administrative centers were usually in control of many villages and hamlets, from which came the surplus to support Wari urbanism. Based on the work we have already done, I expect to find full confirmation of this pattern in the Chicha Valley.

The 1980 digging season will start on June 1 and continue until the end of September. This year we intend to do test excavations to get an idea of the cultural chronology in the Chicha Valley and to establish an artifact sequence that can be used to date sites accurately from their surface material. A section through several agricultural terraces will be made to establish their method of construction and to find out if their distribution throughout the valley is linked to the exploitation of specific microenvironments. We hope that our efforts will continue to add to the currently small amount of knowledge of the Wari Empire and perhaps lead to clues that will reveal the actual causes of its mysterious decline and disappearance.

LONG-TERM HUMAN SURVIVAL AT VERY HIGH ALTITUDES

 NICOLAS JAEGER
Honorable Mention, Rolex Awards for Enterprise
31, Avenue de La Motte-Picquet, 75007 Paris, France

French, born October 20, 1946. Last seen alive at 8000 meters, above his base camp on the mountain Lhotse, on April 25, 1980.

In Tribute and in Memoriam

Dr. Nicolas Jaeger, a specialist in Sport Medicine and High Altitude Physiology, a High Mountain Guide since 1975, and an outstanding writer, photographer, and lecturer, widely known and respected throughout the demanding world of international alpinism, lost his life in the pursuit of the project described below. A long-time contributor to humanity's improving understanding of life in high-altitude environments, Dr. Jaeger's courage and dedication, in addition to the excellence of his project, led to his being awarded a posthumous Honorable Mention by the Selection Committee of the Rolex Awards for Enterprise at its November 1980 meeting in Geneva.

I plan to carry out a survival test in very high-altitude surroundings that will involve four men living together above 7000 meters for a period of at least one month. Included in the test will be studies of a medical and physiological nature with up-to-date equipment, the socio-psychological analysis of a small group isolated in a hostile and wild environment, the study of specific high-altitude surroundings, and a thorough study and testing of various kinds of specialized equipment and food supplies.

Nepal has been chosen as the most convenient country, due to its abundance of mountains higher than 7000 meters. In most instances it will be possible to have helicopters bring supplies up to a 5000-meter level, from which point they must be packed up. The exact location for the survival test will be chosen during 1980 after preliminary scouting and through discussions with the Nepalese government. We will seek to carry out the test in the post-monsoon season, in order not to be forced to halt the experiment due to bad weather.

Our planning is based on the following timetable. During 1980 and the first half of 1981, we will be gathering the necessary authorizations and local help necessary in the Kingdom of Nepal, organizing funding from various private and public sources, and reviewing the most recent equipment and foodstuffs available. We will be determining the medical observations to be made and the most appropriate equipment for these purposes. The organization and arrangements for shooting a 16-mm film of the expedition will be carried out, and arrangements for transport to Nepal of the team and all the freight will be made.

We plan to fly from Paris to Kathmandu on August 20, 1981, and to be installed at our base camp, approximately 5000 meters high, by between September 1 and 10. From September 10 to 30, we will be establishing the altitude camp above 7000 meters, settling in with equipment and food carried from base camp. The period of the test itself is planned to run from October 1 to November 1–15, depending upon conditions and capabilities. We should return to Paris by the end of November.

Though the survival-testing experience will cover several areas, our principal objectives will focus on medical and physiological observations, and we will use the most modern techniques and equipment available.

The environment known as "very high altitude" is poorly understood, even today, in terms of its impact on humans. It is emphatically not simply a state of reduced barometric pressure. The "very high altitude" surroundings themselves set very strong stresses on the human body and mind. Recent advances in the art of mountain climbing have in many instances outstripped the gradual growth of scientific knowledge about life in the high altitudes. Science now needs to be adapted to a new cast of men and women who are spending, each year, long periods above the height of 4000 meters.

Therefore, in our work at the high altitudes, we will be concentrating on a variety of testing and observation parameters. Each of us will be given extensive medical check-ups before and after the experience. At the altitude camp daily measurements will be taken, most of them being radio transmitted to a small computer established at base camp. To the extent possible, we will be using new techniques to study such information as cardiac frequency, electroencephalography, central temperatures, measurements of small blood samples for glucose, and oxygen in the blood.

Broadly speaking, the scientific study program will focus on six different general areas of interest:

Neuropsychic study, with memory, attention, equilibrium, and coordination psychological tests, and electroencephalogram work.

Cardiac and circulatory study, with blood pressure, cardiac frequency, respiratory volumes and frequency, dynamic and static efforts, and electrocardiogram work.

Metabolic and food study, with body weight recording, strength and volume of muscle measurements, food input and composition, fluid input and output recordings.

Blood study, with red-cell count, hemoglobin, hematocrit testing, blood content of oxygen and carbon dioxide, pH, and measuring of glucose, sodium ions, and potassium ions.

Urine study, with research on irregular components, sampling for urea, sodium ions, and potassium ions, and hormone sampling.

General study, recording central temperatures, rhythm and analysis of sleep, maximum oxygen uptake, and skin, hair, and nails assessments.

The information collected during this experience should bring to a higher level that knowledge we possess of human possibilities for adaptation to high altitude, and therefore contribute to a better understanding of the effects of stresses on the human body.

As leader of the expedition, I bring experience as a member of the French 1978 Everest expedition and leadership of four expeditions (in Peru and Nepal) prior to this one. Of particular interest, I believe, is the completion of an original experience in 1979, a sixty-day solo survival test at 6700 meters on the summit of the Andes' highest mountain, Nevado Huascaran. During this experience, I wrote a book, shot a film, and carried out medical observations for a medical thesis.

THE ENVIRONMENT

The projects appearing in this section were submitted in competition under "The Environment" category, which was defined in the Official Application Form as follows:

Projects in this category will be concerned primarily with our environment, and should seek to protect and preserve, or to improve, the world around us.

The 'Aurelian' lily ('Honeydew' × 'Tundra'). The blooms are about 6 inches across, and the plant has dark green glossy foliage.

The 'Auratum' lily ('Tiki' × 'Moon Crater'). The bloom is 10 inches across. The plant is extremely vigorous and seems to withstand a higher water table level than average.

HYBRIDIZING AND RAISING BEAUTIFUL NEW PLANTS

PATRICIA L. GREENFIELD
16 Coronation Street, Takapuna, Auckland 9, New Zealand

English, born March 8, 1946. Staff typist. Self-educated in horticulture and hybridizing in New Zealand.

I am involved in the hybridization of various flowering plants, with the ultimate aim of improving a particular variety in a particular area, such as achieving a particular flower color or increasing health and vigor. The plants I am working with are: (1) the Hybrid Tea Rose; (2) the Lily, specifically 'Aurelian' and 'Auratum' varieties; (3) the Hippeastrum; and (4) the Hawaiian Hibiscus.

I started the breeding of various flowering plants in 1974, prompted by not being able to obtain what I wanted through the usual commercial sources, and also by the lack of health and vigor in some plants whose color I liked but whose constitution was poor.

Since I have no horticultural qualifications, I had to obtain information concerning hybridizing from books in my local library. Knowledgeable people dealing in my particular field were also consulted, and, armed with this basic information, I started my various projects.

In the past four years, I have learned and observed much that is not available in books; for example, certain parents will nearly always throw particular traits. Seed and pollen parents are not always compatible with each other, perhaps due to a poor combination of genes, or the ploidy might be wrong. A triploid, for example, is supposed to be sterile according to the books, but this is not always the case. A particular example is the rose 'Diamond Jubilee.' This is a triploid and supposedly virtually sterile as a seed parent. Books won't tell you that this rose sometimes throws two types of flower. One you can breed from, and the other you can't. This, and other information, is gleaned from observation over a period of time.

The Hybrid Tea Rose

The Hybrid Tea Rose is the most difficult of my plant subjects to work with, as there are many variables that don't always show up at the first flowering stage. Roses usually flower within four months of germination but may take another two or three years to show their full worth. Good parents are only discovered after time-consuming method of trial and error. Two parents I have found to be fairly consistent are the Floribunda 'Arthur Bell,' a vigorous, very healthy yellow, and the Hybrid Tea 'Duet,' a vigorous, extremely free-flowering two-tone pink rose. Difficulty can be experienced with some crosses due to an unexplained incompatibility of genes. For example, 'Duet' crossed onto 'Grand Nord' has produced some nice seedlings. 'Duet' crossed onto the huge pink rose 'Portrait' produced nothing of consequence at all. That is why records are so necessary.

I have been working with the triploid rose 'Diamond Jubilee,' and my best seedling with this one so far appears to be from the cross 'Whiskey Mac' × 'Diamond Jubilee.' It has a wonderful petal texture and is so far free of the balling habit of the pollen parent. The stems are very stiff and thus stand up well to rain. Its disease resistance is only fair, so I will be crossing the very healthy variety 'Arthur Bell' onto it. This seedling's main fault so far is its color instability, which can be traced back to 'Whiskey Mac,' which has a tendency to throw this defect.

Seedling roses that look fabulous early on may turn out to be duds in their second season. Conversely, other seedlings may not show much at all during their first year of growth and then really leap away in the second season. Assessment of roses is difficult in the early stages, and it is all too easy to discard too soon. Habit of growth, shape and color of flower, capability to withstand hot sun and pouring rain—all of these things take time to assess, and usually three full growing seasons are required before a final assessment can be made on a promising new variety, which, due to my high standards, are few and far between.

The Lily

With the 'Aurelian' variety, I have no particular aims apart from the raising of good, reliable garden plants. As I have three good seedlings in this group, I will not be developing this line any further ('Aurelian' lily seedlings take eighteen months from germination to the flower for the first time).

With the 'Auratum' variety, I will be working with a seedling that germinated in the open garden without going through a period of dormancy first.

'Auratum' seed usually needs a warm period to produce a bulb, then a cold period to induce leaf production, generally spanning a period of about six months. This seedling germinated in two months. It is extremely vigorous and healthy and has survived admirably our very wet winter in soil that had a high water table for long periods of time. It flowered first on December 31, 1979, with two blooms on, each measuring 10 inches across and being flat-faced. The color was a very deep pink/red, darker in the center of the petals. Texture was extremely good. (These seedlings usually take two-and-a-half years from germination to flower for the first time.)

The Hippeastrum

I have no particular aims in this field, apart from the raising of vigorous, free-flowering varieties. I have used the variety 'Intokazi' (white with a green throat) as a base and have crossed several varieties onto it. Two of the best seedlings are 'Intokazi' × 'Desert Dawn' and 'Intokazi' × 'Apple Blossom.' The former is basically a huge, well-formed white flower splashed with orange/red. This is extremely vigorous and had foliage measuring more than 3 inches across with the leading flower being 9 inches across. The latter is a green-white flower with a green throat. Hippeastrums take two-and-a-half to three years from germination to flower for the first time.

Hawaiian Hibiscus

Here I wanted a good, deep red, and I obtained nine seedlings from my only successful cross to date ('Kitty Beebe' × 'Molly Cummings'). I kept one, the best, and discarded the others. I judge all of my seedlings on vigor and health and discard before flowering if not up to my standards. The one that survived is a lovely deep smokey red flower, ranging from 6 to 9 inches across. It is vigorous and healthy but not quite as free-flowering as I would like. I have not advanced further with this work, primarily through lack of space; also, it is extremely hard to get a successful "take." I believe only about three out of a hundred attempts will yield any viable seed. Hibiscus takes about eighteen months from germination to produce its first flower. (The germination times quoted for these plants are pertinent to New Zealand growing conditions and may differ from countries having more extreme climates.)

Among my choice of subjects have been plants that can be quite difficult to work with. Each have their correct germination techniques, special growing conditions, and a host of other things that would be difficult to put into words. I am only interested in the very best, as my photographs indicate.

A BLUEPRINT FOR SAVING MALAWI'S EVERGREEN FOREST BIRDS

 ROBERT J. DOWSETT
Honorable Mention, Rolex Awards for Enterprise
Nyika National Park, Private Bag Chilinda, Post Office Rumphi,
Malawi

British, born April 16, 1942. Freelance research ornithologist, attached to the Malawi Department of National Parks and Wildlife. Chartered biologist, educated in England.

T his project is a two-stage attempt to provide a blueprint for saving the endangered bird species of the evergreen forests in Malawi. The first stage started in October 1979, when my wife Françoise (a Belgian zoologist) and I came to live on the Nyika Plateau, to continue studies of the birds I had begun during brief visits to the area since 1969. Because of the numerous patches of evergreen forest and the long-lived, stable (in relationship to the environment they inhabit) populations of forest birds, studies of their population, movements, productivity, and so on require several seasons of work. Then, with firm knowledge of the situation in an undisturbed area, we will turn in 1982 to a two-year study of forest birds elsewhere in Malawi, where few other mountain forests are protected and some bird populations are endangered.

On the Nyika Plateau in Malawi (which rises to over 2600 meters and is a national park), numerous isolated patches of evergreen forest of varying size provide a microcosm of the "islands" of evergreen forest that exist throughout the tropics. Here the effects of forest size, structure, isolation, fire, and other factors—very difficult to study in larger forest areas—can be determined.

Our study consists of two parts. First, we make frequent inventories of the breeding birds in as many forest patches as possible, relating results to such factors as forest size, structure, altitude, and isolation. During the first four months of research, we have investigated a continuum of seventy-five forests, ranging in size from .16 hectares to 90 hectares. Although small by standards elsewhere, these forests contain many of the breeding species of the Central African mountains, in natural conditions that are easy to study.

The second part of the study consists of color marking, for individual recognition, as many as possible of the birds breeding in part of this area—in a section of the larger forest and in a grouping of smaller patches. These birds are caught in mist nets, marked with numbered and colored leg rings for future individual recognition (without the need for recapture) and released unharmed. To date, since 1972, we have ringed more than 1500 birds, and many of the oldest are still alive and monitored regularly. Studies elsewhere in the tropics suggest that we may expect some of our smallest forest birds to live some sixteen to eighteen years. Our results so far show that most species comprise stable populations; living in circumscribed areas, they are extremely vulnerable to the modification or reduction of their habitats. During our Nyika study, the ringed birds will give us information on interforest "island" movements at different times of year, and on productivity.

We need to know how the birds are affected by the size of their forest habitat. Forests reduced below a certain size can be expected to lose—through extinction or emigration—the least tolerant and rarest species. Even more important is our discovery that the numbers of individuals of each species present do not increase in direct proportion to forest size. The effects of territorial behavior in every species studied indicate that although a single pair may breed successfully in a very small remnant, it may take forest space from four to twenty-five times the size of the smallest territory (depending on the species concerned) before a second pair will be admitted. It is necessary to know which species can and will "wander" for food outside their specific habitat, which species are capable of dispersing to other nearby or distant forest "islands," and the extent to which such movements are carried out. To date, such data have been the subject of speculation in the tropics; our Nyika project will provide real evidence.

By 1982, after three breeding seasons on Nyika, we hope to have a much clearer indication of the factors influencing the existence of African mountain evergreen forest birds. We will then apply this knowledge to a whole country, where the conservation of the natural environment gives considerable cause for concern. Malawi contains some forty isolated mountain forests, greatest of the Central African countries. We plan to prepare inventories, as on Nyika, of as many as possible of these forest avifaunas, with particular emphasis on areas with rare species. Plans for the conservation of key areas will then be presented to the Malawi authorities.

THE UNIVERSITY OF DEVELOPMENT

PISIT SARAWICHITR

Doctoral Programs, Graduate School, Srinakharinwirot University, Sukhumwit 23, Bangkok 11, Thailand

Thai, born September 2, 1938. Assistant Professor, Head of Native Community Development Program. Educated in Thailand, the United States, and the United Kingdom.

T he University of Development Project is my attempt to rebuild my native community into a center of learning and culture. The project was begun in March 1963 and is planned to come to fruition 24 years later, in September 1987. I have devoted the main thrust of my adult life to this project, for both personal and professional reasons, on behalf of my people and country.

The background is as follows. I was born in Ban Napho, one of five small villages that make up an area known as Tambol Nahaeo, some 50 square miles in size, situated in Dansai District, Loey Province, in the northeastern part of Thailand. Nearly surrounded by mountains, the area is made up of hills, forests, and mountain ranges. Some 1200 people, descendants of the Thais who came to settle here about 300 years ago, still live in the area, though the population has declined sharply from the 3000 people who lived here at the beginning of this century. Colonization by the French, the ravages of World War II, and the brutal killing of people by Laotian revolutionary soldiers all contributed to disastrous changes in this peaceful, freedom-loving, and prosperous community, and many people moved away to the interior of Thailand.

I had the good fortune, after 10 years of living in my village, of being able to leave home and continue my education in Loey Province, Dhonburi, and Bangkok. Then I was fortunate enough to win a Thai government scholarship that enabled me to complete my Ph.D. studies in the United

States and to study in England. I resolved to return some of the benefits I had received from my education to my own community in Tambol Nahaeo.

My project started from scratch, without money, power, influence, or cooperating friends—just the will to rebuild a native community, the desire to render useful service to humanity, and the sincere wish to be able to devote my life and efforts to revitalizing and rebuilding the community I love.

The project centers on establishing the University of Development, for which a site of 10,000 acres of undeveloped land has been chosen. The purposes of the project include the rekindling of pride, love, and hope in one's motherland; the development and betterment of Tambol Nahaeo; the teaching of vocational and agricultural skills and self-development techniques for successful and efficient living; and the preservation, protection, and improvement of the natural setting, plants, mountains, rivers, waterfalls, and surroundings of Tambol Nahaeo. The ultimate reality will be a university community in which all people live, learn, work, and help each other to grow, so that human beings and other natural things can cohabit with bounty, happiness, and satisfaction for generations to come.

I have mapped the site of the University of Development, drawn up plans for the facilities, photographed the natural wonders that will be an integral part of the environment, and secured the beginnings of the financial and administrative needs of the project. In the local villages, I have established scholarships and academic prizes designed to encourage the local children to continue with their education and to bring them to the level of university entrance requirements. This has been done, in part, by persuading various family members and friends to establish awards in their own names to promote a strong sense of community among the people in the area.

In 1974, the University of Development Foundation was started on an informal basis to serve as a center for a variety of assistance aids, either grants in cash or equipment or expert help and advice. Also established in 1974 were University of Development Awards, again offered to local schoolchildren to promote their awareness of an academic goal. I have already established a small library for use by the University of Development and hope that this will serve as a further focal point of interest and help to the community.

I have applied for various governmental support programs, using in many cases a document I have written on the entire project. Entitled "A Preliminary Study of the Problems, Needs, Educational Aspirations, Economic Status and General Outlooks of the People and Pupils in Tambol Nahaeo," this 395-page report was released and distributed in about 165 copies. It has been helpful in obtaining small grants, which have been totally and effectively used to further the project. It is my strongest wish to be able to open the University of Development in 1987.

A Himalayan snow leopard.

RADIO-TRACKING THE SNOW LEOPARD IN THE HIMALAYAS

RODNEY M. JACKSON
Rolex Laureate, Rolex Awards for Enterprise
c/o Bodega Bay Institute, 315 Fort Mason, San Francisco,
California 94123, U.S.A.

British, born January 19, 1944. Wildlife biologist, and one of the principals in a biological consulting firm. B.Sc. Honors in Zoology and Botany through the University of Rhodesia, a college of the University of London, and M.A. in Zoology from the University of California at Berkeley.

I wish to investigate the movements, home range, habitat preferences and use patterns, predator-prey relationships, and aspects of the social organization of the endangered snow leopard in the Nepal Himalaya.

This rare carnivore is now largely restricted to remote valleys and mountains, where it finds tenuous sanctuary from humans. Virtually nothing is known about the snow leopard's ecology. I propose to live-trap and radio-collar up to five animals, and to track them over at least eight consecutive months. Data gathered by radio-tracking will be supplemented by intensive tracking of sign, censusing of major prey species, habitat characterization, and interviews with local residents. This study will be a difficult and challenging one; a rigorous level of effort is required. I have selected a study area I visited in 1976–1977 to survey for snow leopards. The development of ecologically viable management strategies for snow leopards is an important goal of the project.

As background, it must be stated that environmental degradation in the Himalaya of Nepal has reached unprecedented levels; population growth has forced farmers onto ever steeper slopes, villagers forage farther from home for firewood as the forests disappear under axe and plow, and shepherds are maintaining larger herds for longer periods of time in fragile alpine pastures. All these activities have forced native wildlife to retreat into remote and sparsely populated terrain where the remnant populations may be making their last stands.

The increasing rarity of the beautiful snow leopard perhaps best epitomizes the precarious status of Himalayan wildlife and the difficulty of protecting wide-ranging predators. Despite the establishment of parks and restrictions on the trade of pelts, snow leopards are now often found only in the most remote valleys and ranges of the Himalaya; their presence in Nepal's three mountain national parks has not been confirmed. Information on the snow leopard in the wild is very limited because of its secretive habits, inaccessible and rugged habitat, low numbers, and sparse distribution. Almost nothing is known about its movements, home range, food habits, hunting behavior, or social organization. In George Schaller's words, it remains "a creature of mystery." As I am aware from personal experience, wild snow leopards are very difficult to study. Radio-telemetry is the only feasible approach, and one that I believe can be successfully applied.

The study will be difficult and challenging because it focuses on a solitary, largely nocturnal and shy cat that is time-consuming to live-trap and hard to radio-track. The selection of a suitable study area (I have chosen the Kanjiroba Himal of West Nepal) is crucial, since radio-tracking requires a study population that is reasonably dense, as undisturbed as possible, and located in country relatively conducive to ground-based tracking (aerial surveillance is politically and logistically prohibited). Given the parameters, I believe I have selected the optimum study area.

Animals will be live-trapped in winter, when their range is most constricted and when it is easiest to track them. Traps will be placed at strategic, pre-baited locations. In several places in the Langu Khola, topography funnels leopards to cliffside trails several feet wide; I successfully baited an animal there in the winter of 1976. Trapped leopards will be tranquilized using a blow-pipe projected syringe.

In the radio-tracking itself, line-of-sight conditions will generally be required for location fixing. My knowledge of the study area will aid in tracking, which will be conducted from ridgelines by two mobile teams, the first led by me, the second by my local counterpart. The mountains will act as barriers to deflect the radio signals. Although the "bounce-effect" may make radio-location difficult, we are confident that our techniques will reduce, if not eliminate, such problems.

Insofar as logistics and living conditions are concerned, I am very familiar with the idiosyncrasies of expedition portage in West Nepal and am aware of the need for thorough preparation in advance. I will be almost entirely self-sufficient in terms of food, which will be air-freighted to Jumla and carried by porters to a base camp at Dalphu village. Winter camping is feasible because of the presence of warmer, south-facing slopes and protected valleys in my study area.

The prospects of receiving governmental permission for making the study are good, due to interest in a radio-tracking study expressed to me while I was in Nepal in 1977; I plan to follow this up during the fall of 1980 in person in Kathmandu. I will also recruit a wildlife biologist from the Nepal Office of National Parks and Wildlife Conservation to serve as co-investigator.

In addition to the radio-tracking, the strong tendency of the cats to use well-defined routes and to leave sign (scats, scrapings, and scentings) at prominent locations improves the effectiveness of tracking in otherwise difficult terrain. A method used to estimate mountain lion relative abundance in California will be tested for applicability to snow leopards in the Himalaya. The presence of the radio-tagged animals will aid in determining population levels by making it easier to tally individual animals.

Snow leopard food habits will be studied by analyzing scats and examining known or suspected leopard kills. Diet will be evaluated with respect to prey preference and availability and size, sex, age, and health of prey. The ecological distribution and abundance of prey animals like the bharal or blue sheep and the Himalayan tahr will be studied by regular censusing, the observation of sign, and by interviewing local residents. Sex and age composition counts will provide information on prey population recruitment, survival, and mortality rates, although I will have to rely heavily on previous studies of these herbivores for much of this data.

I will make special efforts to seek answers to such questions as what factors affect the size of the snow leopard's home range and what proportion of the population is nomadic. Do females occupy overlapping ranges shared partially or wholly with males? Are males territorial? How does this cat compare with other solitary cats, like the forest leopard and the mountain lion? To what extent are they dependent upon domestic livestock for their food supply? How can coexistence between humanity and the cat be fostered?

While the species does not appear to face imminent extinction in the Himalaya, its future urgently needs to be secured. The management plan I propose to develop in consultation with local officials and residents will: (1) identify critical ecological requirements of snow leopard and prey species; (2) evaluate environmental conflicts and trade-offs; (3) identify ways to encourage conservation on local, regional, and national levels; and (4) provide a basis for follow-up work by my collaborator, which could include the implementation of a snow leopard recovery plan for each one of Nepal's mountain national parks.

HALTING THE IMPACT OF MECHANIZED DRY FARMING NEAR THE BLUE NILE

ABU EL GASIM MOHAMED SULEIMAN
c/o Forests Office, P.O. Box 31, Damazin, Sudan, Africa

Sudanese, born January 1, 1933. Director of Forest Conservation for Southern Blue Nile Province, Sudan. Educated in Sudan, Sweden, the United Kingdom, and the United States.

My project is concerned with documenting the damage being done by mechanized dry farming near the Blue Nile in Sudan and establishing appropriate safeguards for the environment of this area.

The period of the early 1950's saw the beginnings of an enormous change in the natural ecological balance of the clay plains of the Blue Nile Province in Sudan. During this time, mechanized dry farming was introduced on these plains because the conditions of soil and climate had been found to be favorable for growing sorghum, sesame, cotton, and other crops. The Dali area, an accessible, large, flat plain, was the first area to be cleared for mechanized dry farming. Overall, the area cleared at Dali amounted to some 300,000 feddans (1 feddan is equal to about 1.03 acres). The cash return on this kind of farming was quickly proven to be very profitable and quite high enough to encourage more people to enter this kind of agriculture. Recognizing this fact, the Sudan government consequently drew up plans for reconnaissance and demarcation of more lands into which to extend mechanized dry farming.

The areas cleared to date for this method of agriculture are very large, with estimates ranging upward of 5 million feddans in the low-rainfall, woodland savanna belt in Sudan. This figure, perhaps more than any other, clearly provides a picture of what is happening in this part of the world. The damage that has been done is so great that, in spite of nature's ability to adapt to varying conditions, a major change has taken place in the flora and fauna of what had been a well-balanced environment:

Loss of the rich topsoil, with all its microorganic elements. The remaining soil has been severely damaged by the sun, wind, and water. The tree cover has been destroyed by uprooting and burning all tree species.

Run-off of rainwater is more rapid than it used to be, due to the absence of tree cover and retaining grasses, which has created many new water courses across the plains, which has increased erosion of the valuable soil.

Though not yet scientifically proven, there appears to have been a drop in rainfall in some northern areas, a dangerous change.

Repeated plowing and cultivation of the plains, in spite of crop rotation practices, has led to a drop in soil fertility and a resulting drop in crop productivity.

Destruction of an entire habitat for many types of wildlife, including Sommering gazelle, Dorcus gazelle, and guinea fowls. It is virtually impossible to find any of these animals or birds on these plains, which once were teeming with rich wildlife.

Dust storms are now frequent, with their inconveniences and hazards.

Nomads face difficulty in moving freely and in grazing their cattle and sheep, as they have done for centuries on these plains. Their land was taken for agriculture, and most of their traditional routes to grazing areas and water points have been blocked by farming, causing conflicts with farmers.

The protection of the environment in this part of the world is not a luxury; it is a necessity. The misuse of land and destruction of vegetation cover will ultimately lead to a great loss of soil, a situation that will deprive as-yet-unborn generations of their own prosperity and future welfare. It is the duty and responsibility of today's generation to ensure that those who come after will inherit rich and fertile soil and be able to enjoy living in a balanced environment.

My project seeks to create forest reserves and establish shelter-belts and windbreaks as intersections on the plains in order to check the most adverse factors acting upon the soil and to re-create suitable habitats for the native wildlife, thus keeping nature's cycle intact. I am attempting to introduce afforestation programs using tree species that may effectively conserve and protect the particular environment of these plains. I am working to establish irrigated forest plantations, in those areas where water is readily available, to serve as an alternative cash crop for the people. I seek the imposition of fire protection measures that will protect these forests. And finally, I am trying to create a separate government administration to cope with these problems in order to protect the future of Sudan and the children to come.

A VIDEOTAPE LIBRARY
OF HISTORICALLY
SIGNIFICANT ARCHITECTURE

BARBARA J. GILBERT
212 Race Street, Philadelphia, Pennsylvania 19106, U.S.A.

American, born June 4, 1951. Architectural Designer and Urban Planner; partner in design firm. Educated in the United States.

T he purpose of this project is to design and apply a new format for recording architecturally significant structures and urban spaces through the use of videotapes. Six structures of varying use, age, and scale will be filmed in the first stage of this project, with appropriate narratives to be provided by well-known experts in architectural history and theory. These narratives will be geared to a wide audience of divergent education and interests. At the conclusion of this initial phase of work, all supporting materials and films will be made available to libraries, community groups, educational television programs, and schools.

Architecture is the design and creation of three-dimensional environments in support of human activities and in furtherance of social goals. As contemporary architects and architectural historians have attempted to make their work understandable to a broad range of people, they have been frustrated by the difficulties non-professionals have in visualizing an environment through reading drawings and viewing single photographs or slides. Although the traditional methods of recording architecture are invaluable from the standpoint of precise measurements, they do not allow the viewer to experience a building as it was meant to be experienced by its designer or builder, in three dimensions.

This project intends to experiment with the application of video filming techniques to architectural study and to begin the accumulation of a library of video recordings. Each of the recordings would be valuable, from a historical and educational point of view, in three ways; first, as an expressive and accurate documentation of a culturally important piece of architecture; second, as a recording of valuable contemporary architectural thought through the use of expert architectural historians and theorists as narrators; and third, as an experimental application of the relatively new field of video recording to architectural history. This product will make architectural critiques equally accessible and legible, for the first time, to both the professional and non-professional public. It is a technique that could prove to be valuable to designers who wish to involve the public in the work that they do and to educators who wish to present architectural history to students with little previous training in this field.

The first stage of this project, for which funding is being sought, includes these activities:

1. Tape-record preliminary interviews with architectural historians to select the first six structures or environments to be documented. At this time, a team of television producers and related specialists will design the format for the video recordings. A diverse group of buildings of historical merit will be selected from the following categories: (a) an urban exterior space, such as a plaza or a square, (b) three types of residential structures—one rural structure, one single-family urban structure, and one multifamily urban structure, (c) a monumental civic structure, and (d) a large-scale urban design scheme or project involving multiple uses, such as institutional, civic, religious, commercial, and residential facilities.

2. Videotape each environment using appropriate narratives by the selected experts.

3. Provide a packet of background materials for each film, including architectural drawings and a bibliography of selected readings.

4. Create a pamphlet describing the projects that have been recorded and the availability of these recordings to schools, libraries, and television. Place the videotapes with corresponding background material and brochures in the care of a non-profit institution.

The goal of this project is to complete these six videotapes as the basis or core of an ongoing program of videotaping great historical architectural structures, some of which can be considered already to be on the "endangered species" list. Not only should they be preserved, but their eloquence, significance, grandeur, or simple beauty should be brought to those thousands or millions of people who might not otherwise be able to appreciate them.

A typical well in Mauritania's desert regions.

Equipment installed in the Taouaz, near Atar, Mauritania.

SPECIAL WELL EQUIPMENT TO FIGHT MAURITANIA'S DEADLY DROUGHT

 OTTOMAR A. J. AMEIS
Honorable Mention, Rolex Awards for Enterprise
Schleusenredder 21, 2000 Hamburg 65, West Germany

German, born August 19, 1926. Administrative supervisor in the Hamburg city transit system. Educated in Germany.

T his enterprise involves the acquisition of eighteen specialized pieces of well-constructing equipment in Germany, their transportation to Mauritania in West Africa, and the mounting of them at suitable places in the desert in order to provide vitally needed water in an area of killing drought.

This project was inspired by the distress of the people and their animals in the West Sahara described in an article by Mme. Dr. Hilde Gauthier-Pilters, a French zoologist, in *Kosmos* magazine of January 1975. The German government documented the loss of 80 percent of the cattle, 60 percent of the sheep and goats, and 30 percent of the camels during the long drought that had run from 1969 to 1973 as due to the lack of well-equipped watering places in Mauritania.

My wife and I decided to start an aid program, in cooperation with Dr. Gauthier, of improving the existing wells in Mauritania to secure a more constant water supply for both humans and animals. We went to Mauritania first in 1976, where we improved two wells by means of a construction of concrete and ready-made galvanized iron parts. Though these steps were successful, they were not, in my opinion, effective enough when compared with the cost involved (DM 25,000). Therefore, when we returned home, I tried to find a solution that would allow the carrying of eight or ten units on a single truck. Instead of taking a week to install a unit, we should be able to install each one in a single day.

Since the concrete form we had used in 1976 was made of steel sheets, I decided to build the complete unit of stainless steel sheets and galvanized iron parts. Only the superior quality of the stainless material can withstand use by the people and cattle and exposure to the ever-present sunshine. With the aid of a locksmith's workshop, we fabricated nine well-rings with attached pours, with basins connected to the pours by a strong chain. Additionally, a small crane with two wheels was made, with all joints constructed of galvanized iron. All these parts had to be stackable, since it was necessary to stow them under the seats and the floor of our 20-year-old truck.

In the unit we designed, the well-rings are to be installed to protect the well-hole from sand and animal droppings, which are normally blown into the wells. They also prevent humans and animals from accidentally falling into the wells. The basins guarantee a more rapid supply of water to the numerous camels, cattle, donkeys, sheep, and goats. The cranes themselves facilitate pulling up the waterbags from depths that extend as far as 60 meters.

Gifts from two local church communities in Hamburg covered approximately 50 percent of all our expenses. The balance was paid by my wife and me, as well as our complete expenses for the 1976 trip.

In 1979, with the assistance of two friends, the Catholic Mission in Nouakchott, and our native guide in Atar, Mauritania, we succeeded in constructing another eight well-equipment units. We have found that our new system serves its purpose and that it is well accepted by the natives.

Our third project is being planned for 1982. We intend to install another eighteen units of the same type. The two specialized trucks required for the transport will be bought second-hand from the army, because we have not sufficient money for better trucks in addition to all the other costs.

The passenger fare for three or four persons from Marseilles to Dakar, plus two trucks through Keller Shipping S.A. of Basel, is at least 10,000 Swiss francs. (Due to political reasons, it is impossible for us to drive the trucks cross-country to our intended sites of installation.) Expenses for food, fuel, the guide, and the return voyage would also be included.

I will undertake this enterprise with my wife, one or two of my sons, and any other person capable and willing to accompany us. I will have to complete the project in three months, the amount of time I can take away from my job. The planned time for the expedition is approximately February 1982 to April 1982.

We hope our local church will again be able to help finance the project, providing up to 10,000 Swiss francs. Although they supported the 1979 project (our second visit to Mauritania), it is uncertain whether they can assist us again. At present we have no other sources of contributions. No further applications to other organizations have been made. (I tried to do this in 1976, but did not succeed; there is very little hope for a private person to receive official financial aid.)

Any award or gift will be for the benefit of the poor people in the West African desert, who have now come to appreciate what this new well system can do for them and their lives. In summary, some of the advantages of our new system are: (1) it is easily and quickly mounted; (2) the basin can easily be turned and cleaned, helping prevent infections and the transmission of disease; (3) the whole system is removable and replaceable, in case of destruction or the need for relocation; (4) it can easily be removed to another well when its location dries up.

We believe the system could be used for many wells in the Sahel and Sahara, and perhaps in other desert regions of the world. We believe it is more useful to the people and animals of these countries to have several watering-places with average capacities than only a few with huge capacities.

We know that complicated machinery, such as fuel-engine pumps, cannot be maintained in desert areas. We have therefore decided to accommodate our system to those that have been used by the natives in the Sahara for hundreds of years. It appears that this approach has been successful, and we would like to continue to offer such help to those people who need it.

THE "WORLD OF WUVULU"

PAUL M. STOCKER
Alaba Lodge, Wuvulu Island, P.O. Box 437, Wewak,
Papua New Guinea

*American, born March 16, 1924. Founder/Director of two Papua New Guinea
companies. Educated in the United States.*

The "World of Wuvulu" project is dedicated to the protection of an endangered people, the Wuvulu Islanders. The first phase of the project is a program to eradicate malaria on Wuvulu. Subsequent phases involve the protection of the Wuvuluian way of life.

Wuvulu Island is found in the Bismarck Sea, about 200 kilometers northwest of Wewak, Papua New Guinea. The Islanders have a unique oceanic heritage; their appearance as well as their language is distinctly different from their closest mainland neighbors. They have their own art, fables, myths, and folklore unique to the island.

My wife, my son, and I are the only Europeans in residence. Our daughter-in-law and our two grandchildren are Islanders.

We live in a society that is family-oriented. There is no need for police or government agents on Wuvulu. Families share the fish that are caught and the food that is grown, and they even exchange children to raise. A woman without her own child is given several to raise and to love. Elderly people are respected and cared for by the village. Wuvuluians live for the moment. They do not worry about tomorrow or grieve about yesterday.

Wuvulu is composed of a coral mantle grown on the pinnacle of a submarine mountain. Its 1820 hectares now support 550 Islanders. It is entirely surrounded by a barrier reef, which forms its frontier. In 1543, a European navigator reported an attempt to land on Wuvulu and noted the opposition he encountered from brave, light-skinned warriors.

For several hundred years, Wuvulu has been exposed to the negative influences of the "other world" without the corresponding advantages. Malaria and other diseases were brought to the island, and in a few generations the population had declined from 2000 to 200.

In the Anchorite Islands to the northeast of Wuvulu, an entire population, save for a small boy, was decimated by malaria. This sole survivor, whose name was Bulu, was rescued by a German planter and brought to Wuvulu Island. Bulu died this last year at the age of 82. Bulu was the great-grandfather of my grandson Paefa and our teacher of the Wuvulu way of life.

The Wuvulu Islanders are now fighting for their survival. Even remote Wuvulu must prepare for the future or be overwhelmed by the "other world." My Wuvulu project is separated into categories of priorities.

First, we had to create a village industry to finance needed improvements, keeping in mind always that nothing should impair the island way of life. For over seven years, we worked without generators or power tools to build a lodge of native hardwoods. It is now complete, and our first scuba divers are starting to arrive at Alaba (Turtle) Lodge. It will probably take three years more before a net profit will be realized. The Rolex Award could move our clock forward on the following currently planned projects.

1. The eradication of the malaria-parasite-bearing anopheles mosquito from the island by the use of the most modern methods is our most urgent task.

I have talked with the malaria control officers in Australia and Papua New Guinea and have visited Mauritius, where malaria was successfully defeated. Aided by the official Mauritius report, I am coordinating with Dr. Farrell, who is the Senior Health Officer at Wewak. Our campaign involves an attack on the vector mosquito and a complete medication of each man, woman, and child on the island with malarial suppressants. We must either drain the swamp on the island or coat it with antilarval oil. The huts must be sprayed at least once a month, and the swamp taro patches must be covered with vegetable oil. We figure it will take us three years to rectify the damage of 300 years of exposure to the "other world" in this critical health area.

2. We seek to improve the island's general health standards.

3. We wish to continue the work of preserving the unique oral language of the Wuvulu people, their customs, fables, folklore, and art.

4. We are determined to protect one of the finest reefs in the entire world.

Our family is not connected with any religious or secular organization. As G. B. Shaw said, "This is the true joy in life, the being used for a purpose recognized by yourself as a mighty one."

DAGA FARMERS' SELF-HELP IN PAPUA NEW GUINEA

 CLEMENT D. BATEMAN
Honorable Mention, Rolex Awards for Enterprise
Daga Farmers, Anglican Church PMB, Agaun via Alotau,
Milne Bay Province, Papua New Guinea

Papua New Guinean, born December 12, 1926. Priest-agronomist in Papua New Guinea for Church of England since 1959. Educated in England and Australia (Diploma in Tropical Agronomy from University of Queensland).

The Daga Farmers, at Agaun in the Daga Mountains area of Papua New Guinea, are a group of young school-leavers who have completed grade six at primary school, and who previously had no way of making an adequate income. Annual cash income in this society is about $10.00 per year from coffee crops. In this developing country, only a very few young people have the chance to go on to secondary education.

Started in 1969, the Daga Farmers Beef and Dairy Cattle Project is aimed at enabling school-leavers to make a cash income and avoid the unemployment problem that exists in many developing lands. This particular area was chosen because it is the poorest and least-developed district in the country, and because of the presence of the local "cargo cults"—a movement that expects the miraculous appearance of valuable "cargo" from the skies as the result of wartime military airlifts. To clarify to participants in this project that cash income from industry is not magic but the result of planning and hard work, we decided to start this project with no assets and to build up everything from practically nothing. In the last ten years, there has been considerable development.

In 1969 I was asked by a student from the area to help set up a cattle industry in this remote mountainous end of Milne Bay Province. With no money to start the project, I began making concrete blocks with the student for sale to local builders. By 1971 there was a surplus of $900 from this activity, which was used to purchase six heifers and a bull and hire a small plane to fly them into the airstrip at Agaun by the end of 1972.

From 1973 to 1976, we had fifteen school-leavers attend a three-year course in cattle farming, with the promise of a loan of some cattle to set up their own family cattle farm if they completed the course. The fifteen students represented five different clans, or families, and by 1979 these five clans were given cattle bred from the original imports. During these years, the five farms have steadily planted improved pasture grasses and legumes for their cattle and have gradually extended barbed-wire fencing by the sale of a small amount of coffee.

We are now considering the future market for beef and dairy products. Beef can be bought only by the small number of wage earners here—staff at the local hospital, some local government personnel, and the teachers at the local school. Except for a short time after the annual coffee market, village families have no money for buying meat. With the local market for beef at about two beasts per month, the remainder must be sold outside this area, which will help bring cash into the local economy.

As the closest outside market is on the coast over 50 kilometers to the south, we are planning to build a road by hand with pick and shovel, since there is no road-making equipment available. The road is planned for bullocks and horses with packs, as a vehicular road would be washed away with the high rainfall and damaged by landslides on the nearly vertical slopes. Thus, both the animals and the coffee can be walked to the market. Although the road has been started, it will take some years to complete.

For the local beef market, which calls for the ability to freeze the meat and the subsequent need for freezer units and electric power, the farmers have spent two years digging a water-supply route from around the mountain, using a higher stream for hydroelectric power in a self-made plant that now supplies enough power for the freezers and lighting. This hydroelectric plant was made from salvaged road-machinery parts, sprockets, and chains, with an overhead 2.5-meter drive-wheel, and a salvaged 3-kilowatt alternator.

The purpose of this description is to show a notable degree of spirit, initiative, and perseverance by a group of young men in an underdeveloped country—a country that has only very recently emerged from the Stone Age.

The dedication of this group of Daga Farmers is shown by their willingness to start their cattle projects independently, with no outside help or finance at the initial stage. Their perseverance has lasted continuously for over ten years, in a very difficult part of this tropical island, and has included a great amount of hard physical work and intelligent planning.

A herd of West Indian manatees gathered in the warm-water discharge of the Riviera Power Plant (Riviera Beach, Florida) on a cold winter morning (air temperature 1°C).

A POWER COMPANY AND ENDANGERED SPECIES: EXAMPLES OF COEXISTENCE

J. ROSS WILCOX
c/o Florida Power & Light Company,
Licensing and Environmental Planning, P.O. Box 529100,
Miami, Florida 33152, U.S.A.

American, born January 13, 1942. Ecologist at Florida Power & Light Company. Biology and oceanography education (Ph.D.) in the United States.

Florida Power & Light Company (FPL) has interacted with nine rare and endangered species, and for the most part we have experienced no direct conflicts. The animals involved are the West Indian manatee, the American crocodile, the southern bald eagle, three species of sea turtles, the American alligator, the indigo snake, and the Everglade kite.

Through research and monitoring, the company is documenting ways in which endangered or threatened species can coexist with the production and transmission of electricity. Where real or potential conflicts are identified, FPL has taken positive action to eliminate or minimize adverse consequences.

FPL is the sixth-largest utility in the United States, serving more than two million customers in an area covering approximately half the area of Florida. The company owns and manages large tracts of land in both rural and urban areas. Much of this property is undeveloped land, used as a buffer zone to isolate power plants from residential and agricultural areas. These buffer zones serve as wildlife habitats for many species, both common and endangered; this situation in effect places FPL in the wildlife business.

To date, the company has had no direct conflicts in its interacting with the animals, due largely to a specific program of research and management. With a sense of stewardship and good business practice, the company is documenting that the well-being of these endangered species is compatible with the production and transmission of electricity. Examples of the coexistence of industrial needs and the welfare of endangered species are given here.

West Indian Manatee

This air-breathing, aquatic herbivore, often called the sea cow, grows to a length of 3.5 meters and weighs up to 1000 kilograms. Classified as endangered, the manatee is found in shallow coastal waters, bays, lagoons, estuaries, rivers, and inland lakes of tropical and subtropical Central and North America. In the United States, its present-day distribution is limited to peninsular Florida during the winter months, and isolated individuals are found in Texas and the Carolinas during the summer. The total manatee population is estimated at 1000.

Although the manatee is a slow swimmer, it is capable of quick and swift movements for short distances. The animal is harmless and has no natural predators. In recent years, human activity has been identified as the largest known cause of manatee injury and mortality. All adult manatees bear some type of scar resulting from collision with high-speed motor boats. Control of motor-boat speeds in the winter congregation areas, where large numbers of manatees gather, is therefore a way of protecting the species. FPL has contributed to this solution by catering to a peculiar feature of manatee behavior.

During the winter months only, manatees seek warm-water refuges in Florida. Historically, the animals have congregated around constant-temperature freshwater springs, but the population build-up in Florida and the tapping of aquifers for agricultural purposes have caused many of these natural springs to cease flowing today. The manatees have therefore sought warm-water effluents as refuges. FPL has five plants that operate in a once-through cooling mode. By contracting the Florida Audubon Society to conduct a year-round Aerial Census Program for us, we have documented winter concentrations of manatees at these plants. The results show that up to 60% of the population of an endangered species will congregate in our warm-water discharges.

FPL is working very hard to promote a stewardship with these endangered animals. Through the efforts of the Aerial Census Program, the Florida Audubon Society was able to collect scientifically valid data that, when presented to the Florida Legislature, became the impetus for passage of the Florida Manatee Sanctuary Act of 1978. This act provides for the regulation of boat speed in 13 manatee congregation areas between November 15 and March 31 of each year. Law-enforced speed-zone signs (paid for by FPL) will cover all of these zones, which include all the warm-water discharges of the five FPL plants. FPL has also contracted with the Florida Audubon Society to conduct a Public Awareness Program concerning manatees, to minimize human/manatee confrontations. This program has become very popular.

American Crocodile

This endangered animal ranges in length from 23 centimeters at hatching to 4.6 meters for the larger males and has a present population estimated at 200–400 individuals with approximately 25 breeding females, located at the extreme southern tip of Florida. FPL owns about 8900 hectares of land at the extreme tip of Florida, all of which fall in the critical habitat of the crocodiles. Approximately half this land comprises a plant site, which has an elaborate set of closed-circuit cooling canals for the condensers. The other half of the land is undeveloped.

In 1977 we first discovered that at least one crocodile was living in the southwestern section of the cooling canal system here. A survey documented a rather extensive population of crocodiles at this (Turkey Point) plant site. By locating nests within the berms, which have produced at least eighteen hatchings, our consultants have been able to capture, mark, release, and subsequently recapture specimens, enabling them to construct a growth curve. A particularly fascinating element in this program is the recognition that crocodiles will preferentially seek out and utilize manmade canals and berms for resting and reproduction, because they are in effect in a controlled environment—the adjacent land area of "prime" habitat being less utilized by them than our "disturbed" habitat.

Southern Bald Eagle

A viable population of this bird, endangered on the federal level and threatened on the state level, exists in Florida, with approximately 325 breeding pairs. The species has declined over the last thirty years, however, due to loss of nesting habitat and use of pesticides.

FPL is developing a major power-plant complex on a large tract of land in south-central Florida, which presently includes a 3200-hectare reservoir, two more units under construction, and two more planned. In 1971, as part of the company's commitment to coexist with wildlife, a 160-hectare tract of land with a unique cypress tree stand was preserved by redesigning the reservoir around this area, which includes a southern bald eagle's nest. A pair has used this nest successfully in breeding, actively fishing the reservoir. We have advised plant, construction, and security personnel of the presence of eagles at each of our sites and have advised them not to disturb the animals. A result of this program is a high degree of respect for the eagles on the part of FPL site personnel and a highly protective viewpoint about them.

RECONSTRUCTING EARTHQUAKE-DAMAGED TOWN CLOCKS

EDWIN E. LOPEZ REVOLORIO
9a, C, 6-31, Zona 1, Guatemala City, Guatemala, C.A.

Guatemalan, born June 20, 1948. Watch repairer in charge of jewelry store repair department. Educated and trained in Guatemala and the United States.

I wish to begin rebuilding the grand old tower clocks in the town buildings of my country, which were destroyed in the earthquake of 1976. I wish to participate in your Enterprise competition. I am aware that in your business watches and clocks are everyday items, but in view of your competition and the reasons for it, I hope you will understand my project, which I shall explain as follows.

In 1976, my country was violently shaken by a large earthquake that caused immense loss. Still today, many Guatemalan buildings remain in a state of ruin.

Here in Guatemala, we have many churches and monuments with towers that have been part of our history and life since colonial days. Many of them were built more than 500 years ago. During the years from 1920 to 1934, clocks were installed in the church and monument towers, with from one to four faces, along with their respective bell chimes. Some of these pealed at hourly intervals, others at half-hour intervals, and still others at 15-minute intervals, with different melodies.

Today all of these clocks are out of order. The earthquake, and a lack of maintenance, have deprived the people of Guatemala's towns and villages of an important part of their daily lives.

The mechanisms of these old clocks are old-fashioned in this age of quartz watches and timepieces. It would be possible to replace them with modern mechanisms, but that would be like condemning a species to extinction, in this case, a mechanism specially made for a very special purpose.

I have actually had the opportunity to rebuild one of these clocks here in Guatemala, which was of German manufacture. Having worked for 18 years in the repair of clocks and watches of all types, this experience awakened in me a strong desire to make all the public clocks of my country function again and thus avoid the extinction of an unusual and valuable species.

The tower clocks themselves generally have from three to four different faces, all exposed to the elements on a year-round basis. The faces of this type of clock are made of iron, with black Roman numerals. Due to the earthquake, these faces are either misshapen or broken. To rebuild them, it will be necessary to gather the talents of metalsmiths, painters, bricklayers, and builders under the supervision of a qualified watch repair man.

Internally, there are brass gears and iron rods that connect the faces of the clocks to the main clockwork machine. The repair of these elements involves welding, and because the majority of the churches in the country have repaired their towers already, it may be impossible to do the work on these interior mechanisms. In this case, I should like to dedicate myself to restoring the faces and the presentation of the damaged clock faces themselves. In any case, the building of the brass pieces requires fusing and finishing by hand, a time-consuming task but one that can be overcome with patience once the faces of the clocks are again in order.

The majority of the clocks are made with steel cables and weights, the latter up to some 300 pounds. Of these, the largest is within the main Guatemala City Cathedral (another of the stopped clocks). To repair this particular clock would require assistance from factories in Europe, which might be able to duplicate special parts.

The third area of concern is the repair of the bell ringing mechanisms. There are no problems here apart from the height of the bell towers and the inconvenience of changing the wooden holders from which they swing. The techniques to be used here are those of synchronized bells, which each jeweler uses in order to repair watches and which can easily be applied to a tower clock.

I know that it is illogical for me to think that I can repair all of these clocks by restoring them to their original states. But, in my view, I must begin this work, to avoid the gradual extinction of the tower clock in this country.

The clocks are not living things, perhaps, but they are the fingerprints of humanity and should not be allowed to perish simply through the passage of time and lack of care.

CONSERVATION OF THE INDIAN WILD BUFFALO

 KANAK T. BANERJEA
Honorable Mention, Rolex Awards for Enterprise
5/1, Nayapatty Road, Calcutta-700 055, West Bengal, India

Indian, born July 9, 1939. Director of a company; associated with various conservation organizations in India. Educated in India.

There are only five hundred wild buffaloes still surviving in Indian forests. They are extinct from Peninsular India and are now found only in Assam and on the Bhutan border. Until 1908, these fine animals were found in the Sundarbans—the southern riverine and coastal forests of West Bengal and Bangladesh.

Contamination by rinderpest and mixing with domestic buffalo are the two causes most responsible for the rapid disappearance of these animals from Orissa, Andhra Pradesh, and Madhya Pradesh states of India. Only segregation of these beasts from domestic animals and populated areas can save them from extinction or degeneration. I propose they be rehabilitated in the Sundarbans.

The Indian wild buffalo stands some 5–6 feet in height and weighs 1–$1\frac{1}{2}$ tons. It is distinctly separate from its cousins in Africa and Southwest Asia. It looks charcoal gray and deep black in forests and possesses massive horns of great proportions. A single horn, kept in the British Museum, measures $78\frac{1}{2}$ inches along the outer curve. The animals have bifurcated hooves, suitable for movement in muddy and swampy habitats.

In earlier times, the animals were found all over the monsoon forests of India, including the Sundarbans. Feeding on grass, reeds, tree leaves, and creepers, they prefer dwelling in muddy areas and enjoy wallowing in pools and rivers. Very moody, these animals are unpredictable in nature, and hence much of their behavior pattern is unknown to us. We do know that they like to live in herds, though occasional "lone bulls" are seen. The young are born after a 310-day gestation period and become sexually mature at two or three years.

Humans have been the greatest enemy of the Indian wild buffalo. When domesticated, the animals are very docile; they serve as useful beasts of burden, produce milk at low maintenance cost, and represent wealth to their owners. The passage of rinderpest from domestic cattle to the wild buffalo further decreases its numbers, again a result of human intervention in its natural ecology. It is imperative that we give the wild buffalo its own home, and I wish to do this in its old, and naturally ideal, habitat of the Sundarbans, on one of the southernmost of these estuarine islands. There is already a Tiger Project functioning in the northern fringe of the Sundarbans, and it would not be difficult to procure one of these islands (about 6 square kilometers) from the West Bengal government to use for the wild buffalo.

There are about forty herds of Indian wild buffalo still surviving in the forests of Assam, under the control of the government of India. We would collect a small herd of adolescent calves for introduction to the new island site. The island will provide adequate fodder in the form of grasslands. Digging of some water holes may be necessary to assure sweet subsoil water for drinking, as the estuary water can be too saline for the buffalo.

Protection of the animals from natural enemies such as tigers and panthers will be accomplished by the island location. Crocodiles and sharks, patrolling the surrounding waters, will provide a natural and effective obstacle to the buffalo's inclination to move from its location. Since the tidal flow in the estuary sweeps into the islands every six hours, flooding the lowlands, it is difficult for humans to enter.

By placing a herd of Indian wild buffalo on one of the Sundarban islands, we will be able not only to restore this imposing beast to one of its original homes but also to closely examine it in a natural habitat, free from the debilitating influences of in-breeding with domestic stock and away from the crippling effects of disease carried by domestic animals.

I anticipate that the project will take two to three years. It will be carried out in two phases of stocking, in order that we can learn from the observations of the initial herd what the most appropriate additions to it should be, what population the island can support, and other key data that will help us to re-establish the Indian wild buffalo in its natural habitat.

The first step in disposing of organic waste: the worm bed.

A COMPLETE RESOURCE RECOVERY SYSTEM FOR SOLID WASTE IN THE THIRD WORLD

 BASIL A. B. ROSSI
Honorable Mention, Rolex Awards for Enterprise
Rossi–Nayve Consultancy Services, Inc.,
House of Montinola, San Vicente St.,
Sta. Clara Subd., Bacolod City, Philippines

*Australian, born July 3, 1931. Company President and Asian Recycling Association
President. Educated in Australia.*

The cities and towns of the Third World are literally becoming buried in garbage. Currently dumped in unsanitary smoking mountains, this so-called waste is a hazard to health, a polluter of water supplies, and a rising cost to authorities that they can ill afford.

I would like to prove that it is possible to turn this "waste" into prime resources, which will conserve energy, cut import spending, and employ hundreds of thousands of people in areas of high unemployment. Such a scheme will also result in the improvement of agricultural land and produce badly needed protein—all at minimal capital costs.

Studies have shown that the average garbage produced in Asia (or rather that which is presently collected and dumped) weighs 0.2 ton per capita per year. This means that excluding China, Asia produces some 200 million tons of household waste annually, and the figure is rising rapidly. Agricultural and animal waste could multiply this figure, as could planned collection, which cities cannot afford at present. Even present collection and unsanitary dumping cost billions of U.S. dollars a year.

This waste is 80–85 percent organic putrescible and 15–20 percent inorganic plus plastic. Of the organic putrescible, as much as 15 percent is paper. Of the inorganic, as much as 6 percent is steel/tin can scrap, 3 percent glass, and 5 percent plastic. In considering the recycling of this waste, one of the plus factors in developing areas is the relatively low cost of available labor, so that separation can be achieved by hand. Sophisticated separation methods—for example, the magnetic separation of ferrous scrap—do not work well in the tropics because of the high moisture content of the garbage. The main problem has been that the Western system of organic disposal—composting—does not resolve the organic disposal problem in Asia due to the high risk of spreading disease. Another reason for not composting is that the end product (the soil improver) is unacceptable for the farmer with bare feet because of its broken glass content, plus the general lack of need for the product in tropical and subtropical areas.

Following Japanese successes using earthworms to convert putrescibles to product, a concept going back to Artistotle and Darwin, I have proven that in the tropics, earthworms—particularly the North American red worm or manure worm—will eat their own weight and more of wet waste in a day. Thus, 1 ton of worms will devour $1-1\frac{1}{2}$ tons of wet waste per day. Their castings, when blended on a 40/60 basis with conventional chemical fertilizers into a granule, will produce crop increases up to 40 percent, improve the soil, and help to prevent nitrate run-off (a problem in high rainfall areas) as well. A ton of wet garbage will produce 40 percent of dry castings. Sewage sludge, animal waste, certain factory wastes (paper mill sludge, food packing wastes) will give similar results.

The worms breed rapidly (one worm will produce 1000 offspring in one year; 1,000,000 in two years). Surplus worms can be dried to worm meal (20–25 percent of wet weight), which is 64 percent protein plus amino acids—an excellent feed for animals, fish, and humans. It is, in fact, better than soybean meal and even has advantages over fish and meat meals.

Through this worm conversion, the garbage that may have cost $10 per ton to dump takes on minimum plus value of $40 with labor and collection costs taken into account. Very important considerations are that minimal mechanization is needed and that the system can be placed wherever quantities of appropriate wet garbage occur, rather than transporting the waste over long distances to central dumps at high cost on congested Asian city roads. This localization is significant. In fact, my first tests were conducted on the seventh-floor balcony of a Manila apartment building. Since worms deodorize the waste, we had no smell or fly problem, and a kilogram of worms disposed of our four-person family waste. Such a system can be installed in the middle of residential areas, saving on transport.

The treatment of inorganics can be considered after the treatment of organics has been settled. Paper-making machines are available at $700 that are capable of producing one-third of a ton of paper per day (compared to conventional plant costs of $100,000 capital per-ton production). Detinning plants can be established in rural locations that can handle down to 2000 tons per year. Glass waste can be formed into insulation sheet, making use of waste heat sources from the plants. Plastics can be used to line irrigation canals, fishponds, and water storage areas; rubber can be converted back to product; leather can be turned into acoustic tiles; and textiles can be turned into paper or wipers.

I wish to establish pilot projects in two different testing environments: a village of 500 families, and a town of 20,000 people. These sites will illustrate the viability and flexibility of the integrated resource recovery system. The capital cost of establishing the village unit will not exceed $2000. At the town level, costs are estimated to be less than $20,000, with land for the unit provided by local authorities. The return on capital will be high and will permit rapid expansion of the basic inorganic disposal system into more capital-intensive miniaturized inorganic treatment facilities. Handling metals, glass, plastics, and so on will then be possible.

One ton of garbage per day can employ an average 1.2 persons; thus South Asia's 200 million tons of garbage waste could employ some 650,000 well-paid workers and produce end-products worth some $8 billion annually, with a product range salable not only in Asia, but also exportable to areas like the Middle East.

Realizing that garbage is one of the few potential assets of many developing countries, I believe that such a scheme should begin as soon as possible. It must be remembered that, in most Third World countries, demonstration of a *working* system is the only thing that can "sell" a project, however good it may be on paper or in limited laboratory-type experiments. Conducting the two projects I wish to undertake and operate will, I believe, open the doors to assistance from governments and international agencies.

I have assembled what may be one of the world's largest libraries on the specific subject of this kind of localized recycling opportunity, presented papers in numerous talks on the subject, and operate a pilot production facility for further research into the potential of this approach to one of the world's great problems. Any assistance in furthering this idea will be appreciated.

PROJECT PRO-BRAZILIAN FAUNA: RAISING A COUNTRY'S ECOLOGY CONSCIOUSNESS

SYNESIO ASCENCIO
Av. República do Líbano, 2131-CEP:04501, Saõ Paulo, SP, Brazil

Brazilian, born December 28, 1929. Magazine owner and publisher. Educated in Brazil.

I n Brazil, the problem of endangered animal species has been faced in very subjective and emotional ways. Only a very few motivated individuals are developing serious projects, and they do so with the help of extremely limited government support. Our list of animals now threatened with extinction totals more than 80 species.

I wish, by means of project Pro-Brazilian Fauna, to make our people accept the transcendental importance of maintaining our animal life in a healthy state of preservation. We have numerous examples that this kind of effort is possible, in countries like the United States, Germany, and Italy, and what these measures have meant for the quality of life in these countries.

Brazil has 8,511,685 square kilometers of land, a population estimated at 125 million, and an estimated 2 million hunters. Of the latter number, probably not more than 30,000 to 40,000 are duly registered in hunting and shooting clubs in all our states. Of the remainder, about 50 percent are furtive, illegal hunters, or poachers. And of the fraction that is left over, virtually all are from poor families that live close to the wilds, on the banks of rivers, very far from small villages and civilized centers.

In this context, in 1970, some 20 million wild animals were massacred. Though somewhat reduced since then in terms of annual killings, the situation has continued, which led me to set up the Brazilian Hunting Association in 1978. The principal objective of this association was to get together the people of good will of this country, especially conscientious hunters, and work for the conservation of Brazil's natural renewable resources on all fronts where this was possible.

I have obtained some results, nowadays shared among several companions, in conveying a conservationist philosophy throughout the country. By publishing *Troféu Magazine*, the organ that has led all of the initiatives in the direction of conservationism, we have been able to slowly build an awareness of the real problems facing our fauna and an awareness of the value of ecological thinking.

We have, however, a very small circulation, proportional to the limited amount of money that comes in from advertisers. With a monthly circulation rate of under 10,000 copies, a quantity that is practically nothing considering our population and potential readers, we are nevertheless encouraged by various results. It is gratifying to know, for example, that some Brazilian mayors orient their citizens toward ecology by means of articles published in *Troféu Magazine*. Secretaries of Education in important Brazilian states request permission to include articles from *Troféu* in their state's school curriculum.

This force of culture and information of *Troféu Magazine* would be still more intense, frequent, and ample if we could increase the number of pages and the circulation of the magazine.

In a recent survey taken in four of the principal Brazilian capitals, thousands of people were asked if they had ever heard of ecology. Some 36 to 43 percent had no recollection of having heard of ecology. If this happens in our principal population and cultural centers, imagine what the results would be if less privileged states were also researched. Confirming this lack of ecological knowledge, let us look at statistics relative to some species hunted professionally in 1970. Of the well-known species, here are the numbers killed: giant otter, 304,188; capybara, 186,134; wildcat, 6,593,222; Maracaja wildcat, 5,278,059; collared peccary, 1,308,988; deer, 730,437; cayman, 2,433,284; and lizzara, 2,505,975. It is worthwhile noting here that Law No. 5197, of January 5, 1967, says, among other things (Art. I) "The animals of any species, in any state of development and which live naturally out of captivity, constituting the wild fauna, as well as their nests, dens and natural breeding places are property of the State, being absolutely forbidden their utilization, persecution, destruction, hunting or apprehension." (Art. II) "The exercise of professional hunting is forbidden."

Obviously, the lack of a plan of education for the people that would follow the promulgation of the law, plus other reasons, has brought the species mentioned above to the brink of extinction.

This is my great objective: to educate, through *Troféu Magazine,* all those citizens who have not yet understood their responsibility with regard to preservation of Brazil's wild animals. I seek both financial support and knowhow for the furtherance of *Troféu Magazine,* which I believe is a leading and constructive element in making a nation conscious of ecology.

MAKING A NEW LIFE CYCLE IN HARMONY WITH NATURE

TADASHI INAMOTO
Makigahora, Kiyomi-mura, Ohno-gun, Gifu-ken, Japan

Japanese, born February 5, 1945. The Representative of Oak Village, subject of this project. Educated in Japan.

W e human beings have never come so close to possible extermination as a species as we are now. Recent advances in science and technology have certainly enriched and expanded our lives in a material sense, but they have also led us into destroying nature and to feeling insecure about our world. In this sense, the myth of industrialization as the salvation of human problems has almost lost its appeal and power. At the same time, there is no point in denying the advantages of technology and attempting to return to a primitive state.

I believe now is the time we should make as many efforts as we can to establish the ideal environment in which both nature and human beings can exist in harmony. With the cooperation of the members of Oak Village, I would like to establish a new lifestyle, in which we can supply our own needs for food and energy, and do so with the least possible destruction to our environment. At the same time, we would like to pursue an "ideal environment," by using technology and science within nature at either the minimum possible damage or no damage at all to that nature.

We, the members of Oak Village, started our effort in 1976 by establishing a community on about 35,000 square meters of land. We have been very concerned about how we made use of land, and how our small society would work together in harmony with nature and its own members. We located our workhouse in the center of the land, put a lumberroom and houses around it, planted trees, plowed fields, and raised cattle.

We began our work with the production of woodworks made of oak from the surrounding trees that we cut with machines and finished in lacquer with our own hands. In the following years, our members began to make textiles and certain wooden hardware. We are now well established as a workshop community that creates items consistent with our policy.

Each piece of work that emerges from Oak Village is created by one person, from beginning to end, thus reflecting each worker's personality. Each of these personalities is, of course, influenced by his or her environment, as well as by each person's background.

The world of Oak Village has progressed well since its founding, and we are now planning to build a water-power plant that will make use of the river that flows through our land. We also are exploring the possibility of installing a solar-heating unit to further raise the level of our self-sufficient energy base. In another area, we are attempting to increase our agricultural abundance and dairy production to get our food self-sufficiency up over the 80 percent level, through the construction of a fish farm and a greenhouse.

While all of these efforts are individually significant for us, the most important thing for us is how we establish a system of harmonious relationships between humans and nature in this environment. We have now reached the half-way point in our plan for this self-contained and complementary "life cycle," and believe we will have it fully operating in 1985. Our river provides us with adequate water supplies and is a source of energy through the water-power plant. From the trees we get our lumber, from which we make furniture, hardware, and housing elements. Wood scraps from the work are burned for our boiler and hot water, and wood chips go into our composting tank, which also feeds into a heat collector. The solar collector will contribute to raising the output of this energy source. Our rice field, greenhouse, orchard, and garden provide rice, wheat, beans, vegetables, and fruits. The fish farm and cattle, chickens, and goats provide other foods, and the excreta from the animals are cycled into the composting operation.

In 1979, we published a small brochure, outlining our views and expressing our opinions about what we were creating. It tried to respond to the world's idea about the term "hand-made," which we believe is too easily used as a shallow phrase of fashion. The brochure also attempted to answer questions raised by our many visitors, some of whom were interested in our experiment and some of whom wished to become workers in wood. A few lines in the brochure attest to our main policy: "Our personality is always reflected in our works. The personality, based on each individual's characteristics, is determined by how he or she is connected with nature, materials and people. This is why we are not only engaged in making furniture, etc., but occupied with building a village. . . ."

Sperm whales off the southern coast of California.

The Jojoba plant growing in Phoenix, Arizona.

FIELD PLANTING JOJOBA— SALVATION FOR THE WHALES?

MILAN MIRKOVIC
Rolex Laureate, Rolex Awards for Enterprise
P.O. Box 69, West Perth, West Australia 6005, Australia

Australian, born August 25, 1951. Cartographic draftsman for the Metropolitan Water Board in Perth. Partner in a nursery and orchard business. Educated in cartography and horticulture in Australia.

This project revolves around the economic development of large, cultivated areas of Jojoba (*Simmondsia chinensis*) plants. These plants yield a bean containing 50 percent by weight of a remarkable oil—an oil virtually identical to sperm whale oil. An effective, viable, and economic development of this plant and its oil will mean the end of the slaughter of sperm whales, a process that continues in spite of international efforts to reduce their killing to so-called manageable levels or to end it altogether.

At present, field planting of the Jojoba seed is unsuccessful unless accompanied by irrigation, a costly method that is not always possible. We are developing a method of field planting pre-germinated seeds in a polystyrene container in the ground. By using a newly developed water-absorbent polymer in the soil, the plants need only be watered once each month—250 milliliters per plant. Jojoba plantings on a large scale will then become economically possible, and the sperm whale will be protected.

The Jojoba plant is native to arid areas of Mexico and the southwestern United States. Because of its ability to grow in low-rainfall or desert conditions, it is a suitable crop for dry areas, both in the United States and in Australia. The name, Jojoba, is derived from an American Indian word and is pronounced "Ho ho' ba."

We have been establishing Jojoba plants here in West Australia for four years. The major problem, worldwide, in attempting to cultivate the plants has been the difficulty in field planting seeds directly into the ground. Until now, plantations have been established only by using container-grown plants. This method is unsatisfactory for several reasons. First, it is very expensive. Second, plants suffer severe transplant shock. Large numbers of plants are involved, 1300 per acre, which leads to problems with transport of containers. Digging holes, planting, and then filling in is a massive undertaking when considering areas of hundreds of acres. Because of these reasons world interest in the Jojoba is focused on field planting. Only by using irrigation and keeping the soil moist for a period of 3 to 4 weeks is field planting moderately successful. This is, however, an expensive and unsatisfactory method for cultivating large areas. Water is usually expensive and often not available in the quantities needed. Our method of field planting will overcome these problems.

The basis of our system is a relatively new product, the SGP absorbent polymer. This polymer is a starch derivative that absorbs water. Although water insoluble, this polymer can absorb up to 1000 times its own weight of water. This water can be removed from the polymer by plant roots. Adding water will recharge the polymer.

Our planting method involves mixing the water-saturated polymer with soil, pouring this into a polystyrene container, then adding pre-germinated seeds. The container is then placed in a prepared hole in the ground. Further watering will not be needed for four weeks, at which time 250 milliliters of water will be added. Applications of 250 milliliters of water will continue every four weeks until the first autumn rains. Watering will then cease.

Planting will take place in spring, when the frost danger is over and temperatures become warmer. As the plant grows, its root system will take water from the polymer. The root system will grow on through the polymer, seeking subsoil moisture. This moisture, plus that drawn from the polymer, will sustain the plant adequately through the first summer of its life. The root system will continue to develop during the winter months, following which further watering will then be unnecessary, as the plant will be able to sustain itself.

At present, we are using polystyrene containers manufactured for the soft-drink take-away trade as our basic planting module. These containers are approximately 10 inches high, 3 inches in diameter at the top, and about $2\frac{1}{2}$ inches in diameter at the bottom. We are experimenting to determine the most practical and economical size and shape for the containers we will ultimately use. We plan to continue to use polystyrene for the containers, as it insulates the water-absorbent polymer from the soil. This prevents loss of moisture into the surrounding soil. As the plant grows, the container will not restrict growth but will break apart without difficulty.

Extensive field planting using this technique will be carried out during September/October 1980. Although we are planting the containers by hand in this initial trial stage, the knowledge gained through hand planting will enable us to develop a mechanical field planter. A device of this sort will be needed to enable large-scale field planting to be practical and successful.

Jojobas are planted hedgerow style, about 4–5 feet apart in the rows, and the rows about 12–13 feet apart, to allow for future mechanical harvesting. This gives about 1625 plants per hectare. With one male for every seven females for pollination purposes (males should be planted upwind, as the Jojoba is wind-pollinated), this gives 1421 females per hectare. Current yields in America are about 2 kilograms per female bush, without cultivation, for mature bushes. Yields of up to 5 kilograms per bush are not unreasonable under intense cultivation. A yield of 1.5 kilograms per bush can be expected starting in the seventh year. At 1.5 kilograms per bush, and 1421 females per hectare, the yield should be about 2121 kilograms/hectare (1725 pounds/acre). Approximately half the weight of the seed is oil, so the oil yield should be half of that quoted for the nuts.

Demand for Jojoba oil is high, and the Jojoba industry will grow and develop. However, the Jojoba is still basically a wild plant, and much work remains to be done to domesticate it.

If our method of planting is successful, we will have determined a new way of planting successfully in arid lands. Using this method, large areas could then be economically planted to Jojobas, thereby protecting a unique animal—the sperm whale—from extinction.

Since legislation and well-publicized notices of the danger to the sperm whale still have not guaranteed the survival of this endangered animal, perhaps it is time that we seek the solution by attacking the reason it is endangered. If adequate supplies of Jojoba oil can reach the market place at competitive prices, the pressures from industry and business to continue the killing of the sperm whale will abate.

AVOIDING FLOOD HAZARDS WITH COMPUTERIZED TERRAIN MODELLING

ROBERT L. COLLIN
50, Maesceinion, Waun Fawr, Aberystwyth, Dyfed, Wales, U.K.

British, born January 3, 1946. Lecturer in Geography, The University College of Wales, Aberystwyth. Educated in the United Kingdom.

T he purpose of this project, already underway, is the development of a practical method of modelling the extent of river inundation to assist in flood hazard prediction and the delimitation of flood liable lands. The enquiry is investigating methods of combining available hydrologic and flood data with a detailed terrain model gained by photogrammetric measurement, enabling a computer-based simulation of inundation to be formed. Outputs will include the extent, depth, and sequence of river inundation given various predicted river levels.

This idea is an entirely original one and has already been the subject of some preliminary investigations, during which the potential of the method suggested has become evident. The aim of this application is to assist in the continuance of these investigations into a system that may have considerable human and environmental benefits.

In summary, the system has the following stages.

Input Processes. Four major elements are included here. The first involves collecting available hydrological data, both past observations and current records. Second, flood observations from previous inundations will be entered in the system. Third, we will enter certain assumptions, still under investigation, regarding the theoretical numerical form of the flood surfaces over all, or parts, of the river valley in question. Last, photogrammetric (i.e., aerial photo) observations of the terrain, in the form of a detailed digital terrain model for the relevant parts of the valley will be entered in the systems input section.

Computing Processes. This will involve three steps. First, we must sort and store the data. Then we will need to derive and compute the flood surfaces. Finally, there will be a combination of the ground model and the flood surfaces to predict the extent of inundation (among other things, such as speed of flow). This combining process will be the key to the success of the project.

Output Processes. We expect to have two areas here. First, the system should provide the extent and depth of inundation over the valley for as many observed or predicted flood levels as necessary. This information is of critical value in areas where human occupancy is already established, but also in planning of areas where residential, industrial, agricultural, or other development may be projected. Second, the system should provide the sequence of inundation for anticipated flooding situations, thus indicating priorities in a hazard or potential hazard case.

As indicated, some preliminary work has already been carried out. However, the ideas are still at a relatively early stage, and much detailed investigation of all existing or potential stages of the process must be undertaken to ensure that the system has wide applicability. Although present work is in a British context, it is believed that its application may be just as valuable in all other parts of the world where a flooding problem exists.

For the present, it is proposed that the development of ideas and techniques take place in the context of a number of test areas where a flooding problem is known to exist, and where typical information is available, but also wherein observed flood outlines may be used to act as verification of the computer simulation. These will be selected to be contrasting in floodplain morphology and human development.

Work will, as far as possible, be carried out with the backing, in terms of information, of the relevant water authorities in this country. However, in certain aspects of the project, notably the provision of suitable aerial photography and the execution of relevant field work, we may well have to provide our own resources.

Technical expertise is in the form of the two principal investigators, and suitable equipment is available through the University, although some of the lines of development will produce pressures for resources other than those currently at our disposal.

CHIPANGALI WILDLIFE ORPHANAGE—RESCUES AND RETURNS

VIVIAN J. WILSON
Chipangali Wildlife Orphanage, P.O. Box 1057, Bulawayo, Zimbabwe

Zimbabwean, born October 31, 1932. Director of the Chipangali Wildlife Orphanage. Educated in South Africa and the United Kingdom.

I wish to establish a Wildlife Rescue/Release Unit, here at the Chipangali Wildlife Orphanage, for (a) rescuing orphaned, sick, or injured wild animals and ex-pets, (b) preparation and subsequent release of animals back into the wild once they are well enough, or sufficiently trained, to be set free, and (c) providing better facilities at the Orphanage, such as larger and more natural cages and enclosures for rare and endangered animals, and equipping the animal hospital, laboratory, and nursery.

As background on the Chipangali Wildlife Orphanage, which is run by me, my wife, and 20 African staff, I have enclosed my book, *Orphans of the Wild*, which details how my wife and I came to start the Orphanage, eventually purchasing 100 acres of land about 25 miles from Bulawayo, and beginning to care for the many animals brought to us by people who knew of our work. After many years as a Museum Director, with much work in the field, I had seen numerous examples of young animals whose loss of parent(s) through hunting had left them unable to survive in safety through to adult life. Resolving to provide some kind of home for these infants, we established Chipangali as a private effort. As word spread of what we were doing, members of the public, soldiers, and farmers all began to bring us "orphaned" wild animal young. Our "family" of such youngsters grew rapidly, and though we had invested virtually all of our own funds in trying to maintain them on a private basis, it became necessary, if we were to feed them, to open Chipangali to visitors for a small fee. Fortunately, many people responded to our situation, and visitors, various small gifts, and the sale of photographs and paintings of the animals helped us to continue the Orphanage.

What we are now seeking to accomplish is an improvement in our ability to continue our work and better our efforts on behalf of these animals. Specifically, there are four areas of interest for us in this application: (1) creating a more effective Rescue/Return unit, (2) obtaining equipment for the hospital and laboratory, plus nursery cages, (3) acquisition of a 16 mm Bolex Cine camera and projector, and (4) construction of larger enclosures for rare and endangered species.

For the Wildlife Rescue/Return Unit, we need better transportation, a trailer, crates and cages, game nets and darting equipment, citizen band radios and camping equipment. I am frequently called out to rescue an animal, or to collect sick, injured, or abandoned wild animals, or to pick up wild animals previously kept as pets, such as vervet monkeys, baboons, small antelope, or ostrich. In both the rescue and release (in appropriate habitats) of these animals, I have had only a small truck in which to carry members of my staff, crates, equipment, etc. The lack of better equipment makes some of these missions not only difficult, but also occasionally dangerous.

For our hospital, which opened in May 1977, we need laboratory equipment to update what is mostly second-hand instrumentation kindly donated to our effort by friendly medical practitioners. Large numbers of sick or injured animals are brought in with broken limbs, shattered wings, etc., while many of the ex-pets have wounds from rope or chain leads, or are suffering from malnutrition. These animals require special hospital cages in which to recover from their wounds or injuries before being released back into the wild, or, if further care is needed, before being introduced into enclosures.

We should like to be able to do a better job of recording the animals and our experiences with them on film. Though I presently use a 20-year-old motion picture camera, its small magazine capacity makes it difficult for us to record operations easily, for subsequent showing to visiting school groups, etc.

Lastly, we should like to be able to build larger enclosures for a number of the rare and endangered species we have to house. These include aardwolf, servals, large birds of prey, and the brown hyena. In each case, larger enclosures would serve to enable breeding endangered species, so that the young could be returned to the wild, and where the animals can be trained to a more natural habitat before being released. In the case of primates, larger enclosures are essential for introducing individual animals to one another, before they can be released. Further, such larger enclosures would allow research and observations that would be of significant scientific value in determining how best to accustom the animals to the transition back to the wild.

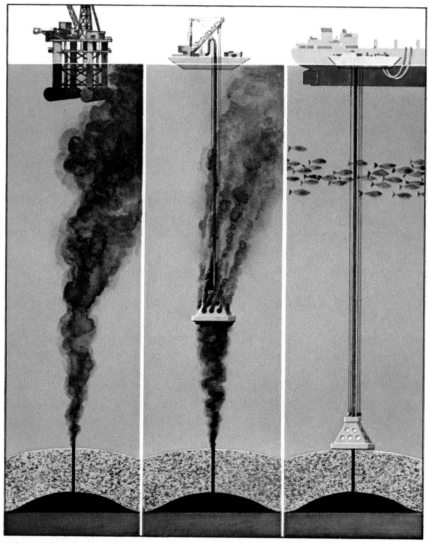

After an oil leak, the bell is lowered with apertures open. Then the apertures are closed, and the oil is pumped up to a waiting tanker.

"CAPPING" UNDERSEA OIL LEAKS

JEAN-PIERRE DUPONT
3, Avenue du Bouchet, 1209 Geneva

Swiss, born August 11, 1942. Safety and security agent at Geneva airport. Educated in Switzerland.

I have invented and developed, in scale model form, an apparatus that should benefit both industry and the marine environment in underwater oil-related mishaps or catastrophes. This patented device will collect the oil escaping from a submarine oil well or other source, thus preventing the loss of this valuable resource and at the same time preventing or minimizing the polluting effect of the oil on marine life.

Recent publicity regarding oil-related accidents has shown what a massive problem they can be, not only in direct economic losses (the value of the lost oil, the cost of attempting to contain its spread and stop its further flow) but also in the degradation of a wide variety of marine-connected environments: marine fauna, the fishing industry, coastal and seaside industry, and others. Given the increasing size of underwater oil installations, accidents are more and more likely to be major. An explosion on an offshore platform, a faulty connection to an undersea oil source, or a similar mishap can occur through mistakes on the part of human engineers and oil technicians. Natural disasters, such as earth tremors or undersea earthquakes, tidal waves, or severe storms, can also wreak havoc on even the most well-constructed oil pumping and processing stations at sea. Such a catastrophe can be felt far from the actual happening, as was the case with the major undersea oil burst at IXTOC I, off the Mexican coast.

Until now, there has been no good way to stop the petroleum escaping into the sea in a quick and easy operation. The invention I propose as the solution to this problem is an apparatus that can be created in different sizes, basically in the form of an inverted funnel, which is placed vertically over an oil well that has gone out of control and "chokes up" the oil well at the source of the leak. A major advantage of this device is that it can be brought to the scene of such an accident with virtually no delay, by helicopter transport of the various pieces involved, and assembled quickly at the site, on board a waiting ship or oil platform. The invention allows immediate extraction of the oil and provides the degree of control over the leak required to make permanent repairs.

The simplicity of the apparatus permits it to be lowered to any depth of sea under virtually any conditions. Its operations are not dependent upon the ascending force of the petroleum streams, which may vary widely according to weather and water conditions, and it can do all this in a minimum of time.

The bell of the device's "funnel" is perforated with 20 apertures, arranged around its circumference. Each of these apertures has a specially designed closing mechanism that slides a sealing plate gradually across the aperture when the device is in place. During the lowering of the device to the source of the oil leak, these apertures are all open, allowing for a free flow of both oil and water up through the bell-shaped funnel. As the bell descends toward the source of the leak, it "rides" the rising oil stream down to the source. As oil is captured at the top of the bell, it is recovered through a large pipe of flexible tubing attached to the top of the bell and pumped to the surface for transfer to waiting containers.

The apparatus should, for maximum security, be placed on site at a boring area in advance of critical operations, at those times when accidents are most likely to happen. It can be stored simply on an appropriate barge.

Essentially, the device consists of only five major parts: four similar side plates and a pyramidal top section that joins each of the four side plates to make the final pyramid-shaped bell. Each of the side plates contains five round "windows" that are individually equipped with reduction motors that turn flat valves into place over the windows on command from the surface supervision team.

The topmost part of the pyramid is equipped with winches and hooking devices for raising and lowering the bell and, of course, the apparatus for connecting the bell to the necessary extracting pipe.

A simple, three-step operation can be put into effect quickly and easily:

1. Equipment is brought to the accident site and installed on a barge or on the existing platform. An empty tanker is positioned, or arrangements are made to connect the recovering piping to existing transport piping.

2. The device is assembled, lowered into the sea, and the extracting pipe is connected to the tanker. The apertures are open. At the source of the leak, the device is positioned over the escaping flow, and ballasted automatically to remain in a level position.

3. Once in position, the upward flow of the oil through the device's opened windows is gradually reduced through the electric closing of the windows and pumping extraction commences through the connected tubing.

The pollution is immediately stopped and the oil is recovered. Beyond this immediate use of the device, further undersea efforts are foreseen, utilizing the same principle, lightly modified, to reach the sea floor effectively and easily.

The scale model of the bell.

REHABILITATION OF A VALLEY: ITS FLORA, FAUNA, AND PEOPLE

 TISSA B. PILIMATALAUWE
Honorable Mention, Rolex Awards for Enterprise
Stockholm, Upcot, Sri Lanka

*Sri Lankan, born April 8, 1929. Manager of a tea plantation.
Schooled in Sri Lanka.*

I wish to "rehabilitate" an entire valley, which has suffered from over 100 years of exploitation, as an example of what can be done to reverse a system of economic and ecological decline in Sri Lanka.

The Poonagalla Valley, in the Bandarawela District of the Uva Province is in the hill country dry zone of Sri Lanka. Once covered with forests that were protected on pain of death by the Sinhalese kings, the land was sold to British colonists starting about the 1850's. When the vanquished Sinhalese refused to work on the land, indentured Tamil people from India were brought in, first to work the coffee, and when that failed, the tea plantations that took the place of the vast forest lands that covered the now denuded hills.

The problem today is that the ubiquitous tea plantations are clean weeded—nothing other than tea and shade trees is allowed to grow. Chemical fertilizers have been used for decades, and the soil has become too acidic to support any crop other than tea. The Sinhalese, who were confined to the huts on the periphery of their paddy fields after the forests were cut down, have grown in population and become poorer. Only a few have been able to find employment on the adjoining tea estates, worked by the Tamils where friction exists between the two groups. The Tamils are employed on a daily basis, and in the long drought periods, there is very little work for them, sometimes as little as three days in the week.

In short, thousands of able-bodied workers are underemployed on the tea plantations in the hills, during certain periods of the year, and an equal or greater number are underemployed in the villages in the valley below. And there are thousands of acres of patnas, as the arid hillsides covered with coarse grass are known, along with some run-down tea plantations that are no longer economical.

What I propose to do is to organize the underemployed labor to rejuvenate and reforest the hillsides, and grow new crops that will provide work for both peoples of the valley. The old problem of land ownership no longer arises because the State now owns it all, since the Land Reform Commission took over in 1975. The tea plantations have the expertise at the managerial, supervisory, and labor levels to get the maximum work done at greatest efficiency. I propose that this effort be carried out in the Poonagalla Valley in a well-planned development program that will take several years.

The key to the undertaking will be the deliberate reclaiming of the arid soil lands through the use of Guatemala Grass, which the tea industry has found to be the most efficient soil reconditioner. It must be planted as closely as possible, lopped twice a year, and left to enrich the soil from 2 to 5 years, depending on the soil. After roads and drains have been cut, and lime applied, the Guatemala Grass should be replaced with fodder and pasture grasses. These will be a basis for a cattle breeding industry for the Tamil population, who have much experience with cows.

Fast growing varieties of trees, such as toona, grevillea, mahogany, hora, and albizzia should be planted to provide the needed timber for building on the island, and large areas of the patnas will be reserved for this important, work-producing industry. Eucalyptus is a rapidly growing timber that could provide much of the thousands of yards of firewood consumed by the tea factories yearly, in place of the expensive fuel oil that increasingly must be imported to meet their needs.

A strip of land 100 meters wide on either side of streams in the valley would be reserved exclusively for the propagation of flora exclusive to the hill country dry zone. This would allow the cultivation and study of plants that belong in the area, which should continue to be a part of the valley's ecosystem. Similarly, when new forest areas are sufficiently developed, the bigger animals such as deer, and even elephants, can be re-introduced, with appropriate protection against poaching.

The project is undoubtedly a long one, with 3 to 10 years the time span envisaged to accomplish the rehabilitation of the valley. I believe, however, that its progress will encourage similar efforts elsewhere, thus giving the project an inherent worth long before we have finished rebuilding the valley, its flora, fauna, and the socio-economic lives of its people.

INDUCED UPWELLING TO MAKE A LAGOONAL ECOSYSTEM

EDWARD RATIGAN

2525 Knightdale Drive, Graham, North Carolina 27253, U.S.A.

American, born April 30, 1943. Physical Oceanographer for Western Electric, in Oceanographic Department. Educated in the United States.

My project proposes the use of wind energy to generate electric power that would drive water pumps to create artificial oceanic upwellings. These upwellings would be the primary means of supplying food (nutrients) to a mariculture farm in the atolls of the Marshall Islands Trust Territory of the Pacific.

Upwelling, considered one of the most dynamic of all oceanic processes, is a phenomenon by which nature brings nutrient-rich water from the depths to the sunlit surface layers to provide food to tiny one-celled photosynthetic plants. These plants multiply rapidly into large masses offering feasting grounds for zooplankton and fish, and create the most productive fish-producing regions in the world. The so-called standing crops in these upwelled regions are at least a thousand times higher than in other oceanic areas. Although these upwelled regions represent only one-tenth of 1 percent of the total of the world's oceans, they are estimated to contain more than half of the oceanic fish catch of 40 million metric tons a year.

Scientists think artificial upwellings are possible, and I propose to test the theory through use of a mathematical model designed to demonstrate the feasiblity of mariculture through an artificially constructed upwelling. Specifically, I propose to use the free energy source of the wind as the means for providing power and food requirements to a marine farm.

The wind could be harnessed by a windmill-type apparatus coupled to water pumps, which would lift deep nutrient-rich water to the surface. The energy requirement for this would be small because the water does not need to be raised from great depths; only the friction head of the pipe carrying it must be considered, plus the small static head caused by the difference in density of the cold deep water and the average vertical density from the surface to the bottom of the suction pipe. This nutrient-rich water, once brought to the surface, would be directed into ponds, lagoons, hatchery tanks, or special pens, as food for phytoplankton, which would be food for the next higher marine life on the trophic ladder. Once this is accomplished, some of the anticipated benefits can be calculated.

Initial calculations indicated that it would be possible to raise approximately 3 metric tons of anchovies per year in an area of 209 square meters. To sustain this yield, the nutrient-rich water would have to be pumped at a rate of 168 gallons/minute. According to my calculations, this could easily be handled by the wind energy scheme proposed here, and further, that the prime location for such a project would be in the Marshall Islands, the 32 small, low-lying (5–25 feet above sea level) coral atolls and islands some 2200 miles southwest of Hawaii. The uniqueness of their geography makes them ideal for this mariculture effort.

The Marshall Islands have large, deep natural lagoons that could be used for farming areas, close proximity to deep oceanic waters that would make pumping operations more efficient, virtually continuous strong trade winds that could be used for the pumping energy source, and an abundance of sunshine vital to the multiplication of the photosynthetic phytoplankton primary producers in the food chain. Freedom from severe storms and typhoons allow for year-round operation at low risk to capital investments in machinery and supporting equipment. The Islands' location is nearly ideal for access to world markets because the area is frequented by ocean-going vessels that fish the equatorial counter-current.

For the Marshall Islanders themselves, there could be a number of significant benefits, including readily accessible electrical energy from the wind turbines (as opposed to the gas generators now required), a new industry in fishing (to complement, or supplant, the single copra industry on which the economy is now precariously balanced), and a new source of fresh water. This latter possibility would be a useful side benefit of the upwelling plan's systems. Estimates show that about 3000 gallons of fresh water could be produced by cooling moisture laden air (77–80 percent humidity) to about 5°C (the approximate temperature of our deep nutrient-rich water). This output of fresh water would require pumping about 300 gallons/minute of cold seawater over 60 square feet of cupra-bronze fin-tubing, filled with liquid freon. All of this is possible with today's "off-the-shelf" technology and the amount of wind available as an energy source in the Marshall Islands.

Most immobilization is performed in the coolness of night, but the aggressive lions are darted during the day.

STUDYING THE ECOLOGY AND BEHAVIOR OF LIONS AND HYENAS IN THE KALAHARI

 MARK J. OWENS
Honorable Mention, Rolex Awards for Enterprise
Central Kalahari Game Reserve, via Box 40, Maun, Botswana,
Africa

*American, born May 17, 1944. Wildlife ecologist currently involved in the subject
project. Educated in the United States.*

For the past six years, as a husband and wife team (Celia, also a wildlife ecologist, and I are both Ph.D. candidates at this writing), we have conducted behavioral-ecological research on Kalahari lions and brown hyenas along the previously unexplored ancient river systems of the Central Kalahari Game Reserve in Botswana.

This 55,000-square-kilometer reserve is an enormous tract of pristine wilderness, where there are no roads or human development of any kind. It is one of the most remote areas left in Africa and the largest game protectorate in the world. Except for a few bands of roving Bushmen, we are the only inhabitants of the entire reserve.

Despite the problems of logistics and supply in such a remote area—we must haul food, water, and supplies 150 kilometers over sand tracks—we have learned more about the natural history of the Kalahari lions and the endangered brown hyena populations than ever before recorded. The information from our research is urgently needed for the conservation of these two carnivores and their unique fossil river habitat.

We initiated the research in January 1974, having spent the previous two years working independently of university or conservation organizations to develop our plans for the research program and save enough of our funds to field the project in a rudimentary fashion.

On our arrival in Africa, we bought a third-hand Land Rover, and spent the next four months searching for a completely natural area as a site. In

May, after three days of crashing through desert bush on a compass course 150 kilometers from the nearest African village, we discovered Deception Valley. Limited funds made our early existence quite harsh. With no money for tents, the Land Rover was our bedroom, kitchen, research lab, and shelter. Our first camp was literally a fireplace and a stack of tinned foods under a tree. We were so isolated that almost no one even knew where Deception Valley was, or that we were there. We had no communication with the outside world for months at a time.

Meanwhile, we were teaching ourselves the field techniques needed for the study of the elusive, highly mobile Kalahari lions and brown hyenas. As we badly needed to ear-tag lions and brown hyenas to learn about their range movements and social organization, we borrowed and fixed up a carbon dioxide darting rifle and successfully immobilized and ear-tagged a number of the animals.

Because no maps of the area had good detail, we acquired a surplus World War II bubble sextant for navigation in the desert. Locating our research subjects was a problem, solved only by driving for hours along the dry fossil riverbed at night, using a spotlight in the hope of encountering a lion or hyena, and then following it until we lost it in the thick bush.

These pioneering efforts developed into what is today one of the most sophisticated wildlife research projects in Africa, involving the use of a project aircraft with radio telemetry equipment for the location of radio-collared lions and brown hyenas. We have gained the financial support of such organizations as the National Geographic Society, the Frankfurt Zoological Society, and the California Academy of Sciences.

Despite the inconveniences of living on 10 gallons of water each per week, and having communications links 150 kilometers away, our living conditions and research techniques have become much refined with sponsorship. We now live in tents, with some shelter from temperatures that range from -8°C (18°F) during winter nights to 48°C (118°F) midday in the hot season. With no electricity, all cooking is over an open fire. Such trials as surviving the heat under wet towels have their compensation, however, when a lion, which has never before seen man, comes into camp to drink the dishwater, with us standing 2 meters away!

Since 1977, we have had an aircraft, provided by the Frankfurt Zoological Society, which has made locating, tracking, and collaring the predators much easier. To date, we have darted over 50 lions, and we have placed radio collars on members of five prides that roam an area of 5000 square kilometers. We have ear-tagged or collared 16 brown hyenas, from two clans.

During the days, we tape record notes on kills, habitat utilization, group member associations, and prey availability. At night, we follow one of the collared lions or brown hyenas, which has been located from the plane, in the 4-wheel drive truck with the radio gear. Often covering 30 kilometers or more in a night, we take notes on the carnivore's feeding ecology, range movements, and social behavior. A detailed compass log of the animal's range movements is kept for our records, but also so that we can find our way back to camp! To date, we have logged over 2000 position fixes for brown hyenas and lions on maps of the research area that we made using aerial photos and the sextant.

Though lions have been studied elsewhere, never before has the Kalahari lion population been the object of an uninterrupted, long-term research project. Fundamental information on population densities, range sizes, and even diet was almost totally lacking. Our research is providing original information with direct management implications on predator-prey populations in an area of over 160,000 square kilometers in which no wildlife research had ever been conducted.

For the first time an estimate of the Kalahari lion population density is possible; a realistic picture of lion range requirements can be made; and the importance of the fossil river bed system to their existence is recognized. These factors are urgently needed for lion management programs because only through an understanding of such data will the Botswana government be able to protect both the animals and the land from those who shoot the lions and those who would destroy the terrain in the search of natural resources (such as the prospecting team that will invade Deception Valley in 1980 to pursue aerial indications of uranium to be found in the area).

Our research on the rare and secretive brown hyena is one of the first two projects and the longest ever conducted in the wild on this endangered species. Exclusively nocturnal, extremely cautious by nature, it is almost exclusively a scavenger. Contrary to earlier views, we have learned that the brown hyena is not solitary, but one of the most socially sophisticated of all the social carnivores. They are not a threat to livestock, but as scavengers their management must be coupled with other predators' protection, in order that they can continue to subsist.

To date, we have produced a wealth of material, both for scientific and lay articles, in addition to the quarterly reports we submit to the Botswana Department of Wildlife. Our goals include continuation of our detailed investigation of the ecology and behavior of the Kalahari lion and brown hyena, developing the Central Kalahari Research Institute where scientists from various disciplines can gather to conduct in-depth field research on the physical and biological Central Kalahari environment, and disseminating information on the Kalahari lion, the brown hyena, and their ecosystems accumulated during the past six years of research.

EXPLORING THE QATTARA DEPRESSION IN EGYPT BEFORE THE FLOOD

TREVOR D. DAVIES
Church Cottage, Blackhorse Lane, Runhall,
Norwich NR9 4DR, U.K.

British, born March 29, 1946. University lecturer in meteorology and climatology, and explorer. Educated in the United Kingdom.

T he Qattara Depression in Egypt (19,000 square kilometers) is to be flooded by seawater as part of a hydroelectric power scheme. The Depression lies below sea level and represents a unique environment in the eastern Sahara. The Depression bed and slopes hold much valuable information on past climates, geology, anthropology, and desert ecology. By itself, it is the largest and most spectacular old lake in the Sahara. *It has hardly been investigated.* This unique environment is soon to vanish beneath salt water. This expedition represents an attempt to save some of the Depression's wealth of scientific and human information before it is lost forever.

Before mounting the main scientific study in January and February, 1982, a full-scale reconnaissance will be mounted in September and October, 1980, to coincide with the fortieth anniversary of the first operational patrol of the Long Range Desert Group (LRDG). On that occasion (in 1940), two Italian trucks were captured and dumped in the Gilf Kebir. Although one was later recovered during the War, the other could not be started, and as far as anyone knows is still there to this day. An attempt will be made to locate this or other World War II vehicles and to establish the feasibility of recovering them at a later date.

The 1980 reconnaissance will enable the Scientific Team leaders to visit those locations in and near the Qattara Depression where their future studies will be conducted. Additionally, a Military Archaeological Team will visit the Gilf Kebir in an attempt to locate the WW II Italian vehicle. Four vehicles will be used, leaving from Alexandria to Siwa via Matrah. The findings of the reconnaissance survey will be used to govern the final location and type of work to be undertaken on the scientific survey. The scientists will find the military involvement of great help with the logistics of the survey. In the actual Scientific Survey (1981–1982), there will be four teams at work.

The Environmental Sciences Team will look at the Depression bed's information on past climates. This information is imperative to build as complete a picture as possible of the changing climate in North Africa over many thousands of years. The Depression bed will be cored for tens of meters and the cores returned to the United Kingdom for analysis of particulates, isotopic analysis, and pollen analysis. The present-day ecology of the Depression and the existing small lakes will be examined. The geology of the area will also be studied. It is expected that geologists from the Egyptian Geological Survey will accompany the expedition. Six scientists (lecturers) from the School of Environmental Sciences, University of East Anglia, will comprise the team.

The Anthropological Team. On the slopes of the Depression, the old shorelines of the former lake, are the remains of human settlements going back about 10,000 years. Human remains are also scattered around the Depression. These have hardly been examined and will be lost forever once flooding occurs. Dr. Nicole Petite-Maire is Maitre de Recherche at the Department of Quaternary Studies, University of Marseilles. She has an international reputation in the study of old lake-shore settlements in the western Sahara. She will be bringing her research team.

Ornithological Team. This four-man team is being sponsored by the Middle East Ornithological Society. Their objective is to study breeding and migratory habits in the region.

Agricultural Team. The creation of a man-made lake will obviously have a measurable effect on the agricultural balance of the area. In order to assess these effects, the present-day agriculture will be studied in detail by an agricultural science team from the University of Florida.

Recent History Project. Besides the scientific investigations, the military historians will continue to pursue their recovery of World War II relics.

In addition, Dorothy Bovey will be accompanying the expedition. Famous for her wonderful paintings of flowers, she has more recently turned to the art of photojournalism and will document the work and experiences of the expedition, in this soon-to-vanish mystery spot of the Sahara.

COMMUNITY ENVIRONMENT AND RESOURCES DEVELOPMENT IN A NIGERIAN TOWN

GODWIN O. MBABUIKE
Computer Services Department, Faculty of Science,
Bayero University, P.M.B. 3011, Kano, Nigeria

Nigerian, born May 24, 1937. Principal Systems Analyst, Computer Services Department, Bayero University. Educated in Nigeria and the United Kingdom.

My project is concerned with the development of the community environment and its resources at Ihube Town, Okigwe, Imo State, in Nigeria. I wish to carry out a three-phase program designed to create a model community that can serve as an example and an inspiration to other rural towns and areas in Nigeria. With assistance and encouragement from various governmental bodies, the program involves the establishment of an orchard and palm oil plantation, the organizing of a model agribusiness project, and an industrial and human resources development program.

Initially, we anticipate some 1200 hectares of government land as the basis of overall development program for the township. Approximately 400 hectares of this land, situated east of Umekwe Plain, would be given over to the planting of a range of citrus and exotic fruit species. In this part of the plantation, we plan on having grapefruits, sweet oranges, tangerines, lemons, limes, pawpaws, pineapples, and bananas. Already-budded citrus plants would be brought in from the Governmental Agricultural Research Station at Umudike, Umuahia in Imo State. Subsequent expansion of the orchard will be done with seedling varieties.

Adequate pest control of the orchard can be accomplished through the use of poisoned baits containing a mixture of about 35 cubes of sugar and 5.5 grams of sodium chloride in a liter of water. Such an anti-pest program is necessary against local animals to protect the orchard's crops and to avoid the cost of expensive fencing. This measure will contribute substantially to the increase in yield of the orchard, the output of which will be used for both home and export consumption. Furthermore, pest control measures and scientifically controlled growing methods will extend the productive life of the citrus plants under development and cultivation.

On the remaining 800 hectares of the farming land, we would plant a grove of oil palms. The source of supply for palm seedlings is the Nigerian Palm Produce Board, from the depot at the Nigerian Institute for Palm Research, Benin City, Bendel State. Not only would the Board provide this initial assistance and much technical advice, it would also be a ready purchaser of most of the palm fruit yield from the plantation. A Farm Service Center and access roads into the Orchard and Plantation site are items of primary consideration, in order to assure ease of transport for both products and employees.

The second phase of the program is to be located nearby on the Umekwe Plain, and involves integrating a variety of agribusiness programs into a unified whole. First consideration in this phase will be given to crop production. As the main local food crops are maize and cassava, emphasis will be placed on cultivation of these foods with scientific techniques, including the use of fertilizers and sprays, to produce much higher yields than those presently achieved. This will form the basis of a local crop processing industry, and include storage facilities for export of excess yield.

A game reserve, using a portion of the Owhuru Woodland near the Umekwe Plain, is suitable for the proposed preservation area. It will be used for rearing endangered local species, such as the antelopes, brown and green monkeys, partridges, guinea fowl, and turkeys, some of which are in high demand as bushmeat. Careful cropping of such game species, under legislated control, can serve not only to preserve the species, but also to provide the local people with customary elements of their meat diets.

Lastly, in this phase, a livestock farm is envisioned, using cattle with high pest and climate resistance. This farm will not only improve the meat diet of the local people, but also reduce the pressure on the wild game in the area.

The last phase of the community development project is to use the various elements described above as the basis for certain industrial and human resources structuring. Anticipated industrial processes include glucose and starch factories, based on the cassava production; a cornmeal factory, utilizing the output of the maize farm; a meat processing factory from the livestock farm; tourist development based on the game reserve; and the training of the local people in various skills and obtaining their involvement in resource utilization so as to provide them with a higher standard of living.

On a step-by-step basis, the goal of this project is to show how an area rich in natural resources can be made to function much more productively for the benefit of its inhabitants and in harmony with its natural environment.

Lowering a ferro-concrete panel through the grooves in the masonry piers.

PREFABRICATED, ADJUSTABLE DAMS— A LOW-TECHNOLOGY LAND SAVER

SATHE SHRIDAR RAMCHANDRA
418 Narayan Peth, Pune   411 030, India

Indian, born November 1, 1909. Manufacturer of cotton mattresses and cushioning materials. Educated in India.

I n developing countries like India, in spite of sufficient rains at many places, rural areas face severe water shortage problems for much of the year. As a result, not only is agricultural output reduced, but the local people are forced to earn their living by cutting an excessive amount of wood in surrounding forests, thus reducing the greenery and causing a steady decline in the climate and topography. In due course, these people abandon the barren territory and rush to the cities.

Conventional dams are needed for storing the surging waters of our seasonal rains. At the end of the monsoon season, however, a large quantity of water at low velocity is available for storage by temporary dams. The aim of my project is to collect this substantial run-off by using a low-cost, removable, easy-to-operate dam system that shall, in addition to solving day-to-day problems, help local people restore deteriorating environments.

Working on this since 1965, I have developed prefabricated, removable curved sheets of ferro-concrete with tie rods, which can be handled easily by uneducated village people. The sheets can be used for any width of a stream or a river, and the height of the water storage is adjustable. In India alone, thousands of villages can benefit from this system.

We have portable radios, TV sets, even portable bridges. But what about portable dams? Come to think of it. A portable dam! Dams hold and conserve water, which can be useful in so many ways: (a) they fill wells with water, (b) they help afforestation, which attracts rain, and above all, (c) they supply water when it is needed most in the dry season.

A portable dam could work wonders in a country like India, where it is said that agriculture is a gamble on the rains. Only a small portion of India's vast agricultural lands is irrigated. One of the reasons for this, undoubtedly, is shortage of the rains themselves. Another, however, is the heavy cost of storing what little water does come. Lastly, even the scanty water supply we get from the rains is not utilized to the maximum. The quantities that are just wasted are enormous, and this unnecessary and undesirable waste can be avoided if portable dams are constructed.

The advantages of such dams can be briefly stated: Standardization of transportable basic elements, which allows manufacture in an efficient local setting and minimizes the need for highly skilled technical or engineering personnel at the dam site. Low cost, through prefabrication of the basic elements, so that villages don't have to undertake the capital requirements of building a dam "from scratch." An easily constructed base platform, which is well within the capabilities of local village labor. Simple adjustability, allowing for control of the water height without complicated machinery.

In my initial designs, I used curved steel plates to achieve the desired strength for the sliding panels that were inserted in slots built into the stone or brick columns that formed the dams' framework. Patent rights were awarded for this design, and it was the subject of a Maratha Chamber of Commerce award. As steel became more and more expensive, however, it became apparent that price would overcome the entire point of making such dams available to rural communities. It was imperative that a new material be found.

I finally settled on ferro-concrete as the material, and decided upon the present shape and size (curved sheets with a tie rod, and dimensions of 214 cm $\times$ 62 cm $\times$ 2.5 cm thick). Subsequently, a mold was developed for prefabricating these ferro-concrete sheets. The mold allows the incorporation of many small details, such as clamping and lifting hooks, and a groove for waterproofing and packing arrangements.

The first full-scale dam was constructed on a river near the village of Chakan, District Poona, with a width of 165 feet and a height of storage of 14 feet. Existing masonry piers (pillars) at intervals were used as supports for the curved ferro-concrete sheets in addition to supporting a walkway across the river. Toward the end of the monsoon season, local people lowered and fixed the sheets in place in four days.

The sheets were fixed in place using wooden wedges, and ordinary cotton rope was used to prevent leakage at the vertical joints. To prevent horizontal joint leakages, a paste of neat cement, wrapped in a strip of cloth was used. Placed between two sheets, horizontally, the cloth prevents the cement slurry from being washed away, and also facilitates easy removal of the sheets at the onset of the next monsoon season, when the waters must be allowed to move through the fingers of the dam quickly. With this dam, water was successfully stored for the succeeding eight months. At the start of the next rainy season, the sheets were simply and easily lifted from their retaining grooves to allow the surging monsoon waters to pass through.

To date, three dams have been built on a trial basis in the Poona and Kolhapur Districts of Maharashtra State. They have been successful and practicable. Right now, I am not in a financial position to popularize the idea throughout India, but I do believe that the use of these dams should be spread. Both the authorities and the general public required much convincing before the first removable storage system dam could be built, and the efforts of bringing initial acceptance were necessarily financed by myself. Even now, after some 10 years of successful operations of these systems, I still travel to far off places to talk about this new and effective solution to one of India's oldest problems. The costs of such travel are borne by me, which places a limit on how widely I can disperse the knowledge of this useful and valuable system for the storing of badly needed water in our rural areas.

Upstream side of portable dam completed in 1976. The dam has a storage height of 14 feet.

BIOMAP AND PHOTOGRAPHIC ATLAS OF THE MEDITERRANEAN COASTLINE

MARINA CAMPANA
Via Pitagora 14, 20082 Binasco (Milan), Italy

Italian, born December 10, 1949. President and publisher of 'I Quanta s.r.l.' in Milan. Educated in Italy.

For purposes of marine resource management, locating marine parks, and biological monitoring of marine pollution, this project proposes to draw a map of the Mediterranean coastal biocenoses covering a range from sea level to 40 to 60 meters deep, and to create a historical atlas of the same area with photographic references. In order to do this, it is necessary to overcome present difficulties about quantitative ecological research in rocky areas. Our project is meant to give a start to such programs by covering a reasonably large tract of Mediterranean coastline.

Underwater biological research has been widely employed all over the world in the past few decades, and its importance is increasing rapidly in field studies of coastal environments. Among the many techniques used, scuba diving has proved successful in obtaining information about the life of marine animals and plants, the qualitative composition of coastal communities, and the relationships between members of submerged coastal communities.

Though this is true, much work still remains to be done, especially in the field of quantitative ecological research. For example, benthonical biocenoses have been adequately investigated on soft substrata, such as mud and sand, owing to the early development of sampling techniques that could be accomplished out of the water. Rocky areas are definitely less well-known.

Our project has two main aims. First, the development of a standard technology, suitable for performing short-term although relatively thorough, examination of benthic communities in rocky areas. Second, the application of this technology to an area of great naturalistic-ecological-geographical interest—the Ligurian coastline; we intend to draw a precise map of benthic communities in the photic zone of this coast.

We are now routinely performing tests and perfecting materials for the implementation of this project. Our techniques include the following elements. We begin by visually prospecting a 2 to 6 kilometer tract of coastline, using a boat-dragged scuba diver. This gives us a first approximation of our map and provides overall geologic structure, and general biological and abiotic features. This overall prospecting allows identification of characteristic underwater areas, to be accurately investigated in the subsequent steps.

We then carry out surface quantitative plankton sampling (a standard technique), in correspondence with characteristic areas. Bottom quantitative plankton sampling (a new technique, using a gas-operated quantitative plankton suckler) is then carried out, mainly to collect juvenile forms of benthic organisms. This is followed by Improved Plankton Silhouette Photography to obtain *in vivo* pictures of quantitative samples, both of surface and bottom plankton. We then take underwater photographs of sample areas (a statistically defined series of pictures for each characteristic area) in order to make a quantitative assessment of the local community and its overall composition. Underwater macrophotography is carried out on conspicuous and rare specimens in the area.

We then assemble underwater data, collecting such things as temperature, lithological samples, and biological quantitative sampling of small areas correlating well with the general features of the investigated standard area. Additionally, we carry out an underwater population survey to assess the consistency of particular "guide species" of the Mediterranean fishes.

We believe that such procedures provide reasonably accurate and timely means of mapping for a variety of uses. Quantity of data is adequate and relatively quickly usable. Photographic sampling saves time both in collection and filing data and in subsequent comparison of newer data with old in the search for environmental changes. Further, there is the remaining possibility of thorough taxonomic identification because of the contemporary collection of the usual samples.

If this program works as we believe it will, and it can be applied to a large tract of Mediterranean coastline, it could be the first step toward a general map and file of all our coastlines, and give impetus for such work on national or multinational levels. This kind of mapping will be of inestimable value in determining the locations of future underwater parks and for controlling environmentally disadvantageous factors. This kind of mapping will allow for the early detection of environmental changes and, we hope, will permit their early assessment and control.

THE MYSTERY OF THE SUICIDE BIRDS OF ASSAM

PRABAL K. RAY

17, Kailash Bose Street, Calcutta 700 006, India

Indian, born December 18, 1945. Managing Director of a Consulting Engineering company. Educated in India.

In Assam, a state in the eastern part of India, there is a small village named Jatinga, which is about 20 kilometers from Haflong, the headquarters of North Cachar Hill District. At this particular village of Jatinga, every year between the middle of August and the end of October, thousands of certain local species of birds crash half-dead at night around flaming torches; these birds make no attempt to move away, and they ultimately die by self-imposed starvation.

My project envisions studying the reasons for this mysterious suicide of the birds at Jatinga. It will try to find the answers to three basic questions: (1) Why does this phenomenon only happen at Jatinga? (2) Why are the birds attracted to the luminous sources? (3) Why does this collective death wish occur only on occasions when the birds have empty stomachs, several hours after last feeding?

The story of the birds is peculiar. Sometime in 1905, some villagers, who were searching at night for the carcass of a buffalo killed by a tiger, observed that swarms of birds flocked around their flaming torches. By trial and error, they formulated the conditions required for this spectacular event. Each year, in the same period, 1200 Khasias (the local people) feast on thousands of birds that come crashing down, half dead, around the flaming torches that have been set out at night. The birds, as if under hypnotic forces, make no attempt to move away, and they refuse all food. Most of the birds are taken by the local people for food, and the others die of self-imposed starvation.

The suicide spree has been observed for only about a dozen species of local birds, none of which is migratory or nocturnal. All of the species are daytime feeders, generally hovering between 1000 and 3000 meters around the area. They are not great fliers. The most common species are the ruddy kingfisher (*Entemothera coromanda*), the little egret (*Egrette garzetta*), the green pigeon (*Treron*) and the emerald dove (*Chalcophaps indica*).

The suicide spree has been observed to take place only when certain natural and man-made conditions are evident. There will be no moonlight in the sky, and it must rain (being very close to Cherrapunji, it generally rains during this particular period). There should be a steady wind from south to north, at about 15 kilometers per hour. The lamps lighted in the valley should be spherical, as with a flaming torch. The entire phenomenon is confined to 1 square kilometer at Jatinga, 730 meters up the Barail hills.

The birds land at least three or more hours after their last feeding, with empty stomachs. After landing, the birds are nearly immobilized, with their muscles in a state of contraction. Forced feeding is not possible. Generally, the birds die in 24 hours, although some of them carry on for a few days until their fat resources are burned off.

The "hypnotic" spell of the birds may be caused by any of several reasons, some of which are summarized below.

1. The hypnotic spell may be cast through a fine optical illusion caused by the scattering of light rays through the mist and raindrops.
2. The ecophysiographical peculiarities of the place, Jatinga, may make it a death trap for the birds. It may be that the accumulated rainwater and other environmental conditions tend to bend local magnetic force lines, which in turn may affect the endogenous rhythm of the birds.
3. The birds, resting in their high perches after feeding, may imagine an untimely sunrise (from the spherical lamps in particular atmospheric conditions) and are shocked to find their endogenous rhythm going haywire; unable to rely on their "bird sense," they tumble to the earth like broken kites.
4. The birds may become more "photopositive" on an empty stomach. It is not known whether the light rays affect them through the eyes or through the photoreceptor cells located around the temples.
5. The quasi-paralytic state of the birds' central nervous systems after landing may be the after-effect of sudden toxicity or some hormonal change.

It is my intention to study all these aspects in detail, in hopes of solving the winged mystery that takes place at Jatinga, Assam.

1978.

1980.

THE MINTER GARDENS: NATURE IN FULL BLOOM

BRIAN E. MINTER
46129 Hope River Road, Chilliwack, British Columbia V2P 3P1, Canada

Canadian, born February 26, 1947. President and General Manager of a greenhouse/nursery/garden supply company. Educated in Canada.

The project is a huge and remarkable Garden Showcase in British Columbia. It has been created to harmonize splendidly with a unique natural setting. Nine distinctive gardens are featured to provide a series of different nooks, sights, colors, and sounds, all contributing to the sheer inspirational delectation of the senses.

A rustic building complex, architecturally designed to blend with the local history and natural landscape, is being completed, providing facilities for guests and visitors. This complex incorporates, among other things, a gift and craft shop, which will feature artistic creations and designs from local and regional craftsmen and artists. A restaurant will provide natural foods in a greenhouse atmosphere. The Gardens have been so designed that they can accommodate wheelchairs and the handicapped.

This garden project began as a dream. On Christmas morning, 1977, I was on my way to a family dinner when, for some unknown reason, I ventured off the main road. Along this road I spotted one of the most beautiful properties I had ever set my eyes upon. I could not visualize a more perfect location for a sparkling garden—a garden like no other in the world. It was nestled at the base of the 7000-foot Mt. Cheam and surrounded by the Cascade Mountains. There were meadows, sunken areas, hillside treed expanses of land, and even ravines.

After much consideration and discussion with family and friends, I undertook a feasibility study on the practicality of such a venture. Findings were not favorable. TransCanada Pipeline has a 24-foot oil line running under one area of the garden. British Columbia Hydro and the Department of Highways had right of ways on the property, and the land itself would have to be rezoned for such a project. The cost was also very substantial, and the project rated as a high-risk venture.

Nevertheless, the deep conviction that it was possible to turn a uniquely beautiful area into a magnificent garden development that would provide years of lasting enjoyment to many people prompted me to go ahead. Acquiring two parcels of land totaling 25 acres, I recruited a talented landscaper and architect. Most of the obstacles hindering development were overcome, and by October 1978, work began. Help from many friendly sources played a big role in bringing the plans to fruition. Finance was a major problem in the beginning, so I drew on my present gardening business for bill paying until late 1979, when a local credit union came forth with enough funding to allow the project to open early in 1980.

We think the Gardens are simply overwhelming. So many factors are at play on one's senses. Whereas in most gardens so much is to be seen all at once, here we have tried to make each flower stand out and seem exciting simply by its placement in relation to other plants and land contours. The pathways have been carefully laid to allow a visitor only glimpses of upcoming gardens. As the stroller follows the pathway, more of the Gardens are unfolded, constantly changing the perspective.

In all, there are nine gardens, separated by "gray areas" of lesser interest in terms of excitement and color. This relief between the gardens allows the visitor to collect his or her thoughts and ideas from one garden before entering the next.

The manner in which the gardens are laid out provides alluring excitement and enchantment. For instance, the first garden, which is a lake garden, is designed to welcome people. Through the use of soft colors, water, and weeping pendular trees, the area is quite relaxing. You leave the area through a large bank retained by two beautiful dry rock walls. Suddenly you are exposed to the sound of traffic on the nearby highway and a sharp ravine to your right. Your attention, however, is quickly diverted by a massive flower bed or a large bank on your left. And, before you are aware of it, you are entering a natural arbor of Japanese Shirofugen cherry trees leading you to the secluded rose garden.

This element of delightful surprise is a typical and important factor of the Gardens. Layout and placement of specimens are key considerations. The pathways are all graded at 1:20 to provide complete access for the handicapped. They swing back and forth in such a manner that you see almost everything several times, from several different angles.

One of the features of the Gardens is the generous use of natural stone, either in the dry rock walls or in large stone groupings. The result of slides from 7000-foot Mt. Cheam, above, they are diverse in size and shape, and have made a welcome contribution to the creation of the Gardens' moods and images. Large native trees, which were all carefully preserved during the working phase, provide a unique touch to the landscape, their size and quality giving a sense of maturity to the Gardens. Old stumps mingle with huge birches skyrocketing out; and native dogwoods, weeping willows, firs, and native thujas provide diversity. In addition, a great number of native plants contribute another dimension to the Gardens, with alpine strawberries, bleeding hearts, ferns, species geraniums, huckleberries, and even native roses, affording the naturalist many forms of enjoyment while identifying the species.

While the Gardens have a certain obvious botanical character, the main emphasis is on the use of color through masses of flower bulbs, herbaceous plants, perennials, and annuals. The Gardens are designed not just for gardeners, but for everyone. The intent is to bring people close to nature. Spectacular displays of colors and the natural beauty of the surroundings will spark a spiritual affinity for plant life.

The Gardens will never remain the same, either by month, season, or year. The development shown in the photograph represents only Phase I, and if our dreams are to be fulfilled, we will expand with many new and exciting concepts. Each year will bring changes as surely as each new season brings new colors.

One of the greatest satisfactions of all is the realization that we are creating an asset for our entire region. The benefits from an increase in tourism alone will be significant in our communities. We hope to have been the spark prodding people from all over the world to come and see our beautiful valley. For indeed, it is a truly magnificent place.

AN EXPLORERS' GUIDE
TO PERUVIAN ECOSYSTEMS

MARK C. MARDON
South American Explorers Club, Casilla 3714, Lima 100, Peru

American, born September 25, 1953. Explorer, Chief Researcher and author of this project for the South American Explorers Club. Educated in the United States, Peru, and Bolivia.

This project involves making field surveys and conducting research for the purpose of preparing an ecological profile of Peru, including detailed ecosystem maps, photographs, statistical and narrative descriptions, and a bibliography. This profile will define ecosystems by type, location, and suitability to logical forms of exploration. The results of this research will be published and distributed through the magazine *South American Explorer,* and in the form of an *Explorers' Guide to Peruvian Ecosystems.* The intent of this publication is to actively promote the idea of minimum impact upon the natural environment by explorers, whether they be in the field for educational, commercial, or recreational purposes.

The reasons for this effort include the recognition that an ever-increasing number of naturalists, recreationalists, and commercial enterprises are exploring the natural environment of Peru; that there are few or no guidelines to the character of Peru's various ecosystems that may be used to help such visitors avoid damage to the environment; and that the future of exploring in Peru will be better protected through knowledge of the country's ecosystems and a commensurate respect for them.

We therefore wish to determine the status of both major and minor ecosystems (i.e., their inclusion in, or exclusion from, the National System of Conservation Units), their state of preservation, their durability or fragility, the existence of man-made infrastructures, the interest they hold for the non-indigenous explorer, and the frequency with which they are explored.

The first step in this program is the collection and synthesis of published materials, from both United States and Latin American sources, and the preparation of an extensive bibliography for use by potential explorers. Concurrently, a Background Assistance Information Search will be carried out, through consultation with local and international experts in fields related to ecology and exploration, primary among these being officials managing Peru's National System of Conservation Units.

Drawing upon our organization's own resources, we plan field surveys to make first-hand observations, to verify information gathered in our desk research and interview program, and to augment that information.

Using the system promulgated by L. R. Holdridge, ecologists recognize 84 zones of natural life in Peru, each of which includes an indeterminate number of ecosystems, many of which are unique and of incalculable scientific value. Another classification permits grouping of these 84 into only 10 zones, particularly applicable to wildlife, with the objective of explaining Peruvian ecology in terms that are appropriate but not excessively complex.

Our field studies will be organized with the intent of exploring representative areas of these 10 life zones for the purpose of photography, species identification, trail mapping, and small-scale mapping of particular life zones and their constituent ecosystems. We shall pay particular attention to areas bordering major routes utilized by explorers, such as navigable river systems, pack trails, and areas surrounding commonly visited camp sites and villages. We will talk with field personnel of the National Parks and Reserves to learn which areas are most utilized and which areas might be utilized. In other conversations and field work, we will learn of local residents' reactions to visitors and of less accessible areas of interest to explorers.

We will research with two purposes in mind: first, to describe ecosystems adjacent to such areas as described in order to further appreciation for their scientific and aesthetic value, and second, to examine the possible effects explorers might have upon the ecosystems, such as disruptions of natural animal habitats, pollution of streams, littering, destruction of, or impeding the growth of, natural vegetation, and most especially, disturbance of the lifestyle of indigenous human populations.

Our findings will be used to produce illustrated articles for publication in the South American Explorers Club's quarterly magazine and in an illustrated book. These publications will be designed for the benefit of all explorers—archaeologists, paleontologists, botanists, anthropologists, geologists, and other scientists, as well as white-water runners, backpackers, hikers, mountaineers, and spelunkers—as a handy resource guide for understanding the ecology of areas they are likely to be exploring. We shall describe means by which expeditions and exploration can be made with a minimum of disruption to, and a maximum appreciation for, the ecosystems of this country.

CONSERVATION OF THE ARID-LAND FAUNA OF NIGER

JOHN E. NEWBY
Honorable Mention, Rolex Awards for Enterprise
Wildlife Consultant, Direction des Eaux et Forêts,
B. P. 578, Niamey, Niger

British, born July 28, 1949. Wildlife consultant, working for World Wildlife Fund. Educated in the United Kingdom.

U nless far-reaching measures are taken immediately, many of Africa's arid-land fauna will have disappeared by the end of this century. Large ungulate species, such as the addax, the scimitar-horned oryx, and the dama gazelle, are already critically endangered. In my opinion, the key to the survival of the arid-land ungulates lies in rationally exploiting their superior ability to use and manage the otherwise difficult-to-develop arid habitats. This project is concerned with accomplishing this in the West African state of Niger. It includes a program for the protection of the existing ungulate populations through the establishment of reserves, a reintroduction program, and an educational and training program for Africans in wildlife conservation.

The arid grasslands to the south of the Sahara make up a sizable proportion of several West African countries. Of these, the republics of Mali, Niger, and Chad are among the world's poorest. Because of their aridity, these sub-Saharan grasslands are difficult to develop for human use, and even when this is possible, it is expensive and often ecologically unsound. On the other hand, the grasslands provide an unequaled source of rich grazing, and although nomadic peoples do exploit them periodically, they have in the past been the domain of vast populations of wild ungulates. These species, by virtue of their desert physiology and migratory habits, are perfectly adapted to exploiting arid rangelands that are prone to drought.

The advent of automatic weapons and desert-going vehicles, however, has resulted in a catastrophic decline in the numbers of all these arid-land species. Addax and oryx have disappeared from 90 percent of their former ranges and number as few as 2000 head each in the wild. We know from recent work in Chad that addax and oryx can be protected and encouraged to increase if adequate areas of reserves can be established and diligently managed. Lamentably, the recent civil war in Chad has entirely negated earlier efforts, reducing the scimitar-horned oryx to one of Africa's rarest and most endangered species. The survival of the oryx and the other arid-land species now depends on the rapid establishment of conservation programs based on the tiny populations still to be found in Mali and Niger.

At the request of the government of Niger, I am formulating a conservation program to protect the remaining populations of oryx and addax in Niger. A detailed survey and study of such topics as the feeding, reproductive, and social behavior of the wildlife are underway, relying on both previously published data and *in situ* studies to determine biological and spatial requirements. Based on these findings, reserves will be proposed to answer the needs of the wildlife. Because of the pronounced seasonal migratory behavior of the larger animals, the reserves have to be large and will require trained management that can prevent poaching and harassment, and laws that support the management staff.

Surveillance will not be easy, due to size. The Ouadi Rime reserve in Chad gives some idea of the required size; at 8,000,000 hectares, it is the same size as Scotland, or about double the size of Switzerland. Only a knowledge of the wildlife's behavior can make control viable.

Another major aim of the project is to establish captive breeding groups of the endangered species. The nuclei of these herds will come either from the wild or from overseas zoos and collections (there are about 400 oryx in captivity). Once established, the herds will supply animals for release into the wild, either into areas presently devoid of them or to existing populations.

The third part of the project is in the key area of education and training local populations first to recognize the value of the wildlife and then to an appreciation of a society in which humans and animals complement one another. It has long been clear that the balanced exploitation of the wildlife population can bring significant benefits to the surrounding human community. This part of the project is designed to stimulate and provide an educational campaign both in the classroom and in the bush. Niger has operated an educational television channel for several years, which could explain the long-term value of protecting the ungulate herds and encouraging their growth. Development of a professional conservationist corps in Niger will be a major key to success. Speed of action is critically important if we are not to be too late.

Enchanted Island.

ENCHANTED ISLAND— OUTSTANDING USE OF ALTERNATIVE ENERGY SOURCES

 FERNANDO E. LEE
Honorable Mention, Rolex Awards for Enterprise
Rua Haddock Lobo n°. 403 apt. 23-B, 01414 Sao Paulo, Brazil

Brazilian, born August 19, 1903. Businessman, holding numerous official posts with corporations and associations; researcher in wide variety of ecological/environmental fields. Educated in the United States and Brazil.

T hirty years ago, I took possession of a small, uninhabited island situated approximately one mile off the coast of Brazil. Since then it has been transformed into a research center for the development and application of nature's alternative sources of energy. As the result of constant research and hard work, this deserted and rocky island became self-sufficient for human life, based on natural elements. *Water* from rain is collected and stored by processes that make it pure and available for all needed requirements. *Electrical power* is obtained from the wind at levels that have solved all our energy problems. *Heat,* a distinct necessity, is obtained from the sun. *Wild birds, flowers, and freshwater fish* are raised successfully in a medium averse to human subsistence. *Erosion* was eliminated by planting *Neomarica caerulea,* a wild iris of the family Neomaricaceae. The results of these studies and research are being constantly transmitted in talks made at universities, engineering institutes, and other professional organizations in Brazil. I intend to donate the island and all its installations to a foundation for the development of science and the improvement of the environment.

In early 1950, I had circled in a plane over Arvoredos Island, a tiny spot of rocky land about a mile offshore, north of Brazil's port of Santos. Menacingly steep rock formations explained why, though not far from the coast, it had remained uninhabited. Nevertheless, the northern part of the island was covered with a luscious tropical forest (hence the name, "island of the cluster of trees"), ending at a plateau covered with tall grass; the rest of the surface was barren rock. I took pictures on the flight and was struck by the images suggested to me by the island's shape. I was sparked by a spirit of adventure and definitely by a case of love at first sight. Now, after having dedicated 30 years of imagination and hard work to the creation of this place, with all the research projects that have been realized here, my "Enchanted Island" is a part of my life.

Examples of the projects and researches we have carried out on the island include a wide variety of challenges.

Storing rainwater was our first priority. We built large underground cisterns, lined with white enamel tiles, that can store some 160,000 liters of fresh water. From the roof of the house, which is covered with plastic tiles, rainwater is collected in stainless steel gutters, then taken by glass tubes to a 100-liter decanting tank. Only after filling this tank is the rainwater allowed to flow into the glass fabric filters, and from there to the tile-lined cisterns. The decanting tank automatically empties itself in about two hours. Thus, if it rains again after two hours, the first 100 liters flow into the tank, thereby preventing any salt, insects, or leaves that might have collected on the roof from getting into the cisterns. With average annual rainfall over 1900 milliliters, we collect enough pure fresh water for our drinking, bathing, and cooking needs.

At the lower eastern side of the island is a small spring, where we constructed a large reinforced concrete dam, which holds over 2 million liters of rainwater collected from the coconut grove. Water from this dam, in parts over 4 meters deep, is used for irrigation, for raising freshwater fish, for sanitary use, and for mixing concrete. For beauty's sake, its concrete walls were covered with natural stones.

We also needed a source of energy, because bringing diesel oil from the mainland was not practical. We constructed a large wind generator, with variable-pitch 3-blade propellers 4 meters in diameter, which provided $2\frac{1}{2}$ kilowatts that was stored in large lead-acid batteries. Continuing research led to our current $3\frac{1}{2}$-kilowatt, $5\frac{1}{2}$-meter-diameter, 3-blade-propeller wind alternator, the A.C. power from which is transformed by diodes into D.C. for charging the batteries. This provides all the energy needs of the island, including the large crane that lifts boats out of the sea for storage in the freshwater tank on top of the island. Our work in this research area is forwarded to the Brazilian Air Force, which is working on wind alternators to be installed on several of our coastal islands, along with various international researchers with whom we cooperate.

Solar energy has offered us a continuing and rewarding area of research and practical application. From our start with the earliest flat-plate solar heating equipment, we moved on to adjustable collectors, and are now carrying out experiments with even more efficient methods of converting the sun's energy into useful power. One of our developments was a blinking buoy, which works on sun energy and needs no maintenance; it blinks all night, turned on by a photoelectric eye, and recharges all day. It is now widely used by many navies, as well as in Brazil. We have always made our research results available to interested parties for the pure benefit of science.

Beyond pure survival techniques, we have sought also to make the surrounding environment of Enchanted Island an appealing one in which to live. Wild bobwhite quail eggs were hatched under two tiny setting bantam hens. Raised by the mother hens, after a few generations these very wild birds have become completely tame. As no one is allowed to scare them, we have many species of birds peacefully roaming the island. It is a sight worth witnessing to see a tiny clucking bantam hen followed by a large brood of silver or gold pheasants or other species of wild birds. We have planted many tropical flowering trees, which are now growing in our forest, and made a coconut grove by planting three species of coconut trees from seeds imported from Malay. Not only lovely, but also a welcome source of inexhaustible food. Some 300 orchids have been transplanted from the mainland, and re-positioned (using compass orientation) carefully, so that they bloom as if in their original habitat.

We have extensively and successfully experimented with raising a wide variety of fish—with both predators and prey used to maintain correct population balances, and with attention to how best to integrate the abundant vegetable garden with appropriate food for our "fish farm." We wished to have animals on the island but did not wish to disturb the birds, so after considerable research we obtained a three-toed sloth, taking care to plant its own particular food source, the embauba tree. The pair released into our forest has produced offspring and become quite tame. To fight erosion partly caused, in fact, by the foraging bird population, we located and planted a species of wild iris, which grows in the shade, has roots that penetrate and hold soil, and won't be eaten by the birds!

Creating and executing these research projects has been most rewarding; as a result, Enchanted Island today is self-sufficient, accessible, and delightfully inhabitable, based on natural elements and sources.

CONSTRUCTING AN AERIAL WALKWAY IN CAMEROON'S RAIN FOREST

JOHN R. PARROTT
c/o Miss Tessa Board, 11 Ilchester Mansions,
Abingdon Road, London W8 6AE, U.K.

British, born September 20, 1951. Teacher, ornithologist, conservationist, and writer. Educated in the United Kingdom.

The immediate objective of the project is to build and initiate use of an aerial walkway in the tropical rain forest of Cameroon. The projected walkway will be sited in a National Park and will assure ready access to the canopy for scientists, tourists, and school children. It is anticipated that the interest created by the walkway will attract a steady flow of foreign revenue from tourists and thus will help to consolidate the park's future.

The long-term objective is to stimulate an interest in rain forests among local school children and, through a greater involvement in and understanding of their environment, to initiate a greater impetus for forest conservation within Cameroon. It is hoped that the success of the present project will encourage other developing countries to conserve and more wisely use their dwindling rain forest resources.

Of all the world's biomes, the tropical rain forest is the one with the greatest abundance and diversity of species. It is the least documented or understood, and it is the one that is being most rapidly disrupted. Its value in protecting watersheds, stabilizing river flow, minimizing floods, forming new soils, reducing erosion of existing soils, buffering climatic variation, and supplying opportunity for research, education, recreation, and tourism is undisputed. Its destruction for short-term gain nevertheless continues apace.

The coastal forests of Cameroon are unique. They form part of a forest strip once extending between the Niger and Congo Rivers, much of which has elsewhere been destroyed or degraded by logging activities. With its botanical and faunal history going back to the Pliocene Epoch, Cameroon's rain forests possess one of the most diverse primate faunas in the world, with at least 22 different species, many of which are rare or endangered. These forests are of unique biological importance, holding clues to the theory of continental drift, to patterns of climatic change in past eras, to the history of the African biomes, and to the evolution, radiation, and diversification of the primates. Cameroon is apparently the only country of those with coastal forests that has any firm plans for extensive conservation, and the government has already instituted several actions to promote forest conservation.

Why build a walkway? Development of research and tourism in rain forests has, in the past, been severely hindered by the difficulty in observing much of the flora and fauna. Over 90 percent of the forest's productivity occurs in the canopy layer formed by the crowns of forest trees 25 to 35 meters or more from the ground. Here also, forest trees flower and fruit. These massive sources of food attract a large majority of the forest's fauna. Observations made from the ground are necessarily biased and incomplete. A single simple solution can overcome this problem: build an aerial walkway in the canopy.

An aerial walkway is suspended like a footbridge from tall emergent trees, allowing access to the hitherto remote, sunlit world of the canopy and thereby offering unrivaled opportunities in many fields, not just scientific research. To date, the Drake Expeditions (1979) to Papua New Guinea and Panama, which built temporary walkways for research biologists, have encouraged the building of permanent walkways in Papua New Guinea and Sulawesi, though no plans exist for their development for other purposes.

As a scientific tool, the Cameroon walkway will provide inestimably valuable access to canopy-dwelling species for a variety of programs of critical importance to the survival of these species.

As an educational tool, the walkway provides an exciting and important new perspective on a familiar environment, affording unrivaled opportunities for photography, filming, and field observation for school children, for whom the rain forest should be a heritage.

For tourism, the forest canopy houses many of the most spectacular plants and animals (primates, epiphytic orchids, hornbills, plantain-eaters, tree flowers, and fruits). The walk through the canopy, with its viewing opportunities, will be an experience few visitors are likely to forget, affording Cameroon an excellent addition to its many attractions for tourists.

A choice of accessible sites in Douala-Edea and/or Korup reserves will be made after careful study of the results of phenological and vegetation surveys. The walkway will be suspended from healthy emergent trees and will include observation platforms and hides, especially at higher levels, accessed from the walkway. It will be the first to be sited in a National Park and the first to be developed for use by all interested visitors—scientists, students, and tourists.

AN UNDERWATER PARK FOR SARDINIA—PROTECTING THE SUBMARINE WORLD

HERMANN U. HEBERLEIN
Casa Corallo, CH 6932, Breganzona/Lugano, Switzerland

Swiss, born April 9, 1912. Lawyer; photographer; writer; official Swiss delegate for oceanographic questions. Educated in Switzerland.

I seek to help protect the beauty and value of the underwater world through the establishment of an underwater park in the waters of Sardinia. I have come to this effort by virtue of learning how people can be taught to appreciate an alien environment and to respect its conditions, enjoying it without doing damage to it.

I started diving in 1950. As was customary then, most divers harpooned fish, and so did I. By 1952, however, I began to concentrate on underwater photography and filming, publishing my first report on underwater life, illustrated with my own photos, in that same year. A later expedition to the Persian Gulf completed my transition from diving for pleasure to diving for scientific research. Since then, I have spoken out against the senseless "sport killing" of fish and have considered ways to protect this underwater world. I have concentrated on two main efforts: an intensive fight against competitive spear fishing and the promotion of underwater photography and filming as an alternative to harpooning. It was obvious to me that virtually everyone who became interested in underwater photo and film work quickly lost their interest in harpooning fish. With underwater photography equipment becoming less expensive, this worthwhile new diversion could be encouraged as a replacement for killing.

To give tangible form to the idea of protecting underwater creatures, I began to pursue the idea of creating an underwater park, complete in every sense of that word. It should be open to the public, respected, and protected—a true park in the sea.

I dived in 1968 in the excellent park near Eilat in the Red Sea, and I was deeply impressed in the same year with the Pennekamp Underwater Park near Key Largo in Florida, a superbly protected environment. In 1980, I visited the strictly controlled underwater parks on Mahé Island in the Seychelles, where unsuspicious fish, turtles feeding on the sea bottom, and large rays could be closely observed—an underwater filming paradise. By this time, I had already embarked on a program to convince Italian authorities of the need to establish an underwater park in Sardinia, where I had had personal experience of the loss of the moray eel population.

My effort to set up an underwater park in the Capo Coda Cavallo Bay area was purely private. I wanted to protect this unique submarine zone for the generations coming after us. For more than ten years, this project involved innumerable conversations, worldwide correspondence to as many interested persons as possible, writing and photographing the area's story for a wide variety of publications, and carrying out public relations activities on behalf of the proposed park in lectures, interviews, and radio and television broadcasts.

Today, I am pleased to note that the underwater park has been registered on two maps, and the protected zone has been approved by the competent port authorities of Olbia. I have continued to make requests to the mayor of San Teodoro for official approval of additional measures that will increase the protection afforded to and by the park. This fight for the park, initially an individual venture, has now brought the future of the park into the hands of the authorities of San Teodoro. I have done everything I possibly could to promote the underwater park in Sardinia. I will continue to do so in the future, but help from the outside is not only welcome but necessary.

In the last few years, tourism and land speculation have taken possession of formerly untouched shores, especially near Capo Coda Cavallo. The very last monk seals around Tavolara were killed or dispersed during this period. My own eyes have seen not only that the moray eels and the big fish have disappeared from the bay, but also that the beautiful big shells have been destroyed by skindivers and spearfishers, who are leaving us with wasted shores and dead waters where once there had been the pulsation of life. As I have done before, and will continue to do, I appeal for help in furthering the protection of an endangered underwater world.

Clearing undergrowth can help prevent forest fires such as this one.

A PROGRAM FOR PROTECTING AND IMPROVING THE MEDITERRANEAN FORESTS

ANDRÉ MARTIN
Rolex Laureate, Rolex Awards for Enterprise
83690 Sillans-la-Cascade, France

French, born March 22, 1938. General Manager of a company producing humus products. Educated in Switzerland.

Our project involves integrating present efforts to protect our Mediterranean forests with effective recycling of forest products, and to do this within a self-sufficient energy system.

For many years, we have watched the continuing degradation of forests and agricultural land in the Mediterranean basin, a process inherently headed toward desertification. Using the example of France, this degradation occurs principally in forest fires.

Statistics show that when a forest is not "kept up," it burns systematically every 15 to 25 years. Fire spreads very quickly and sometimes with such power that even the most modern firefighting methods become useless. In the Var department, 500,000 hectares of forest land have burned over the last 50 years. On several of these occasions, fire kindled in the same location, leaving the soil badly eroded and impoverished. As a result, the forest does not have the nutrients to restore full-grown trees. Erosion, impoverishment of soils, changes in local climates and soil moisture are all alarming consequences that affect agriculture and our environment.

The main preventive measure against such fire catastrophes is cleaning the undergrowth so that it will grow into full trees. This guarantees the health of the forests so well that most people declare this method to be the only solution to the problem. The effort needed consists of cleaning the undergrowth of its shrub or brushwood, and thinning and pruning low-hanging branches. Thus, a fire can be controlled easily because of a lack of combustibles. Unfortunately, such safeguarding operations have been very limited because of their high cost and the lack of any economic profit.

Another related development is the continuing concern about the degradation of cultivated land. Some types of intensive agriculture lead to a considerable reduction of humus percentage in the soils, and consequently to serious problems for the future of agriculture. These problems include:

Deterioration of the physical structure of soils

Increase in agricultural work

Increase in the need for water and nutritional substances

Low resistance to diseases; more frequent treatments required

Increased lack of soil balance

Erosion leading to desertification through fertility loss

Pollution increase of agricultural origin

To get economical profit from the safeguarding operations called for in our forests and to improve our deteriorating soils, we suggest recycling vegetable mass obtained from underbrush cleaning into forest compost, which is a source of humus. This humus would then be spread on soils to create the best conditions for cultivation.

Under current practices, when plants are cut down to clear forest undergrowth, they are usually burned or left on the spot, since the aerobic composting that takes place is valuable ecologically. Composting is a well-known process that is common on a small scale in many agricultural and industrial refuse situations.

For woody vegetables, however, the fermenting procedures and techniques are not the same, and are still not very well known by agricultural managers. Producing forest compost on an industrial scale is therefore a new and valuable technique. In our work, we have been able to refine more than 5000 tons of compost into a product we call Promus. This product has some interesting qualities:

It is a potential source of long-life humus with rich organic matter.

It retains water and nutritive substances.

It has a positive action on the physical structure of the soil.

It contains nutritive elements.

It contains a full microbic and mycelium flora. Studies on these organic matters show that Promus might also contain substances that would allow better plant growth and better resistance to disease.

This first product is going to be put on the market for the general public through supermarkets, garden centers, and traditional seedmen. Before taking it to the professional market, however, we need to achieve better quality with relation to prices, and we need to elaborate its use as a soil enrichment for specific crops. Additionally, Promus can be introduced as a complemental ration in cattle feed (first results of our present experiments have been very encouraging).

The technique we use for composting brings the various elements of the project together. The first step is the collection of wild vegetable stock, which is obtained through maintenance and rational farming of the forest biomass. We collect underwood, undergrowth, heath, scrub, and so on through the traditional methods of cleaning the undergrowth—lopping and pruning the underwood. This vegetation is brought to our installation and shredded by grinders. The shredded material is composted through an aerobic, humid process and continually enriched by mineral and natural organic elements. The end product is the organic matter called Promus.

We have compiled considerable documentation on the method of producing Promus, the nature of the product, and the economics of producing it on a larger scale, with the attendant beneficial results of sharply improved forest management. New employment in rural regions can be created by locating small forest-product composting installations in appropriate areas and undertaking this valuable, energy-efficient effort.

THE DIRECTORY OF ANCIENT CITIES IN NORTHEASTERN THAILAND

THIVA SUPAJANYA
180 Mahaisawan Road, Bookalow, Thonburi, Bangkok 6,
Thailand

Thai, born December 24, 1938. Assistant Professor, Geology Department,
Chulalongkorn University, Bangkok. Educated in Thailand and Holland.

Since 1965, first as a hobby and then as serious research, I have been searching for the ancient cities of northeastern Thailand, using aerial photographs as a primary working tool. The area covered by this research is approximately 168,000 square kilometers. The ancient sites discovered will be systematically recorded and compiled in the form of "The Directory of Ancient Cities in Northeastern Thailand." The report will include aerial photographs and map locations of the listed cities. The inventory will be of paramount use to all academic researchers interested in this field. I also believe that this work will stimulate the government's interest in protecting and preserving these ancient sites.

The northeastern part of Thailand has its territory bordered in the north and east by Laos, and in the south by Kampuchea. The evidence uncovered during several archaeological expeditions in the area indicates that this region has been populated for a very long period of time; the date of 6500 B.C. is generally accepted as the beginning of the area's human social history. Numerous ancient sites dating from over 1000 years ago have been found all over the area. According to the study of aerial photographs, some 500 ancient cities are located within Thailand's borders, of which some 300 sites are located in the northeastern area.

The presence of the remains of those ancient cities and towns indicates that this northeastern part of the country was at one time the most densely populated in the region, if not in all of Southeast Asia. Unfortunately, as yet there has been no systematic and comprehensive study of these ancient sites. Many of them will be lost forever as the result of large-scale devastation caused by the construction of irrigation dams, water reservoirs, highways, and buildings that are part of the economic and urban development programs being pursued by the Thai government. There is, therefore, an urgent need to identify their locations to facilitate immediate scholarly attention.

My research utilizes aerial photographs to identify moats, mounds, and "Barai" (large water reservoirs of rectangular shape) as the indicators of locations of ancient cities. All such cities found will be located on the map and systematically described by identifying features. The report will include the picture of each ancient city as seen in the aerial photograph, details of scale, province name, and original name (if the latter is known). An overall map showing the location of all the ancient sites will also be included.

The total number of 300 sites collected to date was compiled through the use of aerial photographs in teaching programs and other research projects. To date, however, these have not been presented in the form of a report or publication. Additional aerial photographs in my possession have not yet been thoroughly studied for indications of yet-unknown sites. The working procedure for this task has this plan:

1. Some 8400 aerial photos (scale 1:50,000) will be searched for more ancient sites. When a city site is located, the map coordinates of its location will be recorded. To confirm the photo interpretation, aerial photos of a scale of 1:15,000 covering the target area will be observed and correlated with any available literature on the area. Some of the more interesting locations will be selected later for further direct observation in the field.

2. A literature survey will be conducted, using historical and archaeological data, for correlation purposes and inclusion, where appropriate, in the report.

3. Field observation will check on uncertainties in photo interpretation.

4. Classification will be made on the basis of the cities' sizes, shapes, geographic conditions, etc., and an attempt will be made to estimate the time of their construction.

5. Photographs will be prepared for publication.

6. A base map (scale 1:250,000) will be prepared, showing the coordinates of the center of each city, with individual maps of specific locations reduced to the necessary scale.

7. A final report will be published in two parts; Part One will include text and maps, and Part Two will include photographs of all the ancient cities found in the target area.

ESTABLISHING A CAPTIVE BREEDING CENTER FOR PARROTS

BRIAN M. FULLICK
608 Shields Drive, Motherwell, Lanarkshire ML1 2EE,
Scotland, U.K.

British, born October 9, 1940. Divisional Security Officer, British Steel Corporation. Educated in the United Kingdom.

I t is the aim of the Parrot Society to open a Captive Breeding Center that will assist the survival of all species of the parrot family. The project will be run by the elected officers and members of the Parrot Society.
the Parrot Society will be about £50,000 to £70,000, plus an annual operat-
interested in the breeding and conservation of parrotlike birds. From a small initial group, the Parrot Society has grown to international membership, open to anyone interested in parrotlike birds. Members include the general public and well-known zoological gardens, for example, the Zoological Society of London, the Jersey Wildlife Fund, and the San Diego Zoo. The Parrot Society has been a registered charity since 1975, with operating costs of the society coming from membership fees.

In 1974, a decision was made to hold an annual prize drawing, the proceeds from which would be set aside and invested, with the ultimate aim of obtaining premises for the breeding and conservation of endangered species of parrots. Though this fund continues to build slowly, rising land and construction costs mean that outside help will be necessary if the project is to be completed.

There has never been a project in the United Kingdom to accomplish the breeding of a complete species of animal or bird in one confinement. Nearly all zoological gardens have parrotlike birds, and many of them breed, but this involves the more common parrots. Within the Parrot Society, there is the capability of doing much more.

When the society published its first breeding register in 1976, 40 percent of the members replied, revealing that 97 different species had been bred by the members, totaling some 10,000 birds. In 1977, 13,250 birds were bred. In 1978, the total birds reared was 15,444. Figures are not yet available at the time of writing for the year 1979. Obviously, however, there has been a great deal of valuable information gained for the society and its members from these registers. The cooperation of the members will be a strong help in establishing the Captive Breeding Center.

The cost to open a breeding establishment to meet the objectives held by the Parrot Society will be about £50,000 to £70,000, plus an annual operating cost of about £15,000. The anticipated operating cost would be largely offset, however, by charging admission fees to the public and sales of books, postcards, tea, etc.

About 10 acres of land would be required to provide for the different aviaries, a shop, cafe, and normal facilities for the public. A portion of the area will be set apart from public visiting to allow for breeding, as this bird garden is to be first and foremost a breeding center. There will be six basic types of aviary: (1) small parakeets, (2) lovebirds, (3) medium parakeets, (4) large parakeets, (5) intermediate parrots, and (6) macaws.

With the expertise, skills, and interest of the members of the Parrot Society, this Captive Breeding Center may well be the salvation of certain of these endangered birds. Parrotlike birds face human destruction of their habitats, thoughtless killing, and illegal capture in many areas of the world. Certain species are now reduced to critically diminished populations. Even nature can take her toll, as when, in 1898, the island of St. Vincent suffered the "Great Hurricane," which nearly obliterated the *Amazona guildingii,* endemic to this island. In 1979, St. Vincent suffered a volcanic explosion, which must have had a further deleterious effect on the population of this bird, then estimated to have been some 450 to 500 in the wild. Elsewhere in the Caribbean, the Imperial Amazon and the Red-Necked Amazon suffered when Hurricane David hit Dominica in 1979. These birds had numbered only 150 and 500, respectively, in the wild, and no one yet knows how much damage was done to their population. In yet another example, there may be only 20 specimens of the Puerto Rican Amazon left in the world. There is a captive breeding program in effect, but, in my opinion, help has come too late for this parrot.

The Parrot Society would like to ensure that such aid does not come too late to other parrotlike birds. We have the interest, capability, and organization to do something about it. What is now needed is the land and the financial wherewithal to proceed with the Captive Breeding Center.

Eland husbandry

WILDLIFE RANCHING AND RESEARCH

DAVID HOPCRAFT
P.O. Box 47272, Nairobi, Kenya

Kenyan, born January 24, 1937. Managing Director of Game Ranching Ltd. Educated in England, the United States (Ph.D.), with post-doctoral work in Kenya.

W ildlife Ranching and Research is the practical demonstration of a new land use system. It is based on the concept of using Africa's greatest resource—the vast grassland plains with their teeming millions of wild animals. By reinstating these animals, we are re-creating the healthy, balanced, and symbiotic environment bequeathed us by nature.

Wildlife Ranching and Research developed after I witnessed the extensive human misery caused by desertification in Africa. The origins of this degrading of once healthy grasslands fascinated me as I observed and studied it further. In analyzing available global data, I came to a startling conclusion: Land was degraded only where man overthrew natural grassland/animal systems in favor of his own system. In areas left with indigenous species, no degradation occurred.

Systems introduced by man supplanted natural species with domestic stock—cattle, sheep, and goats. Introducing these foreign animal species adversely affected the grasslands and left the land vulnerable to water and wind erosion. The delicately balanced ecosystems were disrupted and the deadly syndrome of system destruction begun.

This conclusion revolutionized my thinking. We were not powerless before an uncontrollable specter of death gobbling more than 14,000 acres of productive land a year. We ourselves had created this specter. We created these deserts. Could we now reverse this syndrome? What were the natural instructions? They included indigenous animals within their own environment. But could this "natural technology" be as productive as modern ranching systems?

To test the comparative ecological and economic advantages of the two systems, I obtained a research grant from the U.S. National Science Foundation. The research experiments, from 1965 to 1970, were published in my thesis, "Gazelle vs. Cattle." The results in direct field comparisons were conclusive. Cattle did seriously degrade the land, whereas the indigenous species used, gazelle, proved non-destructive to the vegetation, even enhancing the climax grassland species.

Next, and most surprisingly, the gazelle proved a great deal more profitable, for a number of reasons. First, gazelle produced more meat per acre. Compared with ranch cattle, the lean meat advantage was $3\frac{1}{2}$ times greater. Second, gazelle hides were more valuable per acre—by nearly 30 times. Ten acres of Kenya dry ranching land produced one full-grown cow in three years. Cow hides sold at $5.00. The same 10 acres carried eight gazelle, croppable every year, or 24 hides in three years. Gazelle hides sold at $6.00. Third, cattle costs run 50–70 percent of gross income. Gazelle, adapted to local conditions, are virtually cost-free. They require neither herding, inoculations, nor dipping, a weekly and expensive necessity for cattle to eliminate ticks. Furthermore, they do not need water (explained in the attached documentation), a prohibitive expense in dry lands. The advantages of this are threefold: (a) no cost; (b) no energy loss; and (c) no trekking, which eliminates trampling of vegetation, tracks to water holes, and resulting erosion. These results convinced me that a practical demonstration of this natural land use system was needed, in spite of the obstacles.

No one had seriously envisioned the prospect of using wild animals as a ranching system. Previous game projects had failed. These were generally cropping programs that did not include ownership or management of the land and animals. The questions and criticisms flew. What was game ranching? Was it hunting? Was it cropping? Was it poaching? What of the meat? Was it safe? Was it salable? Game belongs to the king or the government. How could it be privately owned? Which governmental ministry would oversee a game ranch? It couldn't be done, etc., etc.

By 1975, after five years of pushing and proselytizing, I obtained a "no objection" permit from the government. Then began the task of financing and obtaining the land, the perimeter gameproof fence, and the conversions required. Apart from the research components, the only management tool needed for the ranch was the $8\frac{1}{2}$ -foot perimeter fence.

In May 1977, 20,000 acres of low-rainfall grassland plains along with its herds of cattle were purchased 25 miles from Nairobi, and the project began. The 50-kilometer perimeter fence was constructed on the ranch, using a homemade machine, constructed from two old truck axles, connected by a driveshaft, and driven by a single cylinder stationary engine. The crimped wire was woven together by hand. In 1978, when we were just about to begin the operational phase, a shooting ban was passed into law. Another hold. (Were we hunting? Were we poaching? . . .) Permits were delayed. But, with more efforts, agreement was finally given, and the project is being published into law in early 1980.

Over the past three years, the cattle have been reduced by half to make way for the increasing number of game. The indigenous animals have been encouraged and protected using experimental traps, vegetational manipulation, salting, and predator control. From 900 animals in 1977, there are over 6000 today. Each of the 13 different species present (Grant's gazelle, Thomson's gazelle, impala, eland, hartebeeste, wildebeeste, zebra, giraffe, steinbuck, dikdik, duiker, ostrich, and wart hog) forage from a different part of the vegetation spectrum. Together, maximum utilization of the land is achieved.

In the early stages of this utilization phase, we will crop excess males only, leaving intact the breeding stock, until we reach 15,000 head and the cattle are phased out completely. The entire system changeover will be monitored. Research funds have been made available from the Lilly Endowment for the first two years of this study.

Living in conflict with nature is a worldwide peculiarity of our age. We reject the natural multiculture system in favor of monoculture. Apart from the ensuing destruction of our primary resource, the land, imposed systems require large imports of energy. Can we afford to continue on this path with rapidly depleting energy resources at escalating prices?

Our present imports for modern cattle ranching are as high as 10 energy-calories for every calorie of food produced. These include development and distribution of chemicals to fight disease, equipment and machinery to pump water, to say nothing of the expensive expertise required, and fuel to operate the machinery. None of this is necessary with the natural system. It was functioning perfectly before man's intervention.

Phase III, then, is the duplication of this demonstration project in other dry areas of the world. We have received requests and inquiries in this respect from several countries.

We see this project as the re-establishment of a land use system using multicultural indigenous species of flora and fauna—nature's technology—to fulfill human needs while reversing desertification. If we can read the instructions, we can be a participant, not a destructive intruder, in time-honored systems. Man must wake up and cooperate with nature if nature is to continue to support life.

LA BARCA LABORATORIO (THE LAB BOAT)

CLAUDIO STAMPI
Via Loreta, 13, 40138 Bologna, Italy

Italian, born June 19, 1953. Physician and Research Doctor at University of Bologna. Educated in Brazil, Italy, the United States, and Denmark.

L a Barca Laboratorio is a sailing ship devoted to interdisciplinary scientific research. Various scientists—physicians, psychologists, physicists, oceanographers, and ethnologists—will be on board with the aim of studying human behavior in the marine environment under socially deprived conditions. Owing to the high level of scientific interest in the 1981–1982 Whitbread Round The World Race (a regatta especially conceived for sailing ships), La Barca Laboratorio will officially initiate its activity by taking part in this outstanding international event.

Based on the findings of a scientifically organized and sponsored yacht voyage around the world that began in 1975, a 21-meter sailing boat is now being prepared to take part in the Whitbread Round The World Race. The project is to be inaugurated in this international oceanic race because the route and the type of performance required are of great scientific interest. This will bring this unique and highly interesting undertaking to public attention. When the race is over (it is expected to take about a year), La Barca Laboratorio will go on its research program in collaboration with several universities, under the auspices of the Lega Navale Italiana.

The boat itself, due for launching in January 1981, is a light alloy cutter, designed to take advantage of advanced techniques and to provide competitive sailing characteristics as well as to allow for the conduct of a wide variety of experiments and research. Two large labs, suitably equipped, are devoted to research activities. Each of the six 2-berth cabins is connected to the laboratory by means of interphones and cables for the survey of physiological parameters of the crew member scientists. Besides saloon, kitchen block, hygienic facilities, chart table, and navigation instruments, a fully equipped workshop for either yacht or scientific apparatus repairing is available. On-board facilities ensuring maximum autonomy and safety on long-distance journeys have been included: watertight compartments, two transceivers, self-inflatable rafts, watertight emergency ration containers, and so on.

The boat will put out from Portsmouth, England, in 1981, with an itinerary divided into four stages of about 50 days each. Calls of about 20 days each will be made at Cape Town, Auckland, and Rio de Janeiro. More than 27,000 miles will be covered across the Atlantic, Pacific, and Indian Oceans, which include a wide variety of weather and sea conditions.

We will be particularly interested in studies of human chrono-biology in a situation where the solar day is shortened to about 23 hours 40 minutes for more than half the distance of the voyage. Circadian rhythms of several physiological variables will be studied: basal temperature, certain hormones, vigilance levels, muscular power, blood pressure, pulse, and so on. The crew will wear specially adjusted wristwatches that are synchronized to the shortened day. As the work necessarily involves the sharing of shifts, we will be documenting results on how this affects efficiency. The aspects of stress under non-circadian living schedules, combined with the pressure of living in fairly cramped social conditions, will all be sources of data and subjects for research.

Within these experiments, we will also be monitoring sleep patterns, via regular electro-encephalograms, and, among other areas, seeking to correlate the apparent need of maintaining postural position in REM sleep, under conditions where the heaving of the waves may modify or inhibit this form of sleep. Dream activity will be monitored and recorded for subsequent analysis on shore after the voyage. Interpreted in light of how the crew arrange themselves personally, what aggressions occur, etc., these data should be valuable in further assessing known data regarding sleeping habits and results.

La Barca Laboratorio developed from an earlier experiment. As a result of that learning experience, we are including such equipment on board as the electro-encephalographs, cardiographs, and myographs with magnetic recorders, instruments to measure the time of reactions, electronic thermometers, spirometers, equipment for taking and preserving blood and urine samples, plus other scientific instruments. In addition to the capability of connecting the laboratory to the cabins to carry out such monitoring efforts, a soundproof laboratory will also be devoted to further behavioral tests.

In addition to these human tests, we will conduct scientifically useful researches on ocean-related subjects (air-sea parameters, sea-motion studies, plankton studies).

ENVIRONMENTAL EDUCATION "ON THE MOVE"

ELEANOR JORDAN
807 North Drive, Brick Town, New Jersey 08723, U.S.A.

American, born July 8, 1944. School teacher, on leave to complete a Master's Degree. Educated in the United States.

I would like to construct an environmental education bus, to be used to teach about the environment in outdoor settings. The bus would be modified to carry equipment necessary for completing lessons outside and still carry up to 30 students. It would carry home-made teaching aids as well as those purchased from scientific supply companies and other sources. Any environmental vans I have seen or heard about carry just the equipment. Being able to transport a class of children as well would be a tremendous advantage. It allows a teacher great leeway in scheduling trips and provides more opportunities for field trips. The cost of hiring a bus for short trips is frequently unjustifiable.

A used school bus will be purchased. All seats beyond the capacity to hold 30 students will be removed and replaced with roll-out storage units, a sink, and a small icebox. Electrical outlets will be installed for operating audio-visual equipment and scientific equipment, such as microscopes, that may require lighting. Films or filmstrips can be shown in the bus, if needed. The outside of the bus will have snap-on tables for conducting experiments. The tables will be adjustable to various heights, will keep equipment out of sand or dirt, and will provide working surfaces. Vertical as well as horizontal roll-out awnings can be installed to protect equipment from the elements.

Videotaping equipment will be installed so lessons can be taped and used for teacher training in environmental education. Lessons will cover more than just the science areas, as environmental education can be taught with a humanities approach or through social studies, outdoor recreation skills, and even math. Equipment will reflect lessons in all the curriculum areas.

I can include a general breakdown of estimated costs. I am in the process of compiling an equipment list. How much equipment is purchased will depend on the money remaining after the basic conversion costs. Some funds will have to be set aside for maintenance and insurance. Insurance costs will depend on arrangements with my school system.

I am receiving advice from a neighboring school system that has an environmental van. It is a custom-built model that cost $30,000 to build and has an additional $30,000 worth of equipment. The van carries only equipment. I would like to show school systems how they can have more with a lot less money.

I estimate costs to be as follows: used bus, $3000; conversion costs, $3000; equipment (video, $5000; scientific, $8000; social studies/humanities/outdoor pursuits, $2000); and maintenance costs, $0.30 per mile. This totals $21,000 without the insurance.

After initial funds are used, which I hope will not be until I have had a full year's use of the bus, I can seek other funding or charge a fee to cover maintenance costs. I am not seeking to turn this into a profit-making situation. I want to keep control of the bus to ensure that it will be fully utilized. If for some reason I would not be able to continue with the program, I would donate the bus and equipment to the New Jersey School of Conservation, to which over 9000 students go each year for lessons in environmental education. It is the largest residential center of its type in the western hemisphere, operating through the support of a meager state budget and the hard work of many dedicated people. There it would be appreciated and used.

With a bus designed just for environmental studies, any place in the community becomes a classroom—the school site, parks, sewage treatment plants, the ocean, or spots in between.

This does not sound like a very formal application. Dealing with problems in our environment does not require formalities, only people who are willing to work to develop an environmental consciousness in our citizenry. Being concerned about the environment has to become as natural as eating and breathing if we are to continue to eat and breathe. I know there is concern in other countries as well as in the United States, but if any long-lasting changes are to take place in the use of our resources, there has to be a change in our thinking. That change can be brought about through our schools. I feel I am helping to develop a change in attitudes and I feel I can do a lot more. Introducing children and teachers to their community through an environmental perspective is paving the way toward an environmental awareness on a global scale.

The seaplane Halcyon, *perched on the shore awaiting refurbishment.*

PREFLITE—A UNIQUE, NEW OCEANOGRAPHIC UNIVERSITY

JERRY D. STARNES
6204 North Ridge Road, Forth Worth, Texas 76135, U.S.A.

American, born September 3, 1936. Management Training Consultant for an industrial firm. Educated in the United States.

P REFLITE is a unique program currently developing in the field of ocean research and education. Program investigations will cover a wide scope of ocean-related topics. Projects and missions will include investigations into unusual marine phenomena; man-in-the-sea projects; ocean environmental problems; and ocean energy, food, and mineral resources. The program will use a four-engine, double-deck flying boat (seaplane) with a top cruising speed of 250 mph and a 2200-mile range. Mission activities will be filmed and videotaped, using specially designed photographic systems, for student and public education. A student/specialist activities program is planned with international emphasis. The goals are to focus attention on multi-national ocean activities, to encourage active participation in ocean studies, and to help build support for ocean programs ensuring proper ocean resources development.

PREFLITE (Program for Research and Education through Flying Long-range Investigations in Transocean Exploration), the brainchild of a small group of educators, marine scientists, photographers, and specialists, began as a dream some 10 years ago. The concept moved closer to reality four years ago with the purchase of a seaplane, *The Isle of Tahiti*, a giant 47-passenger, British-built Solent Mark III—once the pride of a BOAC fleet of clippers that flew the New Zealand–Australia route. The ship has been renamed *Halcyon* after a bird in ancient legend that was supposed to have a peaceful, calming influence on the sea. The aircraft, now based in the inner harbor of San Francisco, California, is being converted to a flying laboratory.

PREFLITE Oceanographic is composed of a group of imaginative, innovative, energetic, and optimistic men and women who believe it is time to stop talking about the ocean's potential, or bemoaning its increasing pollution, and start doing something constructive about it. We believe the tide of the 1980's will be the "Decade of the Oceans." The oceans, which cover 71 percent of our planet, offer unlimited potential in supplying resources necessary to maintain life on earth. However, in order to initiate dynamic ocean developmental programs, people have to become involved. That is where PREFLITE will focus its energy.

PREFLITE is still in the formative stages of planning and development, under the primary leadership of Richard T. Grant as Program Director and myself as Planning Director. A group of some 80 persons, whom we affectionately call *Friends of PREFLITE,* has provided keen interest and assistance over the years. From this group, we have formed a 7-member Planning Team, which has developed a nine-phase action plan.

Phase I is the Planning and Development sector, which has developed two-year and five-year plans to ensure a sensible matrix for the core of PREFLITE's organization in the years ahead. This includes planning for the various functional responsibilities within the operations, the choice of objectives, budget control, and so on. We seek aid in the form of grants to fulfill subsequent steps.

Phase II is Staffing. We wish to recruit qualified, competent individuals for full-time positions. Should specialized training be needed, we wish to provide it. The staff's responsibilities will be to direct and control the day-to-day operations of PREFLITE, making sure that we reach our chosen objectives. A temporary headquarters will be set up until *Halcyon* is flight-tested and operational.

Phase III is Funding and Research Proposals. A department to handle this area will be established with the objective of researching, indexing, filing, and updating potential sources of funds on a continuing basis. Additionally, however, other financial resources will be developed to permit PREFLITE to become self-supporting relative to ordinary day-in, day-out operating costs (i.e., membership dues, lecture fees, magazine publications, slide and film sales, cost sharing of projects, fees for research and expeditions, etc.).

Phase IV is concerned with Aircraft and Crew Development. Much of the restoration and renovation of the seaplane has been done. The major thrust during Phase IV, however, will be to get *Halcyon* airworthy, flight-tested, certified, and the crew trained and certified. Simulated training missions will be conducted. Aeronautical and marine engineers will assess the capabilities and limitations of the aircraft. Renovations will incorporate the most effective and efficient equipment and techniques meeting the requirements of our proposed missions. Aircraft maintenance equipment and spare parts will be acquired, maintenance crews and schedules established, and training programs will be implemented. All appropriate safety and emergency procedures will be "trained in."

Phase V is Establishment of a Base of Operations. When *Halcyon* is certified and operational, PREFLITE will move to a permanent base of operations. Through efforts expended in Phase II, a site will have been prepared.

Phase VI is the Multi-Media Programs. The seaplane will be equipped with specially mounted cameras to enable the photographing of unique, exciting, and fascinating shots in flight, during take-offs and landings, plus nearby surface activities when on station. A special Multi-Media Team will consist of filming director(s) and necessary diver-photographers charged with responsibilities for documenting mission activities and reproduction for public presentations.

Phase VII is the Student Activities Program. This program will afford high school and university level students the opportunity to work with specialists in their fields of interest. Activities will be coordinated by a PREFLITE staff member to include "sea camps," workshops, self-contained instructions on practical environmental monitoring, coastal marine resources conservation projects, and in some cases actual research problems. This program will serve as a feeder for students into the central PREFLITE program.

Phase VIII will be the Flying Ambassador Program. The centerpiece of the PREFLITE operation, this phase involves the investigation of a wide range of oceanographic topics. An integral part of these investigations will be filming unique and unexplored phenomena. These films will be designed for TV broadcast and use in the Flying Ambassador Program, a campaign to keep the public informed of ongoing research in oceanographics. The Flying Ambassador Program will involve large numbers of individuals in ocean-related activities and will assist in local and regional projects. The *Halcyon* can take the Flying Ambassador Program to any area with an ocean front, lake, river, or reservoir suitable for landing.

Phase IX is Evaluation. Throughout this plan, some phases will be initiated during a preceding phase and run concurrently. We intend to monitor and evaluate all steps continuously to allow appropriate or desirable changes along the way.

The PREFLITE team members are dedicated individuals whose love and concern for the sea, and all that it encompasses, have brought us together as a cohesive group in an effort to preserve and share in this magnificent resource. We believe the implementation of PREFLITE's plan will have a positive and significant impact on national ocean policies and oceanic activities around the world.

ENOUGH CLEAN WATER FOR THE PEOPLE

 CUTHBERT K. OMARI
Honorable Mention, Rolex Awards for Enterprise
University of Dar es Salaam, P.O. Box 35029, Dar es Salaam,
Tanzania

Tanzanian, born July 15, 1936. Sociology Professor. Educated in Tanzania, the United States, and Japan.

The main objective of this project is to make available an adequate supply of clean drinking water to the people and animals of a small Tanzanian village. The village is a tiny rural settlement of some 200 households, with a population of about 2000. It is situated out in the plains, near the Tanga-Moshi highway, about 43 miles south of Mt. Kilimanjaro.

Currently, the only source of water available to the villagers is far away, and the supply is inadequate for the community. In spite of the difficulty, the women of the village spend many hours of trekking daily, simply to haul back minimal amounts of this precious fluid. An alternative source of water, in the form of running water piped into the village, would dramatically change the entire living standard and way of life of this endangered human population. Freed from the time spent fetching water, the women will be able to join more fully in the socioeconomic life of the village and move more easily to a level of equal opportunity to participate in other developmental programs for the village.

I have been researching the "ujamaa" policy (settlement program in Tanzania) for the past few years as it has been implemented in the village of Kiruru-Lwami, in the Mwanza District. Of all the problems encountered in this program, that of procuring water for this village is perhaps the most important. The lack of sufficient clean water means that the villagers (mainly the women) spend up to ten hours daily in search of water, and what they find is not the best water one could wish to have. The present source of water is about 5 miles from the village center.

Although the government is trying its best with limited resources, it cannot provide everything to every village at once. I seek to change this situation in this village for a number of reasons. The absence of adequate water supplies not only upsets other social programs by occupying a large portion of the available work force in unproductive effort, it also forces the villagers to drive their cattle long distances to obtain adequate water. By getting water into the village, not only will the people benefit directly, but they will have ways to control the dangerous erosion of the land in the area, which is a by-product of overgrazing, and they can avoid driving their herds long distances in search of water.

Once water is provided, the women of the village will spend less time fetching it for drinking, cooking, and washing. The energy released from this dreary chore can then be used in other programs of social development, enhancing their participation in the village's other social activities along with the menfolk, as has been prescribed in the Village Act and its corollary organizational structuring.

This project will help me, as a social scientist, to provide basic data for comparisons of progress in the role of women in our social development. Having already collected statistical data on the time expended on fetching water, I will be able to make comparisons with later data on the conversion of that time into other socially involved and useful activities within the community.

The project will commence with the enlistment of the cooperation of the villagers. This will be no problem, as I have already come to know them well during the course of my researches there over the past several years. With their involvement, the project will then become a village program, with much higher prospects for successful completion and operation. Also, in this way, assistance will be provided from the government in the form of plumbers who are skilled in fitting water pipes and their installation. The trench for the water will be dug by the villagers on a self-help basis, which is very popular in this country and in this village in particular. I will be responsible for the administration of funds connected with the project and will see to it that the villagers benefit through the advice and aid of health workers and extension workers.

When the project is completed, I will feel that my ambition has been accomplished and that a contribution has been made to the UN-proclaimed "International Drinking Water Supply Sanitation Decade."

ANTARCTIC GENE BANK

BOGUSŁAW A. MOLSKI
02 938 Warszawa, Orezna 11a, Poland

Polish, born January 5, 1932. Director of Botanic Gardens, Polish Academy of Sciences, Warsaw. Educated in Poland.

The project is to build an Antarctic Gene Bank as a "Noah's Ark" for preservation of the plant genetic resources of the world. The proposed Antarctic Gene Bank will make use of permafrost polar conditions on King George Island, South Shetland Island, Antarctica, as the main repository for seed storage in a tunnel specially driven into the solid rock of the island. The AGB will be easily accessible several months of the year and will be located near the main quarters of the scientists working on the Antarctic Station "H. Arctowski" in Admiralty Bay, at King George Island, operated by the Polish Academy of Sciences at present. The AGB should be under the patronage of the Food and Agriculture Organization of the United Nations (FAO) or other international organizations.

King George Island is covered by a glacier that flows into the surrounding waters. In a few places, however, there are small rock islands. The Polish Academy of Sciences Station "H. Arctowski" is located on a small peninsula unaffected by permanent ice cover. On the station are living facilities for twenty people, a generator station, radio-telex equipment, and the experimental greenhouse—40 square meters of space for biological experiments.

At the pole, permafrost conditions provide permanent low temperatures all year. It would be sufficient to build a permanent tunnel in the permafrost to create a storage area for seeds that would contain the gene resources for the plant world. The storage area should be built in a place of easy access, where the entrance and the cavity are in solid rock. (If the storage area were made in an area affected by glaciers, the moving ice could destroy the chamber and close the entrance.)

The rocks that surround the station on Admiralty Bay are composed of volcanic lava, solid basalt, and andesite, separated by a crystallized layer of compact tuff, ideal for building a seed storage chamber. At one of the rock walls, I propose to form a hall, which will go deep into the permafrost. The hall will have two doors, one to the outside and one that divides the hall into two chambers. The innermost chamber will be used for the storage of seeds, and the first chamber will give protection against influxes of warm air. This first chamber will be used to maintain a constant temperature for the inner storage chamber, which will house the collection of seed samples.

The inner storage chamber would not be less than 150 square meters (5 m by 30 m) and about 3 meters in height. Each of the individual seed collections would hold some 20,000 seeds. In total, the storage chamber should house about 100,000 separate collections of seeds. The chamber floor should be flat, and ordinary lighting can be used.

Overall, the international Antarctic Gene Bank on King George Island would have two basic elements: the chambers hewn into the permafrost to hold the collections, and the surrounding area for laboratories and a documentation center. A card index file would provide information about the germination capacity of the seeds. The experimental greenhouse can also be maintained in the surrounding area, requiring only two trained individuals as operating personnel. Of course, copies of all data and documents would be sent to FAO or the international organizations involved, so that work can be conducted in more than one location simultaneously.

It would be the work of the AGB to keep seeds of recognized valuable varieties of agricultural plants, and wild species that are important to science and the maintenance of humanity. Additionally, this bank should store all possible varieties of seeds for rare and endangered plant species.

Modern gene banks have huge storage areas equipped with freezers that create excellent conditions for storing seeds for many years. The basic conditions for the maintenance of the seeds' viability for long-term storage are low temperatures (these range from $-10\,°C$ to $+4\,°C$) and the reduction of seed humidity (for example, cereals should be dried to a 5 percent humidity and kept in tightly closed glass containers). In these conditions, nearly the entire process of seed respiration is halted, fungus ceases to grow, and all chemical processes proceed at a much slower pace.

All existing gene banks have the same shortcomings; they depend on the permanent delivery of electrical energy to keep temperatures low, and the developed resources belong to the country that maintains the gene bank making international research sharing difficult. The Antarctic Gene Bank would avoid both of these shortcomings by creating an international gene bank in permafrost conditions in the international territory of Antarctica.

A dung-polluted beef cattle pasture in northern New South Wales.

The African dung beetle,
Euoniticellus intermedius.

A 1-liter dung pad.

*The remains of the dung
pad 24 hours later after
attack by the dung beetle.*

FIGHTING PASTURE POLLUTION WITH DUNG BEETLES

 GEORGE F. BORNEMISSZA
Honorable Mention, Rolex Awards for Enterprise
78 Nelson Road, Hobart, Tasmania 7005, Australia

Australian, born February 11, 1924. Ecologist/Senior Principal Research Scientist at CSIRO. Educated in Hungary, Austria, and Germany.

A ustralian native dung beetles are inefficient in clearing away the dung of domestic animals brought by European settlers. The droppings of these animals pollute pastures on a vast scale, resulting in several harmful effects to man and his environment. A project now in progress remedies this situation by introducing dung beetles from the Old World that are fully adapted to recycling cattle dung by burying it in the soil, thereby restoring the balance of the Australian grassland ecosystems.

Since the eighteenth century, Australia has been colonized by European settlers, together with their domestic stock, resulting in a current population of over 200,000,000 herbivorous animals—fauna foreign to the Australian environment. Their ecological impact is particularly striking in cattle pastures, where 32 million cattle are fouling the land at the rate of over 300 million dung pads per day. Most of these pads persist undecomposed on the surface for months, or even for years, which has created a pasture pollution of enormous proportions all through the Australian mainland and Tasmania. This results in continuous losses of plant nutrients and a wasteful accumulation of dung on the soil surface. The undecomposed pads prevent grass growth, and their fouling effect on the surrounding herbage causes an annual fallout of about six million acres of grassland from grazing.

Cattle dung is also the principal breeding habitat of Australia's two major fly pests: the blood-sucking buffalo fly of cattle in the tropics, and the ubiquitous bushfly, which pesters humans and beasts alike. Furthermore, cattle dung serves as a breeding ground for several helminthic parasites and for biting midges of cattle and horses, which are carriers of certain livestock diseases.

Following my arrival as an immigrant to Australia (1951), I was soon struck by the contrast between the grasslands of western Australia, profusely littered with cow pads, and the clean cattle pastures of my native land of Hungary. I immediately started to ponder the reasons. Not until six years later was I able to convince myself, through my own wide travels, that pasture pollution was a countrywide phenomenon in Australia. It was by then also clear to me that the 270 species of native dung beetles adapted to the coarse, textured, pellet droppings of marsupials were eminently unsuccessful to cope adequately with the wet, voluminous cowpads. I felt confident that there was an ecological solution to this environmental situation that had got out of hand. By the end of 1957, I was ready with the rationale of my concept, complete with a remedy: establish a *bovine-dung beetle fauna in Australia.*

I presented these proposals to my superiors in the Commonwealth Scientific & Industrial Research Organization (CSIRO), who received them with interest and some reservations, for they sounded "too simple and too good to be true: how was it nobody had thought of this solution before?" My proposals were shelved due to lack of financial support, for no one in Australia in 1958 would finance an anti-pollution project *per se.* My first publication on this topic in 1960 aroused considerable interest in agricultural and animal husbandry circles both in Australia and overseas, but the first substantial recognition came from the Alexander von Humboldt Foundation, which offered me a fellowship in 1960–1961 for the intensive study of the dung beetle in Bavaria.

With CSIRO's support, my work received positive interest from the Australian Meat Research Committee of the Australian Meat Board. They were motivated by a serious setback in the meat industry because control of the buffalo fly with DDT had been outlawed since it left residual levels in export beef unacceptable to U.S. standards. The AMRC viewed my holistic approach to dung control sympathetically, but emphasized that their priority was control of the buffalo fly, the prime objective of their sponsorship.

At last, my passionate ambition to change the face of the pastoral industry of a whole continent came within my grips: a project was established for the implementation of my concept, and I was put in charge in November 1964. My mandate was explicit: establish an efficient bovine-dung beetle fauna in Australia. The sole criterion of this efficiency would be the speed of dung disposal: if the beetles managed to bury or destroy dung pads during the buffalo/bushfly seasons within 48 hours, both pest and dung control would be fully achieved, along with other benefits. Because of AMRC priority for buffalo fly control, the inclusion into the program of dung-inhabiting predators, such as certain histerid beetles, seemed advisable. For optimal dung beetle activity, proper soil moisture conditions are imperative, whereas histerids can get by during spells of drought with the moisture derived from the dung pads.

Between 1965 and 1970, I established the Australian Program based in Canberra, trained a staff, and developed new techniques for egg sterilization, egg transplant, and mass breeding of beetles. In June 1970, I went to Pretoria to establish the African Program, and I have since surveyed the Old World from Casablanca to Hong Kong, preparing provisional lists of promising species with appropriate recommendations.

To sum up my activity during the last 15 years, I conceived the idea of "Pasture Improvement with Dung Beetles," and secured its acceptance as a thriving and respected project throughout Australia. I have constructed and erected its infrastructure on solid foundations on two continents.

As I have only four years before my retirement at 60, I decided to withdraw from the mainstream of my project to write up the large backlog of my scientific achievements, in a quiet place like Hobart. My other chief reason for coming to Hobart is to speed up the beetle-release program in Tasmania. The native beetles of Tasmania are wholly ineffective, and the pollution of its pastures with cattle and horse dung is in every respect as bad as it was on the Australian mainland. My plans are to receive stocks of climatically suitable beetles from my team in Canberra and step up a vigorous release program over the next 2–3 years here in Tasmania. By monitoring closely the fate of these releases, I intend to collect the established beetles and re-distribute them all over Tasmania as soon as conditions permit.

Without financial assistance, this will not be possible. All funds from AMRC are fully committed to the Australian Program and to running an expanded African Program. In the project I am proposing for Tasmania, I will be the sole participant with no technical assistance.

Though there have been many major achievements developed in the program I have nurtured, and a gratifying number of honors and official appreciations accorded to me for this work, I would not like, after such a creative career, to withdraw into hibernation following my retirement. Working on a personal basis, I would like to achieve for Tasmania the benefits now accruing on the mainland.

THE UNIQUE SOFT CORALS OF TAIWAN'S SOUTH BAY— ENDANGERED BY HEAT

TELO MA
P.O. Box 9-305, Taipei, 37-2, Yang Ming Rd. Sec. 1,
Yang Ming San, Taipei, Taiwan

Taiwanese, born June 1, 1945. Research Associate in Environmental Science, Tunghai University. Educated in Taiwan and Puerto Rico.

I wish to make a film on the unique soft corals that are found now in South Bay in Taiwan to publicize the danger that they face as the result of planned industrial development of the area and, at the very least, to make a record of these beautiful creatures, which may soon be heated out of existence.

We face, as part of our industrial development here in Taiwan, continuing requirements for producing power. As part of this program, a massive new power plant will be erected on the shores of South Bay, in spite of the concern of many people about the effect this plant's heated effluent will have on the bay's marine life, much of it valuable and beautiful.

The construction of the double atomic power plant operations now planned for South Bay will mean the release of massive amounts of thermo-pollution into the bay, affecting many marine species before the temperatures are dispersed in the open sea and carried away by the offshore current. This will critically affect many marine organisms in the bay, which already live at the uppermost temperature levels acceptable to tropical flora and fauna. This is especially true of the very sensitive soft corals, for whom a temperature increase of a mere 2 to 3°C can be fatal, far below the 10°C temperature increase anticipated once the atomic power plants are in operation.

The soft corals are among the most unusual features of South Bay; they are, with rare and less interesting exceptions, unique to this bay. Some fifteen species of soft coral can be distinguished in the bay. They are called "soft" because they lack the mechanism to take up calcium from seawater and thus do not have the hard skeletal body that stony corals do. So far, very little work on the taxonomy of soft corals has been done, because of the difficulty of keeping specimens for examination. Important to the marine world, they provide shelter and a breeding ground for many fishes of commercial value as well as other marine life. Not only are they important in the ecosystem of South Bay, but they also provide one of the great underwater attractions of Taiwan for tourists and divers from around the world.

Before it becomes lost forever, I wish to document the beautiful underwater world of South Bay. A small vessel and several scuba divers will be needed, along with the necessary filming equipment. Several cruising expeditions will be needed to complete the filming.

After editing the film and videotapes of these beautiful soft corals, we would be able to show the people of Taiwan and the world the beauty of these soft corals and let them appreciate the existence of these lovely things in our world.

The claim is made on the part of the power plant authorities that the heated effluent will not affect the corals, that it will stay on top of the water and disperse quickly. But no one knows this for certain, and meanwhile the day of reckoning for the soft corals is rapidly approaching.

Energy is important to modern civilization, and nuclear energy does provide an alternative to fossil fuel. But managing nuclear energy properly and preventing it from causing adverse effects on our only environment is also important. Regardless of recent mishaps in nuclear plants, there will be more nuclear power plant projects installed in many countries of the world. These plants will be especially appealing to underdeveloped countries, many of which lie in latitudes where thermopollution will critically affect their local marine fauna and flora.

Because of this, I think it is critical to film the reality of what thermal pollution may do in tropical waters. Filming in the waters of South Bay will again be done when the heated water begins its inroads in the bay.

People should be able to see the movie and compare for themselves the difference we expect to see between the vivid world of many beautiful organisms living in an underwater tropical garden before the operation of the plant and the dull and dead underwater world covered by a thick layer of temperature-resistant algae afterward. This would be the most worthwhile educational means of showing the general public why humans should avoid this mistake again.

In future nuclear power plant projects, we must find some way to avoid the devastation of our marine environment. We hope that our project will contribute to educating people to thinking this way, as they mourn, with us, the end of a particularly beautiful life form.

NATIONALITY INDEX

NAME INDEX